W9-BPJ-618

IBM

International Technical Support Organization

Building SOA Solutions Using the Rational SDP

April 2007

SG24-7356-00

First Edition (April 2007)

This edition applies to IBM Rational software products, such as Application Developer, ClearCase, ClearQuest, ClearQuest Test Manager, BuildForge, Functional Tester, Manual Tester, Method Composer, Performance Tester, Portfolio Manager, ProjectConsole, RequisitePro, SoDA, Software Architect, Software Modeler, and Unified Process, as well as IBM WebSphere software products, such as Application Server, Business Modeler, Integration Developer, Process Server, and Service Registry and Repository.

Contents

Notices

This information was developed for products and services offered in the U.S.A.

IBM may not offer the products, services, or features discussed in this document in other countries. Consult your local IBM representative for information on the products and services currently available in your area. Any reference to an IBM product, program, or service is not intended to state or imply that only that IBM product, program, or service may be used. Any functionally equivalent product, program, or service that does not infringe any IBM intellectual property right may be used instead. However, it is the user's responsibility to evaluate and verify the operation of any non-IBM product, program, or service.

IBM may have patents or pending patent applications covering subject matter described in this document. The furnishing of this document does not give you any license to these patents. You can send license inquiries, in writing, to:
IBM Director of Licensing, IBM Corporation, North Castle Drive, Armonk, NY 10504-1785 U.S.A.

The following paragraph does not apply to the United Kingdom or any other country where such provisions are inconsistent with local law: INTERNATIONAL BUSINESS MACHINES CORPORATION PROVIDES THIS PUBLICATION "AS IS" WITHOUT WARRANTY OF ANY KIND, EITHER EXPRESS OR IMPLIED, INCLUDING, BUT NOT LIMITED TO, THE IMPLIED WARRANTIES OF NON-INFRINGEMENT, MERCHANTABILITY OR FITNESS FOR A PARTICULAR PURPOSE. Some states do not allow disclaimer of express or implied warranties in certain transactions, therefore, this statement may not apply to you.

This information could include technical inaccuracies or typographical errors. Changes are periodically made to the information herein; these changes will be incorporated in new editions of the publication. IBM may make improvements and/or changes in the product(s) and/or the program(s) described in this publication at any time without notice.

Any references in this information to non-IBM Web sites are provided for convenience only and do not in any manner serve as an endorsement of those Web sites. The materials at those Web sites are not part of the materials for this IBM product and use of those Web sites is at your own risk.

IBM may use or distribute any of the information you supply in any way it believes appropriate without incurring any obligation to you.

Information concerning non-IBM products was obtained from the suppliers of those products, their published announcements or other publicly available sources. IBM has not tested those products and cannot confirm the accuracy of performance, compatibility or any other claims related to non-IBM products. Questions on the capabilities of non-IBM products should be addressed to the suppliers of those products.

This information contains examples of data and reports used in daily business operations. To illustrate them as completely as possible, the examples include the names of individuals, companies, brands, and products. All of these names are fictitious and any similarity to the names and addresses used by an actual business enterprise is entirely coincidental.

COPYRIGHT LICENSE:

This information contains sample application programs in source language, which illustrate programming techniques on various operating platforms. You may copy, modify, and distribute these sample programs in any form without payment to IBM, for the purposes of developing, using, marketing or distributing application programs conforming to the application programming interface for the operating platform for which the sample programs are written. These examples have not been thoroughly tested under all conditions. IBM, therefore, cannot guarantee or imply reliability, serviceability, or function of these programs.

xiii

Trademarks

The following terms are trademarks of the International Business Machines Corporation in the United States, other countries, or both:

developerWorks®	IBM®	Redbooks™
z/OS®	IMS™	Redbooks (logo) ™
Build Forge™	MQSeries®	Requisite®
ClearCase®	Objectory™	RequisitePro®
ClearQuest®	ProjectConsole™	RUP®
Component Business Model™	PureCoverage®	SoDA®
CICS®	PurifyPlus™	Tivoli®
DataPower®	Rational Unified Process®	WebSphere®
DB2®	Rational®	

The following terms are trademarks of other companies:

Oracle, JD Edwards, PeopleSoft, Siebel, and TopLink are registered trademarks of Oracle Corporation and/or its affiliates.

SAP, and SAP logos are trademarks or registered trademarks of SAP AG in Germany and in several other countries.

Oracle, JD Edwards, PeopleSoft, and Siebel are registered trademarks of Oracle Corporation and/or its affiliates.

Enterprise JavaBeans, EJB, Java, Java Naming and Directory Interface, JavaBeans, JavaScript, JavaServer, JavaServer Pages, JSP, J2EE, and all Java-based trademarks are trademarks of Sun Microsystems, Inc. in the United States, other countries, or both.

Microsoft, Visio, Visual Basic, Visual Studio, Windows, and the Windows logo are trademarks of Microsoft Corporation in the United States, other countries, or both.

Pentium, Intel logo, Intel Inside logo, and Intel Centrino logo are trademarks or registered trademarks of Intel Corporation or its subsidiaries in the United States, other countries, or both.

Other company, product, or service names may be trademarks or service marks of others.

Preface

This IBM® Redbooks® publication explains the concepts and practice of developing service-oriented architecture (SOA) based solutions that use the IBM Rational® Software Delivery Platform (SDP). It uses the latest version of IBM Rational Unified Process® (RUP®) that includes service-oriented modeling and architecture (SOMA) content from IBM Global Business Services.

This book aims to help practitioners that are working on SOA-based projects. Practitioners can learn the core concepts behind SOA as well as how to use the tools to automate the tasks involved in developing SOA-based solutions.

The main thread of this book takes business requirements, business architecture, and existing assets as input, and derives the elements of a service-oriented architecture that are needed to realize the business requirements. The book covers architecture in detail, and shows how the architecture is realized through service identification, specification, realization, implementation, and testing. The book is organized around a practical example case study and provides tool and process guidance as well as additional references of key topics.

The team that wrote this IBM Redbooks publication

This book was produced by a team of specialists from around the world working at the International Technical Support Organization, San Jose Center.

Alessandro   Bertrand   Laura   Ueli   Anthony   Gregory

Ueli Wahli is a Consultant IT Specialist at the IBM International Technical Support Organization in San Jose, California. Before joining the ITSO 20 years ago, Ueli worked in technical support at IBM Switzerland. He writes extensively and teaches IBM classes worldwide about WebSphere® Application Server, and WebSphere and Rational application development products. In his ITSO career, Ueli has produced more than 40 IBM Redbooks. Ueli holds a degree in Mathematics from the Swiss Federal Institute of Technology.

Lee Ackerman is a Senior Product Manager with the Rational Learning Services and Solutions team in Canada. He has 12 years of experience in the software development field. He has worked at IBM for seven years. He holds a bachelor's degree in Business Administration from the University of Regina. His areas of expertise include model-driven development, patterns-based engineering, and service-oriented architecture. He has written extensively on these topics and often presents at conferences, workshops, and training events.

Alessandro Di Bari is a Senior IT Architect for IBM Rational Services in Italy. He has 16 years of experience in software development field and nine years using IBM Rational tools. He holds bachelor's degree in Computer Science from the University of Turin. His areas of expertise include the software development process, requirements management, UML modeling, object-oriented programming and software architectures. As part of Rational Services, he provides consultancy to customers on Rational Unified Process adoption and SOA transition.

Gregory Hodgkinson is founder, director, and the SOA lead at *7irene*, an IBM Tier 1 Business Partner in the United Kingdom. He has 10 years experience initially in the field of component-based development (CBD) moving seamlessly into the field of service-oriented architecture (SOA). He holds a bachelor's degree, (Hons) cum laude, in Mathematics and Computer Science from the University of the Orange Free State, South Africa. His area of expertise is the software development process and method, and he assists 7irene and IBM customers in adopting RUP framework-based agile development process and SOA methods. He is still very much a practitioner and has been responsible for service architectures for a number of FTSE 100 companies. He presents on agile SOA process and methods at both IBM and other events.

Anthony Kesterton is a Technical Consultant for IBM Rational Financial Services Sector in the United Kingdom. He has 17 years of experience in IT and 14 years using various IBM Rational tools. He holds a master's degree in Applied Computer Science from Rhodes University in Grahamstown, South Africa. His areas of expertise include the development process, requirements management, business modeling, and analysis and design in UML using the IBM Rational tooling, and helping customers implement process and tools. He frequently presents these topics at external conferences and internal IBM conferences worldwide.

Laura Olson is a Senior IT Specialist for the Global e-Business Transformation group in the Rochester, Minnesota. She has nine years of experience in the technology field. She holds bachelor's degree in Computer Science from the University of Wisconsin, La Crosse. Her areas of expertise in IBM products includes WebSphere Portal, WebSphere Application Server, and Rational SDP.

Bertrand Portier is an IT Architect for IBM Software Group SOA Advanced Technologies in Canada. He holds a diplome d'ingenieur (French Master of Science degree) in Computer Engineering from Polytech' Lille, France. He has worked at IBM for seven years. His areas of expertise include service-oriented architecture, Web services, model-driven and asset-based development. He has written extensively on Java™, Web services, and SOA.

Thanks to the following people for their contributions to this project:

- **Alan Brown**, IBM RTP, **Ali Arsanjani**, IBM Cedar Rapids, **Ava Chun**, IBM Atlanta, for providing help and reviews.

- **Laura Rose**, IBM Raleigh, **Lawrence Smith**, IBM Cupertino, **Christophe Telep**, IBM France, **Charles Shriver**, IBM Austin, and **Karen Smolar**, IBM Poughkeepsie, for their technical expertise, contributions and content reviews of the service testing chapter.

- **Paul Murray,** IBM Glasgow, for his assistance in setting up the ClearQuest® Test Management environment.

- **Peter Eeles**, IBM UK, for reviewing and providing guidance for the chapter about architecture and design.

- **John Smith**, IBM Australia, and **Simon Johnston**, IBM Durham, (along with Ali Arsanjani) for their work on the RUP SOMA plug-in, and their assistance in helping us understand the changes to RUP introduced by the addition of the SOMA content.

- **Robin Bater,** IBM Seattle, for his assistance in the business modeling and requirements chapters. **Jim Heumann**, IBM Seattle, for his suggestions and feedback on the general topic of requirements management and SOA.

Become a published author

Join us for a two- to six-week residency program! Help write an IBM Redbooks publication dealing with specific products or solutions, while getting hands-on experience with leading-edge technologies. You'll have the opportunity to team with IBM technical professionals, Business Partners, and Clients.

Your efforts will help increase product acceptance and customer satisfaction. As a bonus, you will develop a network of contacts in IBM development labs, and increase your productivity and marketability.

Find out more about the residency program, browse the residency index, and apply online at:

`ibm.com/redbooks/residencies.html`

Comments welcome

Your comments are important to us!

We want our Redbooks to be as helpful as possible. Send us your comments about this or other Redbooks in one of the following ways:

► Use the online **Contact us** review Redbooks form found at:

ibm.com/redbooks

► Send your comments in an email to:

redbooks@us.ibm.com

► Mail your comments to:

IBM Corporation, International Technical Support Organization
Dept. HYTD Mail Station P099
2455 South Road
Poughkeepsie, NY 12601-5400

Introduction

This chapter introduces software-oriented architecture (SOA), the IBM SOA foundation and life cycle, and the reference architecture.

We also describe what aspects of SOA application development are not covered in this book.

SOA foundation

The IBM SOA foundation is an integrated, open standards based set of IBM software, best practices, and patterns designed to provide what you need to get started with SOA from an architecture perspective. The key elements of the IBM SOA foundation are the SOA life cycle (model, assemble, deploy, manage), reference architecture, and SOA scenarios.

To gain a better understanding of the SOA foundation we explore the following defining elements:

▶ SOA foundation life cycle
▶ SOA foundation reference architecture
▶ SOA foundation scenarios

> **Note:** For a more detailed explanation of the SOA foundation, refer to *IBM SOA Foundation, An Architectural Introduction and Overview V1.0* found at:
>
> ```
> http://download.boulder.ibm.com/ibmdl/pub/software/dw/webservices/ws-soa-
> whitepaper.pdf
> ```

SOA foundation life cycle

IBM customers have indicated that they think of SOA in terms of a life cycle. As seen in Figure 1-1, the IBM SOA foundation includes the following life cycle phases:

▶ Model
▶ Assemble
▶ Deploy
▶ Manage

There are a couple of key points to consider about the SOA life cycle. First, the SOA life cycle phases apply to all SOA projects. Second, the activities in any part of the SOA life cycle can vary in scale and the level of tooling used depending on the stage of adoption.

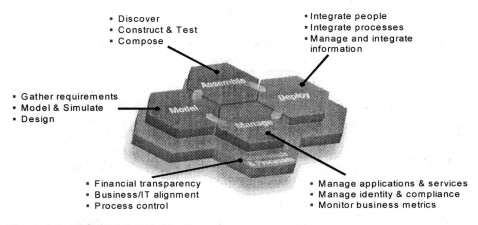

- Discover
- Construct & Test
- Compose

- Integrate people
- Integrate processes
- Manage and integrate information

- Gather requirements
- Model & Simulate
- Design

- Financial transparency
- Business/IT alignment
- Process control

- Manage applications & services
- Manage identity & compliance
- Monitor business metrics

Figure 1-1   IBM SOA foundation life cycle

Model

Modeling is the process of capturing the business design from an understanding of business requirements and objectives. The business requirements are translated into a specification of business processes, goals and assumptions for creating a model of the business. Many businesses do not go through a formal modeling exercise. In some case, businesses that do perform modeling use primitive techniques such as drawing the design in Visio® or using text documents.

Capturing the business design using a sophisticated approach that includes the use of specialized tooling lets you perform what-if scenarios with various parameters the business may experience. The process can then be simulated using those parameters to predict the effect that process has on the business and IT systems. If the achieved results do not match the business objectives, then the process definition can be refined.

The model also captures key performance indicators (KPIs), such as business metrics that are important measurements of your business. For example, this could include a measure of the new accounts that you have opened in a given month. These key performance indicators are input to the assembly of the application. In addition, the indicators can be monitored in production to capture the critical data to measure if the objectives are being met.

Assemble

The business design is used to communicate the business objectives to the IT organization that will assemble the information system artifacts that implement the design. The enterprise architect works closely with the business analyst to convert the business design into a set of business process definitions, as well activities used to derive the required services from the activity definitions. The enterprise architect and business analyst work with the software architect to flesh out the design of the services.

During the process of resolving the design and implementation of the modeled business processes and services, a search should be performed of existing artifacts and applications in an effort to find components that meet the needs of the design. Some applications fit perfectly; some have to be re-factored; and some have to be augmented to meet the requirements of the design.

These existing assets should be rendered as services for assembly into composite applications. Any new services required by the business design have to be created. Software developers should use the SOA programming model to create these new services.

Lastly, the assemble phase includes applying a set of policies and conditions to control how your applications operate in the production runtime environment. For example, these policies and conditions include business and government regulations. In addition, the assemble phase includes critical operational characteristics such as packaging deployment artifacts, localization constraints, resource dependency, integrity control, and access protection.

Deploy

The deploy phase of the life cycle includes a combination of creating the hosting environment for the applications and the deployment tasks of those applications.This includes resolving the application's resource dependencies, operational conditions, capacity requirements, and integrity and access constraints.

A number of concerns are relevant to construction of the hosting environment including the presence of the already existing hosting infrastructure supporting applications and pre-existing services. Beyond that, you need to consider appropriate platform offerings for hosting the user interaction logic, business process flows, business services, access services, and information logic.

Manage

The manage phase includes the tasks, technology and software used to manage and monitor the application assets such as services and business processes that are deployed to the production runtime environment.

Monitoring is a critical element of ensuring the underlying IT systems and application are up and running to maintain the service availability requirements of the business. Monitoring also includes monitoring performance of service requests and timeliness of service responses. In addition, monitoring includes maintaining problem logs to detect failures in various services and system components, as well as localizing failures and restoring the operational state of the system.

Managing the system also involves performing routine maintenance, administering and securing applications, resources and users, and predicting future capacity growth to ensure that resources are available when the demands of the business call for it. The security domain includes such topics as authentication, single sign-on, authorization, federated identity management, and user provisioning.

The manage phase also includes managing the business model, and tuning the operational environment to meet the business objectives expressed in the business design, and measuring success or failure to meet those objectives. SOA is distinguished from other styles of enterprise architecture by its correlation between the business design and the software that implements that design, and its use of policies to express the operational requirements of the business services and processes that codify the business design. The manage phase of the life cycle is directly responsible for ensuring those policies are being enforced, and for relating issues with that enforcement back to the business design.

Governance

SOA governance is critical to the success of any SOA project. Governance helps clients extend the planned SOA across the enterprise in a controlled manner. SOA governance has four core objectives or challenges:

► Establish decision rights
► Define high value business services
► Manage the life cycle of assets
► Measure effectiveness

Note: For more detailed information about SOA governance, refer to Chapter 3, "SOA governance" on page 25.

SOA foundation reference architecture

This section describes the SOA foundation reference architecture (Figure 1-2), which includes the components and middleware services used by applications in the runtime environment.

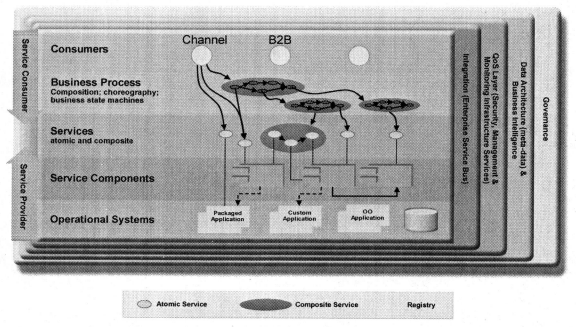

Figure 1-2   SOA foundation reference architecture: Solution view

Figure 1-2 shows the SOA foundation reference architecture solution view used to decompose an SOA design. SOA puts a premium on the role of the enterprise architect, who is responsible for spanning between the business design and the information system that codifies that design.

When taking a top-down approach, the enterprise architect starts by identifying the business processes and business services used by the business users. The business users are consumers of the processes and services. Business processes should be treated as compositions of other business processes and services, and therefore should be decomposed into their subordinate sub-processes and services.

Services and business processes are then detailed into service components. Service components include a detailed set of definition metadata used to describe the service to the information system. Services can be aggregated into module assemblies. The module assemblies are used to establish related design concerns, and begin the planning to determine what teams will collaborate to implement the related services to be deployed as a single unit.

The resulting set of business process definitions, services, and schemas make up the logical architecture of the application. The enterprise architect then needs to map that logical architecture to a physical architecture.

We have included a summary description for each of the services found in the logical architecture shown in Figure 1-3. The services found in the center (Interaction, Process, Information, Partner, Business Application, Access) are the core set of services used by application within the runtime environment when deployed. The other services (outer services) are used in support of the core services.

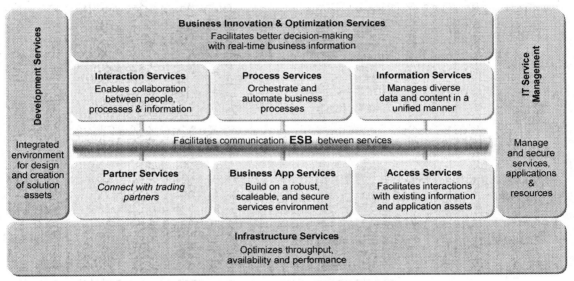

Figure 1-3   SOA Foundation Reference Architecture: Middleware services view

Core components of the logical architecture

This section includes a brief description on the following core components of the logical architecture.

Interaction services

Interaction services provide the capabilities required to deliver IT functions and data to users, meeting their specific preferences.

Process services

Process services provide the control capabilities required to manage the flow and interaction of multiple services in ways that implement business processes.

Business application services

Business application services are called by service consumers. Service consumers include other components in the logical architecture such as portal or a business processes.

Information services

Information services provide the capabilities necessary to federate, replicate and transform disparate data sources.

Access services

Access services provide bridging capabilities between core applications, prepackaged applications, enterprise data stores and the ESB to incorporate services that are delivered through existing application into an SOA.

Partner services

Partner services provide the document, protocol, and partner management capabilities for business processes that involve interaction with the outside partners and suppliers.

Supporting components of the logical architecture

This section includes a brief description of the supporting components of the SOA foundation logical architecture used in support of the core components.

► Enterprise Service Bus
► Business innovation and optimization services
► Development services
► IT service management
► Infrastructure services

Enterprise Service Bus

The Enterprise Service Bus (ESB) or simply bus, provides an infrastructure that removes the direct connection dependency between service consumers and providers. Consumers connect to the bus and not the provider that actually implements the service. This type of connection further insulates the consumer from the provider.

A bus also implements further value add capabilities, such as security and delivery assurance. It is preferred to implement these capabilities centrally within the bus at an infrastructure level rather than within the application. The primary driver for an ESB, however, is that it increases decoupling between service consumers and providers.

Although it is relatively straight forward to build a direct link between a consumer and provider, these links can lead to an interaction pattern that consists of building multiple point-to-point links that perform specific interactions. With a large number of interfaces this quickly leads to the build up of a complex spaghetti of links with multiple security and transaction models. When routing control is distributed throughout the infrastructure, there is typically no consistent approach to logging, monitoring, or systems management. This type of environment is difficult to manage or maintain and inhibits change.

> **Note:** An ESB can be thought of as an architectural pattern, with an implementation to match the deployment needs. There are two IBM ESB products:
> - IBM WebSphere Enterprise Service Bus
> - IBM WebSphere Message Broker
>
> In addition, there are a number of products that extend the capabilities of these ESBs, including DataPower® XML Security Gateway XS40.

Business innovation and optimization services

Business innovation and optimization services are primarily used to represent the tools and the metadata structures for encoding the business design, including the business policies and objectives.

Business innovation and optimization services exist in the architecture to help capture, encode, analyze and iteratively refine the business design. The services also include tools to help simulate the business design. The results are used to predict the effect of the design, including the changes the design has on the business.

Development services

Development services encompass the entire suite of architecture tools, development tools, visual composition tools, assembly tools, methodologies, debugging aids, instrumentation tools, asset repositories, discovery agents, and publishing mechanisms needed to construct an SOA-based application.

IT service management

Once the application has been deployed to the runtime environment it needs to be managed along with the IT infrastructure on which it is hosted. IT service management represents the set of management tools used to monitor your service flows, the health of the underlying system, the utilization of resources, the identification of outages and bottlenecks, the attainment of service goals, the enforcement of administrative policies, and recovery from failures.

Infrastructure service

Infrastructure services form the core of the information technology runtime environment used for hosting SOA applications. These services provide the ability to optimize throughput, availability, performance and management.

SOA foundation scenarios

The SOA foundation scenarios (or simply SOA scenarios) are representative of common scenarios of use of IBM products and solutions for SOA engagements. The SOA scenarios quickly communicate the business value, architecture, and IBM open standards-based software used within the SOA scenario. The SOA scenarios can be implemented as part of an incremental adoption of SOA growing from one scenario to using elements of multiple scenarios together. The concept of realizations are used to provide more specific solution patterns and IBM product mappings within the SOA scenarios.

The SOA scenarios can be used as a reference architecture implementation (starting point) to accelerate the SOA architecture and implementation of your customer scenario. Figure 1-4 displays the SOA scenarios and the relationship between them.

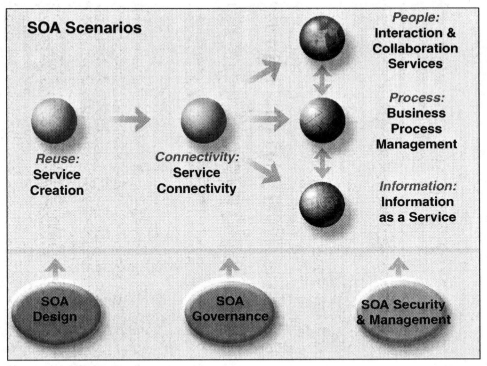

Figure 1-4   SOA scenarios and entry points

► **Service creation**—More details about this scenario can be found in *Patterns: SOA Foundation Service Creation Scenario*, SG24-7240.

► **Service connectivity**—More details about this scenario can be found in *Patterns: SOA Foundation Service Connectivity Scenario*, SG24-7228.

► **Interaction and collaboration services**

► **Business process management**—More details about this scenario can be seen in *Patterns: Business Process Management with the SOA Foundation*, SG24-7234.

► **Information as a service**

The scenarios can be used together and adopted incrementally. For example, the other scenarios commonly include service creation and often want connectivity. In addition, the scenarios can be used together, such as a portal accessing a business process or a portal accessing an information service through an ESB from a service consumer.

SOA design, governance, security, and management should be used in each of the SOA scenarios based on customer requirements.

SOA governance should (or almost must) be used to adopt SOA across the enterprise in a controlled manner with the objective of aligning the SOA initiative with the business objectives. Governance includes setting a baseline for measuring improvements, tracking SOA projects, building a pool of skilled resources, and establishing the structure for making decisions about SOA initiatives.

Companies that adopt an SOA need a solution for managing and monitoring services. In addition, they need of a security model that enables secure business transactions across enterprises and the Internet. The security domain includes topics such as authentication, single sign-on, authorization, federated identity management, and user provisioning.

Out of scope topics with references to other books

In the limited time available to write this IBM Redbooks publication we were not able to cover all the aspects of developing a real business process application using all the facilities of SOA and all the IBM Rational and WebSphere products. In this section we briefly refer to the areas that we do not cover in this book.

Composite applications and business process implementation

When it comes to implementation, this book focuses on individual services, and not composite applications or business processes.

The tasks that are described in detail in this book are the tasks performed by the developer of individual services, and not the integration developer, who would be responsible for the composition or choreography of services to implement a composite application or a business process.

The service implementation tool that is shown in detail in this book is Rational Software Architect, used by developers. The tool that is not showcased is WebSphere Integration Developer, used by integration developers. The main difference is that Software Architect is used to implement services and typically requires developers to be skilled in Java 2 Enterprise Edition (J2EE™), whereas Integration Developer is used to build composite applications (to compose services), and does not require detailed J2EE skills.

The tasks performed in Integration Developer would involve taking the Business Process Execution Language (BPEL) generated by WebSphere Business Modeler, and implement it. To implement the business process, the integration developer would use the services that we have identified, specified, realized, implemented, and tested (as described in detail). The integration developer would use the Web Services Definition Language (WSDL), or even the service implementations, that is, the enterprise archives (EARs). Also, Integration Developer would be used to implement the business rules, state machines, or specify human tasks for the human activities involved in the business process.

The result of this work would be the implementation of the solution required for the JK Enterprises Account Opening business process (see Chapter 2, "JK Enterprises case study" on page 17). This is a fundamental topic, and one can argue that we are not completely explaining how to build SOA solutions if we do not cover this topic. However, we do not talk about because it is already covered in other IBM Redbooks, such as:

► *Business Process Management: Modeling through Monitoring Using WebSphere V6 Products*, SG24-7148

► *Patterns: SOA Foundation - Business Process Management Scenario*, SG24-7234

Reporting and documentation

An important part of any project is the reporting and documentation mechanisms and the tools to automate these tasks. This book does not cover this aspect in any detail, but this section summarizes the key concepts and tools involved.

It has long been our assertion that reporting and documentation should be a side-effect of any useful work on the project. The use of automated tools is absolutely required to facilitate this approach. Reporting and documentation are a vital part of the governance of projects, but we have to be able to prevent this governance obstructing the project's progress.

Each of the tools used in this book provide a reporting mechanism specific to those tools. This is typically the production of one or more of HTML, Microsoft® Word, or comma separated values (CSV) files.

Rational SoDA

In addition to the tool-based reporting, we recommend the use of tools such as IBM Rational SoDA® to produce customized, integrated reports that cross product and role boundaries. The challenge is to work out what reports are really necessary. Here, our process was a key guide on what was really required, and we have tried to reflect this in the development case (see "JK Enterprises development case" on page 114).

Project involving SOA-based solutions can take advantage of the RUP SoDA templates provided as part of the tools and processes to minimize the customization work required in SoDA.

It has been our experience, however, both in the field and while working on the book, that static paper or file-based documentation, while a useful snapshot of the project, quickly becomes only useful for the recycling bin (real or virtual) and this leads to a discussion on real-time and historical data gathering and reporting.

In customer engagements and for internal use at IBM, we have found tools such as Rational ProjectConsole™ and Rational Portfolio Manager provide excellent access to real-time and historical data.

Rational ProjectConsole

ProjectConsole is particularly useful in presenting a real-time view of the project artifacts. For example, anyone with the correct access rights can view requirements, defects, and other project data through a Web interface. ProjectConsole also gathers and stores historic data from the tools to allow metrics, such as defect rates. The useful measures are not the absolute numbers, but rather the first- and second-order derivative measures[1].

The beauty of ProjectConsole is that it automatically gathers the data as people use their desktop and server tools. This means no filling in reports every day, week, or month. Useful metrics are gather just by people working on the project (hence the idea of reporting as a side-effect of doing useful work). We found this approach to gather information quickly becomes invisible to the users. The metrics become particularly interesting when correlations are examined. For example, drilling down into a high defect rate might reveal that the code has been churned just prior to testing. A closer examination reveals that the design was unstable because of some late requirements changes. It is vital that these metrics are not used to conduct a witch-hunt but rather to assist the project team on deciding where to allocate resources more effectively, who needs help, or what aspect of the project requires more focus.

Rational Portfolio Manager

While ProjectConsole tends to look at the technical metrics, Portfolio Manager provides a dashboard for the financial, resource and project planning aspects of

---

[1] A defect count of 100 is not a useful metric for the project manager, a 50% decrease in defects (or increase) since last week, or even the deceleration of defect rates tells us more about the project health. These numbers should be read in the context of our process (these numbers may be great in the middle of a project but a little worrying if we plan to ship the same week). In the past, IBM Rational has used the concept of a "defect glide path" in our internal development teams - where the project and product managers watch the defect rates trajectory towards zero known critical defects as a predictor of when the product is ready to ship

a project, program, or the enterprise. By having the participants use the Portfolio Manager tool in their day-to-day work (for example, creating project proposals, entering time sheets either directly or fed in from a time recording system) the ability to gather and report on this data automatically removes some of the obstacles to getting consistent, updated metrics. However, it is vital that this tool is the authoritative source of data. Project planning by spreadsheet must be abandoned if we want to get a consistent picture of the enterprise.

Another important aspect of Portfolio Manager that is particularly relevant to this book is how we can use our process to generate project plans. Our process and development case (created in Rational Method Composer) can be used to generate a work breakdown structure that is used as a template for project plans. There is scope for contiguous process improvement by adjusting our process and development case based on examination of the project actuals or details.

Any project produces work products as the project takes its course. An important decision is which work products are useful only for that project, and which work products should be contributed to the living documentation for the services under development. Models assume a much greater significance when the many aspects of the final service implementation can be generated from the models using the tooling.

We have touched on some aspects of IBM Rational SoDA, IBM Rational ProjectConsole, and IBM Rational Portfolio Manager. The use of these tools is a good topic for a future IBM Redbooks publication.

Software configuration management

Software configuration management is the *control and synchronization of work products of a software system* [RUP V7]. Good software configuration management avoids the problems of overlapping and conflicting changes on work products, and the potential confusion caused by multiple versions of a work product.

All the work products in this Redbooks publication were placed under software configuration management. Good management of the work products is even more important for SOA-based solutions. In the JK Enterprises example, we demonstrate how to build a set of services. Typically, this would only be the start of the life of these services. We would keep the work products produced in this document as part of the ongoing documentation for the services. We have to make sure that the service implementations are matched to the rest of their work products.

IBM Rational's key solution for software configuration management are IBM Rational ClearCase® and IBM Rational ClearQuest. These products provide a secure repository for storing changes and tieing these changes into the reason for the change. ClearCase is the place we store different versions of a work product. ClearQuest stores the defects and enhancement requests, and manages tests for these work products. While both products can be used on their own, the main advantage is to combine these products so that each of the versions stored in ClearCase are tightly coupled to the defect or change request associated with this change.

More information about ClearCase and ClearQuest can be found in the IBM Redbooks:

- *Software Configuration Management: A Clear Case for IBM Rational ClearCase and ClearQuest UCM*, SG24-6399
- *Rational Business Driven Development for Compliance,* SG24-7244
- *Rational Application Developer V6 Programming Guide*, SG24-6449

Governance

We cover SOA governance in Chapter 3, "SOA governance" on page 25, but a comprehensive treatment of governance is not intended by this document.

Summary

This introductory chapter introduces the key concepts behind SOA, the SOA life cycle, and IBM SOA reference architecture.

We also describe some of the aspects of developing solutions and the relevant IBM tooling that is not covered in detail in this document.

JK Enterprises case study

This chapter introduces the case study used throughout this book. This chapter contains these topics:

► An overview of JK Enterprises, the company

► JK Enterprises business problems

► The proposed solution

► Assumptions

Introduction

This book uses the a single example throughout to illustrate the use of IBM tooling and processes to build SOA-based solutions. JK Enterprises is a purely fictitious supply company that has specific goals and constraints that provide a typical set of challenges for the team implementing an SOA-based solution. JK Enterprises is an example that appears in other IBM material. We have adapted the example in some places to illustrate particular points relevant to building SOA solutions using the IBM Software Delivery Platform (SDP).

An overview of JK Enterprises

JK Enterprises has approached us to assist in building a solution to meet some specific business goals. As part of our initial discussions with the company, we meet the CEO and CIO of the company.

CEO interview

The CEO of JK Enterprises turns out to have a very positive outlook on the company's future and has told us this about the company:

► "JK Enterprises is a premier supplier to retail, small business and corporate customers. The company started in 1935, and currently has 11000 employees in 900 offices in 6 countries. This includes 6 call centres and 8 data centres. Our success is based on a high-touch interaction with customers. Part of this high-touch approach is that customers can use multiple channels to interact with the company. The company wants to offer the best customer service at the lowest cost."

► "JK enterprises already has an e-business site (JKe) with the lowest cost per order in the industry. We recently acquired Jensen Inc. and this has allowed us to strengthen our corporate customer base. We treat our corporate customers as true business partners."

► "We want to be the most profitable, high-touch company in the industry. We are pursuing aggressive growth while minimizing risk. We will optimize our corporate organization to maximize company responsiveness. We will maxims our strategic investments in the best Web site in the industry, the best sales force in the industry, a global CRM and sales-focused call centers."

CIO interview

The CIO of JK Enterprises is slightly less cheerful and clearly has been having a difficult time in the last few years. He now has a plan to address many of the issues he faces and we are part of that plan. His view on the company is as follows:

► "We cover multiple market segments, and through multiple channels. The integration with Jensen, which we started in 2000, is still in progress."

► "We have eight data centres and about 200 IT staff. We have a mixture of build and buy applications including SAP®, Siebel®, CICS®, and batch applications. We have applications that we acquired as part of the Jensen purchase that have yet to be integrated. We have a new CRM system that is still being implemented and we add analytics. We have multiple platforms and a heterogeneous topology. To be frank, we have very little reuse of components and skills across the company and this is something I want to address."

► "As we transition to SOA, we have a series of challenges ahead. We have set up an organization to support shared services. HR was first, and SAP ERP was next, but it took a long time to complete (it came from Jensen). CRM is the current project. We have a single database, but still keep information in different schemas according to the area of business they relate to. There is a resistance to sharing customer information across the lines of business (LoB). We have no common terminology and cannot get the LoBs to agree. Before we can implement SOA on a large scale, we have to get the LoBs aligned, normalizing their requirements and designing services with the right level of granularity."

► "We have 2000 IT staff using more than 50 different development tools and environments. We have no end-to-end methodology. Governance is a big issue that we have to address. You have heard about our business technology optimization program. This will support a major development based on SOA."

► "Thankfully, we have identified the key business processes that need optimization. We do have a good idea of the current processes in this area and how they have to look. Fixing these key business processes will help us achieve our business goals. Implementing the automation aspects of a solution will test our new methodology based on the IBM Rational Unified Process for SOMA."

After a double espresso or two, we dive a little deeper into the particular challenges the company is facing.

Business problems

Opening an account is one of the key business processes that is in need of improvement and automation. This process covers four different functions in the business: Account sales, application, verification, and activation.

We capture the key issues for each business function:

► **Account sales** issues are:

- Account application processing delays: Customers want to use their accounts as soon as possible.

- Account status is unavailable while the account is being set up: The business cannot answer customer queries about how the account application is progressing.

► **Account application** issues are:

- Complex application forms

- Different format and information required for applications for different products, when they could use the same format.

- Errors due to re-keying of information. Information is re-keyed from paper applications as well as between different, disconnected systems.

- Lack of single customer view. There are multiple systems that include customer and account information at the company. The primary system is an operational CRM, which is considered to be the master source of data for customer name, address and relationship information.

► **Account verification** issues are:

- No single, consistent view of the customer

- Too many customer applications are declined because of different regional credit scoring policies.

- Credit checks are faxed or called in to the credit checking agency. This takes too long and is too expensive.

- Too many applications are referred for credit checks.

► **Account activation** issues are:

- Manual updates to multiple systems is required to activate the account. The data is re-keyed into the ERP system, a data warehouse and billing system.

Proposed solution

It is clear from the list of business problems that we have a few areas of improvement. This book shows how we:

► Create business use cases.

► Document an improved business process.

► Identify, specify, design, and implement services to support the business process improvements.

► Test the implemented services.

We focus on two areas of the business. The primary area for improvement is sales management, and the secondary area is customer service:

► In the sales management area, we look at improving the *Account Opening* process. We optimize the business process, and then look for areas where automation can reduce the costs and speed up the process. Inside this process, we have an *Account Verification* sub-process that we will improve by speeding up the account eligibility task. This task determines whether we bypass a credit check or send for a full credit report.

► In the customer service area, we will make it possible for prospective customer to check on the progress of their account application.

Account verification improvements

Our solution for account verification involves an integrated way of performing these tasks:

► Verification of customer information

► Retrieval of credit report, if necessary

► Request of additional documentation for a low credit score

► Determination of pricing plan based on customer credit score

► Acceptance of account application and account activation, if the account application is approved, or rejection notification, if not approved

The JK Enterprises case study is used to illustrate improved efficiency, reduced costs and latency, and increased customer satisfaction of account management. The specific business goals and objectives are to optimize account setup to:

► Improve sales and customer service through increased speed and responsiveness.

► Enhance productivity through reductions in total cost of ownership (TCO).

- ► Reduce regulatory non-compliance risk and increase consistency via rules-based business process management.

To achieve these goals, we need to improve the business process.

An analysis of the business problems and our approach

Even in this simple example, we have problem areas, how the problems affect the business and dependencies between problems can be hard to relate to each other. Reading this information in a series of documents or presentations can be a challenge. Using visualization to analyze the situation makes it possible to rise above the details, abstracting away information that is not relevant at the moment and enables the reader to focus on the issues at hand. Figure 2-1 illustrates these issues and their dependencies using a repurposed class diagram.[1]

Each problem area is represented using a class element with a description of the problem as its name. and the implications of that problem listed as attributes within the class element. Each problem in turn has an impact and dependency on other problems and these are connected using the dashed arrows. In this way, we can look at the problems and easily discern which problems have an impact on other problems.

Take the Account Application problem area. This problem area affects the business because we are not able to provide accurate information about status and related account information (among other things). Solving the Account Application problem requires that we also activate the account (Account Activation), because the Account Application depends on this activation. Account Activation itself has dependencies on Account Verification and feeds to other systems, and so forth.

We analyze the problems by breaking them down into smaller problems, with their implications and dependencies.

---

[1] This diagram is drawn by creating a model in IBM Rational Software Modeler, and then showing the elements in a Unified Modeling Language (UML) class diagram. We represent each problem area using a class, list the implications as attributes of that class, and then use UML dependencies to connect the problem areas. The model could be further manipulated using other class diagram to view subsets of the model as required. This is a powerful way of working with this information. While this is not a standard way of using UML, the technique of using stereotypes on UML elements to represent aspects not considered when UML was first developed is a common practice and is part of the power of both the UML and the IBM tooling that supports UML.

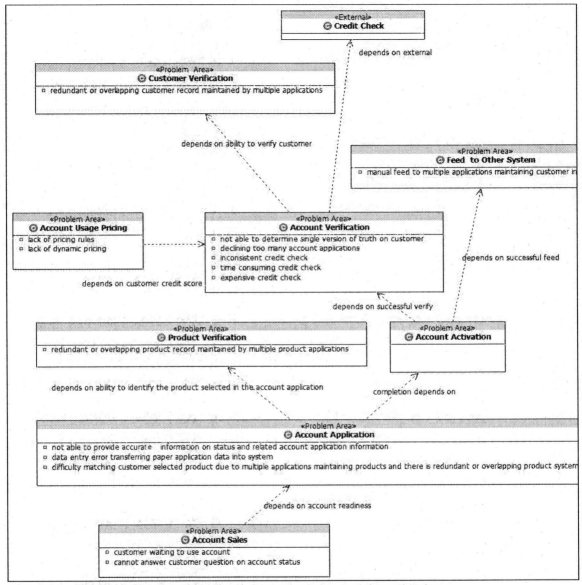

Figure 2-1   Problem areas, their implications for the business, and dependencies

Approach

As mentioned previously, we focus on two areas of the business: Sales Management and Customer Service. Within Sales Management we look at the

Account Opening process to leverage automation to speed up the process and lower costs. Within Customer Service we make it possible for prospective customers to check the status of their application. Based on an analysis of Figure 2-1 and the supporting artifacts, we see that there are a number of problem areas that are interrelated. As such, our approach to address the business problems areas is to focus on the following:

► Improve the Account Opening business process of the sales management functional area under the servicing and sales area business component.

► Improve the Account Application process.

► Improve the Account Activation process.

► Improve the Account Verification process:
  – Improve the Determine Applicant Eligibility process.
  – Improve the Credit Check process.
  – Use an external address verification service.

► Improve Account Inquiry using consistent and accurate account application status and account inquiry.

Assumptions

In an effort to limit the scope of this book, we have made the following assumptions about our work at JK Enterprises:

► JK Enterprises is not undergoing a complete organizational business transformation. We undertake what RUP calls *business improvement*.

► We do not assess the organizational structure and we do not make changes to that structure.

► We limit ourselves to analyzing a subset of the JK Enterprises business problems in the area of Account Management and Customer Service.

► We assume the stakeholders are as followed:
  – Prospective customers
  – Account coordinators
  – Account manager
  – Risk assessors
  – Customer service department head
  – Credit department head
  – Information technology department head
  – Chief Information Officer
  – Chief Executive Officer

► We continue to use our current external credit scoring agencies.

3

SOA governance

SOA governance is necessary for the successful adoption of SOA, partly because of the cross-organizational nature of SOA where service funders, designers, implementers, maintainers, or consumers are not located in the same organization (business, IT, department, LOB, division, enterprise). SOA governance ensures that the value proposition of SOA is achieved.

SOA governance could be the topic of another Redbooks publication. In this chapter, we do not attempt to cover all of SOA governance, but simply to raise your awareness about why it is important, to define what it means, and to show how SOA governance is supported in the IBM products that used for SOA solutions.

This chapter discusses these topics:

► The importance of SOA governance
► SOA governance definition
► Service life cycle
► SOA governance life cycle
► IBM products for SOA governance

Importance of governance

This section talks about the challenges governance addresses, as well its benefits.

Challenges

Challenges addressed by SOA governance include:

- **Establishing decision rights**: Who decides who can use a service and how it can be used? Who owns the service? Who funds shared services? Are the service QoS standards clearly defined?

- **Defining high value services that are business-aligned**: Does IT have a clear understanding of the business value? What are the success factors?

- **Managing the life cycle of assets (including services):** What is the impact of a specific service going down? How are service users notified of change? Who needs to approve changes?

- **Measuring effectiveness**: How can you make sure different departments or divisions with disparate goals all provide business value? What are services performance goals? What service level agreements are needed? How to gather performance metrics?

Benefits

This section lists benefits of adopting governance, quoted from the MIT Sloan school of management:

"Effective IT Governance is the single most important predictor of value an organization generates from IT."

- **Increasing share price**: Professional investors are willing to pay premiums of 18-26% for stock in firms with high governance.

- **Increasing profits**: Top performing enterprises succeed where others fail by implementing effective IT governance to support their strategies. For example, firms with above-average IT governance following a specific strategy (for example, customer intimacy) had more than 20 percent higher profits than firms with poor governance following the same strategy.

- **Increasing market value**: On average, when moving from poorest to best on corporate governance, firms could expect an increase of 10 to 12 percent in market value.

Definitions

This section contains definitions from the IBM Rational Method Composer plug-in for SOA Governance (refer to "Rational Method Composer" on page 32 and "References" on page 38 for more information).

Governance

Governance is about:

► Establishing chains of responsibility, authority, and communication to empower people (decision rights).

► Establishing measurement, policy, and control mechanisms to enable people to carry out their roles and responsibilities.

Governance looks at assigning the rights to make decisions, and deciding what measures to use and what policies to follow to make those decisions. The decision rights are assigned to roles, not to individuals. Management, on the other hand, includes assigning staff to the roles and monitoring the execution of policies.

Compliance

Part of any governance solution is meeting the organization's compliance requirements. Compliance is documenting and proving that governance is in place and is being executed: decisions are documented and decision policies are followed.

Compliance can also be seen as an opportunity for setting up governance, and make you think about what the decisions and roles are. Then, once in place, governance helps with compliance.

You can think of governance as a way of empowering and enabling people, so that decisions can be made that ensure the delivery of successful projects.

Management

Governance determines who has the authority to make decisions, whereas management is the process of making and implementing the decisions.

IT governance

IT governance is the application of governance to an IT organization, its people, processes, and information to guide the way those assets support the needs of the business.

IT governance refers to the aspects of governance that pertain to an organization's information technology processes and the way those processes support business goals.

IT governance may be characterized by assigning decision rights and measures to IT processes.

SOA governance

SOA governance is an extension of IT governance specifically focused on services and the life cycle of other SOA artifacts.

Specifically, SOA governance focuses on the methods and processes around service identification, funding, ownership, design, implementation, deployment, reuse, discovery, access, monitoring, management, and retirement.

SOA governance is a specialization of IT governance that puts the key IT governance decisions within the context of the life cycle of service components, services, and business processes. It is the effective management of this life cycle that is the key goal of SOA governance.

SOA governance ensures that:

► The value proposition of SOA (business process flexibility and improved time to market) is achieved.

► Business risks are mitigated, and control is regained (by maintaining quality and consistency of service).

► Team effectiveness is improved (by measuring the right things and having clear communication between business and IT).

SOA governance addresses challenges such as:

► What new organizational roles and structures facilitate service identification, design, and sharing?

► What metrics support investment, maintenance, vitality, and sharing of services?

► How do businesses decide to invest in service creation and maintenance?

► What is an enterprise's service-orientation maturity?

► What education, training, or mentoring is required?

Service life cycle

The service life cycle comprises the states services may be in and the events that trigger transitions between these states.

Think of a service's life cycle as a business state machine with states (positions) in which services can exist, and transitions that make them evolve from one state to another.

SOA governance is about planning, defining, enabling, and measuring around the service life cycle. SOA governance defines what the service states are, what actions need to happen to move from state to state (transitions), how (processes and methods), and by whom (roles, guards).

For example, SOA governance can define what services states are, such as identified, funded, specified, implemented, approved, operational, published, deprecated, and retired.

The development platform then has to support services through their life cycles and make sure the processes in place are followed. For example, service registries and repositories have to allow users to take action so that services evolve through their life cycle. Collaboration and portfolio management tools need to allow users (and just those who have the rights) to make decisions that move services from one state to another, and notify users that need to take action.

SOA governance life cycle

In "SOA foundation" on page 2 you were introduced to the SOA foundation life cycle, including the underpinning SOA governance life cycle. These two life cycles have to coexist within the organization to ensure that we are successful in our SOA implementation.

The governance life cycle helps us in meeting the challenges mentioned earlier in this chapter, such as decision rights, business alignment, asset life cycle, and effectiveness. By working through the governance life cycle, we position ourselves to succeed as we work through the SOA foundation life cycle, including model, assemble, deploy, and manage. In this section, you learn about the SOA governance life cycle (as shown in Figure 3-1) in more detail.

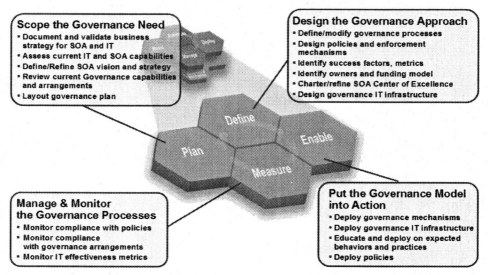

Scope the Governance Need
* Document and validate business strategy for SOA and IT
* Assess current IT and SOA capabilities
* Define/Refine SOA vision and strategy
* Review current Governance capabilities and arrangements
* Layout governance plan

Design the Governance Approach
* Define/modify governance processes
* Design policies and enforcement mechanisms
* Identify success factors, metrics
* Identify owners and funding model
* Charter/refine SOA Center of Excellence
* Design governance IT infrastructure

Manage & Monitor the Governance Processes
* Monitor compliance with policies
* Monitor compliance with governance arrangements
* Monitor IT effectiveness metrics

Put the Governance Model into Action
* Deploy governance mechanisms
* Deploy governance IT infrastructure
* Educate and deploy on expected behaviors and practices
* Deploy policies

Figure 3-1   SOA governance life cycle

The SOA governance life cycle comprises four phases:

► **Plan**: Good IT and SOA governance results in better alignment of the IT organization and business needs. It is in the plan phase that needs and priorities of the business are documented along with the role of the IT organization in meeting these needs. Also, the state and maturity of the current IT organization governance is assessed, and gaps are identified. From this analysis, the governance vision and strategy (as well as the roadmap and plan) are documented. In the plan phase, the governance measures are put in place. These measures are used to assess how well the IT organization is aligned with the business and the business needs are met.

► **Define:** In the define phase, the detailed governance plan is put in place for the current cycle. In particular, the processes to be governed are specified and prioritized, and the decision rights, policies, and measures for these processes are defined. In preparation for the next phase, detailed deployment plans are set. In some cases, these plans may include specifying or updating the structure and staffing of the SOA governance center of excellence (CoE).

► **Enable**: The enable phase is when the defined solution is rolled out to the organization. In this phase, roles are assigned, staff are trained, decision rights may be automated in workflow tools, and metrics collection and report mechanisms are put in place.

► **Measure:** In this phase, the governance approach is executed and tuned. The governance metrics, those that show alignment with the business, are gathered. These metrics are used in the next cycle to revise the governance approach."

Refer to "Rational Method Composer plug-in for SOA Governance" on page 33 for more details.

IBM products for SOA governance

The IBM Rational SDP enables SOA governance with a portfolio of modular, open standard-based products, as illustrated in Figure 3-2. Note that you do not require all of these products to get started with SOA governance; there are adoption roadmaps for different entry points, and your organization's SOA governance dashboard will be a different, one that is customized for your needs.

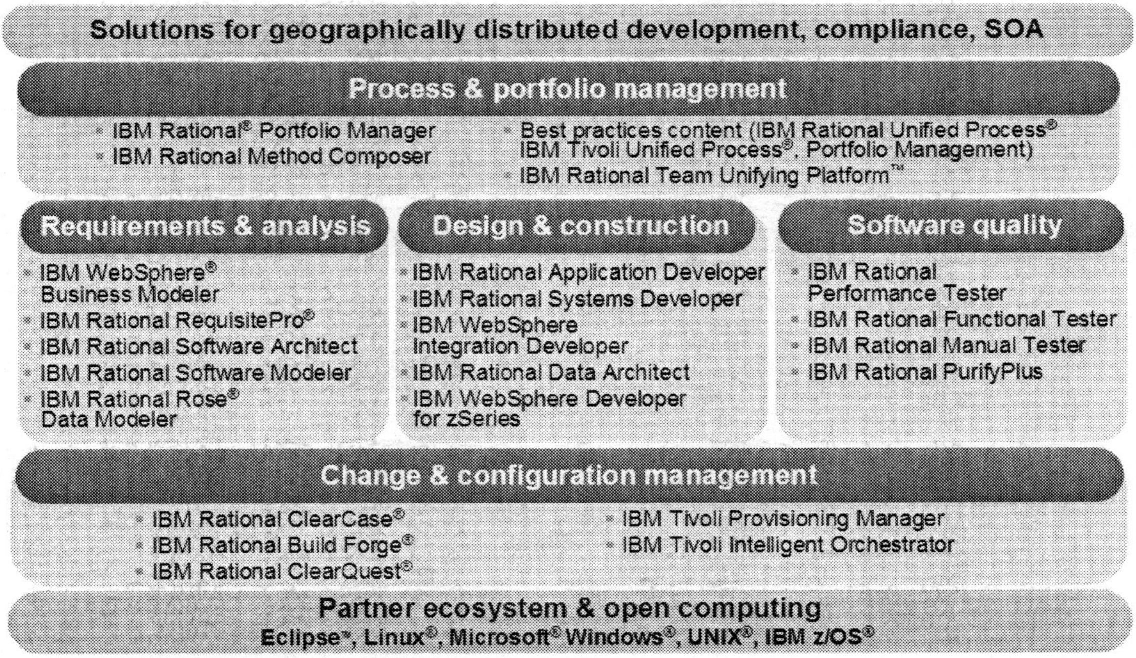

Solutions for geographically distributed development, compliance, SOA

Process & portfolio management
- IBM Rational® Portfolio Manager
- IBM Rational Method Composer
- Best practices content (IBM Rational Unified Process® IBM Tivoli Unified Process®, Portfolio Management)
- IBM Rational Team Unifying Platform™

Requirements & analysis
- IBM WebSphere® Business Modeler
- IBM Rational RequisitePro®
- IBM Rational Software Architect
- IBM Rational Software Modeler
- IBM Rational Rose® Data Modeler

Design & construction
- IBM Rational Application Developer
- IBM Rational Systems Developer
- IBM WebSphere Integration Developer
- IBM Rational Data Architect
- IBM WebSphere Developer for zSeries

Software quality
- IBM Rational Performance Tester
- IBM Rational Functional Tester
- IBM Rational Manual Tester
- IBM Rational PurifyPlus

Change & configuration management
- IBM Rational ClearCase®
- IBM Rational Build Forge®
- IBM Rational ClearQuest®
- IBM Tivoli Provisioning Manager
- IBM Tivoli Intelligent Orchestrator

Partner ecosystem & open computing
Eclipse™, Linux®, Microsoft® Windows®, UNIX®, IBM z/OS®

Figure 3-2   IBM Rational SDP governance dashboard

Key governance aspects supported by the SDP are:

► **Traceability**: Linkages between artifacts spanning the full SOA life cycle. For example, how can you make sure that a requirement is addressed in your design? What is the impact of a change in a requirement on your design? What test case verifies that a specific requirement is addressed?

- ▶ **Geographically distributed teams**: Today, strategy, analysis, design, development, deployment, and management teams are not physically located in the same building and sometimes span across the globe. How can the development platform support geographically distributed teams?

- ▶ **Compliance**: How can the development platform help your organization meet its compliance objectives?

In this section, we describe how specific IBM products (mainly from the governance dashboard) support the four phases of the SOA governance life cycle. Depending on your background, you may relate SOA governance to only one or two specific products. At the end of this section, you should see that more is needed to support effective SOA governance, from planning to defining, enabling, and measuring.

Rational Method Composer

Rational Method Composer is an Eclipse-based framework for process and method authoring, targeting primarily process engineers who want to tailor or create method contents and processes. For example, RUP for SOA has been codified using Method Composer.

Method Composer is the product that replaces Rational Unified Process (RUP) and RUP authoring products such as RUP Process Builder. Method Composer ships with processes, including:

- ▶ Classic RUP
- ▶ RUP for Business Modeling
- ▶ RUP for Service-Oriented Modeling and Architecture (SOMA)

Method Composer is based on the open source Eclipse Process Framework (EPF). The main difference between Method Composer and Process Framework is around process contents, such as the ones listed above. Process Framework only contains limited contents whereas Method Composer has a lot. Also, Method Composer provides additional integration capabilities with other Rational products, such as Rational Portfolio Manager.

Method Composer implements the Unified Method Architecture (UMA) standard, submitted to the Object Management Group (OMG) as Software Process Engineering (SPEM) V2.0. With this standard, everyone uses the same terminology around methods and processes. For example, SPEM defines what tasks, activities, roles, or guidance are.

Method Composer contents are packaged as plug-ins. A new plug-in can be based on an existing one. For example, RUP for SOMA is based on RUP, and provides variations (contributions, extensions, or replacements) for service-orientation.

The main output of Method Composer is an HTML site (formerly RUP site), with method and process contents, that is accessible from a Web browser and from within tools of the SDP, such as Rational Software Architect.

Also, Method Composer bridges the gap between process engineering and project management by providing the capability to export processes as Rational Portfolio Manager or Microsoft Project templates.

It is a key product for SOA governance because it supports the formalization of method and processes defined by SOA governance, which are then made available to entire teams.

Refer to "References" on page 38 for links to more Rational Method Composer or Eclipse Process Framework information.

Rational Method Composer plug-in for SOA Governance

The Rational Method Composer plug-in for SOA Governance V1.0 is available for download on developerWorks®:

```
http://www-128.ibm.com/developerworks/rational/downloads/06/plugins/rmc_soa
_gov/soa_plugin.html
```

The plug-in helps identify appropriate best practices, merged with your existing IT processes, to provide proper governance of the capabilities introduced with SOA. The end result is a project plan to create your organization's unique governance framework.

Refer to "References" on page 38 for a link to the developerWorks Web site.

Rational Portfolio Manager

Rational Portfolio Manager is a project portfolio management (hence its name!) tool targeted at business executives to support them in making decisions. Portfolio Manager helps make business decisions in the area of (sorted in chronological order):

► **Business priorities, alignment and trade-off:** These two activities involve evaluating initiatives based on internal performance and external demand. Then, trade-off decisions are made regarding what to pursue and when. Business alignment is key for SOA, and Portfolio Manager helps select the right initiatives. For example, Portfolio Manager provides a consistent way to look at demands with work and proposal templates. It also provides analytical tools (for example, investment maps and scorecards) to help deciding what the best mix of initiatives makes the best aligned portfolio. Also, initiative approvals are auditable, which supports compliance.

- ▶ **Source or resource:** Following the prioritization of initiatives, the next decision is about identifying the solution needed to meet the initiative's goal. Typically, a particular initiative may involve multiple projects. Decisions are made on using internal resources or outside vendors. Portfolio Manager helps improve resource utilization in geographically distributed teams. Also, it helps understand forecasted resource capacity (for example, supply and demand analysis, what-if analysis, demand scheduling, and real-time resource assignment).

- ▶ **Build or buy, and deployment-ready**: Knowing what resources are available, a decision maker can then decide whether to build from scratch, evolve an existing application, or buy a packaged application. Also, because there is not only a single project running, there is always the need to integrate (projects, people, ...) so that at the end, a solution can be delivered to support the identified initiative(s). Portfolio Manager supports this execution through its integration with Method Composer, which allows project teams to follow consistent methods and processes. Portfolio Manager also provides access to all project information (including historical data from past projects) through its centralized repository. Finally, Portfolio Manager provides an integrated way of assessing risks, issues, and changes.

- ▶ **Value analysis**: It is then critical to know whether the selected initiative brings the intended value to the business. Portfolio Manager provides constant access to measurements and control throughout development. Using Portfolio Manager, IT can prove to the business how much value it delivers (for example, calculating earned value to predict project performance, providing warnings through trends).

- ▶ **Regulatory compliance:** Last but not least, businesses have to ensure regulatory compliance, and Portfolio Manager helps by providing graphical workflows that enforce and automate decision rights and responsibilities, as well as scorecards that show project compliance. Refer to "Compliance" on page 38 for more information.

Portfolio Manager is important for governance because it helps executives make business decisions so that an organization's portfolio is best aligned to business priorities, as is key to the success of SOA. Also, it helps define and enforce decisions right, a central part of governance.

Rational RequisitePro

RequisitePro® is a requirements management tool. It stores requirements (and related information) in an underlying database and provides an easy-to-use (client or Web) interface to sort, search, filter and track dependencies between those requirements. RequisitePro allows for the description of requirements in Microsoft Word, which can then be stored in the RequisitePro database (using RequisitePro menus from under Microsoft Word). The database stores requirement details (attributes, links to other requirements, discussions, and revision history), while documents display the requirement text and context.

Rational Software Architect allows for RequisitePro requirements to be browsed, modified, or created (from within Software Architect, under the Requirement perspective). More importantly, design elements can be created from requirements, or existing design elements can be linked (traced) to requirements. The idea is to record how design decisions address requirements, and then be able to analyze requirements trace, including assessing the impact on the design of a change in requirements.

In addition, RequisitePro can be used in combination with WebSphere Business Modeler to ensure that the needs of the business are being captured and understood. When starting a project, the business, including executives, analysts and architects, can use RequisitePro to record the high-level business needs. The high-level business needs can take the form of goals, including objectives and strategy, as well as business rules. As the project moves forward, WebSphere Business Modeler can be used to add details to the business goals, modeling them as processes, and then using simulation and cost comparison reporting to help the business understand the return on investment. RequisitePro can be used to add business operational details, capturing both functional and non-functional requirements. A key aspect of capturing these additional details within RequisitePro is to find a balance between the needs of the business and the architecture.

RequisitePro supports SOA governance by allowing traceability. from business, design, implementation, or test elements to requirements, and also between requirements. It helps ensure that requirements are addressed throughout the overall development process.

Rational ClearQuest and Rational ClearCase

Rational ClearQuest is a change, test and application life cycle management application that can be used to manage change activities (such as defects and enhancement requests), test cases, and test assets.

ClearQuest enables users to manage any type of change request or test artifact throughout the entire development life cycle. User-defined queries, charts, and reports provide metrics useful to all roles within a project team. Customization capabilities enable ClearQuest to adapt to and help enforce any kind of development process and life cycle.

Rational ClearCase is a change and configuration management (CCM) solution.

ClearCase provides users with transparent access to versioned artifacts. It integrates with Microsoft Windows® Explorer as well as with many popular integrated development environments (IDEs), including Eclipse, the Rational SDP, and Microsoft Visual Studio® .NET. It enables development teams to incorporate configuration management seamlessly into their normal, daily workflow they can work as usual with minimal or no disruption.

ClearCase and ClearQuest support IT governance because they help enforce the process and life cycle that has been defined through Unified Change Management (UCM). They allow developers to know what they own, such as defects or software components. Moreover, it allows developers to make decisions on the artifacts they own. Senior developers own bigger software components or more critical defects, which empowers them to make more important decisions than junior developers can. Also, developers do not have to be aware of the IT governance process. For example, the ClearQuest queue tells them what they need to work on. When work is complete, they just deliver their work on the ClearCase system, and that is it, the ClearQuest state automatically changes (process enforcement). They just have to worry about what they own, and ClearCase and ClearQuest support the IT governance process. This is key to IT governance, and developers usually like to know the boundaries of their work.

As discussed previously, ClearQuest allows you to track any type of change request or test artifact. However, we also have to know how those these artifacts map back to our project requirements. Using the integration between CQ and RequisitePro, we can create links from requirements in RequisitePro to records in ClearQuest.

WebSphere Service Registry and Repository

The WebSphere Service Registry and Repository plays a central role in SOA governance.

The Service Registry and Repository supports the management and governance of services through their life cycles, and helps ensure services provide value to the business. It supports storing, accessing, and managing service metadata, which allows for the selection, management, and invocation of services.

The registry tells what the services are and where they are located. The repository tells about the nature of service usage, and their interactions.

The Service Registry and Repository capabilities are classified around:

- **Publish & Find** services to encourage reuse, including a subscription mechanism that provides dynamic access to service information by runtimes and users.

- **Enrich** services to enable dynamic and efficient service interactions at runtime.

- **Manage** services to optimize service performance, enable the enforcement of policies, do impact analysis, versioning, classification, and usage.

- **Govern** services through their life cycles.

The Service Registry and Repository supports SOA governance as services progress through their life cycle. For example, it supports services access control, monitors service vitality, and manages policies for publishing, using, and retiring services.

Let us explain how the Service Registry and Repository supports service management and governance.

The Service Registry and Repository provides a simple configurable life cycle model that can be used to manage governed entities (services) through their life cycles:

- As explained in "Service life cycle" on page 29, the life cycle is represented as a state machine, with the states indicating the position of the governed entity in its life cycle. Transitions are used to validate changes to the governed entities and apply control (guards) before performing the action represented by the transition.

- Governance is ensured because actions are constrained by the life cycle model. Following a successful transition the governed entity then adopts a new state. Also, changes in states are socialized to users through the notification mechanism, as well as audited when needed.

When a service is developed, its information (in the form of definition and metadata) is stored in the Service Registry and Repository:

- As the service moves towards deployment (through testing and approval), and SOA governance processes start to apply, the Service Registry and Repository ensures that the service complies with company policies and follows best practices.

- Once deployed into production, the service is used and reused. At some point, the governance process in place may determine that the service is no longer operationally needed, which trigger a retirement state transition in the repository.

- This process also enables an assessment of how subscribers are impacted if the service is retired.
- Finally, a service may be de-provisioned, but only when alternatives are in place for subscribers.

Note that the list of IBM products that support governance is not exhaustive. Many products support governance one way or the other, and some of the products listed in this section (for example, Rational Portfolio Manager and WebSphere Service Registry and Repository) play a more important role in SOA governance than others. Also, this section emphasizes the products from the Rational SDP.

Compliance

IT governance and SOA governance are closely related to compliance. Today, companies are required to follow key regulations, standards, and policies to comply with the law in regard to how they conduct their business.

This book does not cover any compliance issues. For information about compliance, refer to the IBM Redbooks publication *Rational Business Driven Development for Compliance*, SG24-7244.

The RUP plug-in for Compliance Management is a RUP-based method for strengthening the auditability of an organization's software development process and the work products it produces. The goal of this plug-in is to enhance an organization's ability to comply with internal and external policies and standards.

References

Visit the Web sites listed here for more information.

- IBM SOA governance page at:

  `http://www-306.ibm.com/software/solutions/soa/gov/`

- Download the IBM Rational Method Composer plug-in for SOA Governance V1.0 at:

  `http://www-128.ibm.com/developerworks/rational/downloads/06/plugins/rmc_soa_gov/soa_plugin.html`

- Download the IBM Rational Method Composer plug-in for SOMA at:

  `http://www-128.ibm.com/developerworks/rational/downloads/06/rmc_soma/`

- ► Download the IBM Rational Method Composer plug-in for Compliance Management V1.0 Beta at:

  `http://www-128.ibm.com/developerworks/rational/downloads/v7_0/compl_mgmt/`

- ► Consider the IBM SOA Governance Business Briefing:

  `http://www-128.ibm.com/developerworks/offers/techbriefings/details/governance.html`

- ► Read the Rational Method Composer developerWorks article series at:

  `http://www-128.ibm.com/developerworks/rational/library/dec05/haumer/`

- ► Refer to the Eclipse Process Framework site at:

  `http://www.eclipse.org/epf/`

- ► The CBDI Forum contains resources on SOA governance:

  `http://www.cbdiforum.com/`

Architecture and design

This chapter explores a central theme of SOA, that of architecture, along with its companion design.

This chapter addresses these topics:

► Is there still an application in an SOA environment?

► What does a service architecture look like?

► When does architecture end and design start?

► How are the goals of reuse achieved?

► How is software integration addressed in an SOA environment?

► Architectural styles and design patterns

As with the rest of the chapters in the book, we relate this chapter to the JK Enterprises case study.

What is an application in an SOA environment?

We take a tour through some important service architecture concepts by addressing the question "what is an application in an SOA environment?"

Traditional software applications

The term application (as an abbreviated form of application software) has been used for many years to describe the class of software systems that employ the capabilities of a computer to directly support a task that the user wishes to perform. The scale of application we consider in this book are those that exist in large enterprises (business or organization).

Traditionally applications have been built in a silo fashion. In other words, standalone applications that meet very specific business requirements with no inherent integration at either a process or data level (Figure 4-1). This has two effects:

► These applications do not support business processes well because they were not designed with business processes in mind.

► Integration between these applications is costly and piece-meal.

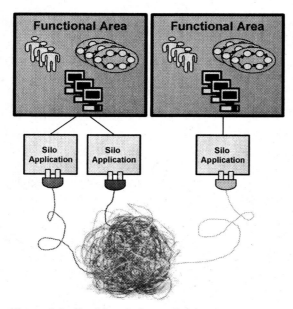

Figure 4-1   Traditional silo applications

Architecture of software systems

To look at how SOA improves the way applications are built, let us look at the definitions of two central concepts: *Architecture* and *system*.

- ► **Architecture**—From Latin *architectura* and ultimately from the Greek word for master builder : "*The art and science of designing structures where the structure of something is how the parts of it relate and how it is put together.*"

- ► **System**—From Latin *systema* and from the Greek *systema*: "*An assembly of entities/objects, real or abstract, comprising a whole with each and every component/element interacting or related to another one.*"

So architecture is specifically related to structure—which as we note is itself a fundamental property of every system—therefore these two terms are related. Indeed, we cannot talk about architecture without talking about the structure of the thing being architected. In our case we refer to this thing as the software system (and also we note that we are talking about software architecture here; business architecture is discussed in "Business architecture" on page 174).

There are two aspects to the *off-the-shelf* meaning of system that we have to be wary of:

- ► The division/aggregation of objects/entities into systems is a subjective abstract concept.

- ► The term system is usually relative, that is, a system may be part of a super-system and its parts may be sub-systems.

We want the service architecture we create to be clearly and finitely defined. Therefore, we really want our systems to be <u>less</u> subjective and <u>less</u> relative. To accomplish this, we make use of proven architecture styles, reference architectures and patterns, as discussed in "Reusing architecture and design experience" on page 73.

Note that we consider the terms *software system* and *software application* to be interchangeable. The term software system places more emphasis on the structure of the software, where as software application emphasizes the usage of the software—which is to directly support some user task or tasks.

> **Note:** In CMMI the term system is specifically used to include hardware (computational and non-computational), software and human workers. RUP for Systems Engineering provides system engineering guidance for this style of project.
>
> In this book we use the word system in the standard RUP sense to refer to software systems.

Service-oriented IT systems

In SOA, when we discuss architecture, our software is structured in terms of services, service consumers, and service providers. We define these here:

▶ **Service**—A service is a discoverable software resource that executes a repeatable task, and is described by an externalized service specification.

▶ **Service consumer**—A client of a service (or set of services).

▶ **Service provider**—A provider or implementer of a service (or, again, set of services).

So in an enterprise that is practicing SOA, if you peeked under the covers of its software applications and took a look at its internal structure you would find the things we have mentioned above: Services, service consumers, and service providers.

At the enterprise scale if you considered the insides of all of the software applications, the picture would rapidly become quite complex. To make this more manageable, we define three levels of software system (Figure 4-2):

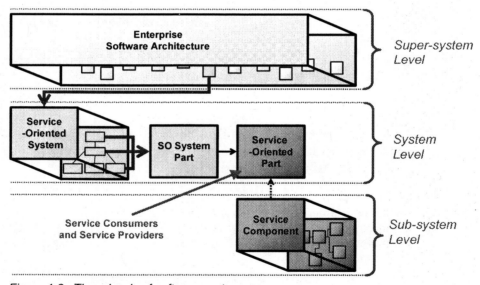

Figure 4-2   Three levels of software system

▶ **Enterprise software architecture** (super-system)—The sum total of all service-oriented software in the organization.

- ▶ **Service-oriented (SO) system** (system)—A set of service-oriented software assembled to form a composite application. Its parts are called SO system parts, themselves being created from service-oriented parts (which are individual pieces of service-oriented software specification that can be used in multiple SO systems). SO parts come in two flavours: Service consumers and service providers.

- ▶ **Service component** (sub-system)—An individual atomic piece of service oriented software design (at least, atomic from an architecturally significant point of view—see "Architecturally significant services" on page 57).

The service-oriented system (SO system) is about the closest thing in this picture to what we would traditionally call an application. So we discover that the first way in which our applications are different in an SOA environment has to do with what they look like on the inside.

> **Of interest:** There is an entire interdisciplinary field called *Systems Theory* that studies the theoretical properties of systems relationships as a whole. This science seeks to bring together theoretical concepts and principles from ontology, philosophy of science, physics, biology and engineering and has found applications in further fields such as organizational theory, management, economics and sociology. *Cybernetics* is a closely related.
>
> It is comforting to note that IT systems are relatively simple compared to some other types of systems out there!

Business-aligned systems

In order to improve the life span of our SOA software, we place more emphasis on understanding the business context for our applications.

Of primary importance here is an understanding of the functional areas in the business. The definition of these is the concern of business architecture which is described in further detail in "Business architecture" on page 174. However, for the purposes of the discussion here, we note that the business can be viewed as a set of functional areas. Each of these functional areas comprises (Figure 4-3):

- ▶ **People**: the people (roles) involved in the functional area.

- ▶ **Process**: The business processes that touch the functional area.

- ▶ **Technology**: The technology that supports the functional area. This includes the software systems (and in our case SO systems) that support this functional area.

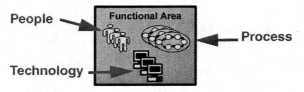

Figure 4-3   People, process and technology in functional areas

Besides simply ensuring that our SO systems support the business processes owned by the functional area, it is common for them to actually be driven by executable versions of these business processes. These executable business processes take the form of Business Process Execution Language (BPEL) artifacts.

These BPEL-implemented executable business processes tie together tasks performed by people in functional areas across the business, and therefore cross traditional application boundaries (Figure 4-4). Note two key differences with Figure 4-1 on page 42:

► There are no integration couplings required as the applications are integrated due to sharing the same underlying services.

► The workflow of the users is integrated by executable business processes.

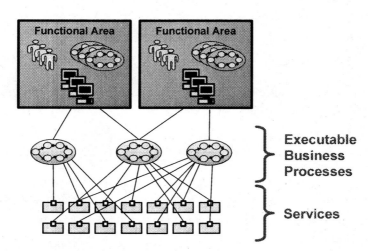

Figure 4-4   SOA-style applications

Note it might seem that the *applications* in Figure 4-4 have more to do with a perspective on the software from the point of view of a specific set of users rather than being some tangible software as with our traditional silo applications in Figure 4-1 on page 42.

To a degree this is true. But as reasoned in the previous section, it is useful to partition our SOA software into logical systems (which we have termed SO systems) to make the overall software picture more manageable (both at development-time and at runtime). Figure 4-5 shows an SO system in the context of the enterprise software SOA, and shows where the executable business process would fit in.

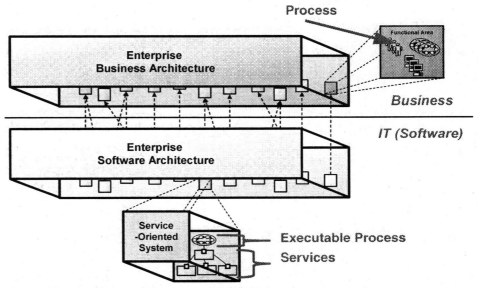

Figure 4-5   Business process-driven SO systems

Figure 4-5 shows us:

► Our business architecture is described in terms of functional areas; for more information refer to "Component business modeling" on page 175 which introduces component business modeling (CBM).

► We organize our service-oriented software into SO systems which can be placed in the context of the functional areas that they support (technology). Note that this is not necessarily a 1-to-1 mapping (although for simplicity the examples in this book use a 1-to-1 mapping).

► The business processes that we model and that we identify as touching the functional areas can be used to create executable business processes that drive our SO systems.

- Although it is not specifically shown in the diagram, in the same way that business processes can span across functional areas, executable business processes can span across SO systems—or to put it another way, the same executable business process can be a consumer in more than one SO system.

So the answer is...

So let us get back to our original question: "What is an application in an SOA environment?"

We answer by summarizing the concepts introduced thus far as statements about such an application:

- It is architected as a system of services, service consumers, and service providers.

- It does not exist as a single piece of software, but rather it is composed from a number of software parts.

- It is aligned with things in the business—specifically a functional area. It provides automation of parts of the business processes that are supported by the functional area.

- It is inherently integrated as its parts are shared across applications.

Why did we pose the question in the first place? Well it is a useful way to introduce a number of the key concepts that we expand on further in the rest of this chapter.

Modeling service architectures

The primary focus of this chapter (and indeed of the entire book) is on services. From the point of view of architecture, we care about the service consumers and service providers, and the applications or systems into which they are assembled to provide business benefit.

Before we start looking at the detail of how we model these applications or systems, we have to get a good feel for what the concepts are that these models are based on. It is of no use describing a model without first providing a description of the things that it is meant to represent.

Different forms of a service

The first aspect that we look at is the different forms of a service.

It may seem obvious as to what the thing is that we are referring to when we speak about a service. In reality, what we are referring to as a service can exist in a number of different forms.

We list the following perspectives to provide context for our forms:

► **Architecture specification**—In a software context, we use the term *architecture specification* to describe the black-box view of the parts of a software system. It also describes how these parts are joined together to form a software system.

► **Detailed design**—In this context we use the word design to describe the white-box view of a part of a software system. This describes the design realization of the specification.

► **Implementation**—Here we use the term implementation to refer to the source code (and corresponding binary) that implement the software designs.

► **Assembly**—This is about assembling service implementations in-line with the original architecture specification and deploying them to the target environment.

► **Runtime**—This perspective looks at the running software. In contrast the previous four perspectives are on development-time—in other words, their view is on the artifacts of the software development project as opposed to the running artifacts produced by a development project.

Now that we have listed this set of perspectives, let us examine the forms a service can take.

As we can see in Figure 4-6, the notion of a service extends across each of the perspectives (enclosed by the dotted-line box).

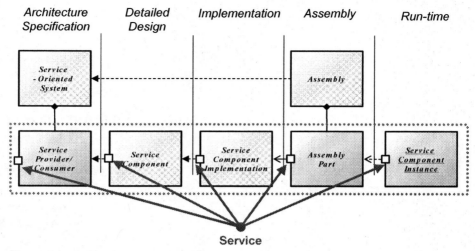

Figure 4-6 Different forms of a service

Architecture specification

In our architecture specification, services are either consumed or provided by a *service consumer* or *service provider*, respectively. The service itself is specified using a service specification.

An example service provider with associated service specification is shown in Figure 4-7 (service provider CustomerAccountMgr at the top providing CustomerAccount and AccountApplication services; service specification AccountApplication below, along with associated parameter types and messages).

The service architecture is specified as a number of service-oriented (SO) systems, whose parts are based on service consumers and providers.

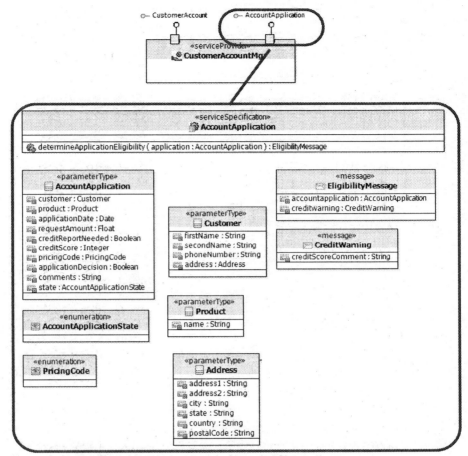

Figure 4-7   Example service provider and service specification

An example SO system is shown in Figure 4-8. In this diagram we can see a service consumer part, `accountOpeningProcess`, which is based on the service consumer, `AccountOpeningsProcess`. Similarly an example service provider part is `salesManagementComposite`, which is based on the service provider, `SalesManagementComposite`.

Note that the service consumers and service providers exist independently of the SO system—which is why we differentiate between the parts of the SO system (SO system parts that are an owned part of an SO system) and the service consumers or service providers they are based on (SO parts that live independently of the SO systems).

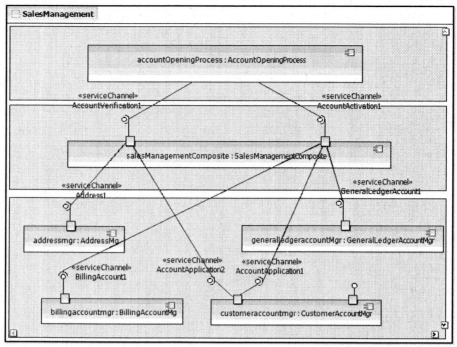

Figure 4-8   An example SO system specification

Detailed design

The *service component* is the modeling artifact that realizes the architectural specification of a service. Note we are still modeling our software at this stage (as opposed to writing code). However, we are modeling at a lower level of abstraction than that of our service architecture, and we include further design constraints that we want to place on the implementers of the specification.

> **Note:** There are other elements to design other than service components. These are outside the scope of this book. An example would be user interface component design.

An example of a service component detailed design is shown in Figure 4-9:

► Here we have a service component, AccountApplicationSC, which realizes the AccountApplication service specification provided by the CustomerAccountMgr service provider.

► The AccountApplication service specification provides our architecture specification, where as AccountApplicationSC is our detailed design.

- The design elements that form the detailed design (white-box internals) of `AccountApplicationSC` are `AccountApplicationFacade`, `AccountApplicationImpl`, and `AccountApplication`.
- We can see that some sort of facade design pattern has been used in the design of `AccountApplicationSC`.

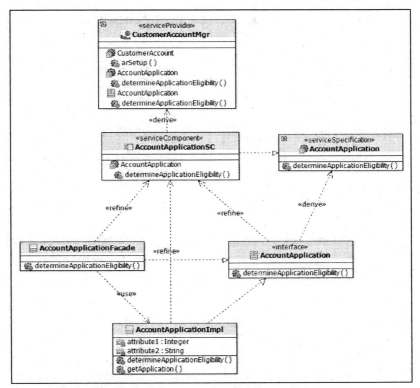

Figure 4-9   Example service component detailed design

Implementation

The *service component implementation* represents the actual software that realizes our architecture specification and detailed design models (and respects the constraints detailed in these models). Normally—but dependent on the implementation technology used—the service component implementation has two different forms itself: A source code form and a binary form. These can be classified as *service component source* and *service component binary*.

Assembly

Once we have service component implementations for each of the service consumers and service providers that have been identified in the SO system, it is time to start putting these pieces together into deployable units.

For each part in our SOA assembly, we take the relevant service component binary and configure it to form an *assembly part*. In Java Enterprise Edition the equivalent is a JAR file containing configuration (including runtime identity) and executable.

Figure 4-10 shows an example of a model element representing an assembly part. In this case AccountApplicationAP is the assembly part formed by configuring and building (in other words, creating a binary) a service component implementation that corresponds with the AccountApplicationSC service component.

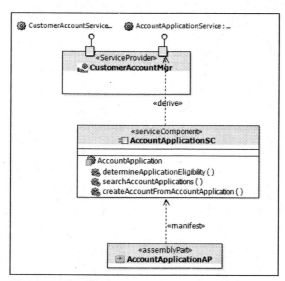

Figure 4-10   An example of an assembly part

Assembly parts are assembled to form *assemblies*. These assemblies combine a number of assembly parts into a larger grained unit for deployment. In Java Enterprise Edition the service assembly is an EAR file.

An example of this can be seen in Figure 4-11. The service assembly LocalSharedServicesAssembly assembles the parts BillingAccountAP, AccountApplicationAP, CustomerAccountAP, and GeneralLedgerAccountAP for deployment.

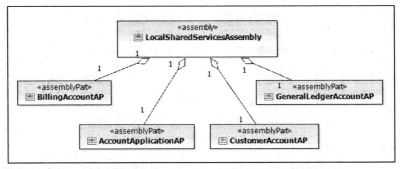

Figure 4-11   An example of a service assembly specification

One or more assemblies congregates a number of assembly parts to realize the original architectural specification as described by the SO system. An example of this is shown in Figure 4-12, which corresponds to the SO system specification shown in Figure 4-8 on page 52. The corresponding assembly parts have been separated into two assemblies, one containing the business process service consumer and the composite business application service provider, and the other containing the atomic business application service providers.

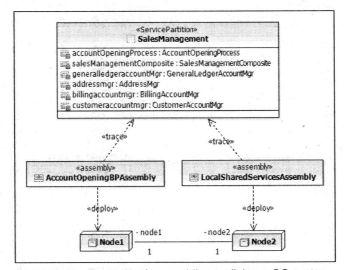

Figure 4-12   Example of assemblies realizing a SO system

Runtime

Finally, once the service assembly has been deployed and "started", the final form of the service appears—The *service component instance*. This is literally the service component as it is manifested at runtime—the process threads and state.

Note that the even though from a technology point of view there may be many threads running deployed on multiple nodes, there is still only one service component instance for each assembly part (this is described in further detail in "Decomposition and re-assembly of applications" on page 59).

With reference to Figure 4-13 we note that there are three different scales of software concepts:

► **SO system scale** (right column): SO system, deployed as an assembly, and existing at runtime as an assembly instance (which is a running instance of an assembly).

► **SO part scale** (left column): SO part, realized by the detailed design of a service component, and implemented in the form of a service component implementation.

► **SO system part scale** (middle column): SO system part (where we use a SO part in the context of an SO system), deployed as assembly parts, and existing at runtime as service component instances (running instances of the assembly parts).

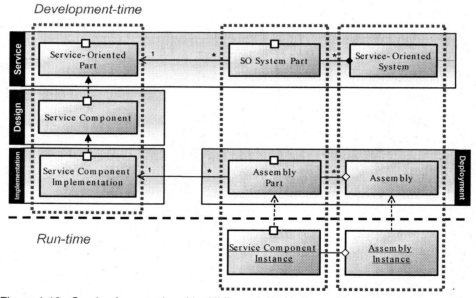

Figure 4-13   Service forms ordered by UML model and grouped by scale

All of the elements in Figure 4-13 are architecturally significant. We describe in the next section what we mean by this.

Architecturally significant services

As the name would suggest, in SOA we especially care about services at an architecturally significant level, hence the fact that we orientate our architectural view in terms of services.

At this point it would be useful to refer to the concepts of black-box versus white-box views. We make the following two simple definitions:

Black-box view   A view of something where the internal parts are not visible

White-box view   A view of something where the internal parts <u>are</u> visible

The black-box/white-box paradigm could be recursively applied to elements in a system as you "open up" its parts. However, the problem with a recursive view is that it provides no guideline as to when you are moving beyond the boundaries of architecture as you continue to open up the parts.

We feel strongly that it is necessary to know when the elements you are modeling are architecturally significant and when they are not. Otherwise:

► How do you show someone a clear and easy to understand picture that completely describes the system from an architectural level?

► How do you focus on modeling those things that have the most significance and impact on your software?

► How do you organize your service repository? It is very useful to be able to separate architecturally significant assets from those assets that are reused only in implementing architecturally significant assets (otherwise you just end up with a really big list of software assets and confusion about which assets to use in combination with each other).

► How do you know when you are finished with your architecture for a given perspective?

► How do you split up responsibilities/tasks between roles on the team, for example, between a software architect and a designer?

Preferably, we rather create quite a clear boundary between those elements that are architecturally significant from those that are not. This view is presented in Figure 4-14.

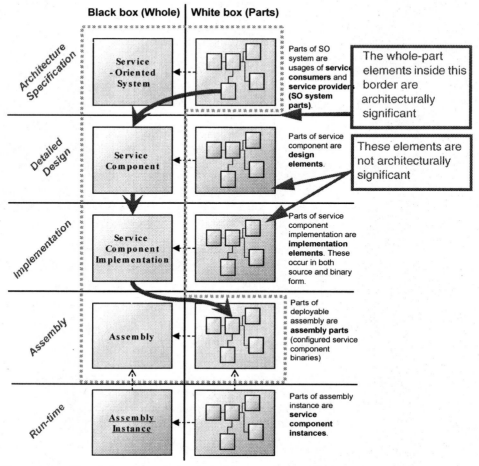

Figure 4-14   The delineation of what is architecturally significant in our models

▶ The dotted-line boundary defines which of the model elements are considered to be *architecturally significant*. Note that we specifically show that there are two sets of parts (white box views) that exist but do not fall within our architectural view—design elements and implementation elements. However, it is important to note that even though these elements themselves do not exist in the architecture, they are represented in the architecture by service component and service component implementation respectively.

▶ A whole-part relationship exists across each of the perspectives that we defined in "Different forms of a service" on page 49. Instead of recursively repeating this relationship to infinity, Figure 4-14 describes a fixed set of defined whole-part relationships (however in the design perspective, the design model elements that are parts of the service component can be nested as whole-part relationships as many times as you may care to).

► Figure 4-14 hints at the architect → assemble workflow (if you follow the curved arrows). This is further described in "Decomposition and re-assembly of applications" below.

With these observations as a backdrop, we provide a definition of what we mean by architecturally significant:

An architecturally significant element has a wide impact on the structure of the system and on its performance, robustness, evolvability, and scalability. It is an element that is important for understanding the system [Kruchten].

Architectural significance is also hinted at in the following quotation:

Architecture is what remains when you cannot take away any more things and still understand the system and explain how it works [Kruchten].

Decomposition and re-assembly of applications

In our brave new SOA world, one of our aspirations is to increasingly satisfy business requirements by assembling existing software assets instead of having to build new software.

The key reasons for this are:

► As your organization and software development processes become better geared towards this style of development, you are able to meet business requirements faster (as there is less new software that needs to be written).

► There is less software produced (in terms of lines of code or similar) to satisfy the same set of business requirements. And less overall software means that less software to maintain, which reduces the total cost of ownership (TCO) for your applications.

► Systems are integrated *out-of-the-box* as they share functionality and state. This is further described in "SO systems and integration" on page 69.

At this point, let us note two points:

1. To assemble a set of parts to create a new application, you have to start with a view of the parts that you require for the application.

2. To increase the chances of having a suitable component on the shelf to reuse, you must have a common architectural style that these components adhere to, and a corresponding set of architectural techniques for identifying components. By common we mean that they have to be rolled out across the organization.

The first point justifies our focus on architecture specification. The second point is described more fully in "Reusing architecture and design experience" on page 73.

Let us now look at the workflow for decomposing and re-assembling applications (Figure 4-15).

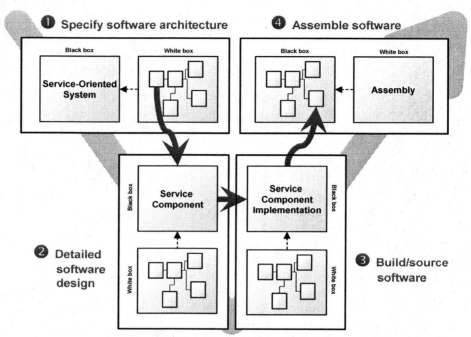

Figure 4-15   Overview of the workflow of part of the model → assemble SOA life cycle

Note: Figure 4-15 only provides a simplified workflow for the purpose of discussion. Specifically note that:

► The diagram makes the workflow look like a waterfall. In reality, the work done is sequenced using phases and iterations.

► The diagram only suggest the structural diagrams of the various models. The models additionally describe software behavior using behavioral diagrams.

► The diagram only covers part of the Model → Assemble → Deploy → Manage SOA life cycle.

1. Specify software architecture

Based on the requirements as they have been described for the project, an SO system is specified that supports these requirements (in some cases more than one SO system depending on the size of the project). The SO system(s) are either brand new, or they may be existing SO systems that require modification, or a combination of both.

For each of these SOA systems we describe their internals with a set of SO system parts that are based on SO parts (service consumers/providers).

These SO parts are either created or *sourced*.

> **Note:** We use the term *source* here and further in this section to mean "retrieve from an asset repository." This is where reuse comes into play and is a key advantage to the SOA approach, reusing specifications, designs, implementations and runtime instances in the creation of new systems.

Therefore, to summarize, the specification of our service architecture consists of:

► The specification of the structure of our SO system in terms of SO system parts

► The specification of each of the individual SO parts (service consumers and providers) that these SO system parts are based on

2. Detail software design

Once the service architecture has been specified, each part specified can now be designed separately.

We note again that we may be reusing an existing service component's detailed design rather than designing one from scratch.

3. Build or source software

Based on the detailed design of our service components, the next step would be to either create or source a service component implementation.

Each of these service component implementations can be unit tested on its own. Testing is described further in Chapter 14, "Service testing" on page 483.

4. Assemble software

Now that we have implementations for each of the parts in the SO system, we can put the pieces back together again as service assembly parts that combine in the form of a service assembly. These deployable assemblies are the deployable realization of our SO system specification.

Once a service assembly has been created, integration and system testing can be carried out. Again, testing is described further in Chapter 14, "Service testing" on page 483.

Referring back to Figure 4-14 on page 58, at runtime we see a service assembly instance. It is very powerful that we can trace these back to our software models in such a clear way:

► Running software can be traced back to our business requirements (in their various forms—business goals, KPIs, process policies, rules).

► Runtime metrics can be traced back to the corresponding business KPIs.

► Runtime problems can be traced back to the corresponding design and implementation artifacts.

► Communications within the project team between different roles across the different disciplines is much easier.

Services and reuse

The notion of reuse in the context of services is especially important and deserves some detailed treatment.

Specifically we describe:

► Some different types of reuse
► What can be reused?
► What needs to be in place to enable reuse?

Some different types of reuse

The following set of figures introduce a few different types of reuse scenarios.

As-is reuse of a service by multiple systems

Figure 4-16 shows probably the most obvious reuse scenario which is where the same service gets reused as-is by a second SO system.

Note that just because the second system is using the same service provider, it does not necessarily imply that the same service component design, service component implementation, service assembly, or service assembly instance is also reused.

For further information refer to "What can be reused?" on page 66.

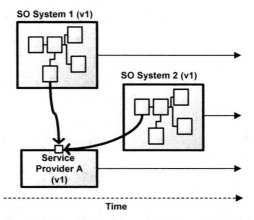

Figure 4-16   Reuse of a service provider version in multiple SO systems

Reuse of a service by successive versions of the same system

Figure 4-17 shows the most common reuse scenario, although it is not one which we would obviously recognize as reuse.

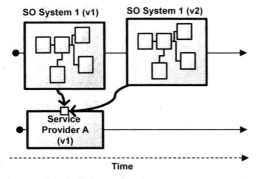

Figure 4-17   Reuse of a service provider version by two versions of the same SO system

This is the scenario when a new version of an existing SO system is created. Depending on the changes between the two versions of the system, most if not all of the services used in the original version are used in the new system. This means that the specifications of the SO system and the service consumers and providers that it uses can be used, the design of the service components, the service component implementations, the assemblies, and the assembly instances.

Reuse of a service with modification

Figure 4-18 can be a variation of both of the previous reuse scenarios. In this case, the service is modified before it is reused. Either the original system is migrated onto the new version of the service (which should be backward compatible) or the original version runs alongside the new version to satisfy its consumers.

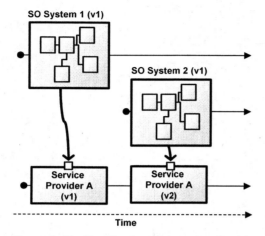

Figure 4-18   Modification of a service provider version for reuse in a second SO system

Usage of the same service twice in one system

Figure 4-19 shows one of the less common but still important types of reuse—that of the same service being used more than once in the same system.

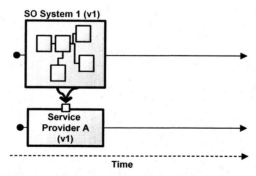

Figure 4-19   Reuse of a service provider by two different parts of the same SO system

This is easiest to explain with an example (Figure 4-20):

► Let us say that you have a contact management service which allows contact details to be stored and then searched against and retrieved.

► Further assume that contact details have to be held in a system for both customers as well as suppliers. In this case, the same service could be used for both—although you do not want your customer data and your supplier data getting mixed up.

► You could specify two SO parts for the SO system, both based on the same service provider.

► At deployment time you would have two different assembly parts, based on the same service component implementation, and being in the same assembly. Each assembly part would have a different configuration, specifically their runtime identity and data/state persistence area would be different in this case.

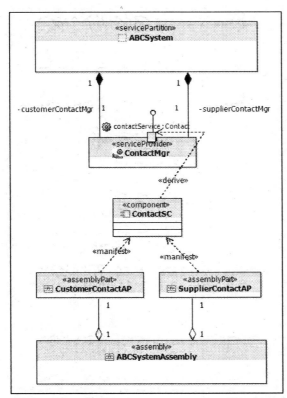

Figure 4-20   Example of same service used twice in same system

Figure 4-20 shows the ContactMgr (providing the Contact service) service provider being used as both the customerContactMgr and supplierContactMgr SO system parts in the ABCSystem SO system. The corresponding assembly parts are CustomerContactAP and SupplierContactAP, which are assembled into the ABCSystemAssembly. At runtime there would be two service component instances, one for each of the parts above. Each would have its own runtime identity and state (with these details being defined as part of their service assembly part specifications).

What can be reused?

The simple answer to this question is "As much as is sensible!"

A more thorough treatment of the various types of reuse in the context of asset-based development is provided in Chapter 15, "Creating reusable assets" on page 533 (especially an explanation of when it is sensible to make something reusable). In this section we discuss some specific points around the reuse of different forms of our service software (Figure 4-21).

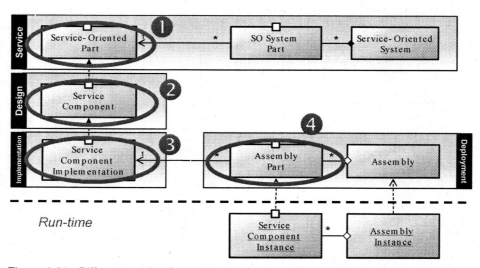

Figure 4-21   Different service forms that can be reused

The following descriptions relate to the numbers in Figure 4-21, which attempts to highlight the various forms of services that can be reused:

1. **Specification reuse**: The first artifact that can be considered for reuse is the UML package containing the specifications of the SO parts (service consumers and service providers). These can be reused as SO system parts in the specifications of new SO systems.

2. **Design reuse**: Second to reusing specifications, your can also reuse the UML package containing the service component and its detailed design. This can be reused instead of creating a new design.

3. **Implementation reuse**: If you reuse the service component and its detailed design, then it is likely that you also reuse the corresponding service component implementation. However in some cases you may have to create a new implementation for an existing design—possibly because the non-functional requirements are different (for example the implementation needs to be faster, or needs to scale more, or has different distribution characteristics).

4. **Runtime instance reuse**: If you reuse the implementation then it is likely that you also reuse the runtime instance. However, this is not always the case as we described in "Usage of the same service twice in one system" on page 64.

In general, if each of the numbered items in the list is thought of as a level, then reusing something at lower level implies also reusing each of the higher levels. However, reuse at a higher level does not automatically imply reusing the corresponding lower level artifacts.

Outside of the artifacts mentioned above, the following would also be candidates for reuse:

► Business processes
► Use case specifications
► Test cases (and matching test data)

Our discussions so far have focused on reusing artifacts that have been created during software development projects. There is also reuse of artifacts which assist in the creation of new artifacts. For example:

► Patterns (both automated and documented—Support for automated patterns in the Rational tooling is discussed in "Architectural patterns" on page 74)

► Transformations (transformations in the Rational tooling is discussed in "Model-driven development" on page 145)

► Templates

What has to be in place to enable reuse?

Keep in mind that reuse does not happen by accident. It requires effort and up-front planning. However once the pattern has been set, reuse should become part of *business-as-usual*.

The most common problems preventing reuse are listed here:

► Poor factoring of artifacts
► Ambiguous and bloated specifications
► Lack of interoperability of artifacts
► No summary level for managing artifacts
► No mechanism for publishing/consuming
► Activities are only project focused
► Lack of trust in artifacts: How do we know it works?

From this list of problems we can form a check list that has to be in place to encourage reuse:

1. Ensure that projects are producing outputs that are appropriate for reuse (increase reuse positives):

   – Shared standards

   – Consistent architectural style/design patterns

   – Usage of asset-oriented templates to create artifacts

2. Ensure that there are no factors that prevent reuse (decrease reuse negatives):

   – Use technologies that support component integration.

   – Ensure that mechanisms are in place to ensure asset stability before they are reused.

   – Ensure that mechanisms are in place that allow assets to change once they have been published without affecting current consumers.

3. Ensure that there is a desire to produce reusable assets:

   – Introduce incentives for producing reusable assets.

   – Monitor and then publish productivity increases caused by reuse.

   – Encourage projects to take a pragmatic approach to asset creation. Encourage projects to structure what they would normally create as assets rather than modeling/implementing a lot of functionality that they do not require because they think someone *might* need it in the future. Special strategic asset-creation projects can be spawned off to pro-actively create assets before they are required, but this takes special planning and funding.

4. Ensure that there is a desire to reuse assets:
   - Introduce incentives for reusing assets.
   - Project development case tasks should include searching for existing assets.
5. Ensure that there is a mechanism for publishing/consuming:
   - Enterprise and project level asset-based method support
   - Repositories for storing assets (with publish/consume capabilities)
   - Create ownership structures within the organization to manage and control asset publishing and consumption.

SO systems and integration

Figure 4-4 on page 46 introduced the notion that integration in SO systems occurs in a special way. We expand a little on that idea here.

First of all, let us look at what we mean by systems integration. In RUP the term used is enterprise application integration (EAI). The summary definition given there is as follows:

> EAI is the process of integrating multiple software applications that were independently developed, use incompatible technology, and remain independently managed. Fundamentally, EAI is about sharing and exchanging data and business processes among the different applications and data sources in the enterprise.

From reading the first part of this definition you may think that only externally bought in applications were the subject of EAI. After all, within an enterprise why would applications be "independently developed, use incompatible technology, and remain independently managed?" For anyone that has worked in IT, you know that this is traditionally more the rule than the exception.

Standard integration levels

RUP defines four main integration levels, which we describe in this section.

Data level

Data level EAI is a database-centric approach that consists of extracting data from one database and updating it in another. Sometimes the extracted data can be transformed before entering it into the target database, for example to apply specific business rules.

Data-level integration is commonly done through extract, transform, load (ETL) tools that can extract, transform, cleanse, and load data from various data sources to a common enterprise data repository.

Application interface level

This EAI level of integration consists of leveraging the interfaces provided by custom or packaged applications to access business processes and simple information. Usually this kind of integration is done in a three-step process:

1. Extract the information from one application through a provided application interface.

2. Convert the data in a format understandable by the target application.

3. Transmit the information to the target application.

The most common approach to implement this kind of integration is called *message broker*, an approach which standardizes and controls the flow of information through a bus or a hub framework.

Method level

This is similar to application interface level, but at a lower level of granularity. The idea here is not to share business functions (as in application interface level), but to share directly the different methods used to compose a given business function. All other enterprise applications that have to implement the same methods can use them directly without having to rewrite them.

The ability to share methods and to reuse business logic make this approach very suited for EAI. But the downside is that it is also the more invasive approach because it supports the modification of existing applications to allow the sharing at such a low level.

User interface level

User interface EAI is also commonly called *refacing* and consists of replacing existing text-based user interfaces of existing systems with a standardized interface, typically browser-based.

This kind of integration is less expensive than the other options, as the code of the existing applications is not modified. However, this approach is also less flexible for the same reason.

SOA and integration

One of the good features of SOA is that it does not try and reinvent the wheel in response to every problem. The SOA approach to integration makes use of a lot of the approaches to integration mentioned in the previous section. However it brings them to bear in an integrated fashion (integration of our integration approaches!) and adds further benefit as we describe in this section.

Two types of application/method level integration

There are two different types of application/method level integration evident in the scenario shown in Figure 4-22.

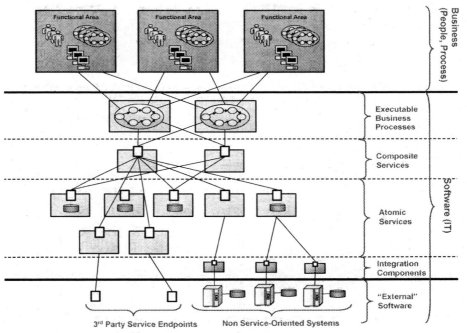

Figure 4-22   Example SOA integration scenario for discussion

Before we mention these, we provide an explanation of the usage of the terms internal and external here. These are terms used relative to our service architecture. Executable business processes, composite services and atomic services—as shown in Figure 4-22—are all internal to our service architecture. As can be seen, non-SO systems and third party service endpoints are all considered external to our service architecture.

Now that we have this definition, let us look at how it applies to application/method integration:

► **External software integration**: We service enable the non-service-oriented software using *integration services.* These are special services that are defined as an exact mapping of the interfaces exposed by the software they are service enabling. Both the third-party services and the integration-service-wrapped non-SO software are called from atomic services in our service architecture. One of the service providers of our atomic services are chosen to *manage* the state of each external system, and on this basis the external software is called from the implementation of the atomic service. This is further described in the architectural pattern "Pattern 7: Service enable non-SO systems" on page 92.

► **Internal software integration**: Inside our service architecture, software is integrated by the sharing of services between SO systems (SO applications). As can be seen in Figure 4-22, our atomic services are called from our composite services and indeed get shared between composite services. These composite services essentially form our new applications. It is important to note that as they share atomic services, they are therefore indirectly sharing state (as our state is either managed directly by the atomic services or by the external software that they are the proxy for).

Having described these two different types of application/method level integration, let us note the following:

► Atomic services become the data (state) integration points

► Atomic services are also where "external" software is integrated into our service architecture.

► We connect non-service oriented software into our service architecture using integration services

► State is managed by atomic services. This is either because the state is directly owned by the implementation of the service, or because the state is managed by some external software that is used from the implementation of the service.

► No business-relevant state is kept in our composite services.

Portals front-ending business processes give UI integration

Although it is not explicitly shown in Figure 4-22, our scenario uses a business portal to front-end the executable business processes. Human tasks in the business process are performed by roles in the various business functional areas using portlets hosted by the business portal.

Portal/portlet technology is widely recognized as being appropriate for achieving user interface integration and is increasingly being used to do so in enterprise implementations.

Note that the type of user interface integration is not as simplistic as just adding a new user interface directly on top of existing applications. Our portal allows us to integrate user interfaces supporting both new functionality and also existing functionality that exists in non-SO applications and systems (that have been integrated into our service architecture as described in "Two types of application/method level integration" on page 71).

Executable business processes result in people integration

Besides software and data integration, the scenario described in Figure 4-22 also achieves a more important kind of integration: *people integration*. The business roles that exist in the business functional areas shown in the diagram are all integrated by the executable business processes that they included in. In other words, the work done by people performing these roles is now integrated by the business processes that define the workflow.

Reusing architecture and design experience

Besides reusing actual artifacts (specifications, source code, and so forth) on a project, we also want to reuse experience in building our solutions. For a software architect or designer, reuse of architecture and design experience is good for a number of reasons:

► Reuse makes the job easier to benefit from existing solutions.

► Across the enterprise, if architects and designers are producing work products following a common set of experience, this improves the interoperability of the work products.

► The overall quality of the work products produced is higher if tried and tested solutions are used.

The form that architecture and design experience can take is best described by introducing the two related concepts of *architectural styles* and *patterns*.

Architectural styles

RUP introduces the subject as follows:

A software architecture may have an attribute called architectural style, which reduces the set of possible forms to choose from, and imposes a certain degree of uniformity to the architecture. The style may be defined by a set of patterns, or by the choice of specific components or connectors as the basic building blocks.

So the style we choose for our architecture can be dictated by defining a set of patterns for our software architects to follow. These patterns influence the shape of our service architectures and ensure that a consist approach is followed by all projects. Figure 4-23 illustrates how architectural style is applied to service architectures.

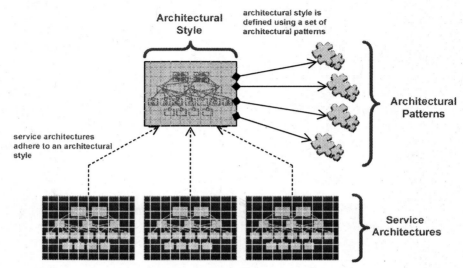

Figure 4-23 Applying architectural style to service architectures

We expand on the notion of what these architectural patterns are in the next section.

Architectural patterns

A *pattern* can be defined as "*a generally repeatable solution to a commonly occurring problem in software design*".

Patterns are a useful mechanism for capturing reusable experience. Typically a pattern has the following parts:

▶ Pattern name: A unique name for the pattern

▶ Context: The context in which the pattern exists

▶ Problem: The problem that the pattern is trying to solve

   – Forces: A list of aspects to the problem

▶ Solution: The solution provided by the pattern

   – Rationale: The reasoning of what the pattern achieves

- Resulting context: The changes in the original context caused by applying the pattern
- Examples: Examples showing the pattern in use

We differentiate between two different levels of patterns:

► **Architectural patterns**—These are patterns that affect architecturally significant software elements. In the context of this book, these patterns affect your service architecture (and therefore primarily your service model) and are used as part of specifying the service architecture (see "1. Specify software architecture" on page 61).

► **Design patterns**—These are patterns that affect the design elements that form the detailed design (insides) of architecturally significant software elements (and therefore primarily your design model). They are used as part of detailing the software designs ("2. Detail software design" on page 61).

So therefore architectural patterns shape architectural specifications and design patterns shape detailed design.

JK Enterprises case study architectural style

We present the architectural style adopted for our JK Enterprises case study in this section by describing a set of twelve architectural patterns.

But first a word of caution. Patterns have a described context and problem for a reason—And that is so that you know when to apply them.

A golden rule for using patterns is to never use a pattern unless you:

1. Understand the benefit that it is providing
2. Are sure that it is relevant to your context

Note that part of the value of a pattern is in getting you to think through your problem from other points of view. This helps you to evaluate a solution that is right for you.

With these words of warning in mind, we present the patterns illustrated in Figure 4-24 for your evaluation.

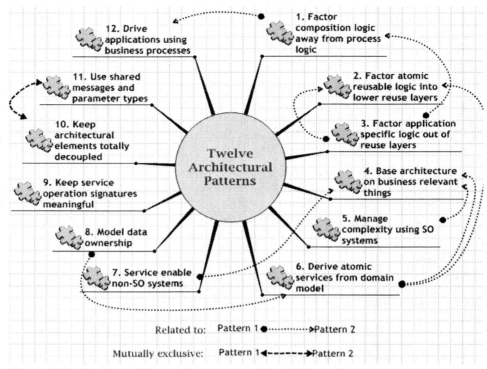

Figure 4-24 Twelve architectural patterns used by JK Enterprises

Pattern 1: Factor composition logic away from process logic

Pattern name	Factor composition logic away from process logic
Context	The emerging de facto standard for building business process-driven SOA solutions is to use the Business Process Execution Language (BPEL) to implement the executable process. Let us look at two specific tasks that BPEL can be used for: ▶ Create an executable version of a Business Process Modeling Notation (BPMN) modeled business process (process flow logic). ▶ Implement a composite service by orchestrating a set of calls on atomic services (composition logic). For any given executable process, both of these tasks can be achieved using a single BPEL artifact describing a sequenced step of Web service invocations.

Problem	Mixing process flow logic and composition logic together in the same implementation artifact has problematic side effects.
► **Forces**	► It makes it more difficult to reuse the composition logic.
	► It makes it more difficult to understand the process flow by looking at the BPEL.
	► The resulting implementation artifact is more complex and therefore more difficult to maintain.
	► It makes it more difficult to split the roles of process developer and service developer.
Solution	Have distinct architectural layers for service consumers and composite business application services.
	Represent executable business processes in your architecture using a service consumer. Place it in the service consumer layer. All business process flow logic exists in the implementation (BPEL) of this service consumer. From an architectural point of view, any user interface required to interact with this process is considered to be a part of this same service consumer SO part.
	This service consumer will consumer the services provided by a service provider which exists in the next architectural layer down - composite business application services. All composition logic exists in the implementation of this service provider. This service provider should provide a separate service specification for each of the processes (or more likely sub-processes) that it supports. It will also have required service specifications for each of the services that this composite service requires (this is what makes it a composite service).
	We note the following:
	► If you use "Pattern 5: Manage complexity using SO systems", then the same service consumer can appear in multiple SO systems. This is because a business process can span across functional areas (and our SO systems are derived from the defined IT systems in these functional areas that support the business processes).
	► The composition logic need not be implemented using BPEL. Oftentimes it is simpler to just use plain old Java. This may depend on the tools and skills of the developer assigned to implementing these components.
	"Pattern 12: Drive applications using business processes" is closely related to this pattern.

► Rationale	Keeping the process logic separate from the composition logic means:
	► It is easier to reuse the composition logic across multiple processes.
	► It is easier to understand the process flow BPEL as it only contains flow logic.
	► The resulting BPEL is simpler and therefore easier to maintain.
	► It is easier to split the roles of process developer and service developer. Process developers implement the business process service consumers. Service developers implement the composite business application services (and any atomic business application services they require).

Examples

In the example shown in Figure 4-25 we see a service consumer called `AccountOpeningProcess`. This can be implemented as a BPEL process (long-running or short-running depending on whether it needed to retain state) using WebSphere Integration Developer, based on a BPMN-based process specification from WebSphere Business Modeler.

We also see a composite business application service provider called `SalesManagementComposite` which provides two services: `AccountVerification` and `AccountActivation`. The service provider using BPEL (as a short-running process) or Java. WebSphere Integration Developer provides tool support for implementing these types of services in the form of SCA bindings, maps, and BPEL editor.

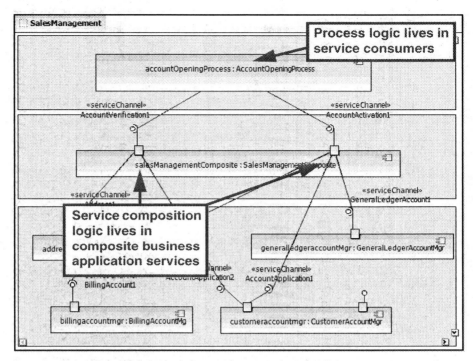

Figure 4-25   Separating composition logic from process logic

Pattern 2: Factor atomic reusable logic into lower reuse layers

Pattern name	Factor atomic reusable logic into lower reuse layers
Context	Today it is common for IT departments to have software reuse as a goal.
Problem	Without a clear policy for factoring reusable logic, the chances for reuse are lower.
▶ Forces	▶ Reuse requires identifiable reusable elements. ▶ Appropriate reuse factoring does not happen by accident.

Solution	Have a clear policy for factoring reusable logic across your architectural layers.
	Reusable logic can be divided into the following two categories:
	► Logic which is strongly relatable to a business object (and therefore a domain type). An example would be customer account setup logic which is related to the domain type `CustomerAccount`.
	► Infrastructure logic. For example, logic that allowed e-mails to be sent or documents printed.
	Both of these types of logic are highly reusable and are respectively factored into the following two service architecture layers:
	► Atomic business application services
	► Infrastructure services
	The layers that these services live in are lower in the architecture than service consumers and composite business application services. These services are generally used from composite business application services (which explains the name).
	Note that although the factoring rules in this pattern are for ensuring that we end up with reusable services that are appropriate for plugging into composite services, it should be noted that service consumers are themselves reusable (specifically across multiple SO systems).
► **Rationale**	Having clearly identified where the reuse points are in our architecture, we can now:
	► Publish these services to a repository for reusable services.
	► Allow the reusable services in this repository to be categorized.
	► Ensure that we factor reusable logic into these services when modeling service interactions (which is when logic gets factored across your architecture—More on this in "Step 2: Design service interactions" on page 359.

Examples

In the example shown in Figure 4-26, there are yellow rectangles for each of our layers.

From top to bottom we have:

► Service consumers
► Composite business application services (and service providers)
► Atomic business application services (and service providers)

Below the last layer, we would also have a further layer (which is omitted in the diagram as there are no infrastructure services in this example):

► Infrastructure services (and service providers)

In our example the following reusable atomic business application services exist:

`Address, BillingAccount, AccountApplication, GeneralLedgerAccount`

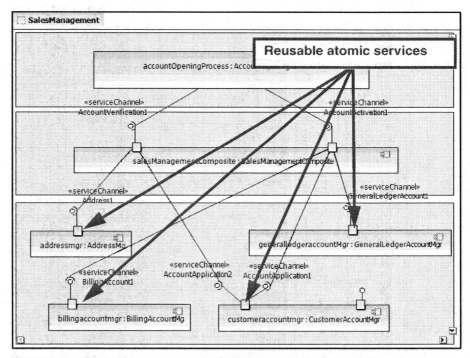

Figure 4-26   Reusable services in the SalesManagement SO system

Pattern 3: Factor application-specific logic out of reuse layers

Pattern name	Factor application-specific logic out of reuse layers
Context	Software reuse can be a goal for IT departments that are building SO systems that are driven by executable business processes.

Problem	Mixing application-specific logic and atomic reusable logic makes it more difficult to reuse the atomic reusable logic from composite services. **Note**: In the context of our business process-driven systems, by application-specific we mean that logic which is unique to the implementation of a specific process (and is not reusable across business processes).
► **Forces**	► Where a service operation contains both the logic that you want to reuse as well as other logic (which therefore causes unwanted behavior), this reduces the likelihood of that operation being reused. ► Appropriate reuse factoring does not happen by accident.
Solution	Factor application-specific logic into the composite business application service layer. This is the layer whose services: ► Are used by service consumers in the higher layer (often, but not always, these are executable business processes). ► Compose (and therefore use) reusable services in the lower layers (atomic business application services and infrastructure services). Note that the behavior provided by a composite business application service is now the sum of: ► The application-specific logic that it implements itself, plus ► The atomic reusable logic that is implemented by each of the atomic business application services and infrastructure services that it calls (composes). As the composite business application services are themselves reusable, this arguably means that they provide a higher-value level of reuse.
► **Rationale**	Keeping application-specific logic separate from atomic reusable logic will: ► Increase the reusability of your atomic reusable services and, ► Provide a further higher-value set of reusable services (the composite business application services themselves).

Examples

As background to the example shown in Figure 4-27, we have a business process called Account Opening, which has sub-processes called Account Verification and Account Activation.

In the diagram we see that the business process appears in the form of a service consumer called `AccountOpeningProcess` which will most likely be implemented as a BPEL process in WebSphere Integration Developer.

For each of our sub-processes we find a service in the composite business application service layer: `AccountVerification` and `AccountActivation`. These are provided by a service provider called `SalesManagementComposite`. The implementation of this service provider consists of:

► Some logic which is unique to the sub-process (application-specific logic)
► Orchestration logic that calls reusable services

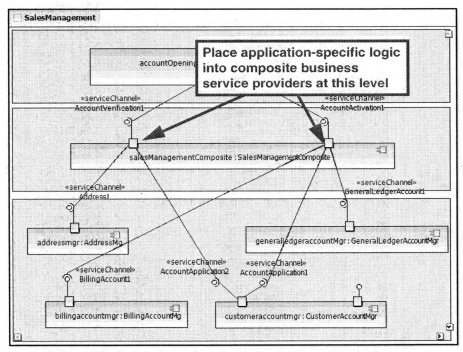

Figure 4-27   Application-specific logic in composite business application services

Pattern 4: Base architecture on business relevant elements

Pattern name	Base architecture on business relevant elements
Context	A software architecture defines the software in terms of a set of parts that together make up distinguishable software systems (See "Architecture of software systems" on page 43). It is common to have in place a standard for identifying, naming and scoping these parts to ensure a common approach is followed across the organization.
Problem	Identifying, naming, and scoping the parts in your service architecture on things that are not part of the business view causes problems. Relevant examples of things outside of the business view are: ► Existing software applications ► Component implementation technologies (for example, EJB™) ► Communications "plumbing" between components
► Forces	► The service architecture is affected unnecessarily if parts are based on things outside of the business view and these things disappear or are changed substantially. ► In general, impacts that cause changes to architectural specifications are more serious than those that only require changes to implementations (changes to one architectural element will typically affect multiple design elements and an even greater number of implementation elements).

Solution	Derive parts of your service architecture on the following business relevant things: ► Functional areas (IT system) ► Business processes ► Business sub-processes ► Domain types Here is a simple set of factoring rules for achieving this: 1. For each service-oriented IT system identified for a functional area, define a SO system (talked about further in "Pattern 5: Manage complexity using SO systems"). 2. For each business process, define a service consumer. This service consumer will consumer any services that support that business process. If executable business processes are being built, then the executable business process will form part of the implementation of the service consumer. 3. For each business sub-process, identify a composite business application service to provide the services that it requires. 4. For each domain type, identify an atomic business application service (this is described further in "Pattern 6: Derive atomic services from domain model").
► **Rationale**	Deriving parts for your service architecture from business things provides a solid architecture. This means: ► Your service architecture should no longer be affected by changes to non-business things (for example retiring and replacing existing applications or choosing a new component implementation technology). ► The architecture should "flex" with changes to the business rather than changes to non-business things. ► This reduces the number of unnecessary specification changes. Changes to the non-business things listed above still requires software change, but such change will be to detailed design and implementation rather than to the architecture. These types of changes have less overall impact.

Examples

Examples of the application of this pattern can be found in part in the following diagrams, ordered by the factoring rules listed above:

► Figure 4-28 on page 89
► Figure 4-25 on page 79
► Figure 4-27 on page 83
► Figure 4-29 on page 91

Tip: Some words of warning in applying this pattern:

- ► Depending on how the business entities themselves have been factored, you may end up with parts that are "too big" if you just apply a simple 1-to-1 derivation. In these cases you may need a further subdivision to create "smaller" parts.

- ► A bit of creativity and experimentation may be required to create factoring rules that work for you. The important point is that these rules have to be based on things in the business view.

Pattern 5: Manage complexity using SO systems

Pattern name	Manage complexity using SO systems
Context	As SOA practices are adopted and rolled-out across an enterprise, the amount of service-oriented software created becomes appreciable.
	The number of individual elements in the service architecture (services, service consumers and service providers) will increase dramatically over time.
Problem	Only having the relatively low-level constructs of service, service consumer and service provider to represent and understand your service architectures causes problems as the number of these things in the enterprise typically becomes large. Some grouping mechanism is required.
► Forces	► Describing and understanding reuse can be difficult without a context for the usage of services, service consumers and service providers. In other words, what is the answer to the question "Where have my service consumers and providers been used?"
	► Managing specifications of service behavior (using for example service collaborations—See "Model element: Service collaboration" on page 250 for a description) without a sensible grouping for these specifications would be difficult. Can you imagine all of the service specification behavior that will exist across the entire enterprise?
	► Understanding (and therefore maintaining) software built by SOA projects without some higher-level architectural specification artifact than service, service consumer, or service provider would be difficult.
	► Not having a higher-level system-size artifact to trace back to the business view means that this traceability is more difficult to understand.

Solution	Use SO systems as a higher level grouping of your service-oriented software (see "Service-oriented IT systems" on page 44 for an introduction). As described in "Pattern 4: Base architecture on business relevant elements", factoring rule 1: One way of deriving SO systems is to create one for each of your identified service-oriented IT systems for your functional area (this assumes that you have well defined functional areas). In the service model we have a single package that contains everything owned by our SO system. Each of our SO systems owns a structural architectural specification and a set of behavioral architectural specifications. These exist in our SO system package as: ► A service partition named after our SO system that contains the structure of our SO system. The parts in this structure are based on service consumers and service providers that can be used as parts in multiple SO systems. ► A set of service collaborations. If use cases are used then these correspond to the set of system use cases that have been defined for the functional area. Each service collaboration has one or more service interactions which each form a behavioral specification. Normally these correspond to flows from the related system use case. We have now grouped our architectural specifications into: ► SO parts that are usable as parts in a SO system service architecture. These are our service consumers and service providers. ► SO systems that own SO system parts based on these SO parts and own the structural and behavioral specifications of our service architectures. **Note**: Definitions for the service model specific terms used here can be found in "Service model work product" on page 234.

► **Rationale**	Grouping service architectures by SO systems (derived from functional areas) provides a scalable way for creating end-to-end architectural models that span the entire enterprise. We note the following:
	► We now have a manageable context for the usage of our services, service consumers and service providers. This is provided by the service partition that represents our SO system.
	► We have a way of grouping the service collaborations that makes it easier to manage them.
	► Understanding the enterprise SOA view is easier now that there is a higher-level architectural specification artifact.
	► Traceability to the business view is simple. There is a SO system providing software to support the automation requirements of each functional area.

Examples

As background to Figure 4-28, let us note that our example has two business functional areas: Customer Service and Sales Management.

Based on inspection of the Account Opening and Account Application Inquiry business processes, we note automation requirements for certain tasks captured in the following system use cases (organized by IT system):

► Sales Management:

  – Determine applicant eligibility
  – Verify address
  – Activate account

► Customer Service:

  – Inquire on application status

In the example we can see that two SO systems exist, one for each of our functional areas: CustomerService and SalesManagement. Each of these SO systems owns:

► A service partition describing its parts

► A set of service collaborations corresponding to the system use cases owned by the corresponding functional area

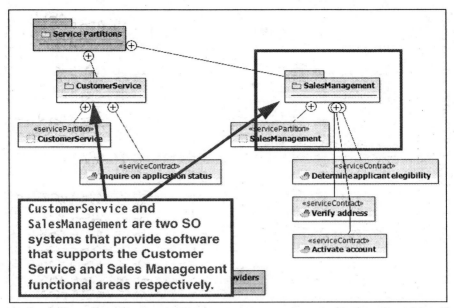

Figure 4-28   Organizing the usage of your service-oriented software using SO systems

Tip: It is important to heed the warning provided after "Pattern 4: Base architecture on business relevant elements" which is relevant to this pattern.

Pattern 6: Derive atomic services from domain model

Pattern name	Derive atomic services from domain model
Context	A domain model represents things that exist in the business world (specific to an identified domain), associations between these things, and any special rules that constrain instances of these things.
	Atomic services (and service providers) do not require any services (at least architecturally significant ones—See "Architecturally significant services" on page 57) in their implementation.
	It is common for business state (data) to be owned by the implementations of atomic services.
Problem	Not having a standard for identifying, naming and scoping atomic services causes data ownership issues.

► **Forces**	► It is difficult to understand which atomic service owns any given piece of business data ► Changes to the domain model are not straightforward to accommodate in the service architecture
Solution	Derive atomic business application services from domain types in the domain model. For each domain type, there should be a corresponding service that whose implementation: ► Contains logic acting on instances of the domain type ► Contains logic that persists instances of the domain type
► **Rationale**	Atomic business application services are where data is owned in your architecture, because it is this business data and the reusable logic that acts upon the data that should be reusable. As your domain model provides a view of the business things that exist and therefore of the data that exists in the enterprise for these things, the domain model is a first choice subject to use to derive your atomic business application services from. Note that: ► It is now easy to see which atomic services own any given piece of business data. ► The impact of changes/additions to your domain model are more straightforward to accommodate in your service architecture.

Examples

In the example shown in Figure 4-29 we see the following domain types:

- ► `Customer`
- ► `Address`
- ► `AccountApplication`
- ► `Product`
- ► `CustomerAccount`
- ► `BillingAccount`
- ► `GeneralLedgerAccount`

Note that this list does not include `PricingCode` and `AccountApplicationState`, which are enumerations. These do not have state but instead describe a fixed set of possible values.

We derive a service specification for each of the domain types.

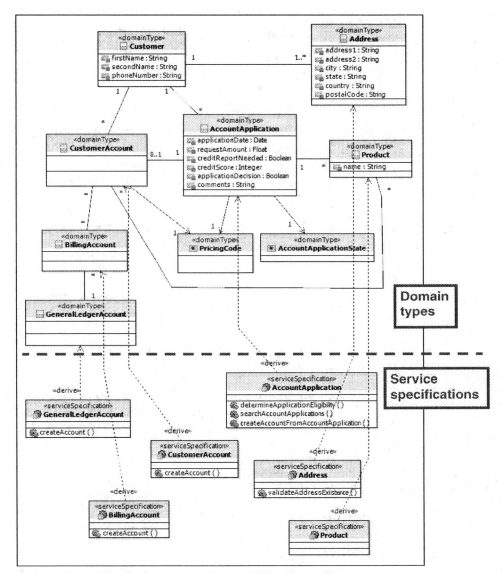

Figure 4-29   Deriving service specifications from domain types

> **Tip:** It is important to heed the warning provided after "Pattern 4: Base architecture on business relevant elements" which is relevant to this pattern.
>
> In this case an alternative factoring rule would be to first consider domain types that are closely related (example whole/part relationships like order/order-line) and only to create a single service that manages both of the domain types (named after the dominant domain type). It is unusual though that the domain types are so large that it causes issues.

Pattern 7: Service enable non-SO systems

Pattern name	Service enable non-SO systems
Context	SOA is a relatively new way of building software systems. All enterprises have a large amount of software systems that are not service-oriented (see "SOA and integration" on page 71).
Problem	There is no clear way to achieve effective application or method level integration (see "Standard integration levels" on page 69) with non-SO systems.
► **Forces**	► The communication technology options for integrating with these systems may differ wildly and using these technologies requires specialist development skills. ► Building point-to-point integrations with these systems from each of the service components that have to integrate with them is inefficient because integration code is duplicated.

Solution	Service-enable non-SO systems using a special kind of service—*Integration services* (these are introduced in "Two types of application/method level integration" on page 71). Integration services are specified using the same kind of artifacts as normal services. However they are different from the types of services we have discussed in our service model. Let us note the following: ► The service specification for an integration service should be a service-based interpretation of a distinguishable interface (or similar) that exists on the non-SO system. ► This interpretation should be as literal as possible. In other words, it should look as close as possible to the existing interface as possible. ► The implementation of the integration service uses an appropriate communication technology to talk to the non-SO system (for example, CICS). This is hidden from consumers of the service who only have to deal with the service using the standard service communications technology in use. ► These services are not architecturally significant and therefore do not appear in the service model. They are design elements and should therefore live in the design model (although it might at first seem as though all services should live in the service model this is not true). ► The data owned by the non-SO system should be owned by an atomic business application service provider. This means that the integration service itself becomes part of the implementation of the atomic business application service provider that owns its data (see "Pattern 8: Model data ownership" for more on this).
► **Rationale**	Wrapping non-SO systems using integration services allows us to: ► Isolate the areas in our software that are implemented using the kind of specialist communication technologies required to integrate with non-SO systems. Even if these technologies are not specialist as such, they most are different to the ones used to communicate *inside* your service architecture between your service consumers and providers. ► Define clear reuse points for integration logic. Note also that the reason that integration services are treated as different to the other kinds of services that we have looked at (in other words those in our service architectures) in line with the reasoning provided in "Pattern 4: Base architecture on business relevant elements".

Pattern 8: Model data ownership

Pattern name	Model data ownership
Context	Most software systems that exist in an enterprise store data using some sort of persistence technology. Normally, but not always, this is a relational database. No matter what the persistence technology, there are some element-level artifacts where the data is stored (for example, a table in a relational database or an object in an object database). We consider that element-level artifact to be owned by a software component if the only thing that is allowed to access the state it contains is that software component.
Problem	Not having clear data ownership makes it impossible to ensure data encapsulation.
► Forces	► It is difficult to know which component has encapsulated a specific data item. ► It is difficult to know what data items a component is responsible for. ► For a given component and data item, it is difficult to know whether the component implementation can access the data item directly or whether the component has to access it through the interface of another component.

Solution	Assign data ownership to service providers that provide atomic business application services. Model this data ownership using information types. For each atomic business application service provider we create an information type to represent each of the data items that it manages. Note the following: ▶ These information types are black box representations of the state that the service provider owns. ▶ By own we mean that the service provider has exclusive access to the data instances in the data structure (internal, white box) that matches the information type (external, black box). ▶ Information types are very useful when using pre-conditions and post-conditions to describe the behavior of service operations. In other words, the pre-conditions and post-conditions describe changes to the state owned by the service provider in terms of the info types. ▶ Information types can be (and should be) derived from domain types. ▶ It is not uncommon for more than one information type, each belonging to a different service provider, to be derived from the same domain type. This is especially common when one service provider only has to store a reference to the identity of a certain business thing, while another service provider persists actual instances of the thing. The approach for determining info types is described in "Model info types for the service providers" on page 331.
▶ **Rationale**	Understanding data ownership is very important in our service architecture. Modeling info types to represent the data owned by each service provider means that: ▶ We can now tell which component has encapsulated a specific data item by checking to see which info types are derived from the domain type, and then checking which service provider owns the info type. ▶ To understand what data items a component is responsible for, we look at which info types its service provider owns. ▶ To determine whether a component implementation can access a data item directly, verify whether the corresponding info type is owned by its service provider.

Examples

Figure 4-30 shows the data ownership of the `CustomerAccountMgr` using information types.

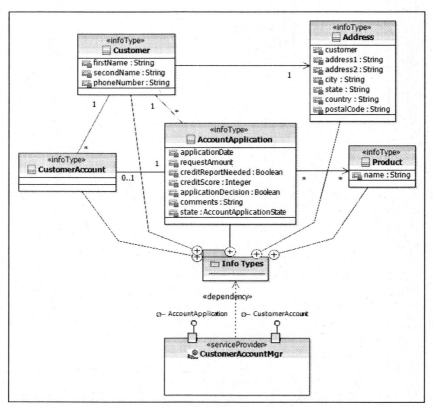

Figure 4-30   Modeling the data ownership of the CustomerAccountMgr service provider

Pattern 9: Keep service operation signatures meaningful

Pattern name	Keep service operation signatures meaningful
Context	RUP defines the *operation* artifact as follows: *This artifact represents a service that can be requested from an object to effect behavior. An operation specifies the name, type, parameters, and constraints for invoking an associated behavior.* Note that the way in which the term service is used in this definition in a different way to the way in which it is used in this book.
Problem	It is difficult to understand what an operation does if its signature is not meaningful.
► Forces	► Modeling an operation signature using a single input and output message reduces the amount of meaning of that signature. ► Often on diagrams, only the signature of an operation might be shown without the structure of the types used in the signature.
Solution	Keep operations as meaningful as possible: ► Avoid modeling your operation using a simple request/response message pair. ► Use meaningful parameter types derived from your domain types to type your parameters. ► Name parameters helpfully (for example, `newCustomer:Customer` for the `createCustomer` operation.
► Rationale	Meaningful operation signatures enable you to convey more meaning in diagrams that only show service specifications without showing the structure of the parameters.

Pattern 10: Keep architectural elements totally decoupled

Pattern name	Keep architectural elements totally de-coupled
Context	RUP provides the following definition for *coupling*: *The degree to which components depend on one another. There are two types of coupling, tight and loose. Loose coupling is desirable to support an extensible software architecture but tight coupling may be necessary for maximum performance. Coupling is increased when the data exchanged between components becomes larger or more complex.* Component as it is used in this definition is a piece of software that is encapsulated and forms a unit of independent deployment and versioning. When components share artifacts it increases the coupling between them. The specification of a component is made up of those artifacts that describe it from a black-box point of view (see "Architecturally significant services" on page 57 for a definition of black-box view). Included in this are the following: ▶ Service specification ▶ Parameter types Even if the implementations of a set of components are totally decoupled, if any of the components share parts of their specification then this increases coupling.
Problem	Sharing specification artifacts between service providers has some problematic side effects.
▶ Forces	▶ Changes to these shared specification artifacts affect multiple service providers. ▶ Where specialized versions of parameter types are required, there is a mixture of shared parameter types and specialized "local" parameter types, which is slightly more complex than just having local parameter types. ▶ The size of the shared service specification artifacts library quickly grows in size. Factoring these out into separate libraries based on some factoring rule itself becomes quite complex.

Solution	Each service provider should own its:
	▶ Parameter types
	▶ Enumerations
	▶ Messages
	▶ Provided service specifications
	Each service provider should also own its info types as well, but this is by definition as info types are used to model data ownership.
	In this way the specification of the service provider is totally decoupled from other specifications. The only resources shared between service providers are primitive types.
	Note that for composite business application services, where a service provides service specifications and required service specifications, there is some coupling between the composite business application service and the service provider providing the services that it requires. You could break this coupling by introducing a local copy of the required service specification.
	Note that although it may seem like a lot of additional work to maintain separate copies of certain specification artifacts (where they look the same across multiple service providers), this can be reduced (or even negated in some cases) by using Rational Software Architect transformations—for example from domain types to parameter types.
▶ **Rationale**	Not sharing specification artifacts prevents dependency issues as follows:
	▶ Changes to the specification artifacts mentioned above only has localized impact.
	▶ It is a lot more clear as to where specification artifacts come from when they are used as they are all local—in other words there is no combination of local and shared specification artifacts in use in a service provider specification.
	▶ No rules are required for when to factor a specification artifact out as a shared artifact.

Examples

The example shown in Figure 4-31 shows the parameter types of two service providers: AddressMgr and CustomerAccountMgr:

▶ The AddressMgr service provider requires a view of addresses as it stores the full set of known addresses for verification against.

▶ The CustomerAccountMgr requires a view of addresses because it stores customer addresses, and therefore an address is passed as parameter with a customer account application.

As can be seen from Figure 4-31, each of these service providers owns their own `Address` parameter type, which is used in the specification of their service operations.

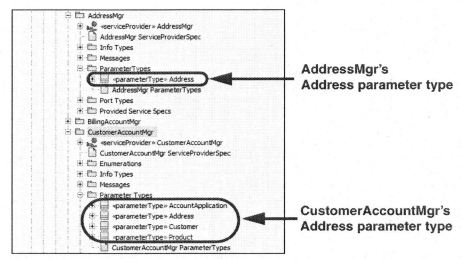

AddressMgr's
Address parameter type

CustomerAccountMgr's
Address parameter type

Figure 4-31   Two service providers, each with their own parameter types

Pattern 11: Use shared messages and parameter types

Pattern name	Use shared messages and parameter types
Context	See the context for "Pattern 10: Keep architectural elements totally decoupled".
Problem	Keeping separate copies of specification artifacts for each service provider as suggested in "Pattern 10: Keep architectural elements totally decoupled" involves additional work.
► Forces	► When a change is made to a domain type, that same change may need to be made to multiple parameter types that are based on that domain type (we say may because in some cases the change to the domain type may be outside of the scope of the parameter type required for a specific service provider). ► Instead of just using a parameter type in a shared library of parameter types, a new parameter type has to be created for each service provider that requires it.

Solution	Create a resource containing specification artifacts that can be shared between service providers. This can contain shared: ▶ Parameter types ▶ Enumerations ▶ Messages
▶ **Rationale**	Having shared specification artifacts means: ▶ You only have to apply changes to shared specification artifacts in one place rather than having to make certain changes to multiple identical specification artifacts. ▶ You do not have to create multiple copies of the same parameter types.

Pattern 12: Drive applications using business processes

Pattern name	Drive applications using business processes
Context	Enterprises adopting SOA commonly also adopt business modeling practices. A key aspect captured in these business models is business process. A de facto standard emerging for implementing business processes in software is the Business Process Execution Language (BPEL).
Problem	It is not immediately apparent where BPEL components should live in a service architecture. Because of this, they may be introduced in inappropriate places.
▶ **Forces**	▶ Using BPEL components in inappropriate places may cause future architectural problems.
Solution	Represent executable business processes in your service architecture using service consumers, and place these in the top layer in your architecture. Limit the usage of BPEL implementations of process flow logic to implementations of these service consumers. These service consumers—acting on triggers from either human actors (through some user interface) or the workflow infrastructure (because a previous task has completed and a new one is starting)—in turn make calls on composite business application services to provide the required automation behavior.

► Rationale	Having a clear guideline for where in your architecture BPEL implemented process logic should live prevents the usage of BPEL in inappropriate places:
	► Prevent BPEL from being used to implement logic that is best implemented in Java language.
	► Prevent process logic being introduced somewhere inappropriate in the architecture. It should be driving the software and therefore should appear in your topmost layer.

Examples

In the example shown in Figure 4-32 we see our `SalesManagement` SO system has a service consumer called `AccountOpeningProcess`. From the example of "Pattern 3: Factor application-specific logic out of reuse layers" on page 81 we know that the Account Opening business process contains two sub-processes: Account Verification and Account Activation.

The `AccountOpeningProcess` service consumer drives system behavior at runtime optionally receiving inputs from the `SalesRepresentative` actor, and in turn calling the `AccountVerification` and `AccountActivation` composite business application services.

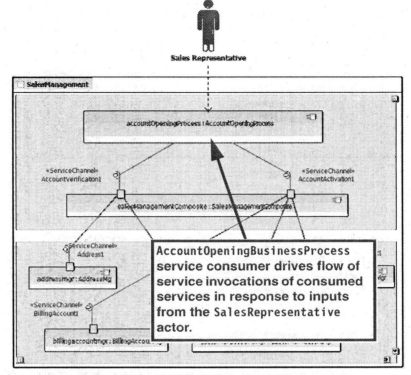

Figure 4-32   Business process driving flow of service invocations

5

Process and methods

This chapter discusses the IBM Rational software development process by describing the basic of Rational Unified Process (RUP) and UML modeling in an SOA context.

Moreover, this chapter describes the development case, or software development process that we follow for this book and JK Enterprises. The chapter also describes, in detail, how to codify the development case in Rational Method Composer.

This chapter is structured around:

► Rational Unified Process
► JK Enterprises development case

Introduction

A fool with a tool is still a fool (anon.)

Every company, project, or team has a method. It may get invented every morning when the team walks through the door, but they have a method—a way of working together. The question is, "Is this the appropriate method for the team?" This chapter introduces the IBM Rational Unified Process and discusses the importance of modeling and architecture. It explains some of the basic concepts of UML. It closes with an overview of the tools the architects use in this book.

IBM Rational Unified Process (RUP)

The IBM Rational Unified Process is an approach that is used to develop software. It contains information about the type of work we need to perform to develop software (tasks), the sets of responsibilities we assign to people (roles), what we have to produce (work products), and assistance in performing this work (guidance).

The process has been developed over the last 26 years as a collection of IBM Rational field experience helping customers develop software and IBM Rational's experience building their own products. This work has led to the OMG standard Software Process Engineering Metamodel (SPEM), and the Eclipse Process Framework project.

► SPEM is a standard way of describing a process[1] and was originally developed by Rational Software, IBM, and other companies.

► The Eclipse Process Framework project is an open-source project that provides tooling to build development and other processes, and provide basic content. IBM and others initiated this project. IBM provided both the initial tooling and content and now uses this open source project as the basis for its commercial IBM Rational Method Composer product. The Web site for the Eclipse Process Framework is at:

`http://www.eclipse.org/epf`

There are a few key definitions we have to understand before we can effectively understand RUP. Figure 5-1 shows these concepts.

---

[1] The more recent versions of RUP and the Eclipse Process Framework project use an updated version of the original SPEM specification. This new version is currently being proposed by IBM and others as SPEM V2.

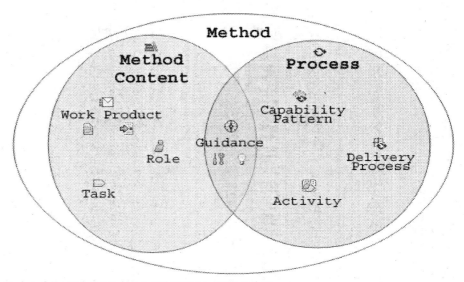

Figure 5-1   Key concepts in RUP [from RUP V7.1]

- **Method** is the combination of method content along with process (the way we combine the method content to create an approach we can follow in a project).

- **Method content** is the information in the process, the words and pictures.

- **Work product** "*...is something meaningful resulting from a process...*" [RUP]

- **Role** "*...a set of related skills, competencies, and responsibilities.*" [RUP]

- **Task** "*...describes a unit of work assigned to a Role that provides a meaningful result.*" [RUP]

- **Guidance** "*...is an abstract concept that generalizes all forms of content whose primary purpose is to provide additional explanations and illustrations to elements such as Roles, Tasks, Work Products, Activities, or Processes.*" [RUP]

- **Process** "*...defines the structured work definitions that need to be performed to develop a system.*" [RUP]

- **Capability pattern** "*...describes a reusable cluster of Activities in common process areas that produces a result of observable value.*" [RUP]

- **Delivery process** "*...describing a complete and integrated approach for performing a specific type of project.*" [RUP]

- **Activity** "*...define the breakdown as well as flow of work.*" [RUP]

We tend to pick a specific delivery process when we start looking for a process for our team or project (for example, RUP for small projects) and then adapt it for our local needs. This local version is called a development case. If we like our adapted process and want to use it elsewhere, we can use the Rational Method Composer to create our own delivery process (for example, JK Enterprises development case).

RUP is delivered as a large set of HTML pages that we use as a library of information. We pick out the parts of the library we need for our project as a development case.

RUP follows a set of core principles that are worth understanding as we use RUP. This forms the motivation for using a process, and specifically for using RUP.

Core principles of RUP

RUP has six core principles that provide the rationale for the process:

► Adapt the process
► Balance competing stake holder priorities
► Collaborate across teams
► Demonstrate value iteratively
► Elevate the level of abstraction
► Focus continuously on quality

Adapt the process

Adapt the process means use the right amount of process for a particular project. Too much process kills projects, too little can lead to unconstrained chaos. an interesting side-effect of having a process that is role-base is the process can be scaled from very small teams to very large teams without changing the core principles. The work products, tasks and other aspects of the process may vary - but we should still be able to recognize a RUP-based process.

Balancing competing stakeholder priorities

Balancing competing stakeholder priorities recognizes the need to constantly balance priorities on a project. Creating a clear set of requirements based on the real needs of the business, and then regularly checking that these needs and requirements have not changed, is one example of this balancing act. Build, buy or reuse of services is another example. There are cost versus time versus functionality balancing acts in this case.

Collaborate across teams

Collaborate across teams refers to the need to motivate the individuals on the team, break down the barriers between different teams or parts of the team, and ultimately extend this collaboration to the business, development and operations. SOA-enabled solutions extend this collaboration to outside the enterprise.

Demonstrate the value iteratively

Demonstrate the value iteratively has several aspects. The first is that we need deliver real code regularly, starting right at the beginning of the project. It gives the stakeholder chance to see what we are doing and provide feedback. The second aspect is that iterations allow the plan to be adapted as the project proceeds. The third is the chance to accept and manage change with changing business priorities and stakeholder expectations. The last aspect is that we drive out risk continuously from the project by demonstrating working software. We also constantly reassess the keys risks and adapt the plans accordingly[2].

Elevate the level of abstraction

Elevate the level of abstraction is a principle aimed at simplifying how we work and communicate. We achieve this by the reuse of existing assets, the use of modeling tools and making use of architecture. A significant benefit of SOA-based solutions relies on this elevation of the level abstraction—services being reused, modeling and transformations to translate business requirements to code as quickly as possible, and the use of SOA as an architectural style.

Focus continuously on quality

Focus continuously on quality emphasizes the need to have quality as a priority throughout the life cycle. Testing is not the discipline that introduces quality into our solution - it can only catch the lack of quality in what has gone before. As each iteration involves some form of testing, we have a regular monitor on quality throughout the project.

Key concepts

The key concepts of RUP include:

- ► RUP summary chart
- ► Iterative development
- ► Phases (inception, elaboration, construction, transition)
- ► Architecture-driven
- ► Use case driven

---

[2] Moving a development team and its stakeholders to an iterative process is hard. Iterative introduces perceived uncertainties such as lack of a stable set of requirements, difficulty in planning and costing work, regular rework and challenges scheduling staff requirements. RUP and the supporting material and training addresses all these issues directly.

RUP summary chart

The RUP summary chart is shown in Figure 5-2.

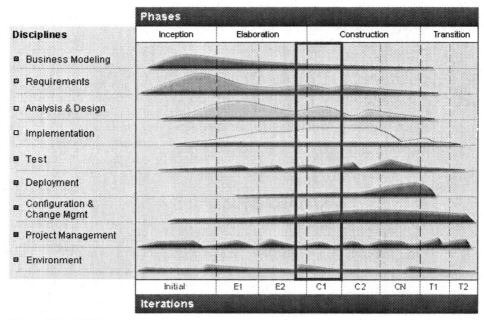

Figure 5-2   RUP summary chart

The RUP summary chart captures many of the concepts in RUP in one diagram. The chart shows a project with time on the x axis, and the disciplines on the y axis. Each RUP project is divided into four phases (Inception, Elaboration, Construction, and Transition). Each phase is broken down into zero or more iterations. An iteration is a vertical slice through the disciplines as shown in Figure 5-2. This iteration is the first iteration in the Construction phase.

The bumps on the chart indicate the level of effort required for each discipline. Notice, for example, how the business modeling and requirements disciplines are biased towards the beginning of the project but still continue into the Transition phase. One of our favorite questions about this chart is based around testing: "Why to the bumps on the testing discipline line get bigger and bigger over time?"[3]

We now look at some of these terms and ideas in more detail.

---

[3] This is because as we build more and more code, we write more and more tests. Each iteration runs the tests of the new code and the tests from the previous iteration. If we managed to identify the really high-risk areas of the project correctly, we will have regression tested these areas to the full extent by the end of the project.

Iterative development

Iterative development is the concept of breaking a project into a set of iterations.

An iteration encompasses the development activities that lead to a product release-a stable, executable version of the product, together with any other peripheral elements necessary to use this release. [RUP]

The project effectively becomes a set of smaller projects. The traditional software development project life cycle of gathering requirements, designing, implementing and testing the solution is discarded. However, an iteration contains these traditional disciplines, hence the idea of an iteration as a mini project. A project consists of a number of iterations.

This approach has many advantages including:

► Faster feedback on all aspects of the project
► Faster exposure (and consequently faster mitigation) of risk
► Ability to validate any estimation techniques within the project

The focus of each iteration is to produce some form of working, tested code. In earlier iterations, this code might be a prototype of a certain aspect of the service or composite services. In later iterations, the working code will be complete builds of the services or composite services but with reduced functionality. This reduced functionality could be stubbed out code, no or reduced handling or simulation of an intended function (for example, a database access and retrieval may be simulated).

Project managers are concentrating on using the iterations to mitigate or expose risk. Contrary to natural inclinations, we encourage projects to attempt the highest risk aspects up front. This in turn allows us to spend the most time on addressing the risks. Each iteration should start with an assessment of what has changed since the start of the last iteration. Risks and priorities changes may steer us to change the plan for this iteration, bring some work forward and pushing some work back.

Phases

Each RUP project is broken into four phases. The phases in order of execution are:

► Inception
► Elaboration
► Construction
► Transition

Inception is the phase where we scope out the project. During the iterations in this phase we define business use cases (or revise them if some already exist). We define our business goals, key performance indicators and metrics. We create initial as-is and to-be business process models. We take initial ideas about the services required and implement a few (with skeleton code if required). We test the services

Elaboration is the phase where we make sure we can have a working end-to-end automated business process or processes. Updates are made to all the work products created in the Inception phase. Some of the code previously stubbed out is filled in. Tests from the previous phase are rerun and expanded to cover the new functionality. Services are automating portions of or whole business processes so we have some useful business functionality.

Construction is where we complete the coding and testing. Many of the work products such as the business process models, requirements, service model, and others are further refined as appropriate and locked down as complete. At the end of the phase, the software is ready to be released to alpha and beta testing. Further changes to requirements based on feedback would be scheduled for future releases, or we could remain in Construction. Given that the stakeholders have already seen running code during the preceding two phases, we have bee tracking changes in business processes and business goals, it is less likely than major changes will surprise us at this point.

Transition is the phase that can vary the most. It entirely depends on what kind of software you are building. For a product release (like a release of IBM Rational tools), transition is focused on alpha and beta testing. We are finishing training materials, marketing materials, deciding on the color of the box or CD, and checking that the copyright notices appear on the accompanying literature[4]. We are fixing any critical defects found in the alpha and beta releases. An internal project for the business will be working with operations to get system and user acceptance testing completed, and planning for deployment. Once transition is complete, further changes to the software require a new project (run iteratively of course). Maintenance has a slightly different shape of project.

Each phase has strict entry and exit criteria or gates. By the end of each phase we require that:

► Inception—Scope of the project has been agreed

► Elaboration—Architecturally significant aspects of the project are up and running as tested code

► Construction—The coding is complete

► Transition—The project is live

---

[4] These tasks can be surprisingly continuous—especially the box color.

It is very important that a project does not proceed to the next phase if these high-level goals have not been achieved. We can add iterations to the phase to enable us to achieve the goals of the phase. This has an obvious impact on schedule, but we may catch up later by accomplishing more in future iterations or we de-scope the functionality we plan to deliver. Iterative development makes this easier as at the end of each successful iteration, we have a stable build of the code and the associated work products that *should* be suitable for release.

Architecture-driven

RUP is an *architecture-driven* process. Defining and building an executable architecture is the focus of the Elaboration phase of any RUP project. An executable architecture means code that demonstrates and proves the effectiveness of our architectural decisions.

Use case driven

Prior to the introduction of SOA concepts, RUP focused on aligning iterations to system use cases. This is still true in that we would expect to take systems use cases through to implementation during a iteration; there are higher-level drivers of the goal of an iteration.

Automating a business process or task becomes the new goal of the iteration. We have to implement system use cases as part of this goal, but now we focus on implementing a thread of the business process from beginning to end. We may not handle all cases in the process and we may not cover all exceptions or branches in the process flow, but we have to implement something useful end-to-end.

If we use business use case realizations as an alternative to business process flows, then we are implementing these business use case realizations. Either way, the focus of the iteration is to deliver some business useful functionality.

How we use RUP in this book

The linear nature of a book means that it looks like we describe a complete project with no iterations. In practice, we have updated and revised business process models, requirements analysis, design, code, test and the other elements as the project has proceeded.

In this book, we are using a new version of RUP V7.1 that incorporates additional information about building SOA-based solutions. This information is a combination of SOA material that was part of earlier versions of RUP, and a lot of content from IBM service-oriented modeling and architecture technique is used by its consultants. Now let us look at our development case.

What is a development case?

A *development case*, as defined by the RUP Environment discipline, consists of a description of a software development process, tailored for an organization or a project.

In our case, we are talking about the development case used to develop the contents of this book, that is the JK Enterprises development case.

The role responsible for creating the development case is the process engineer, responsible for providing teams with the organization's development process.

In this chapter, we use the Rational Method Composer tool, as described in "Rational Method Composer" on page 114, to codify the development case.

JK Enterprises development case

We create a simple development case centered around services and how to make them evolve through their life cycle. It is based on the following processes:

► Rational Unified Process

► Rational Unified Process for Service-Oriented Architecture (RUP for SOA)

► Rational Unified Process for Service-Oriented Modeling and Architecture (RUP for SOMA), which replaces RUP for SOA

► Rational Unified Process for Business Modeling

More importantly, most of the content of the development case comes from proven best practices that we, as the IBM Redbooks authoring team, have applied successfully in the field. These best practices are not yet documented in a formal process such as RUP for SOA. (They are documented in our development case.)

Rational Method Composer

Rational Method Composer is an Eclipse-based framework for process and method authoring, targeting primarily process engineers who want to tailor or create method contents and processes. For example, RUP for SOA has been codified using Method Composer.

Method Composer is the product that replaces Rational Unified Process (RUP) and RUP authoring products, such as RUP Process Builder.

Method Composer ships with processes, including:

- Classic RUP
- RUP for Business Modeling
- RUP for SOMA

Method Composer is based on the Eclipse Process Framework (EPF). The main difference between Method Composer and Process Framework is around process contents, such as the processes listed above. Process Framework only contains limited content, whereas Method Composer has a lot. Also, Method Composer provides additional integration capabilities with other Rational products, such as Rational Portfolio Manager.

Method Composer implements the Unified Method Architecture (UMA) standard, submitted to the Object Management Group (OMG) as Software Process Engineering (SPEM) V2.0. With this standard, everyone uses the same terminology around methods and processes. For example, SPEM defines what tasks, activities, roles, or guidance are.

Method Composer contents are packaged as plug-ins. A new plug-in can be based on an existing plug-in. For example, RUP for SOMA is based on RUP, and provides variations (contributions, extensions, or replacements) for service-orientation.

The main output of Method Composer is an HTML site (formerly RUP site), with method and process contents, that is accessible from a Web browser and from within tools of the SDP, such as Rational Software Architect.

Also, Method Composer bridges the gap between process engineering and project management by providing the capability to export processes as Rational Portfolio Manager or Microsoft Project templates.

Refer to the resources section at the end of this chapter for links to more Rational Method Composer or Eclipse Process Framework information.

The Method Composer Authoring perspective (Figure 5-3) is composed of the following views: Library [1], Editor [2], Properties [3], and Configuration [4].

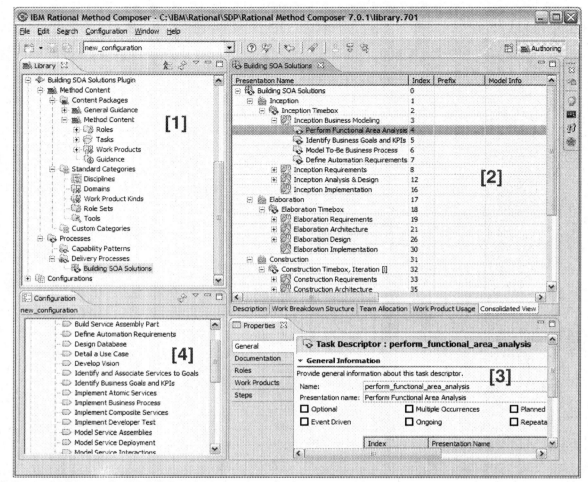

Figure 5-3   Method Composer Authoring perspective

Codify the development case

There are three main activities involved in codifying the development case in Method Composer:

► Create method content
► Create the process
► Publish and export the process

Method Composer differentiates method content from process, as described in the following excerpt from its help system:

> Method Composer separates reusable *method content* from its application in *processes*. The primary method content elements are *tasks, roles, work products, and guidance.* A process engineer uses Method Composer to author these elements, define the relationships between them, and to categorize them. Method content provides step-by-step explanations, describing how specific development goals are achieved independent of the placement of these steps within a development life cycle. Processes take these method elements and relate them into semi-ordered sequences that are customized to specific types of projects.

We create a new plug-in named *Building SOA Solutions* to hold the contents of our development case.

Note that in the case of this Redbooks publication we focus on how you can use Rational Method Composer to build a process that is unique to JK Enterprises. The content for this process is created by the authors of the Redbooks publication to simplify licensing issues and to serve as an example of how you can create these elements yourself. For a real project we would focus on reusing content provided by Rational Method Composer and other plug-ins and try to minimize the amount of content that is custom developed.

Method Composer ships with detailed contents about how to create new plug-ins, method content packages, and others. In this chapter, we do not cover all of the Method Composer details, but emphasize about how to create key elements of our development case.

Create method content

We create the following method content (in order):

► Work products
► Roles
► Tasks
► Steps

Create work products
In this section, we explain how to create the Service Model work product.

► In the Library view, select the *Work Products* folder and *New → Artifact*. The artifact editor opens.

► Type `service_model` in the Name field, and `Service Model` in the presentation name.

You would enter information about the service model in the **Description** tab (Figure 5-4), including the relationship between the artifact and another artifact (contributes, extends, or replaces) if required.

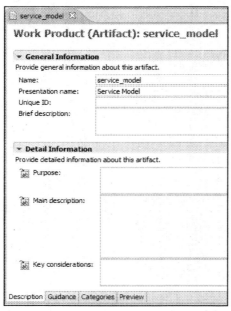

Figure 5-4   Description tab of the work product editor

The **Guidance** tab is where refer to guidance elements that pertain to creating or working on the work product. For example, we could have a *Create a service model using Rational Software Architect* guidance. In simplified case, we have not created guidance elements.

The **Categories** tab is where you enter information that would classify the work product, for example under domains or work product kinds.

Finally, the **Preview** tab is used to view the resulting HTML page.

The service model work product is actually made up of several work products (which it contains). Next, you create the Service Specification work product under the Service Model work product.

▶ Select the Service Model work product in the Library view and *New →
Artifact*.

▶ Name the artifact `service_specification` and `Service Specification`.

We also create the other work products contained under the Service Model as well as other work products. The list of work products in shown in Figure 5-5.

Figure 5-5   Work products in the JK Enterprises development case

We have completed the creation of work products for the development case.

Create roles

We now create the roles that work on work products, for example, the software architect role.

▶ Select the *Roles* folder in the Library view and *New → Role*.

▶ Name the role `software_architect` and `Software Architect`

  You would typically describe the role (main description, skills, ...) in the *Description* tab.

▶ Select the *Work Products* tab and add the `service_model` work product under Responsible for (Figure 5-6).

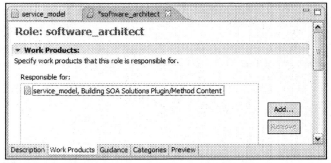

Figure 5-6   The software architect is responsible for the service model work product

► Select the *Preview* tab to see the result (Figure 5-7).

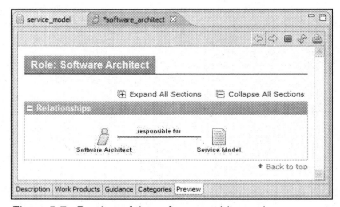

Figure 5-7   Preview of the software architect role

For the JK Enterprises development case we also create other roles (Figure 5-8).

Figure 5-8   JK Enterprises roles

We have completed the creation of roles for the JK Enterprises case study.

Create tasks

In this section we create the tasks for the JK Enterprises case study. Tasks have performing roles and input and output work products. For example, a task for model service interaction:

► Select the *Tasks* folder in the Library view and *New → Task*.

► Name the task model_service_interaction and Model Service Interaction.

► In the *Roles* tab, select software_architect as the primary performer.

► In the *Work Products* tab, add *service_model* as mandatory input and service_contract as outputs.

► The *Preview* tab displays the result (Figure 5-9).

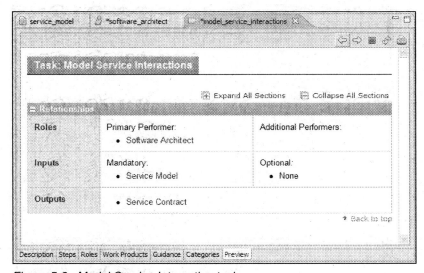

Figure 5-9   Model Service Interaction task

For the development case we have the tasks shown in Figure 5-10.

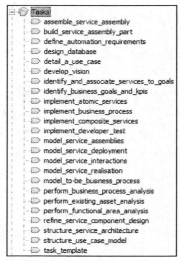

Figure 5-10   JK Enterprises tasks

Create steps

Steps are detailed instructions contained by tasks:

► Open the `structure_service_architecture` task, and select the *Steps* tab.

► Add a step named `Validate and Classify Services`.

► Make sure the `Validate and Classify Service` step is selected, and then enter a description for it (copy and paste from the service specification).

► The result is shown in Figure 5-11.

Figure 5-11   Validate and Classify Services step

We create other steps for the `structure_service_architecture` task (Figure 5-12).

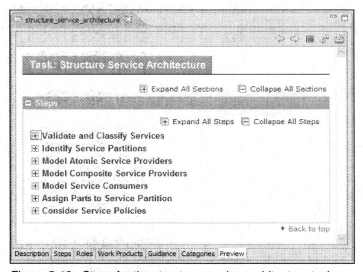

Figure 5-12   Steps for the structure service architecture task

At this stage, we would have to specify the steps for all of the JK Enterprises activities.

After completing the creation of method content we can start to arrange this content in a process.

Create the process

As defined in the Method Composer help: *A process describes how a particular piece of work should be done.* In our case, the piece of work to be done is the JK Enterprises Account Opening project.

We create a delivery process for Building SOA solutions, to arrange method contents into phases and iterations. We perform the following tasks:

► Create phases
► Create iterations
► Create activities
► Create milestones
► Organize tasks in activities

Note that the process elements that we create are heavily influenced by RUP (described in details in "IBM Rational Unified Process (RUP)" on page 106).

► In the Library view, select *Processes* → *Delivery Processes* of the Building SOA Solutions plug-in project, then select *New* → *Delivery Process*.

► In the New Process Component pop-up dialog, name the project `Building SOA Solutions` and select `new_configuration` for the default configuration (Figure 5-13).

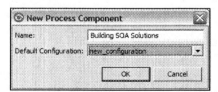

Figure 5-13   New Process Component pop-up window

Note that `new_configuration` is the configuration we create for the JK Enterprises method content and process. By selecting it, the method content is available in the Configuration view.

The delivery process editor should open the new delivery process.

► Type `Development case for JK Enterprises` in the Brief description field.
► Select the *Work Breakdown Structure* tab.

Create phases

As defined in the Method Composer help: *A phase is a special type of activity that represents a significant period in a project, ending with a major management checkpoint, milestone or set of deliverables.*

We first create four phases (from RUP): Inception, Elaboration, Construction, and Transition.

▶ Select the *Building SOA Solutions* delivery process and *New Child → Phase* (Figure 5-14).

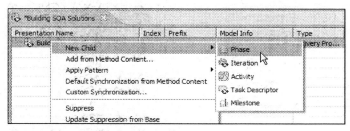

Figure 5-14   Creating a new phase

▶ Name the phase Inception.

▶ Repeat the previous two steps to create Elaboration, Construction, and Transition phases.

▶ The result is shown in Figure 5-15.

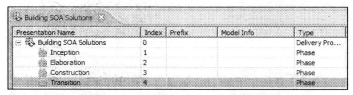

Figure 5-15   Four phases of the Building SOA Solutions delivery process

Create iterations

As defined in the Method Composer help: *Iteration is a group of nested activities that are repeated more than once. Iteration represents an important structuring element to organize work in repetitive cycles.*

We create iterations under the phases. Note that our process is very simple and only has one iteration per phase:

▶ In the *Work Breakdown structure* tab, select the *Inception* phase and *New Child → Iteration*.

- ▶ Name the iteration `Inception Timebox`.
- ▶ Repeat the previous two steps to create one iteration under each phase.
- ▶ The result is shown in Figure 5-16.

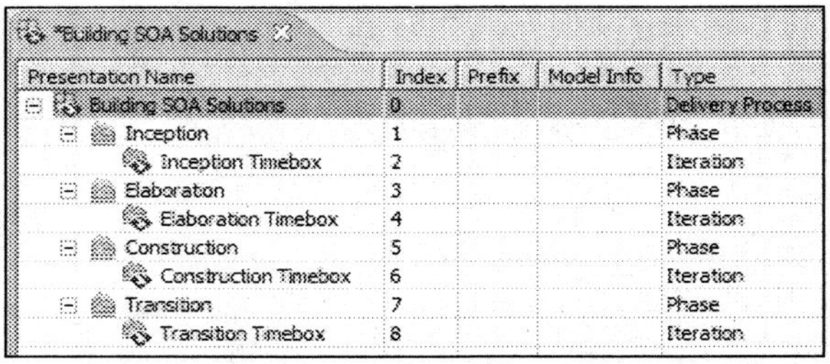

Presentation Name	Index	Prefix	Model Info	Type
Building SOA Solutions	0			Delivery Process
Inception	1			Phase
Inception Timebox	2			Iteration
Elaboration	3			Phase
Elaboration Timebox	4			Iteration
Construction	5			Phase
Construction Timebox	6			Iteration
Transition	7			Phase
Transition Timebox	8			Iteration

Figure 5-16   Four iterations for the Building SOA Solutions delivery process

Create activities

As defined in the Method Composer help: *Activities represent the key building blocks for processes. Activities represent a grouping of breakdown elements such as other activities, task descriptors, role descriptors, work product descriptors, and milestones.*

We create activities under the iterations of our process. The result is shown in Figure 5-17.

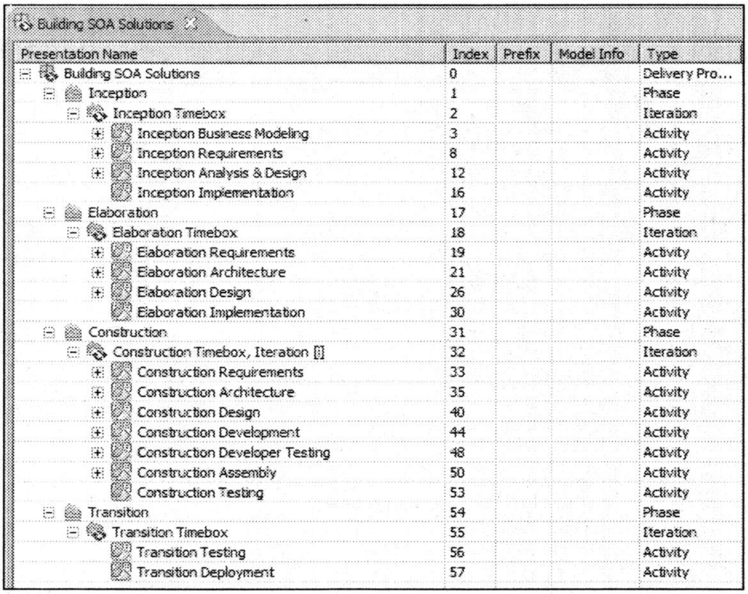

Presentation Name	Index	Prefix	Model Info	Type
Building SOA Solutions	0			Delivery Pro...
Inception	1			Phase
Inception Timebox	2			Iteration
Inception Business Modeling	3			Activity
Inception Requirements	8			Activity
Inception Analysis & Design	12			Activity
Inception Implementation	16			Activity
Elaboration	17			Phase
Elaboration Timebox	18			Iteration
Elaboration Requirements	19			Activity
Elaboration Architecture	21			Activity
Elaboration Design	26			Activity
Elaboration Implementation	30			Activity
Construction	31			Phase
Construction Timebox, Iteration []	32			Iteration
Construction Requirements	33			Activity
Construction Architecture	35			Activity
Construction Design	40			Activity
Construction Development	44			Activity
Construction Developer Testing	48			Activity
Construction Assembly	50			Activity
Construction Testing	53			Activity
Transition	54			Phase
Transition Timebox	55			Iteration
Transition Testing	56			Activity
Transition Deployment	57			Activity

Figure 5-17   Activities for the Building SOA Solutions process

Create milestones

As defined in the Method Composer help: *A milestone describes a significant event in a project, such as a major decision, completion of a deliverable, or meeting of a major dependency such as the completion of a project phase.*

We now create one milestone at the end of each phase (like in RUP).

▶ Select the *Inception* phase and create a new milestone named `Lifecycle Objectives Milestone`.

▶ Make sure the milestone is selected, and then select the *Documentation* tab in the Properties view. Type this text in the Brief Description field (from RUP):

> At the end of the inception phase is the first major project milestone or Lifecycle Objectives Milestone. At this point, you examine the lifecycle objectives of the project, and decide either to proceed with the project or to cancel it.

▶ Similarly, create milestones (in order) at the end of the other phases:

▶ Save the process. The result is shown in Figure 5-18.

Presentation Name	Index	Prefix	Model Info	Type
Building SOA Solutions	0			Delivery Process
Inception	1			Phase
Inception Timebox	2			Iteration
Inception Business Modeling	3			Activity
Inception Requirements	8			Activity
Inception Analysis & Design	12			Activity
Inception Implementation	16			Activity
Lifecyde Objectives Milestone	17			Milestone
Elaboration	18			Phase
Elaboration Timebox	19			Iteration
Elaboration Requirements	20			Activity
Elaboration Architecture	22			Activity
Elaboration Design	27			Activity
Elaboration Implementation	31			Activity
Lifecyde Architecture Milestone	32			Milestone
Construction	33			Phase
Construction Timebox, Iteration [i]	34			Iteration
Construction Requirements	35			Activity
Construction Architecture	37			Activity
Construction Design	42			Activity
Construction Development	46			Activity
Construction Developer Testing	50			Activity
Construction Assembly	52			Activity
Construction Testing	55			Activity
Initial Operational Capabilities Milestone	56			Milestone
Transition	57			Phase
Transition Timebox	58			Iteration
Transition Testing	59			Activity
Transition Deployment	60			Activity
Product Release Milestone	61			Milestone

Figure 5-18   Four milestones for the Building SOA Solutions process

Organize tasks in activities

We now bring the tasks that we created under the appropriate activity of the process.

The tasks are available from under the Configuration view, under *Disciplines* → *Uncategorized Tasks* (Figure 5-19).

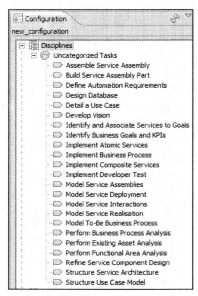

Figure 5-19   Tasks are available in the Configuration view

▶ Drag the `Structure Service Architecture` task from the Configuration view onto the `Elaboration Architecture` activity (under Elaboration Timebox).

  A new task descriptor is created for `Structure Service Architecture`. A task descriptor allows you to modify it without modifying the original task under method content. For example, you can modify the roles or work products for this particular process only. Note that to modify a task descriptor, you have to select it from the Delivery Process Editor, and work in the Properties view.

▶ We compose the other activities into our process. The result is shown in Figure 5-20.

Presentation Name	Index	Prefix	Model Info	Type
Building SOA Solutions	0			Delivery Process
Inception	1			Phase
Inception Timebox	2			Iteration
Inception Business Modeling	3			Activity
Perform Functional Area Analysis	4			Task Descriptor
Identify Business Goals and KPIs	5			Task Descriptor
Model To-Be Business Process	6			Task Descriptor
Define Automation Requirements	7			Task Descriptor
Inception Requirements	8			Activity
Develop Vision	9			Task Descriptor
Structure Use Case Model	10			Task Descriptor
Detail a Use Case for Iteration [1]	11			Task Descriptor
Inception Analysis & Design	12			Activity
Identify and Associate Services to Goals	13			Task Descriptor
Perform Business Process Analysis	14			Task Descriptor
Perform Existing Asset Analysis	15			Task Descriptor
Inception Implementation	16			Activity
Lifecycle Objectives Milestone	17			Milestone
Elaboration	18			Phase
Elaboration Timebox	19			Iteration
Elaboration Requirements	20			Activity
Detail a Use Case for Iteration [2]	21			Task Descriptor
Elaboration Architecture	22			Activity
Structure Service Architecture	23			Task Descriptor
Model Service Interactions for Iteration [1]	24			Task Descriptor
Model Service Assemblies	25			Task Descriptor
Model Service Deployment	26			Task Descriptor
Elaboration Design	27			Activity
Model Service Realisation for Iteration [1]	28			Task Descriptor
Refine Service Component Design for Iteration	29			Task Descriptor
Design Database for Iteration [1]	30			Task Descriptor
Elaboration Implementation	31			Activity
Lifecycle Architecture Milestone	32			Milestone
Construction	33			Phase
Construction Timebox, Iteration [i]	34			Iteration
Construction Requirements	35			Activity
Detail a Use Case for Iteration [i+2]	36			Task Descriptor
Construction Architecture	37			Activity
Refine Service Architecture	38			Task Descriptor
Model Service Interactions for Iteration [i+1]	39			Task Descriptor
Refine Service Assemblies	40			Task Descriptor
Refine Service Deployment	41			Task Descriptor
Construction Design	42			Activity
Model Service Realisation for Iteration [i+1]	43			Task Descriptor
Refine Service Component Design for Iteration	44			Task Descriptor
Design Database for Iteration [i+1]	45			Task Descriptor
Construction Development	46			Activity
Implement Business Process for Iteration [i]	47			Task Descriptor
Implement Composite Services for Iteration [i]	48			Task Descriptor
Implement Atomic Services for Iteration [i]	49			Task Descriptor
Construction Developer Testing	50			Activity
Implement Developer Test for Iteration [i]	51			Task Descriptor
Construction Assembly	52			Activity
Build Service Assembly Part for Iteration [i]	53			Task Descriptor
Assemble Service Assembly for Iteration [i]	54			Task Descriptor

Description | Work Breakdown Structure | Team Allocation | Work Product Usage | Consolidated View

Figure 5-20   Building SOA Solutions tasks organized under activities

Note that because tasks specify performing roles and input and output work product, Method Composer automatically provides views that show what role is needed in each phase or iteration (for example, Software Architect), and what work products are needed. This information is shown under the *Team Allocation* or *Work Product Usage* tabs of the Delivery Process editor. The Consolidated View tab shows both roles and work products (Figure 5-21).

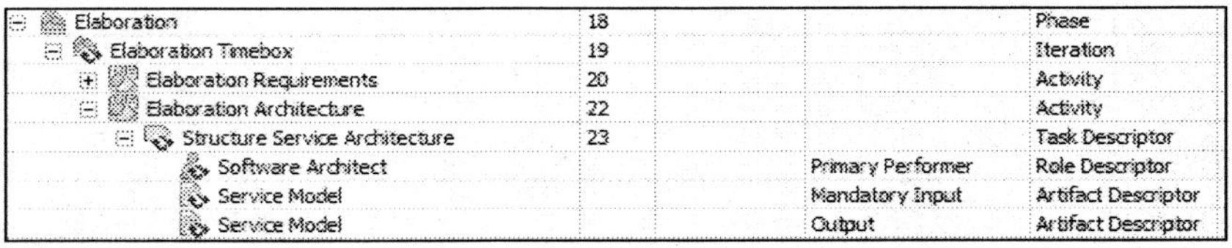

Elaboration	18			Phase
Elaboration Timebox	19			Iteration
Elaboration Requirements	20			Activity
Elaboration Architecture	22			Activity
Structure Service Architecture	23			Task Descriptor
Software Architect			Primary Performer	Role Descriptor
Service Model			Mandatory Input	Artifact Descriptor
Service Model			Output	Artifact Descriptor

Figure 5-21 Consolidated tab of the delivery process editor

We have completed the development of the `Building SOA Solutions` process (including method content) in Method Composer. The next steps are about publishing the process to make it is accessible to JK Enterprises staff.

Publish the process as HTML

Method Composer is a content management application. In this section, we export (publish) the contents that we have produced as a Web (old RUP) site, so that it is available JK Enterprises staff (who do not have Method Composer).

For the purpose of this exercise, we have created three custom categories under our plug-in, one for each of tasks, work products, and roles.

We now edit our configuration so that it includes contents from the three categories:

► Make sure you are in Method Composer in the Authoring perspective. In the Library view, open `new_configuration` (in the Configurations folder).

► In the Configuration editor, select the *Plug-in and Package Selection* tab, and make sure that `Building SOA Solution Plugin` is the only selected content (Figure 5-22).

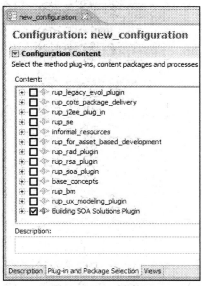

Figure 5-22   Plug-in and Package Selection tab of the configuration editor

We select what contents to include in the published process. For us, it is the content from the three categories (roles, work products, and tasks).

► Select the *Views* tab.

► Click *Add View* and select the *Roles* category.

► Repeat the previous step to add a view for tasks and work products.

► Select the `roles_category` view and click *Make Default*.

► The result is shown in Figure 5-23.

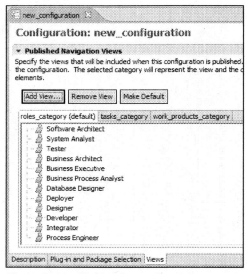

Figure 5-23   Views of a configuration

► Save the configuration.

► Select *Configuration → Publish*.

► Select `new_configuration` in the Select Method Configuration page of the Publish Method Configuration wizard and click *Next* (Figure 5-24).

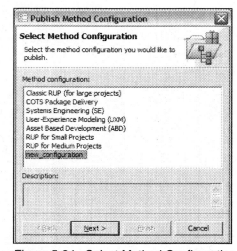

Figure 5-24   Select Method Configuration

► In the Specify Publishing Options page, select a path on the file system to publish the Web site, type JK Enterprises Development Case for the title, and select all options. Click *Finish* (Figure 5-25).

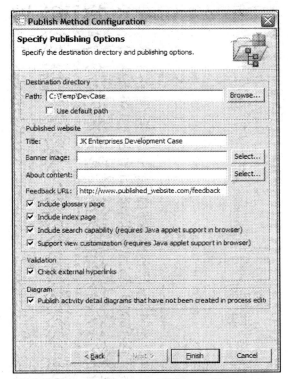

Figure 5-25   Specifying publishing options

► After a couple of minutes, the favorite Web browser should open with the publishing log and the result process Web site.

► Close the log page.

► You can now browse the process (Figure 5-26).

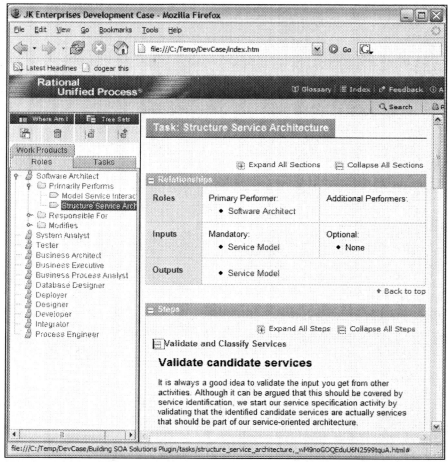

Figure 5-26   Browse the result process

The resulting process site can now be made available to JK Enterprises staff.

Export the process as a project plan

We export the process to Rational Portfolio Manager. Refer to the "Rational Portfolio Manager" on page 33 for more details on this product.

▶ Select *File → Export*.

▶ Select *IBM Rational Portfolio Manager Project Template* and click *Next* (Figure 5-27).

Figure 5-27   IBM Rational Portfolio Manager Project Template

► Select *Delivery Process*, *Build SOA Solutions*, and *new_configuration*. Name
  the project template `BuildSOASolutions`, and specify a directory on the file
  system. Click *Finish* (Figure 5-28).

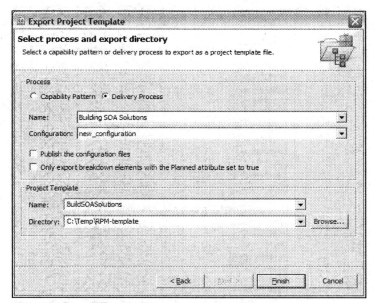

Figure 5-28   Select the process and export directory

A `BuildSOASolutions.xml` file is created by Method Composer. This is a Portfolio
Manager project template.

Export the development case as a plug-in

To export the method plug-in, select *File → Export*. In the Export wizard:

- ▶ Select *Method Plug-ins* and click *Next* (see Figure 5-27 on page 135).
- ▶ In the next page, select the plug-in(s) you want to export, in our case, *Building SOA Solutions*, and click *Next*.
- ▶ In the next page, review the dependencies and click *Next*.
- ▶ In the next page, review the export information and click *Next*.
- ▶ Finally, specify a directory to export the plug-in to and click *Finish*.

The directory you selected contains the exported plug-in. If you want, create a ZIP file of the exported information for distribution.

We provide the Method Composer plug-in of our development case in:

```
C:\SG247356\sampcode\DevelopmentCase\DevCase-RMC-plugin-export.zip
```

Refer to "Rational Method Composer plug-in" on page 591 for instructions about how to import the plug-in.

References

- ▶ Read the Rational Method Composer developerWorks article series at:
  ```
  http://www-128.ibm.com/developerworks/rational/library/dec05/haumer/
  ```
- ▶ Refer to the Eclipse Process Framework site at:
  ```
  http://www.eclipse.org/epf/
  ```
- ▶ IBM developerWorks Rational Unified Process (RUP) and Rational Method Composer site at:
  ```
  http://www-128.ibm.com/developerworks/rational/products/rup
  ```

6

Modeling and tools

This chapter describes the importance of modeling, the Unified Modeling Language (UML), and model-driven development.

After modeling, we describe the importance of architecture and the IBM Rational products that support modeling and architecture.

Importance of modeling

Now it is time to answer to the following question:

"Why do we model?"

In any human technical field, we feel the need to represent concepts in a way easily understandable for our mind; if we are building something small, then the idea itself is a good and reasonable representation; but, if we have to build something more complex, then we begin by creating an abstract representation of its structure and parts by creating pictures, sketches, and blueprints.

Let us consider an example: If we have to build a small paper boat to play with our child, we would likely take some paper, fold it to get the boat shape, and in a few minutes we can try to make it float in the bathtub. If the boat does not work well or it sinks, we could figure out what caused the problem and build another boat to make our child happy.

Now, suppose we have to build a fishing boat for our family. We could start by assembling the tools and raw materials: wood, hammers, nails, and so on. We could then immediately start to build the boat. But maybe this time we want to first figure out some things; so we make some sketches of how the boat will appear; perhaps we still have to agree with our family on some characteristic of the boat: its shape, its dimensions and colors; we may say these are specifications of the boat. This will affect the list of raw materials, the list of tools that we need, and also the steps that we need to follow to build the boat. Indeed creating this specification is a way to reduce the risk of our work ending in failure.

Now imagine that we need a super-customized motorboat. Again we could attempt to start to build it ourselves immediately but there would be many risks—not least of which being that we do not know exactly what we want or even what parts would be required; most probably we will ask a marine engineer to build it for us. The engineer might use some off-the-shelf blueprint or picture to achieve agreement with us on what we want. He might then prepare some scale-model of the motorboat to allow to understand how it will appear, what will be its shape, colors, seat-configuration, and so on. Notice he uses these models for different reasons: first is to gain general agreement with us on what we want; but after this, he will start refining these same models, giving them greater detail and representing with increasing detail what the motorboat will look like. He could place these models into a simulation environment that allows him to test how the motorboat will behave under various conditions, how it will react to certain wind and sea conditions, and so on. This is very useful for him to significantly reduce the risk of the building job and achieve his (and our) goal.

You can easily imagine what kind of models, blueprints, and simulations would be required if we were to build a large supertanker. It would be plain to anyone that starting from a set of tools and materials would be ridiculous.

So the moral of this story is: the more complex you project, the more you need models.

In the world of software we still encounter software development organizations that aim to create complex systems, and are approaching the problem as though they were building something very simple. It is no coincidence therefore that a high percentage of software projects fail.[1] These failures are often directly related to the absence of a development process which mandates the creation of models.

Having models is a recognized practice in many fields: Building architecture, aeronautics, hardware, biology, economics, and sociology.

So basically, a model is a simplified representation of reality. It is possible to have different models on different levels of abstraction, views with different levels of details, and to zoom out or zoom in to a model; it is possible to visualize static or dynamic aspects of a system. Usually we say a good model is a faithful representation of the important parts of a system, hiding the insignificant parts; indeed our mind naturally focuses on the core part of a system when attempting to understand it. When we have to explain to someone, some complex system with pen and paper (the original analysis tools!), we make some sketch of the system representing only core concepts, structure, or main components.

We can see an example of a model and its modeled system in Figure 6-1.

---

[1] Refer to the Standish CHAOS Report, 1994:
    http://www.standishgroup.com/sample_research/chaos_1994_1.php

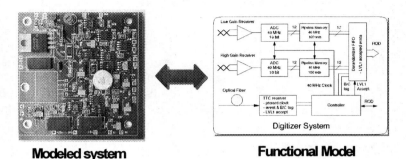

> ⁕ *Engineering model:* A <u>reduced</u> representation of some system that <u>highlights the properties of interest</u> from a given <u>viewpoint</u>
>
> **Modeled system** **Functional Model**
>
> ⁕ *Modeling:* A fundamental technique for coping with complexity
>   - ⁕ We don't see everything at once – only the important stuff = abstraction
>   - ⁕ We use a representation (notation) that is easily understood

Figure 6-1   An example model

According to the UML user guide (see "References" on page 168) there are four reasons for modeling:

1. **Visualize**—Models allows us to visualize and understand better an existing system or one to be built.

2. **Specify**—Models are useful to specify systems characteristic, in terms of their structure and behavior.

3. **Build**—Because a model is usually built using software tools, we can often exploit them to (at least initially) build our solution, by generating other models, code and configurations from them.

4. **Document**—Models are definitely used to document our system or solution.

Another important aspect of modeling, particularly using modeling tools, is that the model itself contains many different types and levels of business context relevant information. Please refer to other chapters of this book for examples of that. With the advent of business driven approach and having value added services in a SOA. There is a need to provide services with business context relevancy. Automated services may have to process the business contextual information in the models.

Unified Modeling Language

The Unified Modeling Language (UML) is the standard for describing models. We start with a brief history and a short overview of UML.

A brief history of UML

In the first part of 1990s several object-oriented languages, such as SmallTalk, C++, Eiffel, and Java were becoming increasingly mainstream. As the software community began to use a variety of software design tools and languages, there were a number of notations all representing similar concepts but with several differences between them. The lack of a standard notation was proving rather confusing for the software community at large.

Majors notations at that times were:

▶ Object Modeling Technique (OMT) by Jim Rumbaugh
▶ Booch Method by Grady Booch
▶ Object-Oriented Software Engineering (OOSE) by Ivar Jacobson

The three methodologists were collectively referred to as the *Three Amigos*, since they were well known to argue frequently with each other regarding methodological preferences.

In 1996 the Three Amigos decided that a Unified Modeling Language was more viable than a Unified Method, and redirected their efforts to respond to the Object Management Group (OMG) Request for Proposal (RFP) for an object modeling language (*Object Analysis & Design RFP-1*, OMG document ad/96-05-01), which was issued in June 1996. Under the technical leadership of the Three Amigos, an international consortium called the *UML Partners* was organized in 1996 to complete the Unified Modeling Language (UML) specification, and propose it as a response to the OMG RFP. The UML Partners' UML 1.0 specification draft was proposed to the OMG in January 1997.

The software community eagerly adopted UML, providing feedback which lead to a number of revisions. UML became a de facto standard and UML 1.1 was adopted by OMG in November 1997.

As a modeling notation, the influence of the OMT notation dominates (for example, using rectangles for classes and objects). Though the Booch *cloud* notation was dropped, the Booch capability to specify lower-level design detail was embraced. The *use case* notation from Objectory™ and the *component* notation from Booch were integrated with the rest of the notation, but the semantic integration was relatively weak in UML 1.1, and was not really fixed until the UML 2.0 major revision.

We can see the major UML version history summarized in Figure 6-2.

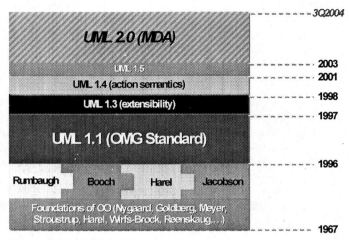

Figure 6-2   UML evolution

> **Note:** Further information about UML can be found at:
>
> http://www.omg.org
> http://www.uml.org

A brief overview of UML

UML is a (visual) language for capturing models about software. As with any language, it has its own syntax and semantics.

There are two main aspects to software in UML: Static and dynamic. This categorization can be applied to the various UML diagram types.

Static diagrams

These types are used to represent the things that must be in the system being modeled. Static diagram types are:

► **Class** diagram—Represents structures: Cases, properties (attributes and associations), and all relationships (see Figure 6-3).

► **Object** diagram—Represents class instances structure.

► **Package** diagram—Represents package structure.

► **Deployment** diagram—Represents deployed elements and topology: Nodes and relations with deployed components, communication association, network connections and so forth.

- **Component** diagram—Represents components, their structure, relationships, and interfaces.

- **Composite structure** diagram—Represents internal part of a classifier, such as class or component. There is a deeper discussion of this later in this section.

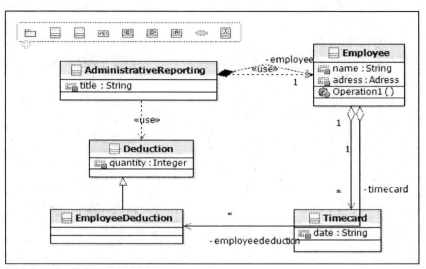

Figure 6-3   A sample class diagram

Dynamic diagrams

These types represent what happens in the system being modeled. Dynamic diagram types are:

- **Use case** diagram—Represents a system from a requirements point of view; we may say from a black-box point of view in terms of system use cases and actors.

- **Activities** diagram—Represents flows of activities, their sequence, conditions, concurrent flows and synchronization points.

- **Sequence** diagram—Represents the sequence of messages that are sent and received between a set of objects (classifier instances), emphasizing their chronological order (the sequence). (See Figure 6-4.)

- **Communication** diagram—Represents communication in a system; they are semantically equivalent to sequence diagrams but they emphasize collaborations between objects.

- **Timing** diagram—Represents timing of events of object(s).

- **State** diagram—Represents objects state machines: We have states, transitions from one state to another, events that fires a transition, guard conditions and so forth.

- **Protocol state machine** diagram—Represent legal transitions (protocols) trough states for an abstract classifier, such as interfaces or ports.

- **Interaction overview** diagram—Represents possible interaction from an high level point of view. They show groups of interactions and the overall flow.

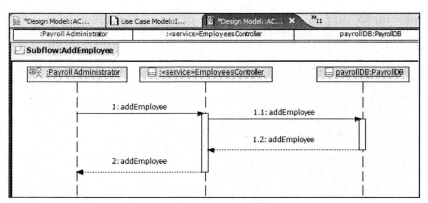

Figure 6-4   Sample sequence diagram

A combination of these diagrams allow to model software from different perspectives. For example, a use case diagram allows us to see our system from a requirement, or *black-box* point of view and help us understand what value the system provides to external actors.

A sequence diagram would provide a *white-box* point of view to help us understand the sequence of messages between objects required to achieve a particular goal.

Another important aspect of UML is that it is a very generic and extensible language. This is one of the primary reasons for the wide-spread adoption and success of UML.

UML defines a few types (we could call them meta classes or classifiers) such as class, operation, property, association, message and so forth.

Additionally, UML defines its own extensibility mechanism based on *profiles*. A profile is a set of information that constrains, customizes and narrows a particular classifier. A profile is made up of *stereotypes*. A stereotype is a way of assigning a type to a particular classifier. Stereotypes give a greater semantic precision to our models.

For example, in Figure 6-4 we can notice an object stereotyped as <<service>>, representing this object will have a *service* behavior and semantics for whatever it means in that context.

> **Note:** For additional material, white papers, and courses on UML, refer to the IBM Rational UML resource center at:
>
> `http://www.ibm.com/software/rational/uml/`

Until now, we have shown various UML characteristics and advantages. However today, in some software development organizations there are still practitioners who doubt the value of modeling. This is often due to considerations related to the accuracy of models. Obviously the less a model is accurate, the less is useful.

We have observed several organizations that developed models with the only goal to document their solutions; this way, models were likely becoming early inaccurate, going far from the actual meaning of underlying code and implementation.

Moreover, an inaccurate model is not just useless but it can also be dangerous, allowing to do assumptions not corresponding to reality. Besides this in software, problems often comes from a very specific detail of the implementation and this may be not caught by a model.

Thus, an important and usual need about models is to keep their semantic near to actual objects (semantic) they represents. However, we have just explained a model is a simplification of reality so how can a model contain the required details?

To solve this apparent paradox, UML has evolved and other initiatives have started such as model-driven architecture (MDA).

Model-driven development

A basic answer on that paradox is to try to have automated tasks that starting from your models, produce underlying implementation; we call these tasks *transformations*.

Considering the historic software engineering evolution, we can notice major improvements in this field have been about raising the level of abstraction: from binary languages to high-level procedural languages to object-oriented languages and so on. Each of these major step have narrowed the gap between human and machines language allowing us to express more powerful concepts and paradigms with a lower coding effort; indeed we say some languages are more expressive than others.

Representing our software solutions with UML models is, in many cases, definitively more expressive and meaningful than using programming languages.

Having models and transformations is a solution to tie two different level of abstraction in a either formal and physical way. This is the point where new modeling technologies, such as model-driven development (MDD), start from. OMG has launched the MDA initiative to define a set of standards to support MDD; these standard include UML, standards to define modeling languages, such as meta-object facility (MOF), to defines automatic transformations and so forth.

Essentially MDD shifts the focus from code to models. Models are becoming primary artifacts representing our solution; they can be transformed to code (or to other models) in an automatic (or manual) way trough transformations. The level of automation may vary from generating only skeleton code to having also some "body" code, structure and so on. This depends on target languages, models, architecture and development processes. As we show in the section "UML 2" on page 149, UML 2 has a much more powerful semantic representation and precision than its previous versions.

> **Abstraction level:** A way to hide implementation details and to emphasize only relevant elements. Clearly, this is a recursive concept: for example a model is a level of abstraction higher than the source code and this is higher than binary code.

We introduced the concept of level of abstraction; however we have not to think just to model and code levels. We have different models on different level of abstraction. We may say code is a model on a lower abstraction level. We show in Figure 6-5 a typical stack of abstraction levels.

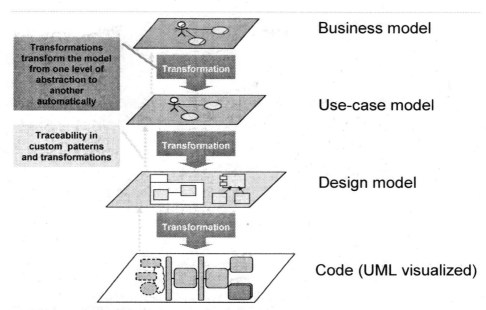

Figure 6-5   *Transformations across levels of abstraction*

Even if it is not necessary to understand each of these level at this time we can just point out the highest abstraction level is relative to the business. We can say it is a business model that does not consider any software but just the business process, its execution, roles, and so forth.

However, this is just an example. What we want to point out here is that when we are focusing on a certain abstraction level, we are hiding details about lower levels. Kinds of models that we represent may vary depending on our context, architecture, organization, and so forth.

Going back to the example, we can expect a use case model is independent from the underlying solution that we called here design model. In the same way we can expect a design model is independent from a technological underlying platform. This way, our organization intelligence is kept and not wasted by changing the underlying software platform, development languages, and so forth.

Through automated and customized transformations, platform specific models are produced. These models usually correspond to code. In that sense we can say that at this level of abstraction, *code is the model*. In this way a model like the design model can be used to generate different *code models*, trough different transformations, targeting different platforms.

Traceability

As we stated before, the greatest improvements in software history are related to raising the level of abstraction. Today, as we explain in other parts of this book, one very important goal for software development organization is business-driven development (BDD).

This implies having methods and tools that supports changing business needs (or requirements) to be immediately supported by IT, in a fluent and agile way. Thus, having models representing business models at an high levels of abstraction implies to have methods to link these models to the others, at a lower levels of abstraction.

Traceability is exactly this tool; it is the ability to know and recognize that a particular model or code at any abstraction level, derives from something else, at a higher level of abstraction. This is very important to allow realizations to be consistent with specifications and to allow to analyze the impact of a change in a business need or requirement.

For example, we can recognize that a change in a requirement specification potentially impacts a particular set of classes in a more abstract model that are in turn linked to correspondent classes in a less abstract model.

Beyond modeling, traceability is related to the whole development process, as we explain in other sections of the book; we can trace from requirements to models, from models to code, from requirements to test and to change management activities, reaching a high level of control across all development life cycle. All this kind of traceabilities are supported by IBM Rational tools.

Transformations

We can have different type of transformations:

- ► **Model to model**—These transformations are used (typically) to create (or update) a model starting from an higher level of abstraction model. Typical examples are: business to use case model, use case to analysis model.

- ► **Model to code**—These transformations are used to generate code starting from (typically UML) models

- ► **Refactoring**—These transformations are used for a particular task on a single model; examples include changing a class name, moving a package, changing stereotypes and so forth.

Transformations generally use UML extensions, such as profiles and stereotypes. These informations can be relevant also to the model they belong or not. For example, in Figure 6-3 we use the stereotype <<service>> for the EmployeeController class. In this case this stereotype is significative for the model itself (because it represent a class "is a service").

Furthermore, this stereotype is used by a transformation from model to code that transforms that class in some underlying component implementing a service (for example, an EJB session bean or a Web service).

In other cases, profile informations are used only by the transformation itself: These informations are not adding any semantic meaning to the model for which they apply. For example, suppose we have an <<entity>> stereotype applied to a persistent class; this stereotype has some additional properties such as PersistenceMechanism that can be assigned to Hibernate, IBatis, or something else. This information is not meaningful from the point of view of the design model from it comes from but it is relevant for a transformation that generates Java code from that model; a particular generation pattern is used to target desired persistence mechanism.

UML 2

UML was born to address primary modeling goals: To have a blueprint of the system to develop and to abstract the system itself keeping in light only important parts. We explained that this was becoming an issue, considering the growing need to have precise models, that are formally linked to implementations. This starts initiatives, such as MDA, and creates the need for a new major release of UML specifications that includes the new initiative. Thus, new UML 2 specifications have been created to address two main points:

► Service-oriented architectures
► Model-driven development

Generally speaking, UML 2 specifications has been designed to have much more precise semantic in the language, to have more expressive power, less ambiguities, to be much more scalable to support large systems and to improve the extensibility of language itself.

UML is based on a *meta model*; UML 2 specifications have strongly changed and improved this meta model, giving it a more precise definition. This meta model is defined by using:

► **Meta-object facility** (MOF), an OMG standard to define meta models that basically is a subset of UML itself

► **Object constraint language** (OCL), a standard language to define constraints

Therefore, we can (informally) say UML is defined by using UML!

For a complete definition of the UML2 specification from a user point of view, refer to the UML 2.0 Superstructure specification at:

```
http://www.uml.org/#UML2.0
```

UML 2 has many improvements and they are about these topics:

- ► Complex structures
- ► Activities
- ► Interactions
- ► State machines

For the scope of this book, we want just to emphasize two of these topics: complex structures and interactions.

Complex structures

Complex structures are designed in UML by using composite structure diagrams. As the name suggests these diagrams belong to the structural part of modeling.

This major UML improvement was necessary because of some limitations in designing structures with previous UML versions: we were able to represent static structures, using *class diagrams*, but this was all at a static (or class) level.

The language was not able to represent structures as they appear at an instance level, we may say at runtime. In other words, we can have different instances of the same class (or component) playing different roles and we have to be able to represent them. Furthermore, we have to represent their relations with the external world.

Structured classes (classes or components) have now an internal structure to allow them to represent their internal instances and the relation between them; in other words we represent internal *collaborations*.

A few very important concepts have been introduced in this area; these are:

- ► **Part**—Represents instances belonging to a structured class. They are basic structural nodes that have one or more interaction points called ports.

- ► **Port**—Represents a structural feature of a classifier that defines interaction between this classifier and the external world.

- ► **Connector**—Specifies a link beween or more instances. This link can be an instance of an association or can derive from any kind of usage of an instance.

Knowing previous versions of UML, it is easy to understand how these new concepts are empowering our modeling notation. With a traditional class diagram, in many cases, it was possible to see just a dependency between two classes and not how, from a structural point of view, the corresponding *objects* were collaborating. Figure 6-6 shows an example.

Structured Classes: Internal Structure

* Structured classes may have an internal structure of (structured class) parts and connectors

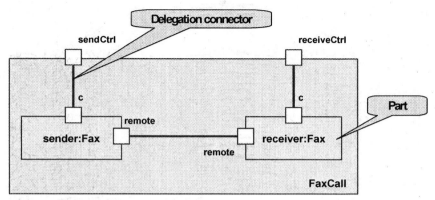

Figure 6-6   *A composite structure sample*

We can easily see how different instances of the Fax class are representing different roles.

One very important concept is related to ports; a port is a *decomposition element*; it is important because it is related to concepts such as decoupling consumers from providers, it creates a clear separation between an internal component realization and the external world.

One may think there is a similarity between port and interface. Indeed these two concept are related; however they are two different concepts: While an interface is a declarative, abstract representation of a behavior, a port is a real object; it is bidirectional and it relates to some interface as we can see in Figure 6-7.

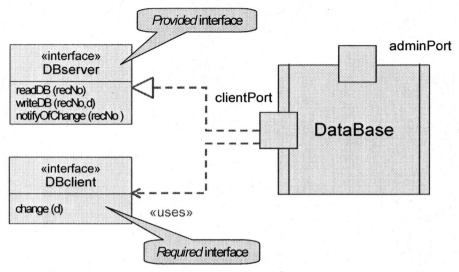

* In general, a port can interact in both directions

Figure 6-7 Relationships between ports and interfaces

In particular, a port receives messages corresponding to the realized interface(s) and sends messages corresponding the provided interface(s).

To summarize, ports provide a complete encapsulation of a component from the external world in both directions.

Interactions

Interactions in UML 1 were represented by sequence or collaboration diagrams and they were semantically equivalent.

Although they were a useful tool to achieve several task such as to represent use case scenarios, they were missing some important capabilities such as reuse of sequences and control flows representation.

UML 2 addresses these issues by defining new interaction elements:

▶ **Interaction occurrence**—When the same sequence is re-used across different contexts, it is possible to define an interaction occurrence to be reused in each context it is needed.

▶ **Option combined fragment**—It is now possible to represent control flows such as loops, conditions, concurrent flows, and so forth.

Moreover, these two capabilities can work together and are recursive; thus it is possible to define a combined fragment that owns some interaction occurrence and both can be composed by others interaction occurrences and combined fragments.

We can see an example of this in Figure 6-8.

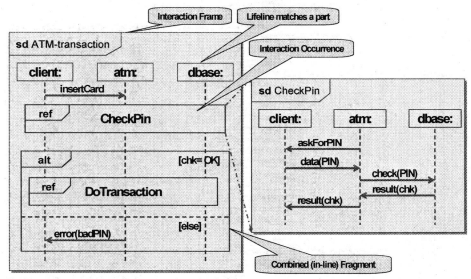

Figure 6-8   UML 2 sample sequence diagram

As we can notice, the CheckPin occurrence is reused in this, more general, ATM transaction interaction. Furthermore we have an alternative fragment that controls the result of CheckPin and, in the positive case, executes the DoTransaction interaction occurrence.

We have shown how these new UML 2 capabilities give much more scalability to the language as it can face very complex project modeling needs.

SOA modeling

Now, we can put things together and define what it means to model SOA solutions.

Following our thread about software historic evolution, we can say that we are facing another important step in raising the level of abstraction. Up to yesterday there were two separated entities in organizations: Business and IT.

Business was defining business processes, business rules, optimizations, organizations, and so forth. IT was trying to create software solutions realizing business needs. However these two entities and points of view were often diverging, were doing different things, using different languages, understanding different goals. So we may say there is a gap between them.

SOA creates a direct connection between business and software solutions. It raises the level of abstraction by identifying *business services* that are directly related to *business tasks* from one side and to *software services* from the other side.

Thus we have to model these services. The SOA modeling life cycle is defined by IBM Service Oriented Modeling and Architecture (SOMA) and is about three main phases:

▶ **Service identification**—This phase has different approaches, such as top-down, meet-in-the-middle, and bottom-up. The top-down-approach, as you can easily imagine, starts directly from the business. We have models representing business processes that are made of business tasks; we begin here to identify services (business services, definitely). This phase is mainly related with business models and you can find further information and samples in Chapter 7, "Business modeling" on page 169.

▶ **Service specification**—This phase is about describing a service: what it offers, what it request, how it is exposed. It also describes dependencies with other services, service composition, and service messages. The main model related to this phase is the *service model*.

A very important aspect related to SOA is, generally speaking, that we are talking about *loosely coupled* business services. This coupling decrease it is very important to allow *reuse* of services to adhere to the general SOA reference architecture. To do this we need models that support this approach; to reduce coupling it is often related to clearly separate external behavior from internal realization (or implementation). We usually achieve this result by seeing services, from the external world, only trough their *business interfaces* and this is, generally speaking, what we call a *service specification*.

Figure 6-9 shows an example of a single service in a service model.

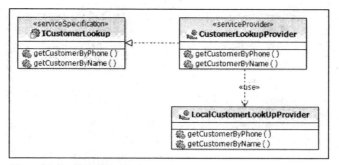

Figure 6-9   Service model sample

► **Service realization**—This phase is about providing a solution for a particular service. We represent here, *how* a service is realized. The model related with this phase is the *design model*. This model has to be traced back to the service model, because it represents its *realization*.

Figure 6-10 shows an example of a service realization in a design model.

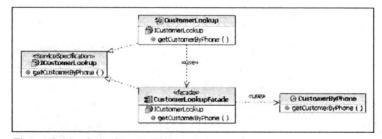

Figure 6-10   A design model sample

Whereas the first example in Figure 6-9 represents the service from a specification point of view, the example in Figure 6-10 is more related to its realization.

Importance of architecture

Architecture considers the design of the target from many dimensions, perspectives, levels, aspects and focus areas. It is driven by the requirements of the owner of the target architecture. The planners are interested in a broad overview of the architecture's purpose. This indicates why it is to be constructed, who is to going to use it, and when it is to be built. The owners supply the purpose and these other details for planning approval. The owners also have other requirements to ensure the architecture meets their specific needs.

Enterprise architecture considers the design and operation of an enterprise also from many perspectives, aspects and focus areas. The catalysts for enterprise architecture are strategic business plans defined by senior management. These address the requirements of the planners and owners of the enterprise.

An enterprise defines its strategic business plans in terms of its mission, vision and values at the highest level. From these, it can establish policies based on specific constraints. These policies are qualitative guidelines defining boundaries of responsibility. They are also used to define the organization structure of the enterprise, made up of business units and functional areas.

Architectural thinking is multi-dimensional, has many levels, perspectives and focused aspects; such as information, network, infrastructure, integration, service and user interface. All these dimensions, levels, perspectives, and aspects are looked at in an interlocking fashion (Figure 6-11).

A successful architecture forms the platform for strategic advantage. Architecture serves both technical and organizational purposes.

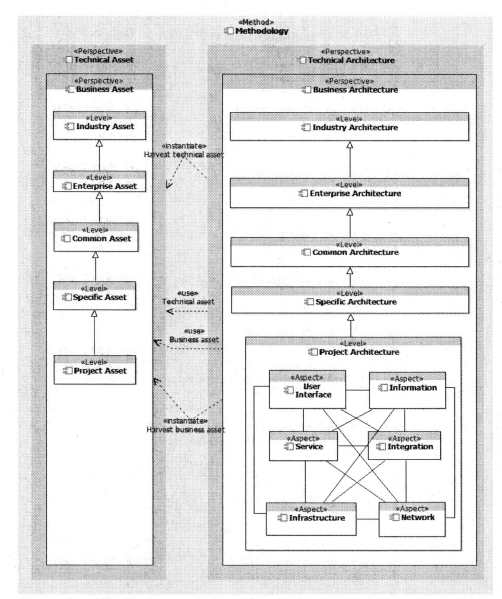

Figure 6-11   Dimensions, levels, perspectives and aspects of architecture

On the organizational side, the architecture helps in:

► **Communicating the high-level design**: A number of stakeholders need to understand the system at a fairly gross level. These include higher-level managers, many of the cross-functional team (for example, marketing, quality assurance, and learning products or user documentation), and may include customers too.

Modeling the system at a high level facilitates communication of the high-level system design or architecture. The reduction in detail makes it easier to grasp the assignment of significant system responsibilities to high-level structures. Moreover, it satisfies the constraint that, though seemingly trivial, has important implications for communication.

► **Providing the system context**: The developers (and future maintainers) also have to understand the overall system. In large systems, developers cannot efficiently understand the details of the entire system. They need a detailed understanding of the more narrowly-scoped portions of the system that they work on. But without an understanding of the responsibilities and interdependencies of the higher-level structures, individual development and optimization of the substructures tend to result in a sub-optimal system. This is both from the point of view of system characteristics such as performance, as well as effort in integration and maintenance.

► **Work allocation**: Where architectures decompose the system into substructures that are relatively independent, have clear responsibilities, and communicate with each other through a limited number of well-defined interfaces, the development work can be partitioned effectively. This allows parallel development work to proceed in relative independence between integration points. This is especially important in large projects, or projects where the teams are geographically dispersed or subcontractors are used.

Moreover, because these units tend to be centers of specialization of function or service, they also afford opportunities for skill specialization among developers. This independence and focus makes development more efficient. The design of the system architecture can be viewed as the dual of designing the organization architecture. If this duality is ignored and the organization architecture is not compatible with the system architecture, then it can influence and degrade the system architecture.

On the technical side, architecture allows us to design better systems and services:

► **Meet system and service requirements and objectives**: Both functional and non-functional requirements can be prioritized as *must have* versus *high want* versus *want*, where must have identifies properties that the system and service must have to be acceptable. An architecture allows us to evaluate and make trade-offs among requirements of differing priority. Though system and service qualities (also known as non-functional requirements) can be compromised later in the development process, many will not be met if not explicitly taken into account at the architectural level.

► **Enable flexible distribution/partitioning of the system and service**: A good architecture enables flexible distribution of the system and service by allowing the system and its constituent applications and services to be partitioned among processors in many different ways without having to redesign the distributable component parts. This requires careful attention to the distribution potential of components early in the architectural design process.

► **Reduce cost of maintenance and evolution**: Architecture can help minimize the costs of maintaining and evolving a given system and service over its entire lifetime by anticipating the main kinds of changes that will occur in the system and service, ensuring that the system's and service's overall design facilitates such changes, and localizing as far as possible the effects of such changes on design documents, code, and other system work products. This can be achieved by the minimization and control of subsystem and services interdependencies.

► **Increase reuse and integrate with existing or earlier and third-party software**: An architecture may be designed to enable and facilitate the (re)use of certain existing components, frameworks, class libraries, existing or earlier, or third-party applications.

Overview of IBM architect tools

Until now we have explained from a conceptual point of view several aspects related to software development process; a strong emphasis has been put on modeling and architecture aspects. We introduced modeling discipline and assets; we explained UML extensibility concepts. Furthermore we have described how an SOA solution should fit into modeling discipline and how it relates to architecture.

Now we move on to more practical aspects.

When talking about modeling tools, we have to exploit all the powerful capabilities of Rational Software Architect and Rational Software Modeler. These tools are all based on Eclipse.

Eclipse

Eclipse has became a very successful open source platform to host software development tools and (with the advent of rich client platform), generic applications.

Eclipse was born in 2001: The proliferation of poorly integrated development tools, methods, formats, repositories and Rational Software Architect, and so on, created the need of a common infrastructure, even across vendors. The initial Board of Stewards of was formed in November 2001 and included: IBM, Borland, MERANT, QNX Software Systems, Rational Software, Red Hat, SuSE, TogetherSoft, and Webgain. Today, more than 100 companies are members of this not-for-profit corporation and all majors and most used development environment are based on this platform.

In particular, for software development tools, Eclipse provides:

► An open, common environment
► A *plug-in based* architecture designed for scalability and extensibility
► A common meta model

Beside these fundamentals, today Eclipse is a fervent community that hosts 10 major projects and more than 50 subprojects.

Plug-ins

From an architectural point of view, Eclipse is based on the plug-in paradigm. We may say in Eclipse *Everything is a plug-in*. Indeed the Eclipse platform core is just a plug-in manager. Up from this point, any Eclipse capability, component or tool is realized by a plug-in (or a set of plug-ins). Any plug-in extends the existing platform and can, in its turn, be extended by other plug-ins.

Trough its descriptor, a plug-in declares its contribution to the platform and therefore, the way the platform will use it. Indeed most important part of a plug-in descriptor are: *extensions* and *extension points*; the first are the existing points the plug-in contributes, where as the seconds (optional) represent the points in which the plug-in can potentially be extended (by other plug-ins). We can visualize this concept in Figure 6-12.

What is a plug-in?

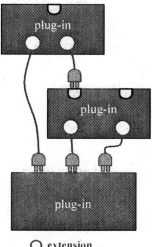

- **plug-in** – set of contributions
  - Smallest unit of Eclipse functionality
  - Big example: HTML editor
  - Declares its pre-requisites
- **extension point**
    Named entity for collecting contributions
- **extension** – a contribution
- Extenders make contributions - **platform controls** and **manages** the contributions

○ extension
▢ extension point

Figure 6-12   Eclipse plug-in mechanism

The Eclipse architecture has been refined from first releases and today we are at Version 3.2 of the platform. Many scalability and performance issues have been faced and solved to allow very powerful tools to be installed and used without impacting the agility and responsiveness of the platform itself.

For any additional information about Eclipse, refer to the Eclipse official site at:

```
http://www.eclipse.org/
```

Rational Software Architect and Rational Software Modeler

Rational Software Architect and Rational Software Modeler include all capabilities needed by the software architect, the designer, and the developer. They are part of a larger picture representing the IBM Rational offering for software development, as we can see in Figure 6-13.

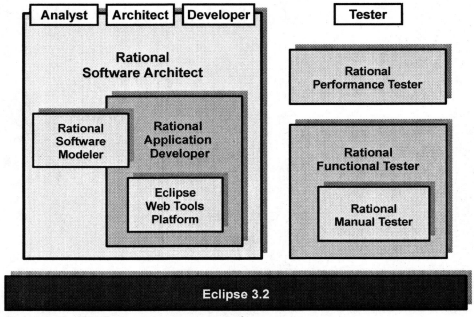

Figure 6-13   IBM Rational development platform

Rational Software Architect includes:

► **Rational Software Modeler**—The tool for designers; it offers all UML 2 modeling capabilities, diagrams and MDD features (transformations and patterns authoring). It is based on some basic Eclipse project such as UML 2 and Eclipse Modeling Framework (EMF).

► **Rational Application Developer**—The tool for developers; it includes all development features such as Web development, J2EE development with EJBs, Web services development, JavaServer™ Faces (JSF) development, UML visualization, component automated test, and run time test environments such as WebSphere Application Server.

► **Eclipse Web Tools Platform (WTP)**—Basic tooling for Web developers; it includes source editors for HTML, JavaScript™, CSS, JSP™, SQL, XML, DTD, XSD, and WSDL; graphical editors for XSD and WSDL; J2EE project natures, builders, and models and a J2EE navigator; a Web service wizard and explorer, and WS-I Test Tools; and database access and query tools and models.

On top of all this, Rational Software Architect offers other features, such as transformations and patterns ready to use. In Version 7, we have a set of useful sample design patterns (including the initial set of patterns document in *Design Patterns: Elements of Reusable Object-Oriented Software*[2]) as shown in the Pattern Explorer of Software Architect V7 (Figure 6-14).

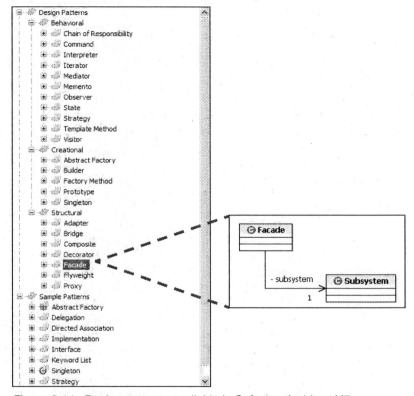

Figure 6-14   Design patterns available in Software Architect V7

Furthermore these transformations are available:

- ► UML to Java 1.4 and Java 1.5
- ► UML to EJB
- ► Java to UML
- ► UML to C++
- ► C++ to UML
- ► UML to WSDL
- ► UML to XSD
- ► UML to CORBA

---

[2] *Design Patterns: Elements of Reusable Object-Oriented Software*, by Erich Gamma, et al, Addison-Wesley, 1995, ISBN 0201633612

Rational Software Architect offers also C++ development, by exploiting a C++ development tool (CDT) from Eclipse; moreover there are proper "architect" functionality such as architectural analysis features: architect can now analyze an existing application by using this capability: Rational Software Architect checks all code for us and discover interesting things such as used patterns, anti-patterns, architectural rules violated and, by automatically creating corresponding UML diagrams.

> **Note:** For information about custom patterns and transformation in Rational Software Architect, refer to "Pattern-based engineering with Rational Software Architect ." on page 545.

UML profile for software services

UML is very generic language, designed for all possible software systems, applications and solutions. Although it would be possible to represent services using only UML itself, it is a better idea to use a specific profile designed for services; this is because you already have SOA elements available to use. Therefore when we have to represent, analyze, and design an SOA solution (with IBM Rational tools) we have to use the *UML profile for Software Services*.

Referring to "SOA modeling" on page 153, we want to point out now that this profile, has to be used mainly in conjunction with the *service identification* and *service specification* phases of SOMA, but not with the *service realization* phase. Therefore, services are identified and specified here, even if this specification is well detailed, it does not represent a white-box view or realization of services. For this goal we use a less abstract model called *design model*.

As any profile does, it extends some existing UML element (we can call them *meta classes*) by defining new stereotypes that provide additional semantic and visual representation on UML meta classes.

In Figure 6-15, we can observe these stereotypes and which meta classes they extend.

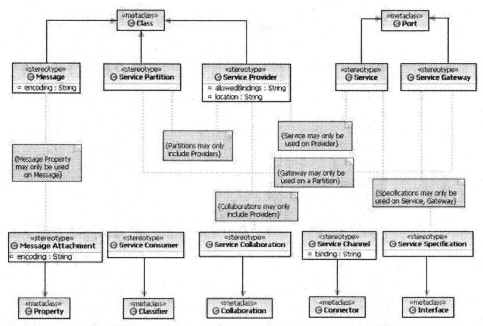

Figure 6-15 UML Profile for Software Services (for Rational Software Architect Version 6)

Note: In Version 6 of the Rational Software Architect, this profile was provided as a tool add-in (through IBM developerWorks), in Rational Software Architect Version 7 this profile is provided in-the-box, with the product.

For a complete description of the profile refer to:

```
http://www-128.ibm.com/developerworks/rational/library/05/419_soa/
```

Note that there are few differences between Rational Software Architect Version 6 and 7 for this profile; some stereotype (such as `<<serviceModel>>`) has been added in Rational Software Architect V7.

Although you can refer to the official documentation to verify formal specifications of the profile, we provide here an introduction to it, by highlighting most significant stereotypes and their meanings.

Service

This stereotype represents the endpoint of a service interaction (and this is defined by a corresponding stereotype). This stereotype extends the UML **Port** meta class and as a port, it decouples the external world from an internal service realization and vice versa. A **<<service>>** element is typed by some interfaces: usually there are provided and required interfaces. Provided interfaces are those offered by the service itself, where as required interfaces are used by the service (see Figure 6-7 for a port sample). For example, a **BankingAccount** service can provide some **BankingAccount** interface and require some **SecureBankingUser** interface.

Service specification

This stereotypes represents a specification of a service. We can view it as what consumers (clients of that service) expect from that service and what it expects from them to be able to execute. However notice that a service can have multiple provided interfaces.

We can notice this stereotype extends the UML Interface meta class and indeed, it acts as an interface. An interface can be informally defined as a set of operation declarations, without any implementation on it; it represents only an agreement between elements that want to realize it and external elements that want use it. See Figure 6-9 on page 155 for an example.

Service provider

A class or a component stereotyped as <<serviceProvider>> represent an element that realize one or more service specifications. A service provider should not expose its internal structure but it has to expose its public ports, stereotyped as <<service>>, trough which, it realizes a (set of) service specification.

Message

A <<message>> represents the element that is used to communicate with a service operation; its definition comes directly from WSDL (Web service definition language) specifications; thus a message is a container of informations having a common meaning between consumers and providers of a service. A message can be composed by other classes (typically from a *domain model*) and can be used either as an operation input or output parameter.

We can see an example of a <<message>> in Figure 6-16.

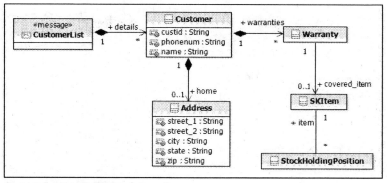

Figure 6-16 Message example

As we can notice from the above figure, the message `CustomerList` is a (UML) *composition* of customers that, on its own, has its structure, associations and so on.

A message can also have a property stereotyped as `<<Message Attachment>>` and this is meaning there is a physical attachment on that message such as a file, an image so on.

Service partition

The stereotype that extends meta class, `class` is used as a container of services. Services can be grouped along several dimensions: for example functional area they belong, different architectural layers and so on. Notice a partition can only contain services or other partitions as internal parts.

Service gateway

A service gateway act as a *proxy* for a target service. a gateway has to be used in conjunction with a partition. It allows internal partition services to be exposed to external consumers and at the same time, to avoid all internal services are exposed to external world. Furthermore a gateway allows to mediate between services interfaces and protocols by introducing a point of decoupling between a consumer and a provider. Notice a gateway stereotype can only be added to a partition and not to a service provider.

References

Read *The Unified Modeling Language User Guide*, by Grady Booch, James Rumbaugh, Ivar Jacobson, Addison Wesley

Read *A Rational approach to model-driven development*, by A. W. Brown, S. Iyengar, and S. Johnston, at:

```
http://www.research.ibm.com/journal/sj/453/brown.html
```

Visit the IBM Rational UML resource center at:

```
http://www-306.ibm.com/software/rational/uml/
```

Visit the Object Management Group UML Web site at:

```
http://www.uml.org
```

7

Business modeling

This chapter describes the use of business models to provide the basis for business-relevant SOA solutions to real business problems.

These topics are described and examples are provided, for:

► Inputs to the business modeling discipline

► Business modeling domain work products

► The tasks required to capture the business use cases, business processes and various other business-related work products and artifacts

► How to use the tools to create these work products and the integrations between these tools.

Introduction

It is an obvious, but often ignored statement that IT systems should support solutions to business problems. The SOA-led approach aligns IT solutions to business needs and constraints more directly than traditional techniques. The service-led approach implicit in any SOA changes the way IT thinks when it looks to provide automated solutions.

Prior to implementing a solution, the business has to decide what the problem is, and the business value in solving that problem. This relates back to the wider problem of business strategy and business alignment. By aligning IT to the strategic business goals and values, SOA-based solutions can lead to very focused deliveries from IT.

Many of the tasks described in this chapter run in parallel with the tasks described in Chapter 8, "Requirements" on page 207. There is a logical sequence of tasks involving business modeling (for example, understand the current business) that will precede tasks of the requirements phase (for example, capture business goals).

Business modeling

The purpose of the RUP business modeling discipline is to:

- ► Understand the current business.
- ► Understand areas for improvement and identify what should be improved
- ► Assess the impact of organizational change
- ► Ensure a common understanding of the business and establish a glossary
- ► Maintain business rules

We would also emphasize that we are looking for a solution that meets the business goals and provides real value to the business. We should understand and capture the key performance indicators and metrics required to prove that the goal has been achieved. We emphasize this last point because many initiatives start without any consideration as to what would be a successful outcome, and how it could be recognized as a success.

In our development case (see "JK Enterprises development case" on page 114), we use the following RUP work products to capture these ideas and goals:

- ► Business vision
- ► Business use case model
- ► Business analysis model
- ► Business goals

- ► Business glossary
- ► Business process model

We show these work products and the relationships between these and other work products in Figure 7-1.

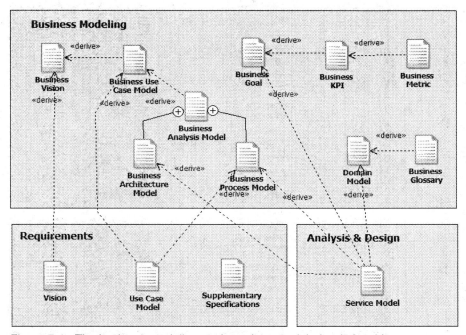

Figure 7-1   The business modeling work products and their relationships

In our JK Enterprises example, we are not starting from scratch. We have existing systems, existing business process models, there has been work done on business process optimization. In many cases, we are expanding on work products that already exist for the system and the enterprise.

Key roles in business modeling

The work products (Figure 7-1) and tasks (Figure 7-3) are performed by different roles in the project (Figure 7-2).

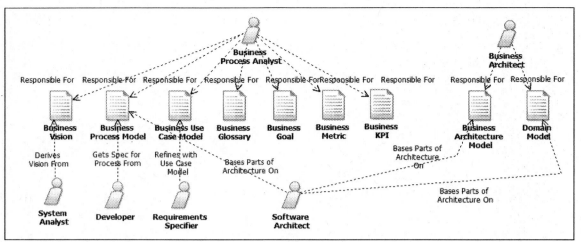

Figure 7-2   Key roles in the business modeling discipline and the related work products

Typical steps in business modeling

The workflow we use for business modeling tasks is shown in Figure 7-3.

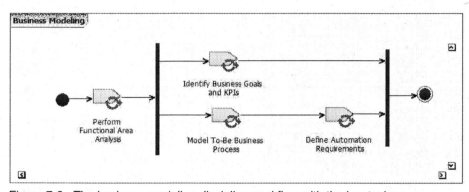

Figure 7-3   The business modeling discipline workflow with the key tasks

The typical sequence of steps to create the business model are:

► Understand the current business.

► Start the business vision and the business glossary

► Create the as-is business use case model (using Rational Software Architect and RequisitePro).

► Create the business analysis model in Software Architect.

- Create business process models that correspond to the business use case realizations created in the as-is model (using WebSphere Business Modeler).
- Extract the business architecture.
- Capture the business vision and goals for the to-be business. Start defining key performance indicators (KPIs) and metrics against the goals.
- Create the to-be business use case model (it may not have changed).
- Create the business analysis model based on the to-be business use case model.
- Create the business process models of the to-be business use case realizations.
- Update the business architecture if required.

Inputs to the business modeling discipline

The business modeling discipline is where our SOA work starts. In our example, we made use of some work that is outside the scope of this IBM Redbooks publication. JK Enterprises has already assessed the business, we show how to document existing (as-is) processes and future business processes (to-be) but we assume we have performed business process optimization. We have a good idea of our goals, and the way we might measure our goals have been achieved.

This chapter demonstrates how to capture this existing information in the IBM tools but we do not describe in detail how to perform these tasks. We have a defined development case for our development process.

In addition, if we have a business that has a mature SOA approach in place, we would have additional inputs to our project. These include domain models, process models, and service models.

A word about tooling

We refer to two IBM RequisitePro projects in this chapter and in Chapter 8, "Requirements" on page 207.

- The first project is for enterprise-level information. This should be relatively stable information and contains the business glossary, business use cases and service policies. All your SOA (and other) projects refer to and contribute to this RequisitePro project.

  This RequisitePro project is named *SOA SDP Redbook Enterprise Content*.

- The second RequisitePro project contains information about our particular piece of work described in our case study. This includes business goals, KPIs, metrics, and other information, which are the basis for some of the design and implementation decisions later on in this book.

  This RequisitePro project is named *SOA SDP Redbook Project Content.*

The rationale for having two separate projects, and using the cross-project traceability in RequisitePro is simple: governance. Access rights to information including read-only and even visibility of information is better controlled by splitting this information into different RequisitePro projects.

If governance is less of a concern in your organization in this context, consider combining the content of these RequisitePro projects. Be aware that good governance is critical to the success of any long-term move to effective SOA-based solutions.

Governance is just one advantage of RequisitePro. There are also the benefits of standardization of templates, the ability to capture and manage information in one central repository, and complete and auditable version histories.

We have created some new RequisitePro document templates for this book, and modified others. Instructions for how to install these templates are outlined in "Loading the RequisitePro projects" on page 577.

We also have various UML and business process models that we refer to and update during this chapter. This includes a business use case model and a domain model held in Rational Software Architect (or Software Modeler) and a business process model held in WebSphere Business Modeler.

Now we discuss the different work products and artifacts from RUP in more detail.

Business architecture

The *business architecture* provides an overview of the significant parts of the business in terms of its products and services, processes, organizational structure, and locations. It is used to capture key features of a business, and in term influences application architecture, services, and other more technical elements of the business.

The business architecture is presented in a business architecture document. This document is typically assembled from sources of information such as business process models, organization charts, market reports, and others.

The following view of the business can be found in a business architecture document:

- ► Market view
- ► Business process view
- ► Organization view
- ► Human resources view
- ► Domain view
- ► Geographic view
- ► Communication view

Not all views may be relevant to your business. For example, no geographic view is required if we conduct our business from a single location. At JK Enterprises, we have already been told that we have many different locations in six countries (see "An overview of JK Enterprises" on page 18).

We have omitted the business architecture document in our JK Enterprises example.

Component business modeling

IBM, specifically IBM Global Business Services, has developed a technique called *component business modeling* (CBM) to help its customers understand their business, the capabilities of the business and identify capability gaps. They break the business down into relatively independent areas to look for potential opportunities for improvements and innovation. The output of this work would be an understanding of how improvement in the certain areas of the business would have maximum positive effect on the business.

A selection of information about CBM can be found at:

```
http://www.haifa.ibm.com/projects/software/cbm/index.html

http://www-935.ibm.com/services/us/index.wss/executivebrief/imc/a1017906?cn
txt=a1005262

http://www-935.ibm.com/services/us/index.wss/executivebrief/imc/a1018920?cn
txt=a1005266
```

Looking at the business from a business strategy perspective gives us a map of the business in terms of domains (for example, Servicing and Sales), levels of responsibility (for example, Directing), and functional areas of the business (for example: Sales Management or Customer Service). In CBM these items are called Business Competencies, Accountability Level, and Business Components respectively. CBM has three accountability levels: Directing, Controlling, and Executing (Figure 7-4).

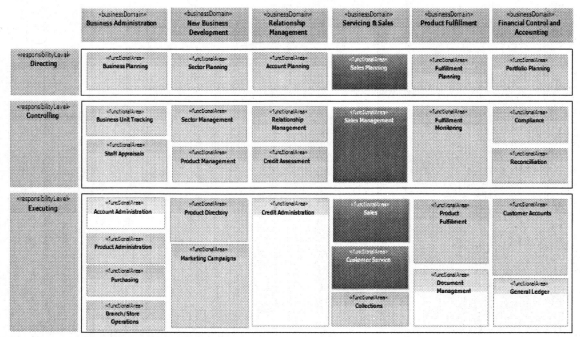

«businessDomain» Business Administration	«businessDomain» New Business Development	«businessDomain» Relationship Management	«businessDomain» Servicing & Sales	«businessDomain» Product Fulfillment	«businessDomain» Financial Control and Accounting
«responsibilityLevel» Directing					
«functionalArea» Business Planning	«functionalArea» Sector Planning	«functionalArea» Account Planning	«functionalArea» Sales Planning	«functionalArea» Fulfillment Planning	«functionalArea» Portfolio Planning
«responsibilityLevel» Controlling					
«functionalArea» Business Unit Tracking	«functionalArea» Sector Management	«functionalArea» Relationship Management	«functionalArea» Sales Management	«functionalArea» Fulfillment Monitoring	«functionalArea» Compliance
«functionalArea» Staff Appraisals	«functionalArea» Product Management	«functionalArea» Credit Assessment			«functionalArea» Reconciliation
«responsibilityLevel» Executing					
«functionalArea» Account Administration	«functionalArea» Product Directory	«functionalArea» Credit Administration	«functionalArea» Sales	«functionalArea» Product Fulfillment	«functionalArea» Customer Accounts
«functionalArea» Product Administration	«functionalArea» Marketing Campaigns		«functionalArea» Customer Service	«functionalArea» Document Management	«functionalArea» General Ledger
«functionalArea» Purchasing			«functionalArea» Collections		
«functionalArea» Branch/Store Operations					

Figure 7-4   Component Business Model™ map for JK Enterprises

We undertake an assessment of these business components, looking at which components are potential targets for improvement. We apply criteria such as costs, revenue potential, strategic fit, alignment between business processes and applications, depending on the current state of the business and its goals. These criteria are not predefined, but tend to be defined by what is being assessed.

The result of the assessment is a set of business components that are targets for improvement. In the JK Enterprises example, the Sales Management business component is being scoped for improvement.

In the next section in this chapter we drill down into this Sales Management business component while performing the Functional Area Analysis task. This is to provide inputs into the business process model.

In the JK Enterprises example, we assume that this process of understanding which areas of the business need improving and what value it would add to the business have already been established.

Functional area analysis

This task is aimed at producing a refined partitioning of the business to create business systems. It is a key step in working out what IT sub-systems might be required in our SOA-based solution.

The initial partitioning would have been derived from previous work (for example, using Component Business Modeling as described earlier in this chapter). Then we break down each functional area into smaller components. Each functional area has specific responsibilities, and collaborates with other functional areas. Ultimately, each area of functionality is mapped to a business system. A business system then supplies services to other business systems. Each business system is then mapped to an IT subsystem. These IT subsystems can be the systems described by system use cases later on in the chapter on requirements.

In our JK Enterprises example, we were told that the Servicing and Sales domain requires our attention.

We also investigate the following initial business components in the Relationship Management domain:

► Relationship management
► Account planning

Customer Services is part of the Servicing and Sales domain. This is a business component. One of the responsibilities of this business component is to handle queries from customers about the status of their account applications. We have been told that this is an area where improvements can be made, as currently customers cannot get the status of their account application.

Business vision

The *business vision* captures the high-level objectives of the business modeling work. In our case, we have created a business vision aimed at the managers of the business, the funding authority, the workers in the organization and the developers of the services so they understand the context and the rationale of the project.

In our JK Enterprises example, the completed business vision work product contains positioning, an overview of the stakeholders, the key needs of the stakeholders and the objectives of the business modeling activities. This content is built up over time during the project.

The positioning includes the business opportunity: Improvements in sales and customer service through increased speed and responsiveness, enhanced productivity through reduction in total cost of ownership (TCO), and reduction of regulatory non-compliance.

The business vision material is specific to this project. We may also have a business vision for the organization.

To create a business vision document, we use Rational RequisitePro. We have a template for the project information called *JK Enterprises Project project*. To use this template, open RequisitePro and select the template from the list of available templates (Figure 7-5). This creates a blank project with predefined packages, requirement types and document types.

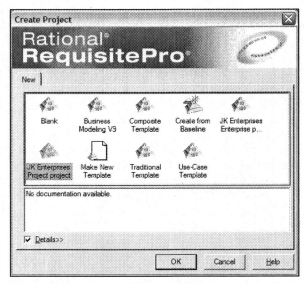

Figure 7-5   Creating a RequisitePro project from the template

Now, select the Business Vision folder and create a new business vision document by selecting *New → Document* (Figure 7-6).

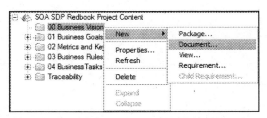

Figure 7-6   Create a Business Vision document

We select the predefined business vision template provided (Figure 7-7).

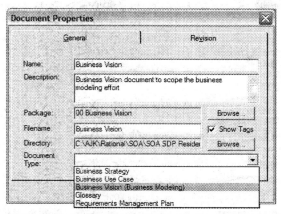

Figure 7-7   Select the Business Vision (Business Modeling) document type

This allows us to encourage the use of standard templates and formats for documentation across multiple projects. As we have potentially many different parts of the organization working on SOA-based solutions, this consistency is important.

Now we can create the business vision document based on the information provided in the case study chapter. We create or mark up the requirements by entering the text in the document, then highlighting the text and selecting *RequisitePro* → *Requirement* → *New Requirement* or use the shortcut button on the Microsoft Word toolbar (Figure 7-8).

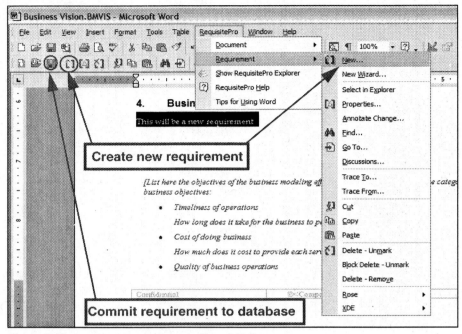

Figure 7-8   create a requirement in RequisitePro

After entering values for any attributes (Figure 7-9)[1], we can save the document by clicking the RequisitePro *Save* icon, which commits the text and its associated attributes to the RequisitePro database.

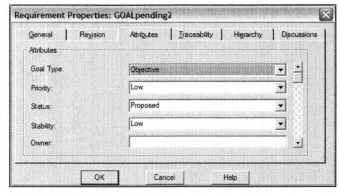

Figure 7-9   Editing attributes for a requirement

---

[1] We discuss the use of attributes on requirements in more detail in the chapter on Requirements Management. Attributes on requirements are additional items of information that relate to that requirement, for example, the priority of the requirement.

We capture the following information in the business vision document:

- ► Business goals
- ► Business opportunities
- ► Metrics
- ► Key performance indicators

These items are captured because they provide both input to other stages in development, and they provide the proof we need to show that we really have solved the business problem. We discuss this traceability throughout this book.

Business glossary

The *business glossary* is the set of common business terms and their definitions. We create a business glossary for our example, you may find your business has a glossary already. Common sources of the business glossary include:

- ► Industry-standards such as Enhanced Telecoms Operations Map (eTOM) by Telemanagement Forum (www.tmforum.org)
- ► Business models such as the model included in IBM Information Framework (IFW) for banking organizations[2]
- ► Work from previous projects
- ► Enterprise or other logical data models

Regardless of the source, we capture the term, and definitions in the following format:

- ► Name of term
- ► Definition of term including any equivalent terms used in the business/

We capture the information in RequisitePro, because this not only enables us to enter the information quickly and easily, but it also provides a full version history and easy access by all interested parties. In this case we enter the terms directly into the RequisitePro database. To enter a requirement into the database directly, open or create an attribute view (Figure 7-10):

---

[2] IFW includes more than just a business model. It provides comprehensive service models and data models for any banking organization. For more details on the IBM Integration Framework models for the financial services industry refer to:

http://www-03.ibm.com/industries/financialservices/doc/content/solution/391981303.html

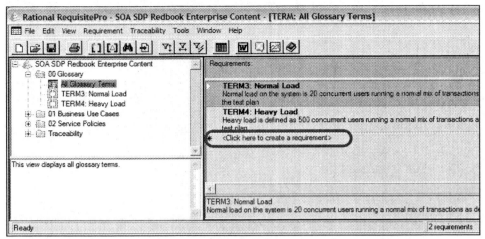

Figure 7-10   Open a View in RequisitePro and click to enter the new glossary term

Click *<Click here to create a requirement>* and enter the term directly
(Figure 7-11).

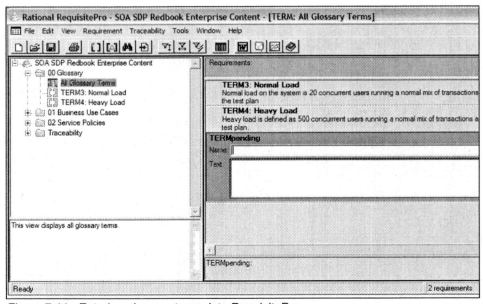

Figure 7-11   Entering glossary terms into RequisitePro

We can link these terms to other elements held in RequisitePro (for example,
other text), Rational Software Modeler, and Rational Software Architect.

The main purpose of having these business glossary terms in RequisitePro is to have a central repository of information that is versioned appropriately; we are not using all the capabilities of RequisitePro for this part of the business modeling effort. We can link the glossary to elements to domain models in Rational Software Architect/Modeler[3].

We have a template for the business glossary in our RequisitePro project. If you want to create a glossary from scratch, you select *File → New → Document*. In our case, we can open the *prepopulated* (already populated) glossary. The glossary is stored in the Glossary folder and is named *JK Enterprises Glossary of Terms* (Figure 7-12). Double-click the document to open it[4].

Figure 7-12   Location of the business glossary in the RequisitePro enterprise-level project

To see how a term has changed over time, right-click any of the terms in the Requirements Explorer and select *Properties* in the pop-up menu.

In the Requirements Properties dialog (Figure 7-13):

▶ Select the *Revision* tab and you can see the current version of the term, when it was lasted edited by whom, and what the change was.

▶ Click *History* to see the full history of all the changes made since the entry was created. Note that even if we change the term and change it back again, all the changes are recorded[5].

Every element stored in the RequisitePro database has a complete revision history.

---

[3] We may also link to enterprise data models in Rational Data Architect or business items in WebSphere Business Modeler.

[4] It is not necessary to use a document with the glossary terms, They can be stored directly in the RequisitePro database if required.

[5] Be careful. Any change committed to the RequisitePro database and the change is recorded. A user cannot remove any entry in the list. We have had customers call the IBM technical support team and beg for entries to be removed without success!

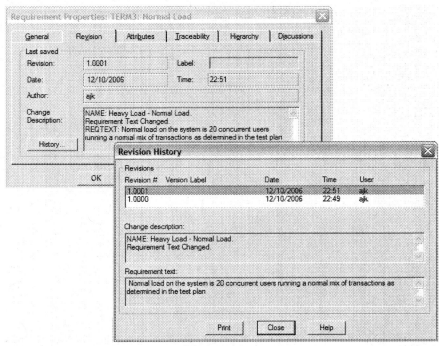

Figure 7-13   Revision history of one the terms in the glossary

At this point we may be asked how people who do not have access to RequisitePro (using the native RequisitePro client or the Web client) can see this information. RequisitePro can produce CSV or Word-format documents based on the views. Alternatively, we use other reporting tools such as IBM Rational SoDA to produce more complex reports that span tools and work products.

Business use cases

Our starting point for thinking about business processes is from the view of the world in which we operate. *Business use cases modeling* is a technique that is used to describe the business from an external viewpoint. More formally, a business use case is *...a sequence of actions that a business performs that yields an observable result of value to a particular business actor, or that shows how the business responds to a business event, to yield a business benefit* [RUP V7.0].

The definition perhaps requires some explanation:

► "...a sequence of actions..." means there is a dialogue between the outside world and the business; it has an order or sequence and it is not a one-sided conversation.

► "...yields an observable result of value..." means there must be an outcome, and it must be visible and of tangible benefit.

► "...to a particular business actor..." means that there is some outside party (the business actor).

► "...or shows how the business responds to a business event, to yield a result of business benefit..." means that as an alternative, the business may be the one deriving the benefit.

The business use case forms the top level view of the business. In practice, this technique is an easy and quick way to get a high level understanding of the business: with whom the business interacts and what the business.

Business actor

To expand on the description of a business actor: It is someone or something outside the business that interacts with the business in some way. Examples include customer, regulator, supplier, and shareholder. It is a role, in the sense that the same external party may take on many roles with respect to the organization or part of the organization under scrutiny. For example, you may have a customer who also supplies you (the business) with goods, so your customer is also your supplier: One party, two roles.

When we name the business actor, we try and refer to the role, not the actual external party. For example, if we have IBM as a supplier of software tools, we would call the role *Software Tools Supplier* and not IBM. This means that our business use case and business actor is still relevant if we change the supplier at some point in the future.

Business process

Business process analysts typically capture the *business process* using tasks and sub-tasks, with flows and decision points. However, these are really what RUP calls business use case realizations (see "Business use case realization" on page 188): How the business operates to satisfy its customers and other external parties.

We think of the business use cases as being the precursor to any business process modeling with workflows and tasks. This allows us to focus on what the business does and how it interacts with the outside world rather than how the process operates inside the business. We show this mapping between a business process and a business use case realization in Figure 7-14.

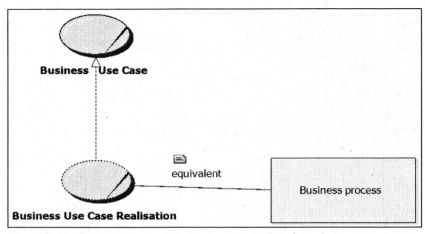

Figure 7-14   Business process to business use case mapping

Practically, we are describing a top-level[6] business process where we recognize that the business has to interact with the outside world (its customers, suppliers, regulatory bodies, and shareholders) and those interactions should deliver some value to the outside world. If there is no value delivered, the processes must be in support of other processes that add value.

The value of using business use cases is that they form a simple expression of the key abstract business processes.

Our business use case for our JK Enterprises example is represented as a UML diagram that shows the outside party (Customer) and what the business is doing for them (setting up an account (Figure 7-15).

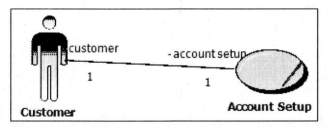

Figure 7-15   JK Enterprises key business use case for Account Setup

The diagram in Figure 7-15 is a convenient way of summarizing the situation, but the real value of a business use case is creating and use the *business use case specification*. This specification contains a textual description of how the outside

---

[6] Also known as a level one business process.

world and the business collaborate to complete the process. Internal workings of the business are not documented here (they go in the business use case realization or the business process model), only the external interactions. The emphasis of the specification is on the order in which the interactions take place, as well as with whom the business interacts for this particular process.

The specification should contain the following information:

► A brief summary of what the business use case is all about

► Any relevant performance goals and what measures are required

► The ordered steps describing the interaction between the outside world and the business.

► Any exceptions

► Any non-functional requirements relevant to this business use case

► Any risks

► The process owner

You can create a business use case in RequisitePro using a standard template (similar to the outline above). Select *New* → *Document* and select *Business Use Case* template as shown in Figure 7-16.

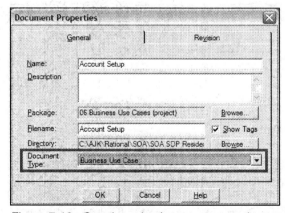

Figure 7-16   Creating a business use case document in RequisitePro

Refining the business use case

As previously noted, the business use case is typically a top level business process. This is also known as a level one business process. We may have to refine this business use case into a set of lower-level business use cases. However, this refinement should be done with care. It is potentially dangerous to split the business use cases into smaller parts as the temptation is to split the business use case into too many pieces. On the other hand, a very high level business use case is difficult to translate in a set of activities in the business process model. Refining the business use case into a set of lower level business use cases should only be done if we have a long running business process, more than one actor or specialization of the actors, and if and only if there is true value delivered to a business actor at these lower levels.

In our example. we do have a long running process but any refinement delivers little or no value to the actor involved (Customer) and there are no other actors involved. Delivering value only to the business itself is not normally a good reason to refine the use case. The business is not a business actor in its own business process.

Business use case realization

A *business use case realization* describes how the resources, business items and tasks are combined to deliver the value described in the business use case. The business use case realization is held in the business analysis model in Rational Software Modeler or Software Architect.

The operations invoked by the workers on the systems form candidate services in the service model later on.

There are other routes to deriving services from the business processes, tasks, and roles, and this is described in the service identification chapter. We do not use the business use case realization for this purpose in our JK Enterprises example.

Business rules

A business rule is ...*a declaration of policy or a condition that must be satisfied* [RUP]. Business rules are either invariant (they always apply) or merely a constraint (they apply if certain conditions apply).

We can capture business rules in the form of UML elements in a UML model, text in RequisitePro, or as part of the business process model. In our JK Enterprises example, we capture some rules in RequisitePro. We also have some conditions in our business process model in WebSphere Business Modeler.

Sample business rule we use in the JK Enterprises example are:

► We accept an account application for < 5000 from any customer.
► The Application Date must precede the Loan Date.

Business rules are used to create decision branches in workflows, and as a source of business logic for service operation implementations. It is considered best practice to separate the rule, or at least the values of its variables from any hard-coded routines.[7]

Business process model

The business process model contains the details of the business process. It captures the activities tasks and subtasks, the flow of data, the roles or systems performing the tasks and other information about the business. Tooling such as WebSphere Business Modeler enables us to capture this information, and run simulations to explore the effects of changing parameters, such as costs, durations, number of workers, and other items.

We create two business process models: The as-is model (how the business works today) and the to-be model (how we want to run the business in the future).

The to-be business process model is created by examining the current business processes. We ask questions such as "how is this done today" and document the answers in our business process model in WebSphere Business Modeler[8]. We want to capture the activities, the roles and the information flowing around the business.

We identify the activities in the organization. In our JK Enterprises example. we would capture how a customer applies for an account, how customers place orders, how orders are processed and delivered. There are represented as tasks in WebSphere Business Modeler.

We then associate the activities with different roles from different parts of the organization. In JK Enterprises, we have roles such as Account Manager and Account Coordinator. We have organizational areas such as Sales and Customer Service.

We want to look at the information that needs to pass around the organization and add to the business process model. Items such as account details, credit reports and rejection messages are all kinds of information we should capture.

---

[7] There are many horror stories of companies hard coding data such as tax rates into applications that would be better separated out as a business rule with configurable data values.

[8] In this chapter we show WebSphere Business Modeler as a standalone application. We can also run Business Modeler in the same Eclipse shell as other IBM products such as Rational Software Architect among others. This requires we are running the appropriate versions of these products. As we wrote this book, we used the latest release of Rational Software Architect (V7) and the current release of WebSphere Business Modeler (V6.0.1 and V6.0.2) that cannot be used in the same Eclipse shell.

Working with IBM WebSphere Business Modeler

To create a new business process model launch IBM WebSphere Business Modeler[9] and create a new workspace. This workspace is a file system directory that holds our business process models for the JK Enterprises example (Figure 7-17).

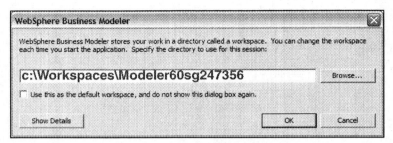

Figure 7-17   Opening Business Modeler and creating a workspace

By default, a Quickstart wizard allows you to create a business process model with a process catalog or folder, and a default process (Figure 7-18).

For example, we enter `JK Enterprises Account Opening` as the project name and `Account Opening` as the process name.

---

[9] This chapter provides basic guidance about how to use WebSphere Business Modeler. For more details, refer to the publication *Business Process Management: Modeling through Monitoring Using WebSphere V6 Products*, SG24-7148.

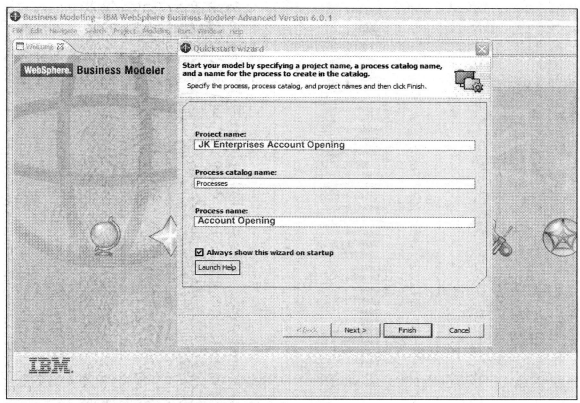

Figure 7-18   WebSphere Business Modeler Quickstart wizard

Initial project

We complete the information in the wizard and this creates the initial (blank) process model (Figure 7-19).

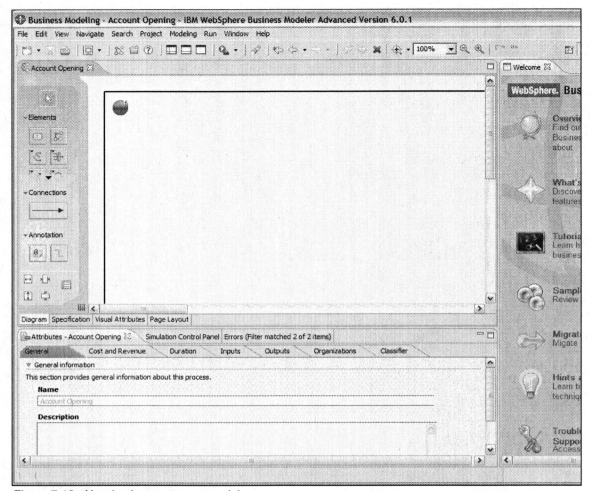

Figure 7-19   New business process model

Four-pane screen layout

There are different ways to arrange the screen layout in Business Modeler. Click the *Apply 4-pane layout* icon 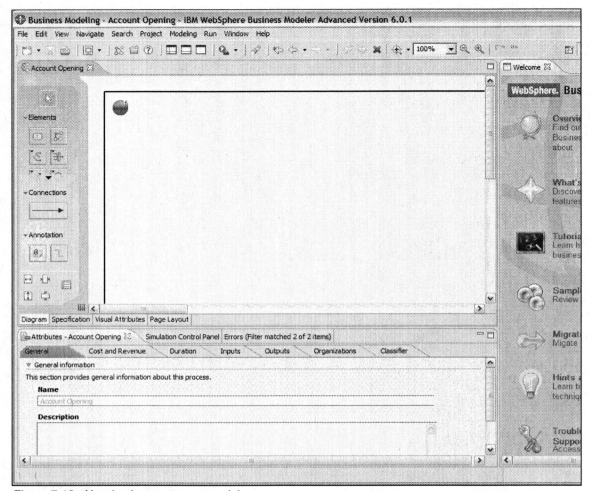 to see the Project Tree and an Outline overview of the model under construction (Figure 7-20).

We also closed the Welcome tab on the right-hand side to get more drawing space. The Errors (2 of 2 items) view is reporting errors because we have not connected the default Start and Stop nodes to anything. We ignore these errors for the moment.

All the elements we can add to the process flow diagram are available on the Palette in the middle of the four-pane view in Business Modeler.

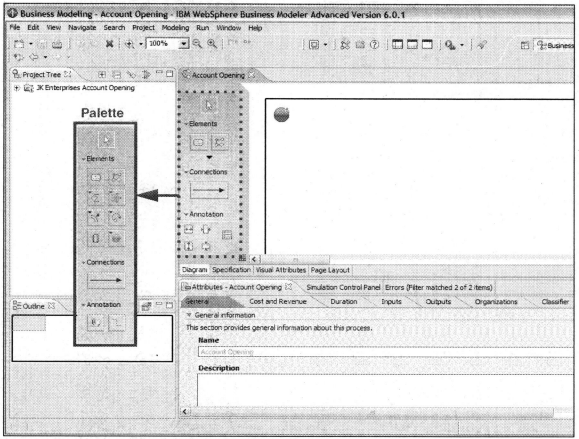

Figure 7-20   Business Modeler in 4-pane view and Palette

Adding elements to the process

Add elements to the process flow by selecting the item in the Palette and clicking on the drawing surface. The property of the element appears in the Attributes view in at the bottom of Modeler. You can edit the name of the task and add other details here (Figure 7-21).

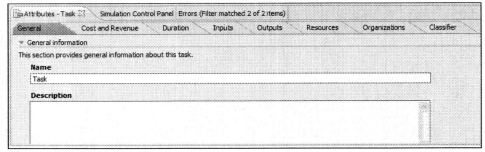

Figure 7-21   Attributes view

Adding connections

Use the Connections section of the Palette to grab a connector. Connect the tasks by clicking on the source node and then click again on the destination node (Figure 7-22). The notation assumes that the source task is the precursor of the destination task.

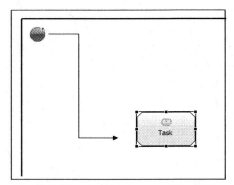

Figure 7-22   Drawing a connector between two tasks

Click the source task and click again on the destination task. Note that Figure 7-22 does not show the cursor (a US-style electrical plug). The cursor shows a *No entry* sign until you move across a suitable target element.

Roles, resources, and business items

Roles, resources, and business items are defined in the Project Tree:

► A role or resource represents who or what performs a task. In our JK Enterprises example, we have an Account Coordinator as a role in the business. Roles are performed by humans, where as resources are machines, tools, computers, and so forth.

- ▶ A business item is information that is passed around the business. In JK Enterprises, we have the customer's account application as one of the business items.

You create an item in the Project Tree select a folder (Business items or *Resources*) and *New* → *<item to be created>*. This menu is context sensitive, so when we select *Business items* we can create types of business items. Select *Resources* and we can create a role or a resource (Figure 7-23).

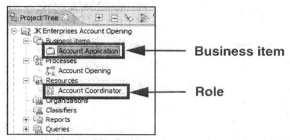

Figure 7-23   Business items and resources in the Project Tree

A role or resource is usually dragged on to a task to indicate the task is performed by that role resource. A business item is usually dragged on to a connector to indicate information flow.

Figure 7-24 shows the expansion of the Account Verification process, which is the focus of our JK Enterprises example. It also highlights some of the modeling elements we have discussed, as well as some new items.

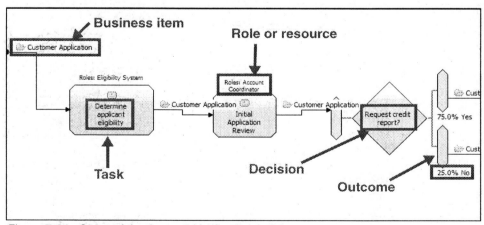

Figure 7-24   Some of the Account Verification tasks

The diagram shows some of the account verification tasks:

- ▶ Recall that time runs from left to right.

- ▶ The large blocks such as *Determine applicant eligibility* represent the tasks or sub-tasks.

- ▶ Above the task block is the resource or role that is responsible for the tasks (for example, *Account Coordinator* performs the task *Initial Application Review*).

- ▶ The arrows represent the flow of information such as the *Customer Application* between tasks.

- ▶ The item that flows between tasks is called a business item.

- ▶ The diamond *Request credit report?* represents a decision with a branch. Note we have assigned percentage probability of the outcomes. These percentages are used when we run a simulation on this model.

There is one other important modeling element relevant to building SOA-based solutions. In addition to a task or sub-task, we can model an external *service* directly in our model. This is useful when we know that we intend to use an *external* service in our process flow. Strictly speaking, this service modeling element is not intended to model an internal service.

Process simulation

Once we have captured the activities, roles and information, we can add the costs and durations to the tasks in the model to simulate the business process and gather meaningful data, such as overall costs and duration. WebSphere Business Modeler allows us to run simulations showing the costs of running a process with a certain number of resources and with a certain input load, and then contrast this to a different usage profile.

The simulations are particularly useful to validate the as-is model against what is really happening in the business. Wild variations in the model simulations from real data obtained in the business is an indication that either the model is wrong, or the data captured by the business today is inaccurate. If a business has no valid baseline with which it can compare any future changes, it becomes very difficult to quantify any improvements.

It is also useful to build up a list of key performance indicators (KPIs) and metrics that can used as to compare the as-is and to-be processes. KPIs and metrics are discussed later in this chapter.

We can repeat these steps of building a business process model but this time modeling the to-be process. By simulating this new process, we can then get an indication of the metrics for the new and hopefully improved, process. We can see if our improvements meet our business goals (described later in this chapter).

Account Opening example

Here is a high-level to-be process model that we construct for our JK Enterprises example (Figure 7-25).

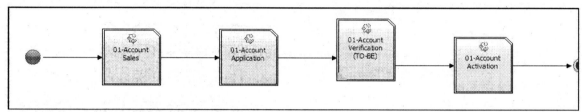

Figure 7-25   Account Opening to-be process

This top-level process in our model is Account Opening. This covers the entire process of account opening from receiving an application from the customer to the customer having an account they can use:

► The first step is to receive the account application (*Account Sales*).

► The next step is for the application to be processed (*Account Application*).

► Then, the account is verified and the customer receives an acceptance or rejection notice (*Account Verification*).

► Finally, the customer's account is activated and it becomes available for use (*Account Activation*).

Each of these processes may have more lower level processes. In Business Modeler, you can right-click each process and open the sub-process diagram by selecting *Launch Global Process Editor*.

Importing the model

Refer to the instructions in "Loading the WebSphere Business Modeler project" on page 579 to import the sample model into WebSphere Business Modeler.

Note that we only implemented one global subprocess of Account Opening: 01-Account Verification (TO-BE).

Visualizing a business model as UML

We can visualize the business process model created in WebSphere Business Modeler in UML. Rational Software Modeler (or Software Architect) accesses the Business Modeler project and create the UML business use case and skeleton business use case realizations.

To visualize the business process model:

► Open Rational Software Modeler (or Software Architect).
► Select *File → Import*.
► Select *General → Existing Projects into Workspace*.
► Navigate to the WebSphere Business Modeler project that you want to import.
► Click *Finish*.

This action displays the project in the Project Explorer. To open the model, expand the project to the models folder and double-click the entry with the same name as the project. We can drag and drop items such as the business processes. flow diagrams, resources, and other items in any UML model and they are displayed as UML (rather than BPMN notation). This is useful to allow the users of Software Modeler to see the business process models in UML format.

Business goal

"A *business goal* is a requirement that must be satisfied by the business. Business goals describe the desired value of a particular measure at some future point in time and can therefore be used to plan and manage the activities of the business" [RUP 7.0].

We use the business goals to make sure that we clearly understand what steps we have to take to achieve the business strategy. Our goals in our JK Enterprises example are listed in Figure 7-26.

We captured these goals in RequisitePro, along with any subgoals. Associated with each goal and subgoal are key performance indicators (KPIs) and the metrics we need to gather to measure if we have achieved these goals (discussed in the next section).

We can use IBM WebSphere Process Server, in conjunction with IBM WebSphere Business Monitor, to capture these metrics directly from the executing business process. We can then calculate the measures to demonstrate the achievement of these goals.

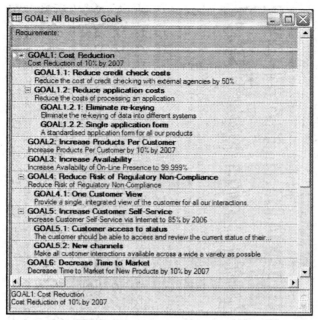

Figure 7-26   Business goals in a RequisitePro View. Note the nested sub-goals.

Key performance indicators and metrics

As we identify business goals, we have to establish the specific measures and the associated values of these measure we are aiming for. The measure is called *key performance indicator* (KPI), and the values we need to record are the *metrics*. Let us define these terms:

► "Key performance indicators represent quantifiable measurable objectives, agreed to beforehand, that reflect the critical success factors of an organization" [RUP].

► "Metrics identify the type of measurements that need to be collected to assess the state of the KPIs" [RUP].

So, metrics are what we measure, and the KPIs are the numbers we are measuring against. This implies we should have mechanism for capturing these metrics; either as part of the service, or the underlying workflow runtime engine as appropriate.

JK Enterprises goals

In the JK Enterprises example, we have a goal of *cost reduction*. The corresponding KPI is *reduce costs by 10% by 1st July 2007*. Note the use of a specific reduction of 10%; otherwise we could reduce by 0.5% and claim success.

There is also the specification of a time scale (by 1st July 2007). Interestingly we originally used the date of 2007, but this was too vague. Did we mean at the beginning of 2007 or the end of 2007? We have to be as specific as possible.

We had this vague date originally by using the Revision History feature of RequisitePro. We right-clicked on the Goal and selected *Properties*, then selected the *Revision* tab, then clicked *History* (Figure 7-27).

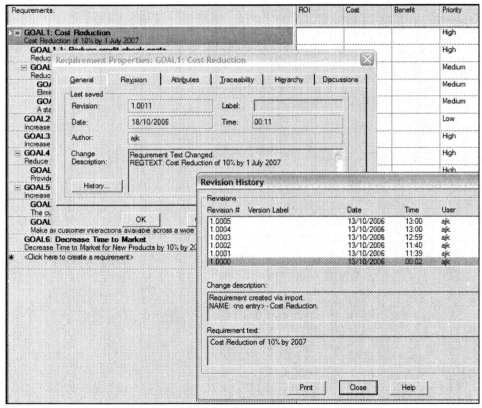

Figure 7-27   Use of the revision history in RequisitePro

Note that the original author (indicated by the initials *ajk*) created this goal on the 13th October, and the current corrected version was entered by the same person on the 18th October. This revision history is an important feature of RequisitePro as it allows us to track changes to goals including who made the change.

To validate whether have met this KPI, we have to record the costs in some fashion. This leads to metrics of cost of processing an account application and the cost of account activation cost. At the moment, the total costs are the sum of these two numbers.

To perform a meaningful comparison, we also have to understand the current costs before we deploy the new SOA-based solution. We may have this information from existing accounting records, or we might use our as-is business process model to calculate this value.

Connecting goals, KPIs, and metrics

It is important to connect goals to the corresponding KPI and the metrics. Changes in any of these items (goals, KPIs, or metrics) imply we may have to change the other items.

RequisitePro provides an effective way to provide this traceability. Every element we capture in RequisitePro has a the ability to trace to or from one or more other elements. This trace can be set up through the properties of the RequisitePro element (Figure 7-28).

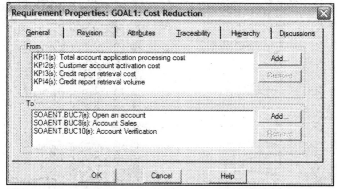

Figure 7-28   Traceability tab of an element property in RequisitePro

Alternatively, we use a RequisitePro Traceability view to show the two sets of elements to be linked, and right-click the intersection of the two elements and select *Trace-to* or *Trace-from* (Figure 7-29).

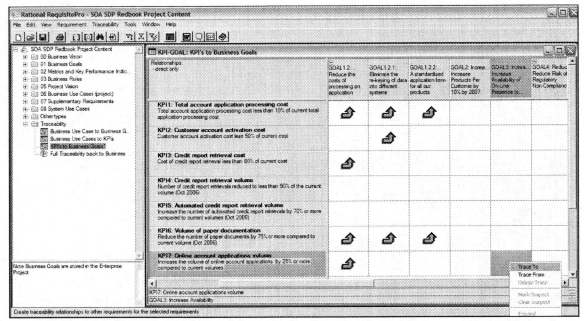

Figure 7-29   Establishing traceability between goals and KPIs through a RequisitePro traceabiity matrix

In a similar fashion, we establish a link between the KPIs and metrics. Then we show the hierarchy from goals to KPI to metrics using the Traceability Tree view (Figure 7-30).

Note the red marks on items in the view indicate that the item has changed. We can use the revision history to establish what has changed.

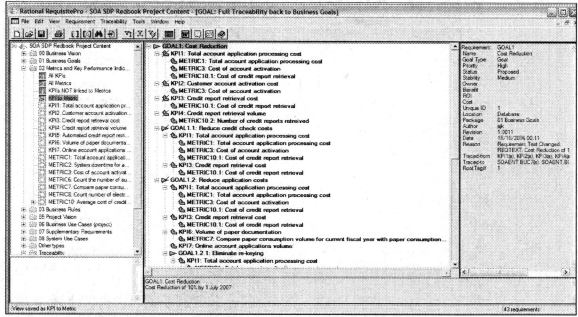

Figure 7-30   Traceability tree view showing goals linked to KPIs to metrics

Defining KPIs and metrics in WebSphere Business Modeler

You can use WebSphere Business Modeler to define the metrics and KPIs that you want to measure using WebSphere Process Server and WebSphere Business Monitor:

► Metrics are typically things that you want to measure, such as elapsed time of the process, number of accounts opened (successful executions), number of accounts that failed verification, and cost of the process.

► KPIs are the goals, typically calculated from metrics, for example the average cost of running the process compared to a given limit or range.

In addition, business analysts want to analyze metrics against business items, for example, failed account opening versus the location of the customers. Such analysis, called *dimensional analysis*, can be performed by Business Monitor if the underlying dimensions (business items) and metrics have been defined in Business Modeler.

Measuring a business process in Business Monitor

Calculations of KPIs, metrics, and dimensional analysis can only be performed if the business process is exported from Business Modeler into WebSphere Integration Developer for implementation and WebSphere Process Server for execution.

In this book we did not follow the path from Business Modeler to Integration Developer and Process Server. Refer to the IBM Redbooks publication *Business Process Management: Modeling through Monitoring Using WebSphere V6 Products*, SG24-7148, for an example of such a business process.

Domain modeling

Domain modeling is the task of capturing a subset of the overall business analysis model, specifically the key business elements and their relationships. Usually, if we have a business analysis model, we do not have to perform this task because we already have a domain model. We also would not have to perform this task if we have already purchased an industry model. Examples of industry models include the domain model part of IBM IFW and IAA models, or any of the other IBM industry models. These models have standard domain models.

In our example, we have a domain model in Rational Software Modeler or Software Architect. This is discussed in "Study the domain model" on page 320.

What do we have now?

By the end of this chapter, our status is as follows:

► We have a clear idea of what the business goals are and how we can measure we have met these goals (metric and KPIs).

► We have a business process model indicating the as-is and to-be situations.

► We have a business use case model showing the relevant part of the business, and with whom that part of the business interacts.

► We have a business process model with process flows, resources and business.

► We have a domain model that gives us an idea of the key abstractions.

References

For further information consult these sources:

▶ *Learn business process modeling basics for the analyst*, developerWorks

http://www-128.ibm.com/developerworks/webservices/library/ws-bpm4analyst/

This paper provides a useful introduction to business modeling using the notation and techniques used in the chapter.

▶ IBM Redbooks publication *Business Process Management: Modeling through Monitoring Using WebSphere V6 Products*, SG24-7148

This book covers the concepts and many details on the use of the tooling for IBM WebSphere Business Modeler and related tooling.

▶ IBM Redbooks publication *Continuous Business Process: Management with HOLOSOFX BPM Suite and IBM MQSeries® Workflow*, SG24-6590

8

Requirements

This chapter discusses requirements management as applied to SOA-based solutions. This chapter should be read in conjunction with Chapter 7, "Business modeling" on page 169 as the two topics are closely related.

These topics are discussed:

► The role of requirements management in SOA-based solutions

► The work products associated with requirements management

► How to use IBM Rational RequisitePro to capture and manage requirements

► Traceability between various work products and the tools

Requirements management in SOA

The usual definition of requirements management is as follows:

Requirements management is a systematic approach to finding, documenting, organizing and tracking the changing requirements of a system. [RUP]

In SOA-based solutions, we need to extend this definition to include "the solution" rather than the system. Requirements management then encompasses information captured in the business domain, the services domain and the system domain. Some of the items that could be termed *business requirements* have been discussed in Chapter 7, "Business modeling" on page 169, such as the glossary, business goals, KPIs, metrics, and business use cases. In this chapter, we discuss the role of service policies, system features, functional and non-functional supplementary requirements, and system use cases.

The key work products for the requirements discipline are illustrated in Figure 8-1.

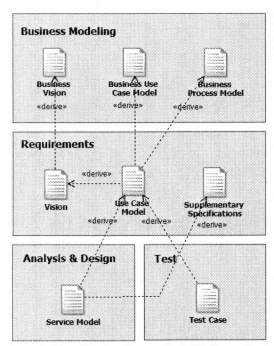

Figure 8-1   Work products for the Requirements discipline, and the traceability

The traceability of the work products are shown in this figure, as well as their impact on work products from other disciplines.

The development process is illustrated in Figure 8-2.

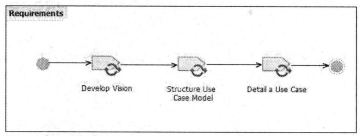

Figure 8-2   *Workflow in the requirements discipline*

It is important to remember that we navigate this workflow every iteration, expanding on and correcting more of the requirements as we go along.

Figure 8-3 shows the roles involved in the requirements discipline and their relationship to the work products.

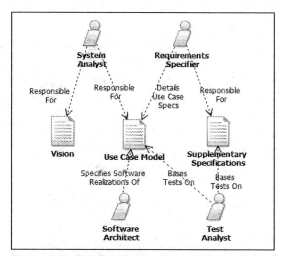

Figure 8-3   *Requirements roles and their relationship to the work products*

The key practices for effective requirements management remain critical, including a clear statement of intent, the creation of testable requirements, and appropriate traceability between requirements, and between requirements and other work products. The structure of our requirements are captured in a requirements management plan.

Requirements management plan

The requirements management plan is a reference document for the project. It captures the following decisions:

► Types of requirements
► Requirement attributes
► Requirement work products
► Traceability between these requirements
► Connection to other work products
► Control mechanisms to manage change of these elements

Generally, this plan can be used from reused from project to project with only minor alterations.

We store this document in IBM Rational RequisitePro and take advantage of the standard outline available in RequisitePro (Figure 8-4). We generally customize this outline to contain our internal standard requirements management plan populated with content, rather than the base annotated template supplied with RUP and RequisitePro.

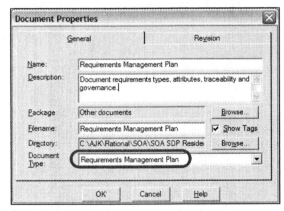

Figure 8-4   Creating a new requirements management plan using the predefined outline

Requirement types and attributes

There are a number of different distinct types of requirements necessary to capture the full spectrum of requirements in any project. For example, a business goal captures the aim of a business, while a feature captures the externally visible capability of a system. We use the requirement types to order and manage the different kinds of requirements.

We use a UML class diagram in to display these types (Figure 8-5). This diagram is typically added to the requirements management plan to provide a convenient view of the types.

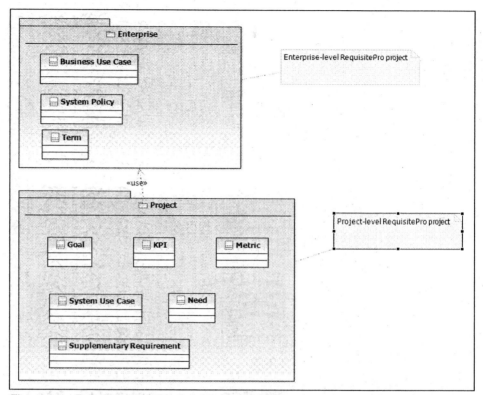

Figure 8-5   Requirement types used in RequisitePro

We also document the traceability relationships between types (Figure 8-6). Note the link to the business use cases in the Enterprise project. This shows the cross-project reference.

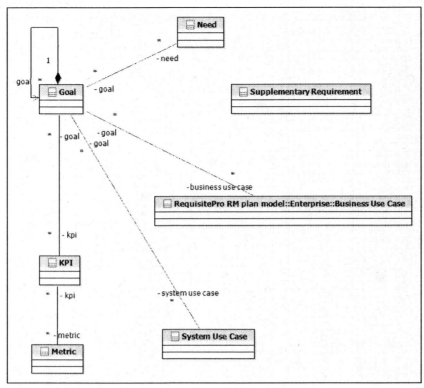

Figure 8-6   Traceability between project-level requirements

Each requirement type has a set of associated attributes. These attributes are used to capture information about the requirement such as priority or source of the requirement (Figure 8-7).

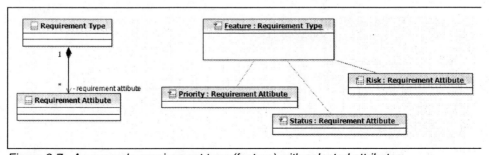

Figure 8-7   An example requirement type (feature) with selected attributes

These attributes are very useful to help manage requirements. For example, for JK Enterprises, the priority of the different business goal helps us decide which goals considered more important that the others, and this influences our decision to look at the account opening process (Figure 8-8).

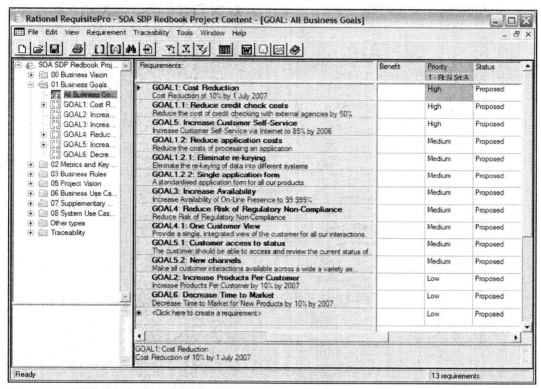

Figure 8-8   Business goals in RequisitePro ordered by priority

Keeping requirements visible

Requirements work products are a combination of requirements, documents and models. The requirements and document-based work products are held in RequisitePro. The UML models held in Rational Software Modeler or Rational Software Architect. Data models are held in Rational Data Architect.

Requirement perspective in development tools

A key feature of the Rational SDP is how we can see requirements in the other tools. Our requirements projects can be seen in the Requirement perspective in Software Modeler, Software Architect (Figure 8-11 on page 215), and Data Architect (Figure 8-12 on page 216).

To open the Requirement perspective in these tools, click the *Perspectives* icon on the top right-hand side of the window (Figure 8-9). Select the Requirement perspective. If Requirement does not appear, click *Other* and select Requirement from the complete list of perspectives.

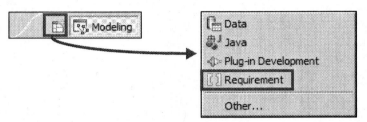

Figure 8-9   Open the Requirement perspective

We should have an empty Requirements Explorer towards the left of the window (Figure 8-10). Click *Open a RequisitePro project* ⬢ (similar to the icon in RequisitePro) to open the selected project (.rqs file).

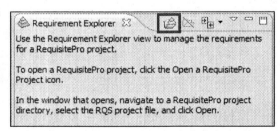

Figure 8-10   Empty Requirement Explorer

We have to make sure we know where the .rqs file is stored on our server or local machine. Typically, the project administrator has set aside space for the RequisitePro files and informed the team of the location.

Rational Software Architect

Figure 8-11 shows the Requirement perspective in Rational Software Architect.

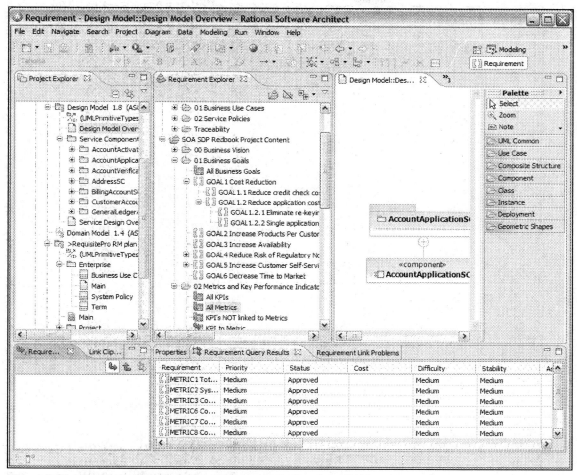

Figure 8-11   Requirement perspective in Rational Software Architect

Rational Data Architect

Figure 8-12 shows the Requirement perspective in Rational Data Architect.

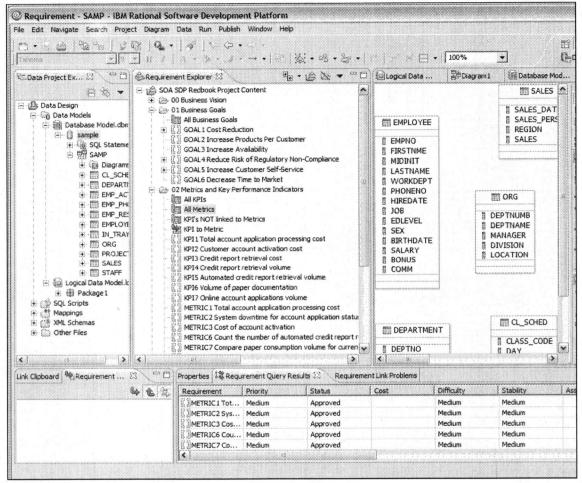

Figure 8-12   Requirement perspective in Rational Data Architect

The Requirement perspective keeps requirements visible and accessible to the other roles working on the project. The RequisitePro integration also allows us to link requirements and model elements to each other as we show later in this chapter.

We also use the Web interface to RequisitePro for remote users who require read/write access, or just read access to the project.

For our project we have a project vision document that contains the stakeholders view of the solution to be developed including the needs and features.

The supplementary specification contains requirements that are not readily captured in terms of features, needs or use cases. The requirements contained in a supplementary requirements include non-functional or system requirements, and functional requirements that do not form part of a system use case.

The system use case is captured textually in a system use case specification, and has a corresponding model item in the UML system use case model. The bulk of the information appears in the system use case specification.

An interesting question is: What does the system use case represent in an SOA-based solution? The system or systems are the underlying applications that provide the services. The system use case forms part of the ongoing system documentation as well as a useful item for project management purposes. In our example, we link the system use cases to business goals. We also verify that system use cases have a corresponding low-level task in the business process model. This linkage is only relevant if low-level details have been added to the business process mode, which is not always the case.

Enterprise-level requirements

As discussed in the Chapter 7, "Business modeling" on page 169, there are two broad categories of requirements. There are a class of requirements that really apply to all projects in the organization: Requirements we term *enterprise-level requirements*. This is not something unique to SOA-based projects or to organizations that move to SOA. SOA-based solutions touch many different parts of an organization and its partners, so there is more opportunities for these requirements to impact a wider audience.

In our JK Enterprises example, we class the following kinds of requirements as enterprise-level:

► Glossary terms
► Business use cases
► Service policies

All these items are elements in RequisitePro, with links into the relevant UML and other models held in tools such as Rational Data Architect.

We connect elements in the enterprise and project-level project. Before we can do this, we have to give the projects a unique prefix. Select *File → Project Administration → Properties* in RequisitePro to set the name as shown in Figure 8-13. Add an appropriate prefix to your enterprise and any project-level RequisitePro projects.

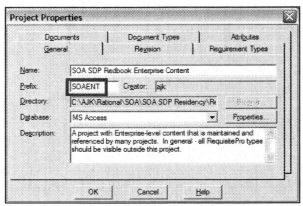

Figure 8-13   Set the project prefix to permit cross-project traceability

We also select which requirements can be see from other projects. Select *File → Project Administration → Properties*, then select the *Requirements Type* tab and select the requirement that should be visible to external projects (Figure 8-14).

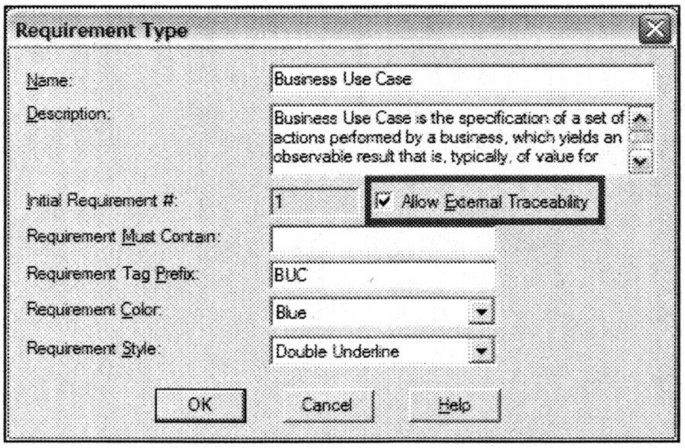

Figure 8-14   Enable external traceability. for each requirement type

Now we can provide access to this enterprise-level project (SOAENT) from our project level project by selecting *File → Project Administration → External projects* and adding the enterprise-level project to the list (Figure 8-15).

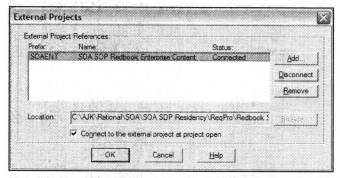

Figure 8-15   Add a project to enable traceability to that project

Glossary

We discussed the purpose and content of the glossary in "Business glossary" on page 181. The defined terms in the glossary are linked to any domain model in Rational Software Architect/Modeler, or any enterprise logical data model held in Rational Data Architect.

Business use cases

We discuss business use cases in detail. We emphasize that the business use cases at the enterprise level are the validated and approved descriptions of what the business does for the outside world.

Business use cases at the project level are used where a new or modified business process is under consideration. The changes have not yet been validated as the new to-be process. In our case, we do not change the business use cases related to account opening or any of the other business use cases. we have changed how they work internally. This implies there are no business use cases in the project-level RequisitePro project.

Once a project has validated the project-level business use cases, they should be copied into the enterprise level project. This is typically a simple export/import process in RequisitePro. Note that the import/export does not retain the history of the changes, but we retain attribute values exported in comma separated values (CSV) format. We also copy across the business use case specification and import that as a document.

Service policies

Effective service development is all about using standards. Any SOA-based initiative in the organization requires a set of standards to make sure that each service provided or consumed by the organization is compatible with other services. Service policies form the reference for service standards. In requirements management terms these policies could be classed as non-functional requirements that apply across the organization, and even outside the organization. There are design time, deployment and runtime aspects to service policy. We discuss the design time aspects here.

Service policies can be broken into four broad categories, from:

```
http://soa-zone.com/index.php?/archives/18-Clearing-up-the-confusion-of-the
-term-policy.html#extended
```

▶ **Schema policies**—Schema policies document requirements related to the schemas of messages that pass between service providers and consumers. We may want to refer to standard XML schemas for messages, for example, Financial products Markup Language (FpML), which is used for complex financial instruments.

▶ **Communication policies**—Communication policies capture any policies that affect the communication between services. This includes message encoding, transport, and security.

▶ **Behavioral policies**—Behavioral policies relate to the behavior of the service as a whole. This is in contrast to the other policies which look at the messages.

We capture these policies in a *service policies* document held in RequisitePro. RequisitePro allows us to use a standard template for the document, and security and version control on the individual policies themselves. It is also useful for individual projects to trace back to these policies, so that the potential impact of any changes to these polices can be assessed.

To create a new policy document in RequisitePro, select *File → New → Document* and select *Service Policies Outline*.

We use the service policies later in Chapter 11, "Service specification" on page 299.

Project-level requirements

We create a project in RequisitePro for requirements and other items that are specific to this project. This project references the enterprise-level project described in "Enterprise-level requirements" on page 217 where appropriate. The bulk of the items discussed in this chapter and in Chapter 7, "Business modeling" on page 169 are held in this project.

Project vision

RUP defines the *project vision* is the *"...the stakeholders view of the product to be developed..."* In this case, we can substitute the term *SOA-based solution* for the term *product*. This document is designed to be an introduction to the solution and should be written in a way that is accessible to the range of stakeholders listed in the document.

The project vision uses RequisitePro to provide a standard template for this document. We create a project vision document by using selecting the relevant package and *New → Document* and select the *Project Vision* outline (Figure 8-16).

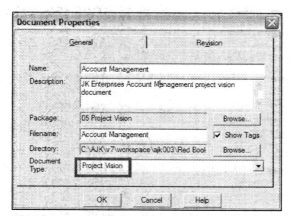

Figure 8-16   Creating a Project Vision document in RequisitePro

A key aspect of the project vision is a list of the key features of the solution. Each requirement should be related back to a goal and need.

Supplementary requirements

Supplementary requirements is the catch-all term to cover both functional and non-functional requirements. The functional requirements are ones that are not readily associated with other types of requirements, such as system use cases. Non-functional requirements provide constraints to help shape the architecture of the system, and are of particular interest to the testing community. These non-functional requirements should be testable and are ideally linked back to test plans and test cases.

Supplementary requirements can be broadly categorized into six different areas according to [Grady]. The FURPS+ categories are as follows (along with some example types of requirements):

► **Functional**—Any requirements related to functionality of the solution that are not use cases. Examples include security, printing, and other functions.

► **Usability**—Focus on user aspects such as user interfaces and training material.

► **Reliability**—Acceptable failure rates, recoverability and other factors.

► **Performance**—Volumes, response times, resource usage

► **Supportability**—How the solution is installed, maintained and retired.

► **+**—Represents any design constraints such as operating system, hardware required or similar.

SOA-based solutions require particular attention to be paid to the reliability, performance and supportability non-functional requirements. This applies particularly to the services themselves. One interesting supportability requirement revolves around how a service might be retired and replaced, or even just upgraded to a new release. The life cycle issues are discussed in "Service life cycle" on page 29.

Supplementary requirements are captured in RequisitePro in a document called the *supplementary requirements specification*. Each requirement is tagged and traced back to the features of the SOA-based solution. Relevant requirements are also traced to a corresponding defect, enhancement request, test case, or test plan held in IBM Rational ClearQuest (Figure 8-17 and Figure 8-18).

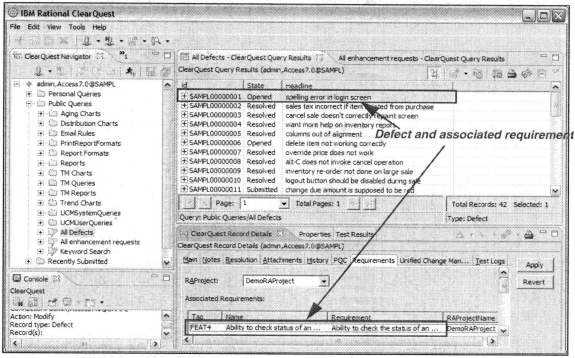

Figure 8-17   Associating a requirement to a defect in ClearQuest[1]

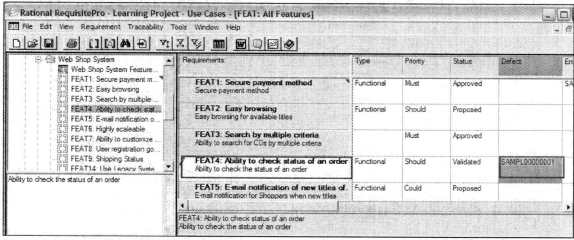

Figure 8-18   The same defect from ClearQuest connected to the requirement in RequisitePro[1]

---

[1] These screen captures are from one of the standard samples and not the JK Enterprises project.

We create a Supplementary requirements document in Registering by selecting *File* → *New* → *Document* and selecting *Supplementary Requirements Specification* outline (Figure 8-19).

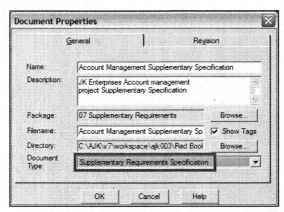

Figure 8-19   Creating a Supplementary Specification in RequisitePro

System use cases

A system use case[2] "*...a sequence of actions a system performs that yields an observable result of value to a particular actor*" [RUP]. Contrast this to the definition of business use cases in the business modeling chapter, they are very similar definitions and this is intentional. A system use case documents the interaction between the world outside the system, and the system itself. It defines the boundaries of the system because we define the actors of the system as someone or something outside the system scope. System use cases define the externally visible functional behavior of the system in a concise and useful way.

In SOA-based solutions, system use cases are used to describe the behavior of the systems that implement the services and composite services. There are different ways we might discover these systems:

▶ **Existing asset analysis**—We have existing systems (see "Perform existing asset analysis" on page 292).

▶ **Automating tasks**—We decide that certain tasks in the business process or the business use case realization are candidates for automation. This implies there is an underlying system or systems involved in providing the services.

---

[2] This definition is actually the definition for a use case instance. In common with many concepts in UML - a use case is a classifier and we tend to work with an instance.

No matter which way we discover these underlying systems, system use cases should be used to document the system behaviors. System use cases allow us to go forward with the design and implementation of service (which might cross more than one system). System use cases form useful input into test planning and test cases. System use cases are also useful for project planning and progress reporting as implementing a use cases and testing it works is a useful milestone. Finally, system use cases form the basis for documentation of the service.

One might be tempted to suggest that a use case is itself just another way of thinking about a service or service operation. However, there are key differences between a service and a use case. A service is typically stateless, as are the operations on a service. A service operation call is a single challenge and response, even though the response is typically asynchronous. Service operations can be called in no particular order. In contrast, a system use case has very specific internal state. A system use case defines a sequence of interactions, a conversation where the sequence of communication is very important. Poorly-formed use cases that ignore the definition of a use case can end up looking like services but we try and avoid this. RUP provides extensive guidelines on use cases, and for even more detailed guidance, we recommend [Bittner and Spence].

Creating a system use case in RequisitePro

We create a use case in the UML model, or as an entry in RequisitePro. If we start with RequisitePro, we select the relevant section of the RequisitePro project, the System Use Case package (or a sub-package if we have already defined a package for each system). Then we select *New → Document* and use the *System Use Case Specification* document type (Figure 8-20). Make sure the name of the document is the same as the name the use case. This makes the document easier to find later on.

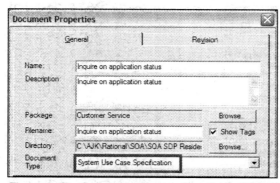

Figure 8-20 Creating a System Use Case document in RequisitePro

We have to edit the generated Word document and add the name of the system use case. The template in RequisitePro uses a Word document property for the name of the use case. This can be edited in Word:

► Select *File* → *Properties* and replacing `<Use-Case Name>` with the actual use case name (for JK Enterprises, `Inquire on application status`).

► We then select the entire document and use the Word **Update Field** command to replace the title in all sections of the document.

► One final edit is required in the document. We change the name of the first section of the system use case template to `Inquire on application status`.

Now we are able to tag this as a requirement in RequisitePro.

To tag the use case name as a requirement, highlight the text in the document, click *Create new requirement* and reenter the name of the use case in the pop-up dialog in the Name field.

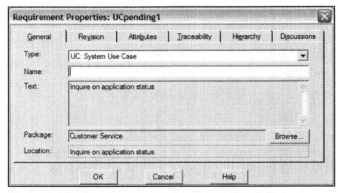

Figure 8-21   Creating a use case: Properties dialog

Click *OK* and save the use case to commit the use case to the RequisitePro repository.

Create a use case model element in Software Architect

The next step is to create a use case model element in Software Modeler or Software Architect.

We open the relevant UML model. In the JK Enterprises example, this is the model entitled Use Case Model. We use the Project Explorer to expand the model and open the Customer Service use case diagram. Once the diagram is open and visible on drawing surface, we switch to the requirements perspective and open the relevant RequisitePro project if required.

We drag and drop the use case from the Requirements Explorer into the Project Explorer as shown in Figure 8-22. This creates a new Use Case model element in the model. We use the same drag and drop technique if we have already created a use case UML element in the model and we want to link the RequisitePro and UML use cases.

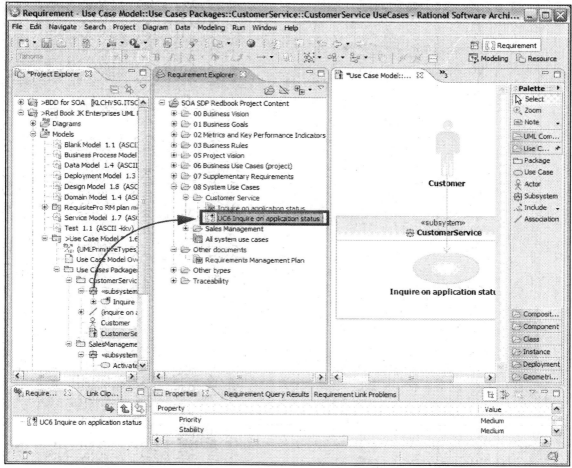

Figure 8-22   Creating a UML use case from a use case held in RequisitePro

As well as connecting the RequisitePro and UML model elements, we should complete the specification of the use case in the Word document managed by RequisitePro. This specification captures the steps of the use case, pre-conditions and post-conditions, as well as any alternate flows or error conditions. These are useful later on as input to design, test and user documentation. The JK Enterprises example project includes a system use case specification for Determine Applicant Eligibility.

Tooling implications

For the JK Enterprises example we are working at a single location or accessing the tools from a central location. If the project is distributed, the following considerations come into play:

► RequisitePro assumes we have a single central repository. Distributed repositories are not supported.

► ClearQuest may be running MultiSite. There are implications for mastership of any ClearQuest records that need to be considered when linking requirements to any ClearQuest records. You have to ensure that you return mastership to the right site (that also hosts the RequisitePro database) before you connect a RequisitePro element to a multi-sited ClearQuest record.

RequisitePro has two versioning cycles:

► The first is the general revision history where any changes to the RequisitePro project are captured.

► The second cycle is called *baselining*. Baselining takes a snapshot of the part or all of the project and this baseline can be added to your version control system (for example, Rational ClearCase). We recommend that backups are made of the information held in other tools at the same time so that any restored version has the correct references between other tools.

For more information about software configuration management, refer to the IBM Redbooks publication *Software Configuration Management: A Clear Case for IBM Rational ClearCase and ClearQuest UCM*, SG24-6399.

Where are we now?

At this point, we have:

► A requirements management plan that explains the kind of requirements we use on this project. We have documented the process to permit changes to these types, associated attributes and traceability.

► A set of business goals with associated KPIs and metrics.

► Business use cases representing the abstract business processes for the business.

► A business process model detailing the activities of the to-be process flows.

- A project vision of the SOA-solution we are developing including key features
- A supplementary specification containing the non-functional requirements
- System use cases for the automated tasks required by the service

References

For further information about requirements management, refer to these resources:

- *Use Case Modeling*, Kurt Bittner and Ian Spence, Addison-Wesley, 2002, ISBN 0201709139.
- *Practical Software Metrics for Project Management and Process Improvement*, Robert Grady, Prentice-Hall, 1992, ISBN 0137203845.

9

Service and design model work products

This chapter describes two key work products that are used for modeling SOA software: Service model and the design model.

These topics are covered:

- ► The purpose of the service model
- ► The contents of the service model (model elements and model diagrams)
- ► The relationships from the service model to other models
- ► The structure of the design model
- ► The contents of the design model
- ► Design model traceability

In this chapter we focus on the work products themselves rather than how they are created and modified. The tasks that touch on the service and design models are covered in the chapters that follow.

Introduction

This chapter describes two key work products used for modeling our service oriented software—the service model and the design model. They are the focus of the analysis and design discipline.

Figure 9-1 shows these models and their relationships to other artifacts in our development case.

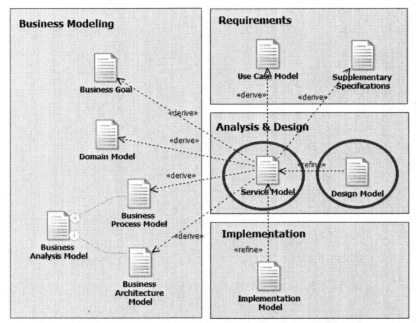

Figure 9-1   Other models related to the service and design models

A quick run-through of the relationships shown in Figure 9-1:

▶ **Service Model → Use Case Model**: Requirements specified as use cases in the use case model have their associated software realization (at an architectural level) described in the service model. Specifically, for each use case in the use case model there is a service collaboration defined in the service model. For a description of service collaborations see "Model element: Service collaboration" on page 250.

▶ **Service Model → Domain Model**: The domain model provides a consolidated view of the business' information. It can be used to influence the scoping of atomic business application service providers. It can also provides cues for forming information types and parameter types. For a description of service providers see "Model element: Service provider" on page 239. For descriptions of information types and parameter types see "Model element: Information type" on page 246 and "Model element: Parameter type" on page 245.

► **Service Model → Business Process Model**: For business process-driven software applications, the modeled business processes can provide an important input into service architecture. The architectural pattern described in "Pattern 12: Drive applications using business processes" on page 101 derives service consumers in our service model from business processes in the business process model. Furthermore, we have services exposed on our composite business application service providers to support the automation requirements of these processes. For a description of service consumers see "Model element: Service consumer" on page 240.

► **Service Model → Business Architecture Model**: The functional areas defined in our business architecture model provide information to scope both our service partitions (in our development case we use these to represent service-oriented systems) and our composite business application service providers. For a description of service partitions see "Model element: Service partition" on page 248. For a description of service providers see "Model element: Service provider" on page 239.

► **Service Model → Supplementary Specifications**: The supplementary specifications influences the service policies that we apply to our service specifications in the service model.

► **Design Model → Service Model**: The design model provides us with detailed designs for each of the service-oriented parts in the service model—namely the service consumers and service providers. The service-oriented parts are realized by design components that each contain a detailed design refinement. For instance, the provided services in the service model will be realized by service components in the design model.

In this chapter, we first cover the service model and then the design model.

> **Note:** The case study and development case in this book are both focused on business-process-driven IT systems. However most of the core concepts described extend to other kinds of IT systems as well.

Service model work product

The service model is defined in RUP SOMA as follows (Figure 9-2):

The service model is a model of the core elements of a service oriented architecture (SOA). The service model is used as an essential input to tasks in implementation and testing.

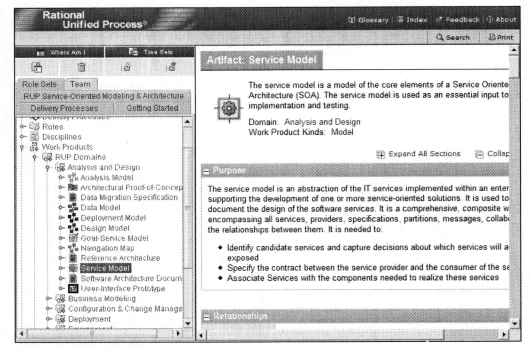

Figure 9-2   Service model defined in RUP SOMA

We expand on this by noting the following facts about the service model:

► The service model is defined as an artifact (of type *Model*) which belongs to the analysis and design domain.

► The service model is used to fully describe both structure and behavior of service-oriented software systems at an architecturally significant level.

► The UML 2 profile for software services provides UML profile support for creating service models. It includes a set of stereotypes for core service model elements.

Purpose of the service model

The service model is used by the software architect to capture the architectural form of the software for a given SOA solution. RUP SOMA describes its purpose as follows:

The service model is an abstraction of the IT services implemented within an enterprise that supports the development of one or more service-oriented solutions. It is used to conceive and document the design of the software services.

It is a comprehensive, composite work product encompassing all services, providers, consumers, specifications, partitions, messages, service collaborations, and the relationships between them.

It is needed to:

– Identify candidate services and capture decisions about which services are exposed

– Specify the contract between the service provider and the consumer of the services

– Associate services with the components needed to realize these services

Figure 9-3 shows the roles in our development case related to the service model.

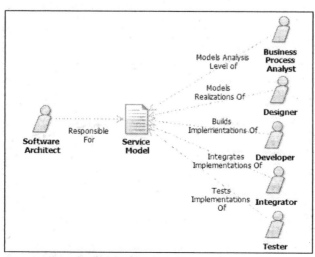

Figure 9-3   The roles related to the service model

Contents of the service model

The service model is an essential part of our development case. It is based on the service model described in RUP SOMA with some extensions. These extensions take the form of additional model elements and a standard set of UML diagrams.

The full set of model elements and diagrams contained in our service model are described in this section. We cover first the model element artifacts, and then the UML diagram artifacts.

Service model elements in our development case

A conceptual model showing the various model elements in our service model and the relationships between them is provided in Figure 9-4.

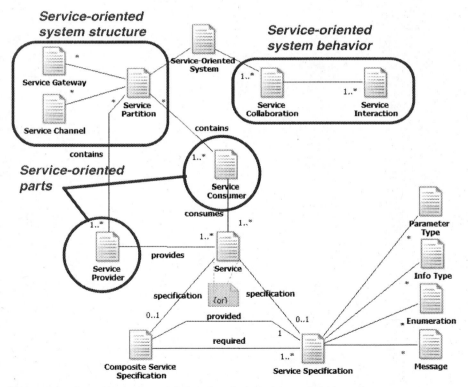

Figure 9-4   A conceptual model showing the service model elements

Each of these model elements is described further below.

Note that for those model elements, where there is a stereotype described in the UML 2 profile for software services, this is mentioned along with the matching icon and the base UML element that the stereotype can be applied to.

For those model elements that are not covered by this profile, the keyword used in our case study to annotate these model elements is mentioned along with the base UML element that this keyword is applied to.

Model element: Service specification

Stereotype:	<<serviceSpecification>>
Icon:	
Base UML element:	Interface

Description

This artifact describes both the structural and behavioral specification for a service.

It acts as a contract between the service client and service implementer; the client understands how to interact with the service and the implementer understands the behavior expected of its implementation.

A service specification also may identify a set of policies governing access to a service or use of the service.

The use of an interface denotes a set of operations provided by a service. Note that a service may implement more than one interface.

By convention it is possible to attach a protocol state machine or UML 2 collaboration to such a specification to denote the order of invocation of operations on a service specification. With such a behavioral specification any implementing service can be validated against not only a static but dynamic specification of its structure and behavior.

> **Note:** In our case study there are no constraints to the order in which our service operations can be called and therefore we have attached state machines to our service specifications.
>
> We do however have service collaborations with defined service interactions that specify interaction scenarios that our services need to support.

Although a service specification can be seen as having a life span of its own. In our case study our service specifications are owned by the service providers that provide them. Therefore the life span of the service specification is tied to the life span of its owning service provider.

Note that the service specification may only provide public features. The ability to include properties on a service specification allows for the modeling of resources.

Purpose

The following roles use the service specifications:

► **Implementers of the services**, for an understanding of the interface the service provides, but also the behavior its clients expect.

► **Implementers of service clients**, for an understanding of the interface the service provides, but also how the service expects to be interacted with.

► **Designers of services**, in understanding the relationship between specifications and the relationship between services and the specifications they implement.

► **Those who design the next version of the system**, to understand the functionality in the service model.

► **Those who test the classes**, to plan testing tasks.

The service specification has to provide both the provider (implementer) of a service and the consumer of a service with a reasonable and complete specification of the following aspects:

► **Interface specification**—This specifies the set of operations provided by a service realizing this specification. Each operation is named and provides a signature composed of input, output, and exception messages. Alternatively, parameter types may be used directly to type the parameters in our service operations.

► **Behavioral specification**—This specifies the protocol between the service and the consumer. A service may be stateful (either explicit or implicit) or it may have certain conversational requirements fulfilled by the client.

► **Policy specification**—This specifies constraints and policies regarding the operation of the service. Examples of policies include security, availability, quality of service and so on; these also represent non-functional requirements of the solution as a whole.

► **Variability specification**—This specifies how the service is configured for deployment and how it can support generic use cases through variability in its behavior both dynamically (messages at runtime) and statically (through configuration parameters).

Related diagrams

▶ **Service specification diagram**—This is the primary diagram for showing the structure of the service specification. It shows the service specification along with its referenced messages, parameter types and enumerations. See Figure 9-6 on page 254 for an example.

▶ **Service provider specification diagram**—This diagram shows how service specifications are used to specify the services that are exposed by a service provider. See Figure 9-8 and Figure 9-9 on page 256 for an example.

▶ **Service consumer specification diagram**—This diagram shows which service specifications are required by a service consumer. See Figure 9-7 on page 255 for an example.

▶ **SOA structure diagram**—This diagram shows where service specifications are used in the overall service architecture. They provide specifications for endpoints of service channels that link service consumers and service providers. See Figure 9-11 on page 258 for an example.

Model element: Service provider

Stereotype:	<<serviceProvider>>
Icon:	
Base UML element:	Class, Component

Description

This artifact groups a related set of services that are provided as a unit in a service architecture.

Service providers can be categorized in any number of ways but the following list describes the types of service providers used in the JK Enterprises architectural style:

▶ Composite business application service provider: Provides composite business software system-specific services from atomic business application services and infrastructure services. See "Model element: Composite service specification" on page 243 for a description of composite service specifications.

▶ Atomic business application service provider: Provides reusable atomic business application services.

▶ Infrastructure service provider: Provides reusable infrastructure services. Note that these are normally also atomic services.

The service provider types listed above are introduced by the architectural patterns described in "Pattern 1: Factor composition logic away from process logic" on page 76, "Pattern 2: Factor atomic reusable logic into lower reuse layers" on page 79, and "Pattern 3: Factor application-specific logic out of reuse layers" on page 81.

The class acting as the service provider may not expose any attributes or operations directly, only public ports may be provided (stereotyped as service) and these are typed by either service specifications or composite service specifications depending on whether the service is atomic or composite.

Purpose

The following roles use the service providers:

► **Implementers**, for an understanding of the aggregation of services and the possible impact on deployment choices.

► **Designers of services**, in understanding the constraints of the grouping of services.

► **Those who design the next version of the system**, to understand the functionality in the service model, and specifically the constraints in moving services between providers.

► **Those who test the classes**, to plan testing tasks.

Related diagrams

► **Service provider specification diagram**—This diagram is the primary diagram for showing the external view of the service provider. It shows the services that are exposed by the service provider, along with the provided and required service specifications for each of these services. See Figure 9-8 and Figure 9-9 on page 256 for an example.

► **SOA structure diagram**—This diagram shows where services providers are used in the overall service architecture. See Figure 9-11 on page 258 for an example.

Model element: Service consumer

Stereotype: <<serviceConsumer>>

Icon: ◇●

Base UML element: Classifier

Description

This artifact represents elements of a service architecture that do not provide services themselves, but rather are clients of services.

They are those parts of the service architecture that exist at the boundary between the system and its external users (described as actors in the use case model).

Service consumers can be seen as the architecturally significant software elements that actors interact with, and which in turn make calls on the services in the service architecture (specifically, according to the pattern that we follow in our case study, they contain executable business processes and make calls on composite services—see "Pattern 12: Drive applications using business processes" on page 101).

We model two things on our service consumers:

▶ The inputs that come from actors interacting with the service consumer.

▶ The required service specifications that are called in response to these inputs.

Where service consumers contain executable business processes we note the following:

▶ The inputs on these service consumers correspond to tasks that exist in the business processes.

▶ Tasks receive their inputs from either human or system actors.

▶ A business process will have a combination of manual and automated tasks. By definition, only automated tasks result in calls on services from the service consumer.

Purpose

The following roles use the service consumers:

▶ **Implementers**, for an understanding of what consumers need implementation in the service architecture.

▶ **Service interaction designers** to represent them in service interactions.

▶ **Those who design the next version of the system**, to understand the functionality in the service model.

▶ **Those who test the classes**, to plan testing tasks.

Related diagrams

▶ **Service consumer specification diagram**—This diagram is the primary diagram for showing the external view of the service consumer. It shows the inputs from actors that interact with this service consumer, along with the required service specifications that are used in response to these inputs. See Figure 9-7 on page 255 for an example.

▶ **SOA structure diagram**—This diagram shows where services providers are used in the overall service architecture. See Figure 9-11 on page 258 for an example.

Model element: Service

Stereotype: `<<service>>`

Icon:

Base UML Element: Port

Description

This artifact represents one of the core elements of a service-oriented architecture (SOA). A service is provided by a service provider and is either an instance of a service specification (for an atomic service) or a composite service specification (for a composite service).

The service provides the end-point for service interaction (in Web service terminology) whereas the definition of these interactions are provided by the service specification.

In the case of a composite service, the service not only identifies the provided service specification but also the required service specifications (see "Model element: Composite service specification").

Purpose

The following roles use the services:

► **Implementers,** for an understanding of the roles the service plays and how the service specification is used by the service.

► **Designers of other services** in the understanding of the collaborations in which services participate.

► **Service interaction designers** to represent them in service interactions.

► **Those who design the next version of the system,** to understand the functionality in the service model.

► **Those who test the classes,** to plan testing tasks.

Related diagrams

► **Service provider specification diagram**—This diagram shows the services exposed by a service provider, along with the provided and required service specifications involved. See Figure 9-8 and Figure 9-9 on page 256 for an example.

► **Service interaction diagram**—This diagram shows the services as they occur in defined service interactions (which exist as part of the definition of a service contract). Figure 9-12 on page 259 for an example.

Model element: Composite service specification

Keyword: <<compositeServiceSpec>>

Base UML element: Class

Description

This artifact is used to specify composite services. What makes them composite services is that they make use of other services in providing their specified behavior.

Therefore a composite service needs more than just the specification of a provided service specification. It also requires the specification of one or more required service specifications. The composite service specification provides the link between these provided and required service specifications.

It *realizes* the provided service specification, and *uses* the required service specifications. It is used to type a service, thereby making it a composite service.

A pattern for creating these artifacts is presented in "Pattern: Composite service specifications" on page 260.

Purpose

The following roles use the composite service specifications:

► **Implementers of the services**, for an understanding of the required service specifications required for implementation.

► **Designers of services**, in understanding the relationship between the provided and required service specifications for a composite service.

► **Those who design the next version of the system**, to understand the functionality in the service model.

► **Those who test the classes**, to plan testing tasks.

Related diagrams

► **Service provider specification diagram**—This diagram shows the services exposed by a service provider and additionally the provided and required service specifications for each of these services. See Figure 9-9 on page 256 for an example.

► **SOA structure diagram**—This diagram shows where composite service specifications are used in the overall service architecture. Specifically, composite service specification are used to type the services provided by composite business application service providers. See Figure 9-11 on page 258 for an example.

Model element: Message

Stereotype: <<message>>

Icon: ▨

Base UML element: Class

Description

This artifact is a container which identifies a subset of an information model or domain model which is passed into or out of a service invocation. A message is always passed by value and should have no defined behavior.

A message represents the concept as defined in the WSDL specification, that is, a container for actual data which has meaning to the service and the consumer. A message may not have operations, it may have properties and associations to other classes (one assumes classes of some domain model—in our development case we use parameter types). A message stereotype has a property to denote its assumed encoding form (SOAP-literal, SOAP-rpc, ASN.1).

The use of this element may be optional in a tool for two reasons.

▶ Firstly the modeler may simply want to use elements from a domain model directly as the parameters to an operation rather than specifying a message.

▶ Secondly the modeler may want to use the convention of specifying a set of input and output messages on an operation, in which case the modeling tool would have to construct an input and output message matching the parameters when generating service descriptions in WSDL.

Purpose

The following roles use the messages:

▶ **Implementers**, for the development of schema describing the implementation-specific message structures.

▶ **Designers**, of other services in the understanding of how information is shared and reused among service specifications.

▶ **Information/data architects**, in understanding the relationship between the implementation-neutral domain model and implementation-specific representations such as database or message schema.

The message is optional and used to disambiguate message structures from other elements representing the same domain model.

For example, there may be a technology-neutral domain model used to represent core business items such as Customer, Product, Order, and so on. This model is related to a set of technology models that represent the same items in specific ways, message structures that take into account the hierarchical nature of XML, database schema that normalize the object model, and so on.

Where there is no separate domain model or where separate models are used for domain and message definition, the use of the explicit message stereotype is unnecessary.

Note: In our case study we have a separate domain model. Although the usage of messages is unnecessary in our case as we use parameter types, we have included them in certain instances in our case study to show how they can be used.

Related diagrams

► **Messages diagram**—This diagram shows the design of the messages.

► **Service specification diagram**—This diagram shows any messages that are used by the service specification. See Figure 9-6 on page 254.

Model element: Parameter type

Keyword: <<parameterType>>

Base UML element: Class

Description

This artifact is used to model information structures that are passed into and out of service operations (as specified as part of service specifications).

They are, as the name implies, used to type the parameters on a service operation. A parameter type contains a set of attributes which may either be typed by a primitive type or in turn by another parameter type.

Where there is a domain model, the parameter types are derived from domain types (the type definitions found in a domain model). Alternatively, they are based on information types (defined next) that are themselves based on domain types.

Purpose

The following roles use the parameter types:

► Implementers, in understanding the behavior provided by a service operation where this behavior is described in terms of pre-conditions and post-conditions which refer to the parameter types.

► **Service interaction designers** to understand what gets passed in and out of a service in a use-case realization.

► **Those who test the classes**, to plan testing tasks.

Related diagrams

► **Service specification diagram**—This diagram shows all of the parameter types used by the service operations of its service specification. The structure of each of these parameter types is shown here. See Figure 9-6 on page 254 for an example.

► **Service interaction diagram**—This diagram shows the signatures of each of the message flows that it specifies. These signatures should include the names of the parameter types that its parameters are based on. See Figure 9-12 on page 259 for an example.

Model element: Information type

Keyword: <<infoType>>

Base UML element: Class

Description

Information types are used to describe persisted data structures in a black-box way (in other words without directly describing the data structures themselves). An artifact such as a database table is considered to be part of the internal design of a service provider and therefore not something that you would want to expose in its specification. Actual data persistence structures may change in shape (possibly for non-functional reasons such as performance) without affecting clients of the specification.

Information types are very useful in service operation pre-condition and post-condition specifications as they provide a mechanism to refer to changes in state in a black-box fashion.

There are two options for package ownership of information types. The can either be owned by service specifications, or service providers.

► In the case where they are owned by service specifications they provide a black-box view of the data managed by that specific service specification.

► In the case where they are owned by service providers, they provide a consolidated black-box view of the data managed by the service provider across all of its provided service specifications.

In our case study we have followed the latter of these two options. This is because it is extremely useful to have a consolidated view of the state owned by the service provider across all of its service specifications. Also remember that our service specifications do not have a life span that is separate from the service providers that provide them (as noted in the Description section of "Model element: Service specification" on page 237).

Purpose

The following roles use the information types:

▶ **Implementers**, in understanding the persistence behavior provided by a service operation where this behavior is described in terms of pre-conditions and post-conditions which refer to the information types. In other words, the information types are used to describe an operation that has persistence behavior (saves something to a database or similar).

▶ **Service interaction designers** to understand what gets persisted by a service in a use-case realization.

▶ **Those who test the classes**, to plan testing tasks.

Related diagrams

▶ **Information diagram**—This diagram shows all of the information types that form part of one information model. As noted above, in our case the information model is owned by a service provider that manages data instances of that model. See Figure 9-10 on page 257 for an example.

Model element: Enumeration

UML element: Enumeration

Description

This artifact is the base UML Enumeration model element. It is presented here for completeness of our description of the contents of the service model. It is used in those cases where a fixed known list of values exist for an attribute on either a parameter type, information type or message.

Note that where an enumeration has been specified, it is normally shared by attributes on both the parameter types and information types for a given service provider (and possibly even its messages as well).

Purpose

The following roles use the enumerations:

▶ **Implementers**, in understanding the possible values taken by an attribute on either a parameter type, an information type or a message.

Related diagrams

▶ **Service specification diagram**—This diagram shows any enumerations that are used to type attributes for either parameter types or messages used in the definition of the service operations of the service specification. See Figure 9-6 on page 254 for an example.

> ▶ **Information diagram**—This diagram shows any enumerations that are used to type attributes for the information types on the diagram. See Figure 9-10 on page 257 for an example.

Model element: Service partition

Stereotype: <<servicePartition>>

Icon: ▢

Base UML element: Class, Component, or Node

Description

This artifact is a model element that provides a logical grouping for elements in our service architectures. The grouping is logical in the sense that the partition structure may reflect a system structure that impacts the way the physical system is deployed, or it may represent a structure that has no impact on deployment, such as the ownership of services by organizations.

In our development case (and therefore our case study) we use service partitions to contain the structural representation of a SO system (these are described in "Pattern 5: Manage complexity using SO systems" on page 86). We furthermore use specific rules for determining the boundaries of our SO systems (and therefore service partitions) that are described in "Pattern 4: Base architecture on business relevant elements" on page 84.

> **Note:** A part cannot be shared between service partitions. To put it in terms of the different service forms shown in Figure 4-2 on page 44, this would mean that in the service model, an SO system part is unique to a given SO system. This is true even though the service-oriented part can be used to create SO system parts for multiple SO systems
>
> In the deployment model though, it is quite acceptable (and even desirable in some cases) for the same deployable part to be shared across deployable assemblies, with the net result that the same running service component instance could realize more than one SO system part across multiple SO systems.

Purpose

The following roles use the service partitions:

> ▶ **Software architects**, to allow for the logical partitioning of a solution.

> ▶ **Designers of services**, in understanding logical organization of the solution.

> ▶ **Those who design the next version of the system**, to understand the functionality in the service model and specifically the logical architecture.

- ► **Those who test the classes**, to plan testing tasks.

Related diagrams

- ► **SOA structure diagrams**—This diagram shows the structural composition of a SO system (as modeled using a service partition). See Figure 9-11 on page 258 for an example.

- ► **Service interaction diagrams**—Although not showing the service partition itself, this diagram shows realizations of service contracts as an interaction of elements in an SO system (again, as modeled using a service partition). See Figure 9-12 on page 259 for an example.

Model element: Service channel

Stereotype: <<serviceChannel>>

Icon:

Base UML element: Connector

Description

This artifact is a model element that represents a connection between two services or between a client and a server over which interaction with the service takes place. Note that the channel does not represent any interaction in particular.

In the Web services world, each service denotes the binding(s) associated with it (so that a client may access it). In a modeling profile, you denote binding either on the communication between services or between a service and consumers. In this way, you can be flexible in understanding the binding requirements.

Purpose

The service channel provides the connection between two services or between a service and a client that allows for communication.

Consider the example of a dedicated telephone line between two parties; the connection is always there even if it is not used and the connection is distinct from any conversation that takes place on it. When modeling collaborations between services and specifically messages being sent between services, these take place over the connection.

Related diagrams

- ► **SOA structure diagram**—This diagram shows the various parts of the service architecture, along with the service channels between them. See Figure 9-11 on page 258 for an example.

Model element: Service collaboration

Stereotype: <<serviceContract>>

Icon:

Base UML element: Collaboration

Description

The standard definition provided for a service collaboration is as follows:

> This artifact is a representation of some set of communication between two or more services usually encapsulated as a new service. In this way, the model can represent services whose implementation is simply the collaboration of a set of existing services.

In our development case (and therefore in the case study), we have extended the usage of service collaboration to specify a collaboration that meets a behavior requirement (in our case this behavior requirement is specified using a system use case).

The parts in these collaborations are:

▶ Actors that interact with our SO system
▶ Service consumers in our SO system
▶ Services in our SO system

Service collaborations have their behavior described by one or more service interactions. In our development case, for each service contract we have one service interaction for each unique flow in the related system use case (Figure 9-5). Use case flows are described in "System use cases" on page 224.

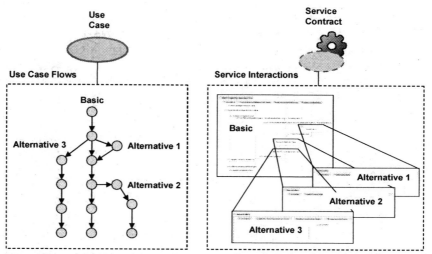

Figure 9-5   Use cases and use case flows related to service collaborations and service interactions

Purpose

Service collaborations exist as a grouping for service interactions, themselves described in "Model element: Service interaction" below. See Purpose in that section for further details.

Related diagrams

Service collaborations do not appear on any of our standard UML diagrams as their purpose is to group a set of one or more service interactions. Note though that it might be useful to create diagrams that show the behavior requirement that a specific service collaboration traces back to. In our case it is obvious as we give our service collaboration the same name as the system use case that it traces to.

Model element: Service interaction

Keyword: <<serviceInteraction>>

Base UML element: Interaction

Description

Service interactions are used to specify a realization of a service collaboration in terms of the parts of a service partition.

A service collaboration has a set of service interactions that together fully specify the behavior of the service collaboration.

These service interactions can be nested, most commonly by having one service interaction that described the basic flow (the default standard behavior), and this referencing a set of service interactions that describe the alternative flows (deviations from the standard behavior). In this way, the service interactions owned by a service contract map one-to-one with the use case flows owned by a system use case. See Figure 9-5 on page 251 shows how nested service interactions relate back to use case flows.

Purpose

The following roles use the service interactions:

- **Software architects**, to describe the behavior of a service partition, and how it maps to a requirements artifact that specifies the behavior in a black box way (where the whole system is a black box).

- **Designers of services**, specifically composite services, to show both the context in which the composite service is used, as well as the atomic services that it calls.

- **Those who design the next version of the system**, to understand the functionality in the service model, specifically from a behavioral point of view.

- **Those who test the classes**, to understand how the requirements have been realized from an architectural point of view, and therefore to help in planning testing tasks.

Related diagrams

- **Service interaction diagram**—This diagram shows the details of the service interaction, along with references to any referenced service interactions. See Figure 9-12 on page 259 for an example.

Model element: Service gateway

Stereotype: `<<serviceGateway>>`

Icon:

Base UML element: Port

Description

This artifact looks very much like a service except that it does not represent an end-point in terms of implementation of a service specification. It only forwards messages from the boundary of a service partition to a service enclosed within the partition. In this way, it allows for partitions to strictly define their interfaces in terms of service gateways.

Note that we have not used service gateways in our case study as our service partitions do not expose services to the outside world. Instead, actors interact with service consumers inside our service partition. The reason that we have modeled things in this way is so that our service partition completely specifies our architecture, including service consumers as well as service providers.

Purpose

The following roles use the service gateways:

► **Software architects**, for an understanding of the communication between partitions.

► **Implementers**, for an understanding of mediation requirements between partitions.

► **Those who design the next version of the system**, to understand the composition of partitions and services in the service model.

Related diagrams

Service gateways do not appear on any of the standard UML diagrams that we have described in our development case.

Service model diagrams in our development case

In this section we present the set of standard diagrams that we have included in our development case, and which therefore appear in our case study.

Diagram: Service specification diagram

Base UML diagram type: Freeform diagram

This diagram shows all parameter types, enumerations and messages used in the definition of the service operations of the service specification.

Included elements

The following model elements appear in this diagram (along with a description of the cardinality with respect to the diagram):

focusServiceSpecification	<<serviceSpecification>> [1]
usedParameterTypes	<<parameterType>> [0..*]
usedMessages	<<message>> [0..*]
usedEnumerations	<<enumeration>> [0..*]

Example

A sample service specification diagram is shown in Figure 9-6.

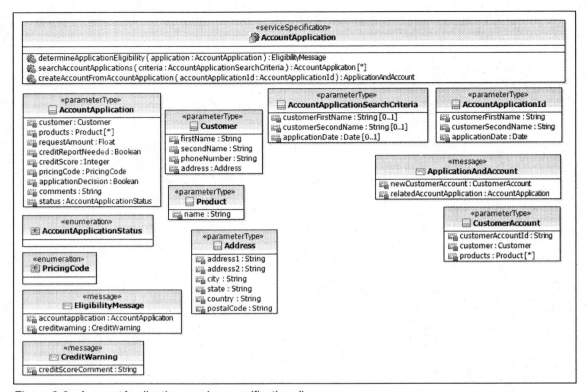

Figure 9-6   AccountApplication service specification diagram

Diagram: Service consumer specification diagram

Base UML diagram type: Freeform diagram

This diagram is the primary diagram for showing the external view of the service consumer. It shows the inputs that are available to the actors that interact with this service consumer, along with the required service specifications that are used in response to these inputs.

Included elements

The following model elements appear in this diagram (along with a description of the cardinality with respect to the diagram):

```
focusServiceConsumer          <<serviceConsumer>> [1]
requiredServiceSpecifications  <<serviceSpecification>> [1..*]
```

Example

A sample service consumer diagram is shown in Figure 9-7.

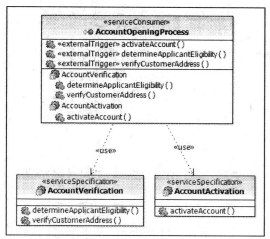

Figure 9-7   *AccountOpeningProcess service consumer specification diagram*

Diagram: Service provider specification diagram

Base UML diagram type: Freeform diagram

This diagram shows the services that are exposed by a service provider, along with their service specifications.

Included elements

The following model elements appear in this diagram (along with a description of the cardinality with respect to the diagram):

focusServiceProvider	<<serviceProvider>> [1]
exposedServices	<<service>> [1..*]

Example

An example of a service provider providing <u>atomic</u> services is shown in Figure 9-8.

An example of a service provider providing <u>composite</u> services is shown in Figure 9-9.

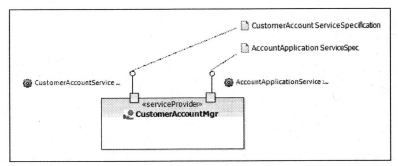

Figure 9-8   *CustomerAccountMgr service provider specification diagram*

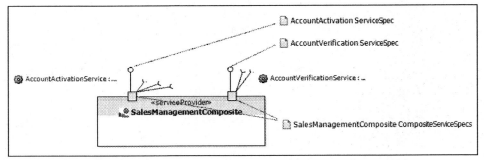

Figure 9-9   *SalesManagementComposite service provider specification diagram*

Tip: Note that the service provider specification diagrams both have diagram shortcuts applied to them. There are links for the related service specification diagrams. And for the composite service provider, there is also a link to the diagram showing the structure of the composite services.

This is good practice as it makes the model easier to navigate. You can click through to the detailed specifications using these links in the tool.

Diagram: Information diagram

Base UML diagram type: Freeform diagram

This diagram shows all of the information types that form part of one information model. In our development case, there is an information models for each service provider that persists state.

Included elements

The following model elements appear in this diagram (along with a description of the cardinality with respect to the diagram):

ownedInfoTypes   <<infoType>> [1..*]

Example

A sample information diagram is shown in Figure 9-10.

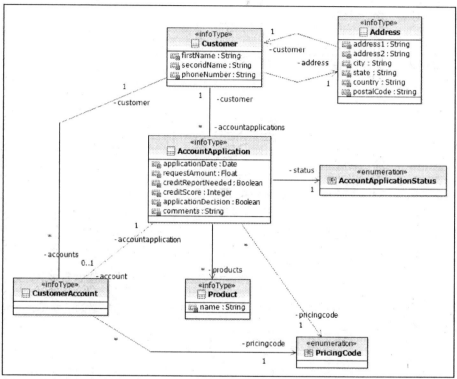

Figure 9-10   CustomerAccountMgr information diagram

Diagram: SOA structure diagram

Base UML diagram type: Composite structure diagram

This diagram shows the parts of an SO system and the service channels between them. The focus is on structure.

In terms of the service forms shown in Figure 4-13 on page 56, the elements in the diagram are SOA parts and the diagram as a whole exists for an SO system (the named element in the top-most compartment shown in the diagram).

Included elements

The following model elements defined in the previous section appear in this diagram (along with a description of the cardinality with respect to the diagram):

focusSOASystem   <<servicePartition>> [1]
serviceConsumerParts   <<serviceConsumer>> [1..*]
serviceProviderParts   <<serviceProvider>> [1..*]
serviceChannels   <<serviceChannel>> [1..*]

Example

A sample SOA structure diagram is shown in Figure 9-11.

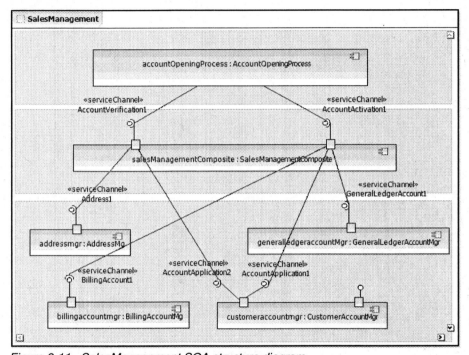

Figure 9-11   SalesManagement SOA structure diagram

Diagram: Service interaction diagram

Base UML diagram type: Sequence diagram

This diagram shows the details of a service interaction. It shows the service architecture elements involved, and the sequence of service operation calls across these service architecture elements that together specify behavior.

Included elements

The following model elements appear in this diagram (along with a description of the cardinality with respect to the diagram):

```
primaryExternalActor       <<actor>> [1]
secondaryExternalActors    <<actor>> [0..*]
serviceConsumer            <<serviceConsumer>> [1]
compositeServices          <<service>> [1]
atomicServices             <<service>> [1..*]
```

Example

An example service interaction diagram is shown in Figure 9-12.

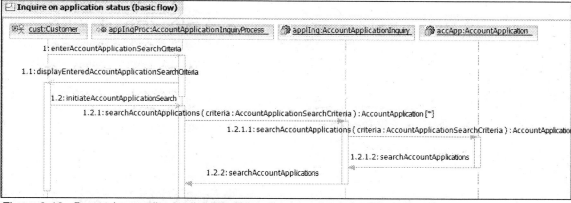

Figure 9-12   Determine applicant eligibility (Basic flow) service interaction diagram

Service model related patterns

"JK Enterprises case study architectural style" on page 75 describes the architectural style used for this book's case study using a set of architectural patterns.

In this section we present a further pattern that is applicable when creating service models: The *composite service specifications pattern*, which is used when creating composite service specification artifacts (see "Model element: Composite service specification" on page 243).

Pattern: Composite service specifications

Pattern name	Composite service specifications
Context	Service providers provide (expose) services. In the case of an atomic service provider, the service provided is fully described by a single service specification. However, not all services are atomic. These non-atomic services are called *composite services*. They have one or more required service specifications in addition to their provided service specification.
Problem	It is not possible to fully specify a composite service using a single service specification.
► Forces	► There is no link between provided service specifications and required service specifications for a composite service. ► The standard mechanism for specifying an atomic service is to use a single service specification, which is insufficient to fully specify a composite service.
Solution	Create composite service specifications to specify composite services. The UML form for this pattern is shown in Figure 9-13. The composite service specification: ► Is based on a UML class ► Realizes a single provided service specification ► Uses one or more required service specifications ► Is used to type a service, thereby making it a composite service (see Figure 9-14)
► Rationale	The composite service specification is used to: ► Link the provided service specifications to one or more required service specifications ► Provide a complete specification for composite services

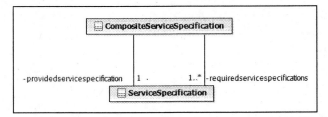

Figure 9-13   UML form of the composite service specifications pattern

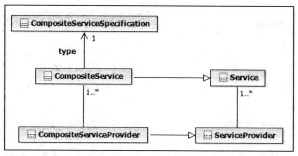

Figure 9-14   Using the CompositeServiceSpecification to type a CompositeService

Examples

Figure 9-15 shows a usage of the composite service specification pattern. Its details are:

Name: AccountActivationCompServSpec

Provided service specification: AccountActivation

Required service specifications: BillingAccount, AccountApplication, GeneralLedgerAccount

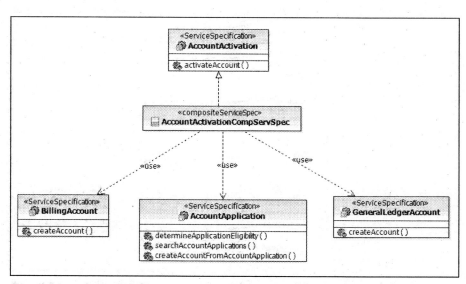

Figure 9-15   AccountActivationCompServSpec composite service specification

Tasks affecting the service model

The overview provided by Figure 9-16 shows the following:

► The tasks affecting the service model, along with the sequencing of these tasks

► The main inputs for these tasks

► The high-level states of the service model caused by these tasks (main outputs of these tasks)

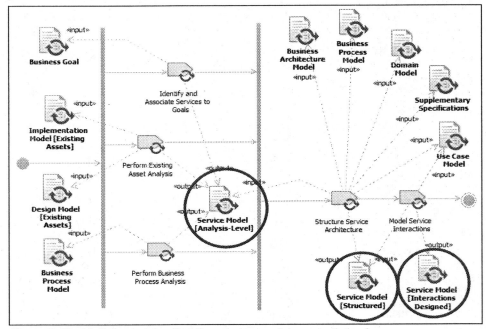

Figure 9-16   High-level states that the service model moves through

The tasks shown in Figure 9-16 are covered in more detail in the following sections:

► **Identify and associates services to goals**: "Identify services from goals" on page 283

► **Perform existing asset analysis**: "Perform existing asset analysis" on page 292

► **Perform business process analysis**: "Perform business process analysis" on page 286

► **Structure service architecture**: "Task 1: Structure service architecture" on page 307

> ► **Model service interactions**: "Task 2: Refine service architecture" on page 356

Design model work product

In the previous section, we described how the service model is structured and that its contents come directly from higher level of abstraction models, such as business models and requirements. In the same way that the service model is mainly related to service specification, the design model is mainly related to service realization (refer to Figure 9-10 on page 257).

Purpose of the design model

The design model has several inputs; however the most important, considering our development case are:

► Service model
► Architecture documents

The main input for the design model is the service model that has to be realized. In other words, we may say the design model *opens the box* of services and represents how individual services are realized. However, this realization has to keep into account other inputs, such as the architecture to be respected, non-functional requirements, and design constraints, as shown in the corresponding RUP work product in Figure 9-17.

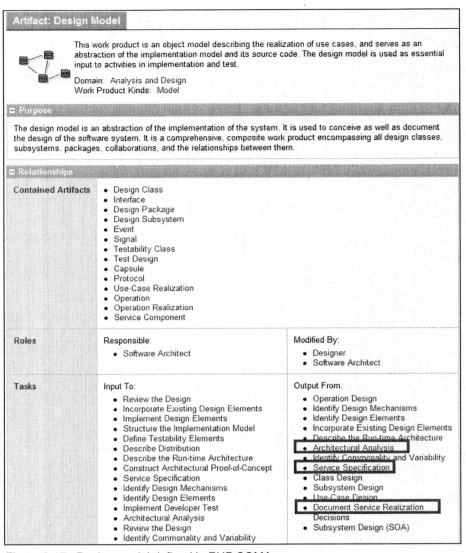

Artifact: Design Model

This work product is an object model describing the realization of use cases, and serves as an abstraction of the implementation model and its source code. The design model is used as essential input to activities in implementation and test.

Domain: Analysis and Design
Work Product Kinds: Model

Purpose

The design model is an abstraction of the implementation of the system. It is used to conceive as well as document the design of the software system. It is a comprehensive, composite work product encompassing all design classes, subsystems, packages, collaborations, and the relationships between them.

Relationships

Contained Artifacts	• Design Class • Interface • Design Package • Design Subsystem • Event • Signal • Testability Class • Test Design • Capsule • Protocol • Use-Case Realization • Operation • Operation Realization • Service Component	
Roles	Responsible: • Software Architect	Modified By: • Designer • Software Architect
Tasks	Input To: • Review the Design • Incorporate Existing Design Elements • Implement Design Elements • Structure the Implementation Model • Define Testability Elements • Describe Distribution • Describe the Run-time Architecture • Construct Architectural Proof-of-Concept • Service Specification • Identify Design Mechanisms • Identify Design Elements • Implement Developer Test • Architectural Analysis • Review the Design • Identify Commonality and Variability	Output From: • Operation Design • Identify Design Mechanisms • Identify Design Elements • Incorporate Existing Design Elements • Describe the Run-time Architecture • Architectural Analysis • Identify Commonality and Variability • Service Specification • Class Design • Subsystem Design • Use-Case Design • Document Service Realization Decisions • Subsystem Design (SOA)

Figure 9-17   Design model defined in RUP SOMA

Notice that there are several tasks influencing the design model. However, given our SOA context and related development case, we want to focus on some of these tasks that are strongly influencing our design model (highlighted in Figure 9-17).

Our focus is on these tasks:

- ► Architectural analysis
- ► Service specification (coming from the service model)
- ► Document service realization decisions. (A snapshot from RUP SOMA is shown in Figure 9-18.)

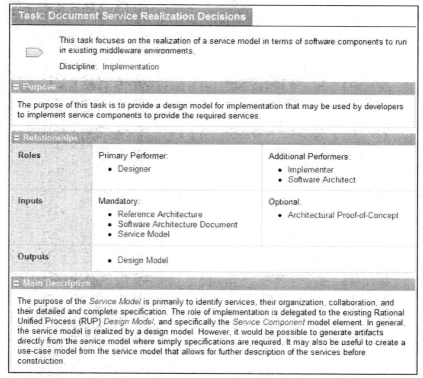

Task: Document Service Realization Decisions

This task focuses on the realization of a service model in terms of software components to run in existing middleware environments.

Discipline: Implementation

Purpose

The purpose of this task is to provide a design model for implementation that may be used by developers to implement service components to provide the required services.

Relationships

Roles	Primary Performer:	Additional Performers:
	• Designer	• Implementer
		• Software Architect
Inputs	Mandatory:	Optional:
	• Reference Architecture	• Architectural Proof-of-Concept
	• Software Architecture Document	
	• Service Model	
Outputs	• Design Model	

Main Description

The purpose of the *Service Model* is primarily to identify services, their organization, collaboration, and their detailed and complete specification. The role of implementation is delegated to the existing Rational Unified Process (RUP) *Design Model*, and specifically the *Service Component* model element. In general, the service model is realized by a design model. However, it would be possible to generate artifacts directly from the service model where simply specifications are required. It may also be useful to create a use-case model from the service model that allows for further description of the services before construction.

Figure 9-18 Document service realization decisions in RUP SOMA

The design model is just one step before implementing services. Indeed, we see later in Chapter 13, "Service implementation" on page 419 how, starting from these models, we are able to generate the lower level of abstraction (the code) structure and basic content, in an automatic way, trough transformations.

The design model represents how services are realized: What a service provider (from service model) becomes, which classes, components, and interfaces are defined to realize it.

Furthermore, in the design model we introduce detailed solution mechanisms, for example hierarchies, design patterns, and detailed structures.

Model structure (samples from JK enterprises case study)

We now describe the design model of our case study.

Profiles

As we explained in "Importance of modeling" on page 138, a profile is a way to extend standard UML elements for a specific domain, trough stereotypes, giving more precise semantics on model elements.

Any model you create in Rational Software Architect has a set of *default profiles*, such as Default, Deployment, and Standard profiles.

If you look at the properties of our design model, you can see there is another profile already applied: *EJBTransformProfile*. This is useful because this model is ready to be transformed to Java or EJB using transformations provided with Rational Software Architect. In our project we are using UML to WSDL and UML to Java transformations, but not the UML to EJB transformation (although the design model is also ready to be transformed to an EJB project).

Type libraries

A model can also have references to *type libraries*. These are containers of (UML) types, with which we can extend our model by adding types belonging to other (non UML) domains. UML has its own primitive types. These are simply:

- String
- Integer
- UnlimitedNatural
- Boolean

The JK Enterprises design model has another type library, named *JavaPrimitiveTypes* that includes all Java primitive types, such as int, boolean, and so forth.

Structure

The (design) model structure depends on the service structure we have in the service model. In particular, we are expanding the 3 - Atomic Business Application Service Providers package in the design model because, as we explain in other sections of the book (for example in Chapter 13, "Service implementation" on page 419), these are services we are going to develop from scratch or from existing assets.

Service component

RUP SOMA describe service component as follows:

> *This artifact is intended for use in describing the realization of a service specification. A service component may provide the realization for one or more services by the realization of multiple service specifications. The set of model elements on the inside of the component represent the concrete realization of the structural, behavioral, and policy contract described by these service specifications.*

We can describe this artifact as the most visible and external element belonging to the design model. The designer and the implementer are responsible for further details, by providing internal component elements, such as classes, interfaces, properties, and operations, building in this way the component structure and behavior.

In our initial design model we have one **<<serviceComponent>>** for each service specification in the service model, and this component is *traced* to its provider, as shown in Figure 9-19.

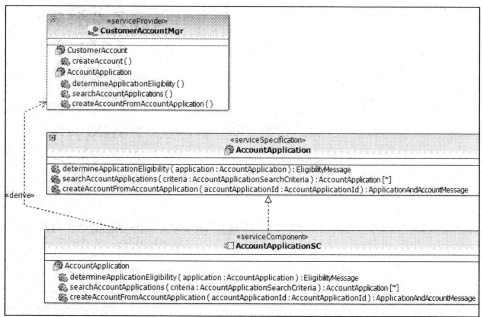

Figure 9-19   Service component trace to service provider and realize service specification

We can have more than one service specification for each service provider as in Figure 9-20.

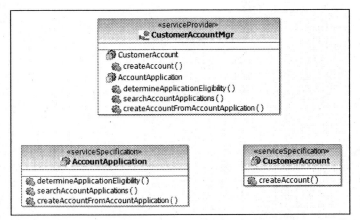

Figure 9-20   A service provider that realizes two service specifications

In this model we focus on the components that are highlighted at the bottom of Figure 9-21 because the other components are realized as *composite services*, by calling atomic services.

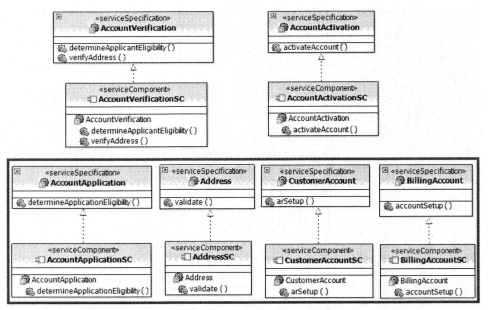

Figure 9-21   Service components in the JK Enterprises design model

The <<serviceComponent>> represents a single step down in abstraction levels; this component is the realization of a service provider and specification. Moreover, this component is refined in the design model, as we explain later in this chapter.

Let us go back to the *structure* of the model. The structure of a model is very important because it is related to several development process aspects, such as managing models, team development, and reusable assets. Therefore this structure is also related to reuse of services; the way we structure a model impacts how service realizations (components) are structured, which kind of dependencies a service (component) has and at the end, how reusable that service is.

With the last argument in mind, we can look at the design model structure (Figure 9-22).

Figure 9-22   Structure of the JK Enterprises design model

In the design model we have a root package called *Service Components* and it represents the set of all components that realize our service model.

Under this package, there is a package for each service component, called with the same name as the service (as it is in the service model) followed by the SC (service component) suffix. This package represents a container for the component itself. We point out a component should be as independent as possible to be reused; therefore we put in this package all architectural elements needed by the component:

► **<<serviceComponent>>** itself that represents the component responsible for realizing the service; this is explained later in this section.

► **All internal classes**, interfaces and elements that compose the component.

► **An Entities package** representing entity classes needed by the service component and that are *owned* by this component or by a group of components that belongs to the same service provider. In this way

► **An Enumeration package** representing utility enumerations that can be used by internal elements of the component.

Contents of the design model

Now that we have explained the design model structure, let us look at the content of the model itself.

For the scope of this book we analyze here only the example that realizes the AccountApplication service specification trough the AccountApplicationSC service component. This component represents the service that we are developing *from scratch*, in a top-down fashion.

Going back to the model root structure (refer to Figure 9-22) we can observe that there is also:

► **A traceability class diagram** representing all traces of this component from internal classes and to elements at higher levels of abstraction.

► **The entities** package keeps a particular kind of classes, stereotyped as <<entity>> that represents a basic business item of our solution. It is derived from the domain model and is owned by the service component.

► **A component** stereotyped as <<serviceComponent>> representing the direct realization of a service provider as we can note from traceability diagrams. This element encompasses all details about the provider realization and realizes the same business interface that we call Service Specification.

If we expand the component (AccountApplicationSC) in the Project Explorer, we can observe the structure shown in Figure 9-23.

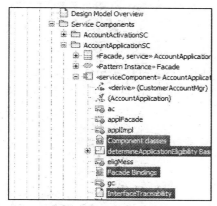

Figure 9-23   Model structure for the AccountApplicationSC service component

In particular we want to point out the meaning of four diagrams:

► **Component classes**—A class diagram that represents actual classes that realize this component.

► **determineApplicationEligibility Basic Flow**—An interaction diagram that represents the behavior for the corresponding operation for a basic flow scenario.

► **Facade bindings**—A class diagram that represents the application of the facade design pattern.

► **Traceability**—A traceability class diagram that represents all traces of this component from internal classes and to elements belonging to higher levels of abstraction.

Finally, we are going to see how our service is realized: For this component, a *facade* design pattern has been used.

A design pattern is a common solution for a recurring problem. we can describe facade pattern in this way:

► **Problem solved:** Dealing with complex subsystem can create too many dependencies on specific subsystem details, such as different methods with different parameters types and so on. This does not allow to have a clear and well defined interface for the subsystem.

► **Solution**: Facade provides a unified interface that hide a set of interfaces in a subsystem. A higher level interface, easier to use is defined for clients.

► **Parameter facade**: This class knows all subsystem details and it delegates all client requests to appropriate subsystem objects.

► **Parameter subsystem**: This is the actual subsystem implementation classes. There is no dependency to the facade.

> **Note:** If you are interested in knowing more about pattern theory and applications, refer to Chapter 16, "Pattern-based engineering with Rational Software Architect ." on page 545.

The pattern has been applied to AccountApplicationServiceFacade and AccountApplicationServiceImpl classes as the <<Facade>> and <<Subsystem>> formal parameters of the pattern.

Thus we can see how the <<PatternInstance>> represents the binding between a pattern and its *bound* classes (Figure 9-24).

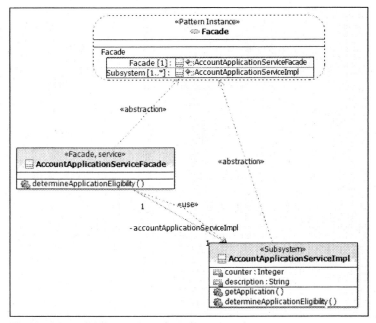

Figure 9-24   JK Enterprises facade pattern instance

We see on this diagram there is a UML collaboration stereotyped as <<PatternInstance>> that represents the bindings we mentioned.

In our solution we want to decouple the internal implementation of the service that is owned by the *impl* class from the external world. This is done typically to simplify and to unify the interfaces of the different classes involved.

Now we can analyze the complete realization, by showing the expected (default) behavior for the `determineApplicationEligibility` operation (Figure 9-25).

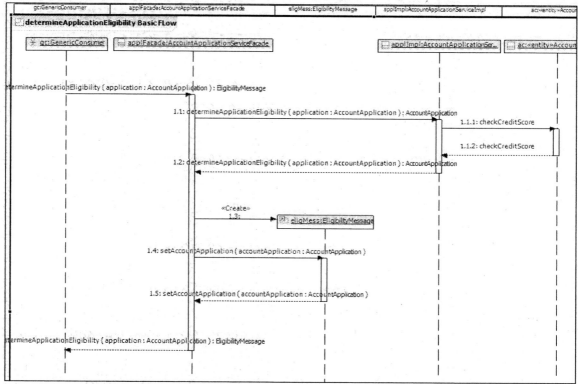

Figure 9-25   determineApplicationEligibility operation sequence diagram basic flow

We can see the facade pattern in action in Figure 9-25, which shows the basic flow for the `determineApplicationEligibility` operation. We notice that the external world (represented here with an actor named *Generic consumer*) expects a very simple interface that directly comes (and is traced to) from the `AccountApplication` service specification. This operation simply expects an `AccountApplication` (parameter type) as the input and returns an `EligibilityMessage`. Notice that both input and output parameters belong to the service model and not the design model. This is because they are part of service specification and our services are fully specified in service model.

Looking at the service model, we can expand the `EligibilityMessage` and see how it is structured (Figure 9-26).

An `EligibilityMessage` is made of one `AccountApplication` parameter type and a collection of warnings.

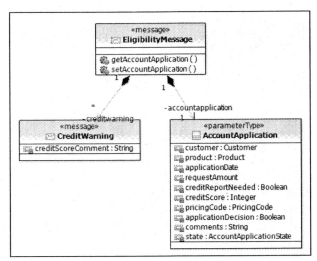

Figure 9-26   Eligibility message from JK Enterprises service model

Going back to Figure 9-25, we notice the internal implementation class, `AccountApplicationServiceImpl`, has a different signature that returns simply an `AccountApplication` parameter type and not a message. This is where the facade actually works: By providing the requested interface (service specification) to the external world and hiding all internal details or more complicated interfaces. This is done by the facade from steps 1.3 to 1.5 in the sequence diagram.

Traceability

As we mentioned several times in this book, for an SOA solution, alignment between business and IT is a key factor. Therefore, traceability becomes very important.

In particular, we can see the design model as a bridge between service model and implementation. Thus we have components, classes and elements that derive from service model and, at the same time, we have implementation work products such as Java classes, interfaces, WSDLs, and so forth, that derive from these design elements.

Analyzing our design model, we can show a traceability diagram for the `AccountApplicationSC` service component—the component we develop top-down in this project (Figure 9-27).

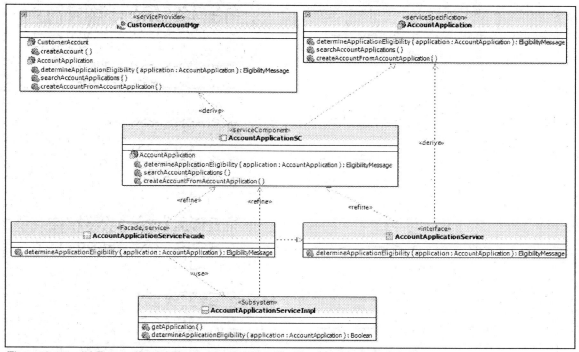

Figure 9-27   *JK Enterprises traces for AccountApplication service component*

Considering Figure 9-27, we can recognize different kinds of (UML) dependencies. Traceability here is represented by two kind of dependencies:

▶ **<<refine>>** dependencies represents a kind of traceability between elements within the same level of abstraction (and therefore the same model). Indeed we can see that we have two classes and one interface that refine the `AccountApplicationSC` service component. This means this elements represent the realization of the component itself.

▶ **<<derive>>** dependencies represents a kind of traceability between elements on different level of abstraction. In this case, we have to point out the component itself is coming from ("derives") the *service provider* we defined in the service model. On the same diagram we can observe as our (design) component is realizing the *service specification* that belongs to service model as well.

The diagram in Figure 9-27 also shows realization relationships:

▶ `AccountApplicationSC` directly realizes the service specification.

▶ `AccountApplicationServiceFacade` realizes the lower level interface, `AccountApplicationService` that is traced to the service specification.

Traceability is important also because it allows us to know *what we are doing and why*, from a lower level perspective and to analyze the impact of a change from a (business) higher level perspective.

Traceability is a general topic that we cover in several sections of this book, corresponding to several disciplines and abstraction levels.

Directly connected to the design model are the service model (on the higher part) and the implementation model (on the lower part). We show an example in Figure 9-28 for the `AccountApplicationService` interface.

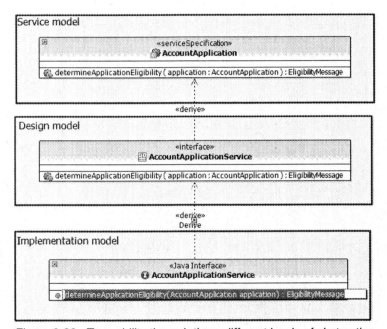

Figure 9-28   Traceability through three different levels of abstraction

Important: Traceability dependencies can be created manually or through automated transformations. Usually a transformation creates a traceability dependency from the target element to the source element.

10

Service identification

This chapter describes the technique associated with identifying services. It describes the inputs and outputs of the service identification activity, and it is structured around these tasks:

► Identify services from goals

► Perform business process analysis

► Perform existing asset analysis

The business modeling and requirements management chapters are very related to identifying services as they describe major inputs to service identification.

Introduction

Service identification is critical to the success of SOA, because it is where *IT meets the business*. Although service identification leverages existing best practices, such as classic RUP, it is an area where SOA brings innovative concepts and ideas that were not addressed by other paradigms.

The goal of service identification is to create an initial set of candidate services and their associated operations.

These identified services are required by and meaningful to the business. To realize this business alignment, business process analyst(s) (additional role) participate in service identification with software architect(s) (main role).

During service identification, the service model work product is created. At the end of service identification, it is handed off to the software architect(s) responsible for service specification. You can think of service identification as producing the analysis level of the service model, and service specification the design level.

Inputs to service identification

This section introduces the main inputs to service identification.

The most critical input to service identification are the existing services an enterprise has access to. These services and information about them are typically stored in a registry and repository such as the IBM WebSphere Service Registry and Repository. JK Enterprises are currently performing their first SOA project. Therefore, there are no existing services they can reuse. The services identified, specified, realized, implemented, tested, and deployed from the Account Opening project will be an input to the service identification of the next project.

An enterprise-level business strategy and business architecture effort may have taken place to identify functional areas that differentiate a business from its competitors. An example of such a strategic effort is the IBM Component Business Modeling (CBM) technique.

As described in "Component business modeling" on page 175, enterprises are made up of business components that are placed on a business architecture map (CBM map) under a specific business competency (domain) and accountability (responsibility) level of direct, control, or execute. Business components own business processes and activities. Also, a key concept of CBM is that business components interact with each other through services that they offer (own) or consume, hence its importance for SOA.

For JK Enterprises, the differentiating business components are under the Servicing & Sales business competency, as shown in Figure 10-1, where dark blue means differentiated, light blue competitive, and white base. The CBM map reflects the fact that JK Enterprises is very proud of the services it offers to customers. Also, other business components such as General Ledger are not considered strategic for JK Enterprises (as it is often the case for other companies).

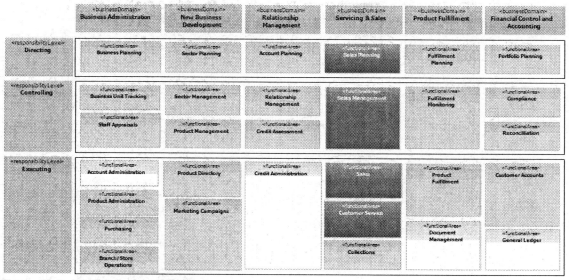

Figure 10-1   JK Enterprises CBM Map

In addition to differentiating business components, the CBM effort also identifies goals and key performance indicators (KPIs) that are used as input to service identification. For example, there is a KPI under Sales Management described as follows:

> *Increase the volume of online account applications by 25% or more compared to current volumes.*

Note that these KPIs should live in and be managed by RequisitePro, as described in Chapter 8, "Requirements" on page 207.

The CBM strategic effort looks in detail at what the business components and the business processes they own are. Service identification takes place in the scope of a differentiator business component and its business processes. Note that the activities that make up a business process may span business components. For example, the Account Opening business process—although owned by the sales management business component—includes activities from the Account Administration business component.

Another important point is that other business components on the CBM map are potential future service consumers of the services you identify, and you should consider them during service identification. Reuse is fundamental for SOA, and you have to think about additional requirements from other service consumers when working on services, so that they can be reused by others.

It is important to note that the CBM enterprise-level strategic effort is not a mandatory input to identifying services, In practice, the scope of services to identify may be set by other things, such as a project's goals and/or a business process only.

Another key input to service identification is the set of business goals and key performance indicators (KPIs) stored in RequisitePro. For example, one of JK Enterprises's goals is to decrease the cost of credit report retrieval by 20%. Goals and KPIs provide additional data used to identify services required by the business.

Last but not least, the existing applications an enterprise owns are its most valuable assets, and they are inputs to service identification. Existing assets include transactions, batch processing, or data structures that are running in production.

These different approaches are visually represented in the SOA solution stack (described in "SOA foundation reference architecture" on page 6, where services play a central role, are used by consumers and are supported by providers (Figure 10-2).

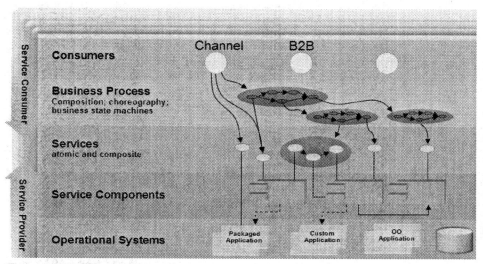

Figure 10-2   SOA solution stack

Tools and models used for service identification

We use Rational Software Architect and its integration features with other tools, such as Rational RequisitePro, and WebSphere Business Modeler to perform service identification.

We create a model named *Service Model - Identification Level*. You can think of this as the analysis level model of the service model. It is the beginning of the service model, and it may simply evolve during service specification. For the purpose of this book, we provide the service model as it is after the service identification, so that you understand the type of information and level of details that relate to service identification.

Identify services from goals

In this section, we describe how business-level artifacts such as business goals and key performance indicators (KPIs) can be refined to a level that is detailed enough for IT design and implementation.

For the JK Enterprises case study, the focus of service identification is the Sales Management business component, and the goals from which we are identifying services support this business component (and other business components used by Sales Management).

Rational Software Architect and RequisitePro integration

Rational Software Architect's RequisitePro integration allows you to work on RequisitePro projects from within the Software Architect IDE. Almost all of the capabilities provided by the RequisitePro native client are also provided, except administration capabilities and the ability to create new projects. There is a Requirement perspective, which supports working with RequisitePro requirements, and the linkage (traceability) of design elements to requirements.

The Requirement perspective is shown on Figure 10-3. It is made up of three views: Requirement Explorer [1], Requirement Trace [2], and Properties [3].

1. The Requirement Explorer allows you to open, browse, and explore requirements stored in RequisitePro. When a specific requirement is selected, you can see more information about it in the other views.

2. The Properties view provides information about individual requirements, such as their attributes (for example, assigned to, cost, or priority).

3. A very informative view is the Requirement Trace view, which allows for the visualization of requirements or model elements traced to and from a specific requirement.

For JK Enterprises, when the PROJGOAL1.1 is selected, the Requirement Trace view informs us that KPI1 is traced to it, and METRIC1 is in turn traced to KPI1, which makes it indirectly traced to PROJGOAL1.

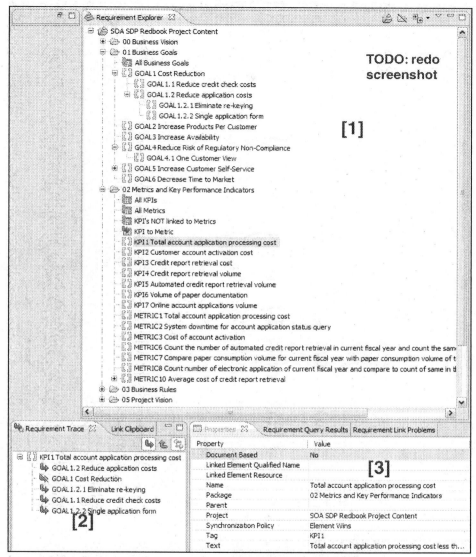

Figure 10-3   Rational Software Architect Requirement perspective

Identify services from goals

In this section, we identify services (model elements), and add traceability links from these services to the requirements they support. The service model elements appear under the Requirement Trace view.

Browsing the JK Enterprises goals, and more particularly PROJGOAL1 and its sub-goals, we notice that they are all related to the activation of customer accounts.

We now create a service named AccountActivation:

▶ In the Project Explorer, open the Services Traced to Goals diagram under Service Model - Identification Level.

▶ When the diagram opens, mouse over an empty area, wait for the action bar to pop up, and then click *Add Stereotyped Class* (Figure 10-4).

Figure 10-4   Create an new instance of a stereotyped class

You are presented with a choice of stereotyped classes to create. Because we have set up the project so that it uses the UML 2.0 profile for software services, the list includes SOA stereotypes.

▶ Select *Create <<serviceSpecification>> Class* and name the newly created service specification AccountActivation (Figure 10-5).

Figure 10-5   AccountActivation, as originally identified from business goals

Create traceability from services to goals

We now trace the identified service back to the goals (requirements) they were identified from:

▶ Drag PROJGOAL1.1 from the Requirement Explorer view into the diagram.

A new model element is created under the Service Model - Identification Level project. This new model element is traced to the PROJGOA1.1 RequisitePro requirement.

Note that because the newly created elements do not live in the RequisitePro project, a new folder is automatically created under the RequisitePro project, named Eclipse Element Proxies. That folder contains information about traces to non RequisitePro elements, including the newly created Software Architect model elements.

- ► To stereotype this element as a business goal (from the business modeling profile), make sure the newly created class is selected, and then from under the Properties view, select the *Stereotypes* tab. Click *Add Stereotypes* and then select *BusinessGoal*.

  The BusinessGoal stereotype is defined by the Business Modeling profile.

- ► In the diagram, mouse over `AccountActivation`, click the outbound arrow (Figure 10-6), then drag the connection to `Decrease customer account activation cost by 50%` and release the mouse button. Select *Create Dependency*.

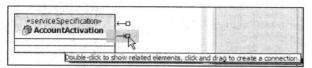

Figure 10-6   Adding a relationship to the AccountActivation serviceSpecification

- ► Make sure the newly created dependency is selected, and then from under the Properties view, select the Stereotypes tab. Click *Add Stereotypes* and then select *Supports*.

- ► Drag `PROJGOAL1.2` into the diagram and repeat the previous two steps to create a `Supports` dependency from `AccountActivation` to the other project goal.

  The resulting diagram is shown in Figure 10-7.

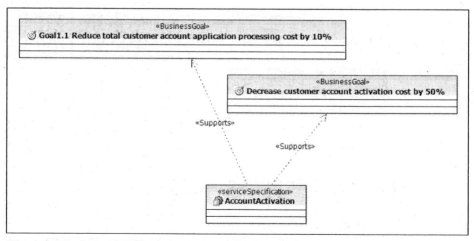

Figure 10-7   AccountActivation traced to two requirements

Note that if you go back to the Requirement perspective and select PROJGOAL1.1 in the Requirement Explorer, you should see the new CLASS2 model element traced to PROJGOAL1.1 (Figure 10-8). CLASS2 is in turn traced to the AccountActivation service specification.

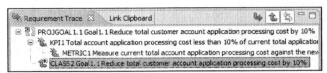

Figure 10-8   Elements traced to the PROJGOAL1.1 business goal

For the purpose of this example, we are done with identifying services from business goals.

Perform business process analysis

Also referred to as *top-down* service identification, business process analysis consists of looking at the set of business processes, their associated sub-processes, activities and tasks, and identify services that would support the elements that can be automated.

As previously mentioned, the business processes used during service identification come from functional area analysis and business process modeling.

One of the first things to do is to look at the business processes and see if they should be decomposed further, so that the leaf-level activities (tasks) are at a level at which services and operations can be identified.

Elements of the service model that are identified from business process analysis include:

▶ **Service consumers**—Usually the business processes themselves

▶ **Service specifications**—Identified from business processes, sub-processes, activities, or tasks

▶ **Service specification operations**—Usually identified from business tasks

▶ **Operation parameters**—Identified for the business items of the business processes

Identify service elements from business process model

For the JK Enterprises case study, the business process modeling effort produced an Account Verification business process (a sub-process of the Account Opening business process), which looks at an application and determines whether or not the application should be approved (Figure 10-9).

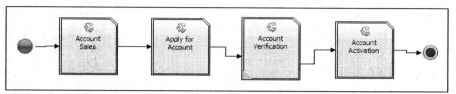

Figure 10-9   Account Opening business process

We identify a service named `AccountVerification` from the Account Verification business (sub-)process.

► If not already open, open the `Services Identified from Business Processes` diagram under the `Service Model - Identification Level`.

► Create a new service specification named `AccountVerification`.

The Account Verification business process has been decomposed into tasks. The first business task of the Account Verification business process is Determine applicant eligibility (Figure 10-10).

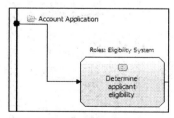

Figure 10-10   Determine applicant eligibility task

Determine applicant eligibility examines a Customer Application, and looks like a good candidate operation for the following reasons:

► It performs a logical finite unit of work.
► It can be reused by many consumers.

We identify a service operation from this business task:

► Find the `AccountVerification` service specification in the Project Explorer. Right-click and then select *Add UML → Operation*. Name the operation `determineApplicationEligibility`.

Note that the `AccountVerification` service specification in the `Services Identified from Business Processes` diagram now shows the operation you just added. There is only one model element for `AccountVerification`, and that single model element can appear under several diagrams. Diagrams provide different views to different people. You can also modify a model element from a diagram, and the change is reflected under the Project Explorer and any diagram the model element appears in[1].

At this stage, it is a good idea to start describing (in English) what the service operation does:

► Select the `determineApplicationEligibility` operation, and then enter this text under the Documentation tab of the Properties view:

> Determines whether or not a customer is eligible for a product, based on an account application that provides information on the customer and the requested product.

At the identification level, service operations do not need to be rigorously specified. However, it is important to give service operations and business items names that are meaningful to the business. These names should be retained through to code.

It is a recommended practice to follow operations naming standards in your organization because consistency promotes reuse. For example, you can name service operations as follows:

► Start with an action (for example, `determine` or `create`).
► Then provide the name of a domain element (for example, `Claim` or `Customer`).

We now detail the operation to specify that it takes the `Account Application` business item as input parameter, and returns a boolean (true or false). We know that we need the Account Application parameter because we see it as being passed as the business item in the business process in Figure 10-10.

We use the Software Architect to WebSphere Business Modeler integration feature, which allows a Business Modeler project to be open as UML in the Modeling perspective. Refer to "References" on page 298 for more information about this feature.

► Open the `Business Process Model`.

► Make sure the `Services Identified from Business Processes` diagram is open. Select the `Account Application` business item under the `Business items` folder and drag it onto the `Services Identified from Business Processes` diagram (Figure 10-11).

---

[1] This is the advantage of using a model with diagrams as different views, rather than bitmaped diagrams. Changes in the underlying model are immediately reflected in the diagrams and we can construct new diagrams based on selected parts of the model without affecting any other diagrams.

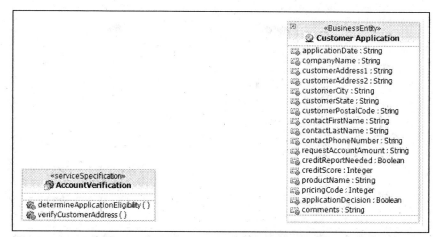

Figure 10-11 Customer Application under Services Identified from business processes

► Select the `determineApplicationEligibility` operation (not the service specification but the operation itself). In the Properties view, select the Parameters tab, and then click *Insert New Parameter* on the right-hand side (Figure 10-12).

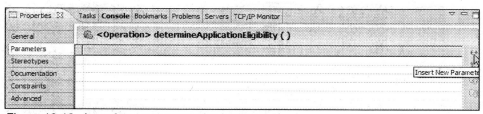

Figure 10-12 Inserting a new operation parameter

► In the Name column, type `application`.

► Click the cell in the Type column and then click ... (Figure 10-13).

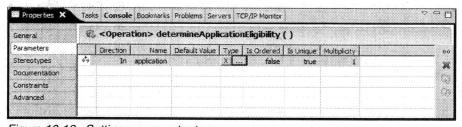

Figure 10-13 Setting a parameter type

► The Select Element for type window opens. Type `Account Application` into the entry field (Figure 10-14).

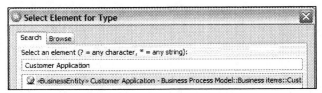

Figure 10-14 Selecting a parameter type

► Make sure `Customer Application` is selected from the results, and click *OK*.

► Select the *General* tab, click *Set Return Type*, and select the *Boolean* type (`UMLPrimitiveTypes::Boolean`).

► Select the `AccountVerification` service specification, right-click, and select *Filters → Show signature*.

► The resulting diagram is shown in Figure 10-15.

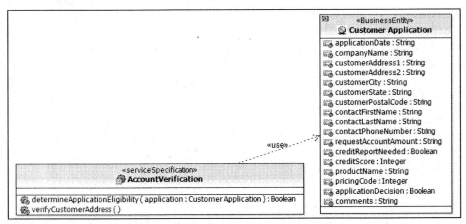

Figure 10-15 Specify determineApplicantEligibility operation parameters

The `Account Opening` business process is a service consumer for `AccountVerification`. We now capture this in the model:

► Open the Identified Service Consumers diagram and create a new service consumer named `AccountOpeningProcess`.

The resulting Identified Service Consumers diagram is shown in Figure 10-16.

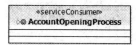

Figure 10-16   Identified service consumers

Other services and operations are also identified from the business process analysis. The final list of services is shown in Figure 10-17:

▶ `AccountActivation` service

▶ `AccountApplicationInquiry` service, with `searchAccountApplications` operation

▶ `AccountVerification` service, with `determineApplicationEligibility` and `verifyCustomerAddress` operations

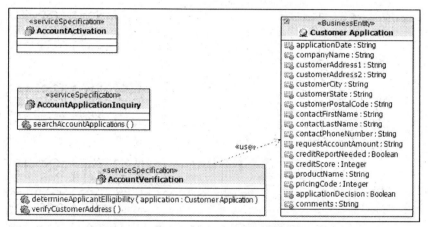

Figure 10-17   Services identified from business process analysis

Note that the service specifications do not trace to the business process elements they were identified from. Two options are available to do so (not explained in details):

▶ Enter the business process elements as requirements in a RequisitePro project. You can think of business process models as being functional requirements, and as such they could live in a RequisitePro project (probably with a RequisitePro template that would define new requirement types such as business activity). Then, you can use the Software Architect RequisitePro integration feature to trace model elements to business process elements in RequisitePro.

► Use the Software Architect WebSphere Business Modeler integration feature to open the WebSphere Business Modeler project in Software Architect as UML. We do not use it here because we want to trace the identified services to business process elements (as in Business Modeler), and not their UML representation.

A significant advantage of identifying services from business goals and business processes is that the identified services are aligned to the business! Sometimes, these services may be difficult or impossible to implement (for example, the service would have to retrieve too much information from too many sources, making the service too slow). One of the first tasks of service specification is to validate those candidate services, including how feasible it is to implement them.

Perform existing asset analysis

Also referred to as *bottom-up* service identification, existing asset analysis consists of looking at an enterprise's existing or earlier applications (including transactions, batch processing, and data structures), and identify services from these. This is sometimes called *exposing legacy application as services*.

Note that any application that is deployed into production is considered an existing or earlier application. Existing or earlier applications are not restricted to mainframe, and could also include, for example, C++ or Java code.

Existing services?

Looking for existing SOA services that can be reused (instead of re-created) is very important, although this activity is typically not considered part of existing asset analysis. Looking for existing services would involve getting information from service registries and repositories, such as the IBM WebSphere Service Registry and Repository.

A service can also be thought of as being packaged as a set of assets, and hosted by a RAS repository. For example, the service and design models would live in one asset, and the service implementation in another asset. These assets are key reusable items that should always be considered during service identification. However, because a lot of organizations do not already have existing services, it is usually omitted, and a detailed description of this is not provided in this book.

Bottom-up and meet-in-the -middle

Bottom-up analysis is a very challenging task. Usually, very few people in the enterprise know what the deployed applications exactly are, how many there are, and what their names or purpose are.

Although analyzing an enterprise's existing assets, such as all of the existing or earlier applications running in production, is a very valuable exercise, reality forbids a complete enterprise-wide effort, usually because of other business pressures. In practice, it is often the case that the existing asset analysis takes place in the context of a business-driven (top-down) exercise. This approach is sometimes referred to as *meet-in-the-middle* (where one identifies existing functionality that can provide what the new (to-be) business goals, processes, and services need.

Existing asset analysis requires the participation of specialists for the systems (for example, IMS™ or CICS) or applications (for example, COBOL programs) being analyzed. Also, it is essential to have appropriate tools that are able to inspect the systems because nobody really knows what all of the deployed applications are.

An IBM product that supports existing asset analysis is WebSphere Studio Asset Analyzer (WSAA). Asset Analyzer provides insight to IT organizations as to what their distributed and mainframe applications are. It helps with the maintenance, extension, reuse (this section), and transformation of applications. Asset Analyzer provides information about applications such as batch jobs, CICS groups, CICS regions, CICS transactions, DB2® systems, IMS subsystems, or IMS transactions.

JK Enterprises

From the business process and goal (top-down) analysis, we know that JK Enterprises requires functionality in the area of Customer. For example, there are business goals around reducing the cost of customer application, and the Account Opening business process has to deal with Customer information. In this section, we analyze existing assets to identify services that would support customer data, and more specifically the creation of customer data, since the business process is about new accounts.

We now request the assistance of the JK Enterprises specialist for CICS (a COBOL programmer). The specialist thinks a program named CUSTDATA handles customer information. Using Asset Analyzer, we determine that there is a data set named JK.CUSTDATA. Asset Analyzer also tells us that a CICS file (online data store) named CUSTFILE refers to this data set. Then, Asset Analyzer tells us that CUSTFILE only has one program named CUSTPROG. Asset Analyzer allows the specialist to access the COBOL source code for CUSTPROG (Figure 10-18).

```
EVALUATE REQUEST-TYPE
     WHEN 'C'        PERFORM 1000-DO-ADD
     WHEN 'c'        PERFORM 1000-DO-ADD
     WHEN 'R'        PERFORM 2000-DO-READ
     WHEN 'r'        PERFORM 2000-DO-READ
     WHEN 'D'        PERFORM 3000-DO-DELETE
     WHEN 'd'        PERFORM 3000-DO-DELETE
     WHEN 'U'        PERFORM 4000-DO-UPDATE
     WHEN 'u'        PERFORM 4000-DO-UPDATE
     WHEN OTHER
          MOVE '04' TO RET-CODE
          MOVE 'ERROR: Invalid customer request received'
               TO RETURN-COMMENT
          PERFORM 7100-RETURN-ERROR-MESSAGE
END-EVALUATE.
EXEC CICS ABEND ABCODE('CUS2') END-EXEC.
```

Figure 10-18   CUSTPROG COBOL source code

From the source code, the specialist can tell that CUSTPROG does create, read, update, and delete on customer entities. At this stage, CUSTPROG is a likely candidate for an existing application that can be exposed as a service. We now analyze CUSTPROG in more details. Asset Analyzer also tells us that one of the source files CUSTPROG uses is CUSTIORQ, and provides access to its source code (Figure 10-19).

```
 1.      **********************************************
 2.      * CUSTOMER FILE I/O REQUEST AREA
 3.      **********************************************
 4.
 5.          03   REQUEST-TYPE              PIC X.
 6.          03   RET-CODE                  PIC XX.
 7.          03   CustomerId                PIC X(8).
 8.          03   CustomerLastName          PIC X(20).
 9.          03   CustomerFirstName         PIC X(20).
10.          03   CustomerCompany           PIC X(30).
11.          03   CustomerAddr1             PIC X(30).
12.          03   CustomerAddr2             PIC X(30).
13.          03   CustomerCity              PIC X(20).
14.          03   CustomerState             PIC X(20).
15.          03   CustomerCountry           PIC X(30).
16.          03   CustomerMailCode          PIC X(20).
17.          03   CustomerPhone             PIC X(20).
18.          03   CustomerLastUpdateDate    PIC X(8).
19.          03   RETURN-COMMENT            PIC X(50).
```

Figure 10-19   CUSTIORQ source code

From the CUSTIORQ source, the specialist can see what the definitions are for CUSTPROG's request and response messages. This confirms that CUSTPROG works on customer data, and more specifically it can create the customer data we need. From the CUSTRPROG COBOL program, we identify a new service named CustomerAccount.

► From Service Model - Identification Level, open the Services Traced to Existing Assets diagram.

- ► Using the action bar (or another technique), create a new class and name it CUSTPROG.

- ► Make sure the CUSTPROG class is selected, and then click the *Stereotypes* tab under the Properties view. Specify COBOL Program in the keyword field.

  Note that we are not using a stereotype defined by a profile, but simply a keyword to add a visual clue that the class is a COBOL program. Except for the visual notation, CUSTPROG is just a class, and as such does not have additional properties.

- ► Make sure the CUSTPROG class is selected, right-click, and then select *Filters → Show/Hide Compartments → Name Compartment only.*

The resulting diagram is shown in Figure 10-20.

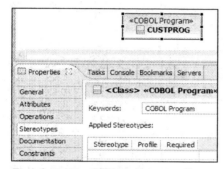

Figure 10-20   COBOL Program keyword for CUSTPROG

- ► Create a new service specification named CustomerAccount.
- ► Add a trace association from CustomerAccount to CUSTPROG.

The resulting diagram is shown in Figure 10-21.

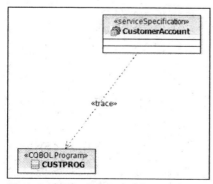

Figure 10-21   CustomerAccount traced to CUSTPROG

Note that we add a trace from the service specification to the existing asset. This may surprise you because usually you would trace to elements that are at a higher level (for example, service to goal). But what we want to show here is how (or why) the service was identified.

So, starting from a given service, we want to be able to trace to the element that made us identify the service:

► Add an operation named `createAccount` under `CustomerAccount`.

   Note that although the COBOL program supports the creation, read, update, and delete of customer accounts, we only create a service specification operation for read, because it is all that is required by the business.

Two other services are also identified. The list of services identified from existing assets is as follows:

► `BillingAccount` service, with `createAccount` operation, identified from the `BILLPROG` COBOL program

► `CustomerAccount` service, with `createAccount` operation, identified from the `CUSTPROG` COBOL program

► `GeneralLedgerAccount` service, with `createAccount` operation, identified from the `GL` SAP program

The resulting diagram is shown in Figure 10-22.

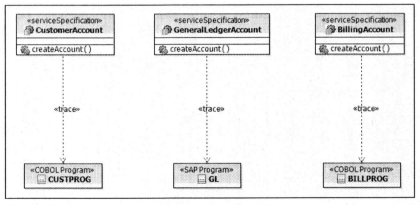

Figure 10-22   Services identified from existing assets

This completes our example of the identification of services from existing assets.

A risk associated with identifying services from existing assets is to "blindly" expose as services any functionality that seems "technically" interesting. For example, existing or earlier applications may provide a lot of functionality around create/read/update/delete (CRUD) of data (such as Customer in our example), and services identified from these may be too fine-grained to provide the value expected of services in an SOA environment. Fortunately, processes such as RUP SOMA provide prescriptive guidance to avoid this. Also, looking at existing assets in the context of business goals or processes helps a lot, as described in this section.

During service identification, we do not look at how services that have been identified from the top-down approach would be supported by existing applications. This exercise belongs to service realization and implementation. After all, in that case, the service has already been identified. Similarly, we do not look at what external service providers could be used to support a service identified from the top-down approach.

Output of service identification for JK Enterprises

For our example, the result of the service identification task is a list of six service specifications and their operations, traced to the artifacts they were identified from. In our example, we have identified the following services:

- ► `AccountActivation` service
- ► `AccountApplicationInquiry` service, with `searchAccountApplications` operation
- ► `AccountVerification` service, with `determineApplicationEligibility` operation
- ► `CustomerAccount` service, with `createAccount` operation
- ► `GeneralLedgerAccount` service, with `createAccount` operation
- ► `BillingAccount` service, with `createAccount` operation

Note that not all of the services that make the service-oriented architecture are listed here. All of the composite services (the ones that call other services) are identified at this stage. But not all of the atomic services (the ones that do not call other services) have. Only during service specification do these appear in the architecture.

We create a diagram named `Identified Services` with the service specifications (Figure 10-23).

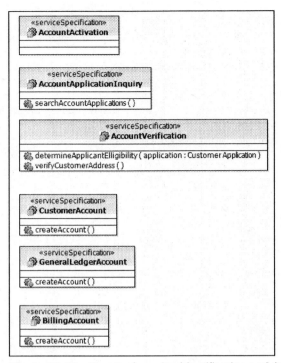

Figure 10-23   Result of service identification activity

References

Read the article on *Business Services Modeling, Integrating WebSphere Business Modeler and Rational Software Modeler* on developerWorks:

    http://www-128.ibm.com/developerworks/rational/library/05/1227_amsden/

11

Service specification

This chapter describes the technique associated with fully specifying the service model work product.

It describes the inputs, outputs, and tools that are used for the service specification activity, and it is structured around these two tasks:

► Structure service architecture

► Refine service architecture

The service identification chapter is relevant to this chapter because it is where we describe how the service model work product is created.

Introduction

The goal of the service specification activity is to fully specify the elements of the SOA design that are architecturally significant, that is the elements of the service model work product. For this reason, service specification is performed primarily by software architects, optionally with the participation of designers.

Service specification only focuses on the services layer of the SOA solution stack (Figure 11-1).

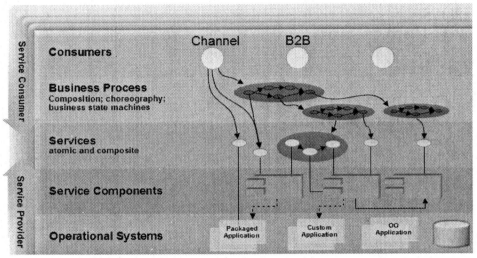

Figure 11-1   SOA solution stack

Service specification is about the *A* of SOA (architecture) and as such is a key activity without which an SOA effort cannot be successful.

Whereas service identification can be seen as the analysis of the service model, service specification can be seen as the design of the service model.

During service specification, the service model is fully specified. After service specification, it is used by the designers responsible for service realization, and the developers responsible for service implementation.

Tools and capabilities used for service specification

In this section, we describe the artifacts that support service specification.

Rational Software Architect

The tool used to perform service specification is Rational Software Architect. More specifically, the work is performed in the Modeling perspective of Software Architect, shown in Figure 11-2.

The modeling perspective includes four views that are helpful in the design of the service model. They are:

1. **Project Explorer**: Shows projects, their diagrams, packages, classes and other model elements.

2. **Diagram Editor**: Where you can edit diagrams, including creating elements from the palette or the action bar, and laying out elements on diagrams. When a diagram is double-clicked in the Project Explorer, the diagram editor opens the diagram.

3. **Properties**: Shows information about the artifact selected. The information is presented in several tabs, depending on the type of artifact selected.

4. **Outline**: Useful when a diagram is large, the outline shows which part of the diagram is currently shown in the editor.

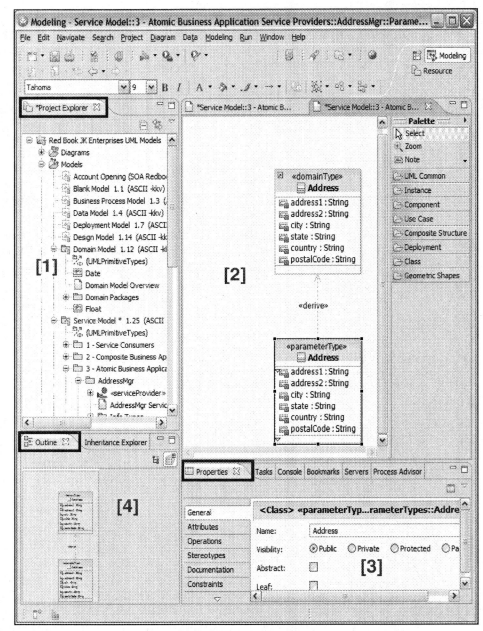

Figure 11-2   Software Architect Modeling perspective

UML and the UML 2 profile for software services

The Unified Modeling Language (UML), as described in "Unified Modeling Language" on page 141, supports the design of the service model. For example, the JK Enterprises service model is an instance of a UML model. Because we are working on a specific domain (SOA), we make use of a UML profile for that domain, that is the UML 2.0 profile for software services (described in "UML profile for software services" on page 164). For example, we are not using base UML interfaces, but interfaces stereotyped as <<serviceSpecification>> for service specifications.

Process guidance

One of the nice things about Software Architect is that it provides integration with the development process JK Enterprises follows.

The JK Enterprises process engineer used Rational Method Composer (see "Rational Method Composer" on page 32) to customize RUP for SOA for JK Enterprises. From Method Composer, the process engineer publishes the customized process and makes it available to JK Enterprises staff. The software architect responsible for the service specification sets the Software Architect process to JK Enterprises. He also specifies that he is performing the role of software architect, and that he is interested in all topics.

Setting process preferences

The process preferences are set in the Preferences dialog:

► Select *Window → Preferences*.

► When the Preferences window opens, type process in the filter text field. Then select *Process*.

► Select *Software Architect* under the Developers category of the Roles you are performing.

► Select *Method Content*, *Process*, and *General Content* under Topics you are interested in.

► For the purpose of this exercise, we do not point to a customized process under Process Configurations Location. However, this is where the developers will point to the JK specific development process.

► Click *Apply* and *OK*.

The process preference window is shown in Figure 11-3.

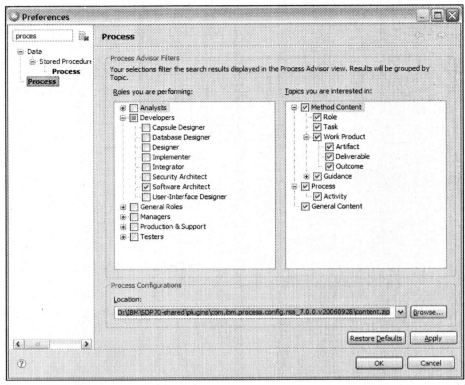

Figure 11-3   Process preferences

Software Architect provides a Process Advisor view and a Process Browser window.

Process Advisor

The Process Advisor view provides context-sensitive guidance for the task at hand. It provides an additional filter to what is set under preferences so that it only displays the contents that pertain to what the user is currently performing.

We display the Process Advisor view by selecting *Help → Process Advisor*.

The Process Advisor view appears at the bottom of the Modeling perspective (Figure 11-4). It provides process and method information under categories such as Tool Mentors or Work Products. When nothing is selected, you can see how many entries each category contains.

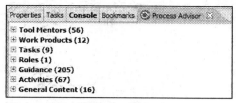

Figure 11-4   Process Advisor

Process Browser

The Process Browser is very similar to the help system, but with process and method contents. It displays HTML pages and also provides navigation aids, such as process view, search query and result, and index.

The Process Browser is opened by selecting *Help → Process Browser*, or by clicking one of the Process Advisor entries.

In the Process Browser, to go to the RUP welcome page select the *Team* tab under Process Views, and then select *Welcome* (Figure 11-5).

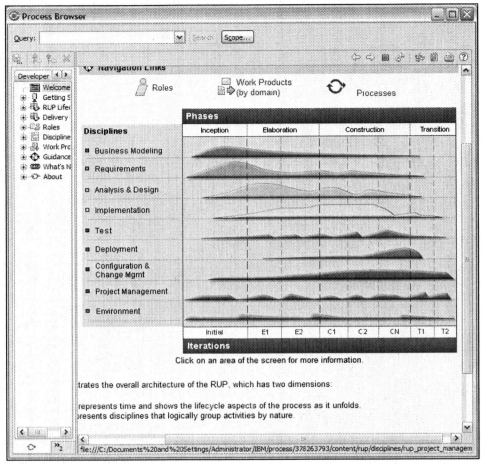

Figure 11-5   Process Browser

Armed with the powerful Software Architect tool, its support for SOA and integrated process guidance, we are now ready to dive into the details of service specification.

Overview of the service specification activity

The service specification tasks are shown in Figure 11-6.

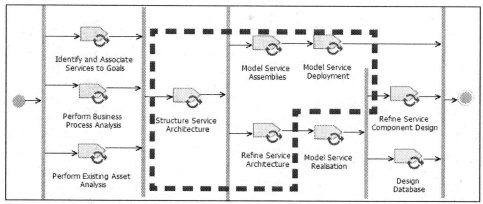

Figure 11-6   The service specification tasks

Service specification consists of making most of the architecturally significant decisions of our design. It mainly consists of architecting our services. For example, it is during service specification that all service consumers, specifications, providers, and partitions are specified in terms of their structure and behavior.

The main input to service specification is the analysis-level **service model** resulting from the service identification activity.

Additional inputs include:

► **Domain model**: Used for the initial structure of the architecture and the service parameter types and message design.

► **System use case model**: Optionally used during service interaction design to determine what behavior is required of the service-oriented (SO) system.

► **Business architecture model:** Used to describe the business architecture context, specifically the business functional areas and the processes and IT systems (including SO systems) that support them.

Task 1: Structure service architecture

This task takes the outputs of service identification (described in Chapter 10, "Service identification" on page 277) and creates a structured service model in preparation for modeling service interactions (described in "Task 2: Refine service architecture" on page 356).

The constituent steps of this task are listed in Figure 11-7. These are described further in this section.

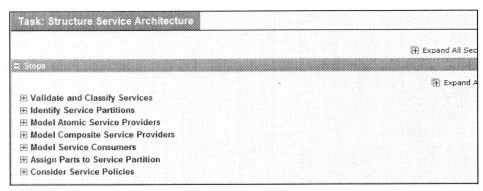

Figure 11-7   Structure service architecture steps

Step 1: Validate and classify services

The first step in structuring the service architecture involves validating and classifying the candidate services created during service identification (see "Output of service identification for JK Enterprises" on page 297).

Validate candidate services

It is always a good idea to validate the input you get from other activities. Although it can be argued that this should be covered by service identification, we start our service specification activity by validating that the identified candidate services are actually services that should be part of our service-oriented architecture.

Also referred to as service litmus test by the IBM Service-Oriented Modeling and Architecture (SOMA) technique, validation includes making sure that all services are:

► **Business-aligned**: All services should be traceable back to a business requirement (for example, goal, sub-goal, or KPI), or business activity from a business process. A very good way to verify business alignment is to ask the business if they would be ready to fund the service through its life cycle!

► **Reusable**: Services and their operations should be generic enough so that they can be used by consumers that were not part of the original requirements. For example: Can a particular service be reused by other functional areas (business components)? Would the service be useful for the projects in plan?

For JK Enterprises, we start by looking at the first criteria, business alignment. In our case, three out of the six identified candidate services are already traced to a business goal or were identified from a business task. Therefore, we only have to look at the other three services, identified from the existing asset analysis (Figure 11-8).

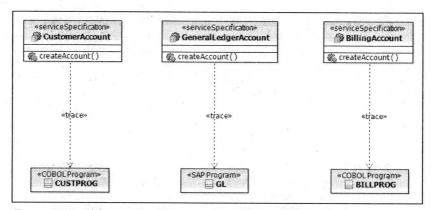

Figure 11-8   Services identified from the existing asset analysis

For example, let us consider the CustomerAccount service specification with the createAccount operation. We talk to the business people that own the JK Enterprises Account Administration business component: They tell us that they had issues with other business entities because the other entities could not create a customer account without manual intervention by someone from Account Administration. They agreed then to fund such a service through its life cycle, as it will help them to mitigate the issues they had with the other entities. This is a very good sign, and we have determined that the CustomerAccount service is business-aligned.

We now consider the reusability criteria for CustomerAccount. We interview people from the JK Enterprises Customer Account business component: They tell us about a project planned for next year that is related to the automation of new account creation. We conclude that the CustomerAccount service is reusable.

Similarly, we study the GeneralLedgerAccount and BillingAccount services and conclude that they are business-aligned and reusable as well.

We indicate that the service specifications are validated by changing the status property from candidate to accepted, which means that they are part of a project.

► Capture this in Software Architect by selecting each of the service specifications, and from the *Stereotypes* tab under Properties, change the value of the status property from *candidate* to *accepted*.

Note that we perform this validation with only a set of service specifications, their operations and descriptions being in plain English, but we also have to perform this test at the end of service specification when the service providers are designed.

Classify services by functional area

In this section we classify services under the functional area that owns them. Ownership here means that functional areas are responsible for meeting services requirements through their life cycle.

Note that in this section, *functional area* is synonymous to *business component*.

The JK Enterprises Component Business Modeling (CBM) map is shown in Figure 11-9.

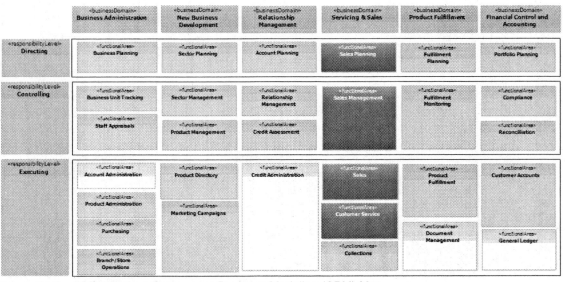

Figure 11-9   JK Enterprises Component Business Modeling (CBM) Map

The list of identified service specifications and operations from the service identification activity is shown in Figure 11-10.

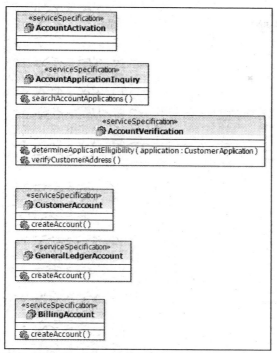

Figure 11-10   List of identified services and their operations

Sales Management was the key functional area being looked at during service identification. However, only a few of the services belong to Sales Management. It would make sense, therefore, if other services were owned by other functional areas.

For JK Enterprises, our classification of services (service specifications) by functional area is as follows:

Sales Management	AccountVerification, AccountApplicationEnquiry
Customer Accounts	AccountActivation, CustomerAccount
Account Administration	BillingAccount
General Ledger	GeneralLedgerAccount

You may have noticed that the Address service does not belong to any of the functional areas. Verifying addresses for existence is not part of what JK Enterprises does and it makes sense for JK Enterprises to use an external service provider for that.

We now describe the initial service model in Software Architect. For the purpose of this exercise, we decided to keep the service model (analysis level) work product, and create a new service model work product. Another option would be to evolve the analysis level work product into a design level work product.

The UML 2 profile for software services (see "UML profile for software services" on page 164) has an associated Service Design Model template, which you can select when you create a UML Modeling project in Software Architect. You get an initial package structure and a set of building blocks (Figure 11-11).

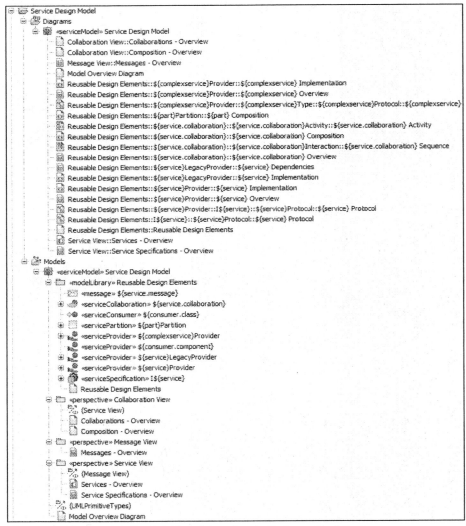

Figure 11-11   Service Design Model template in Software Architect

In our development case, because of the architectural patterns we follow (see "Architectural patterns" on page 74) we do not use the default service design model template, but a different structure, centered on service providers.

We provide the initial structure of the Service Model in the Service Model - Initial Specification model.

▶   In the Software Architect Modeling perspective, open the Service Model - Initial Specification model. Expand the different packages (Figure 11-12).

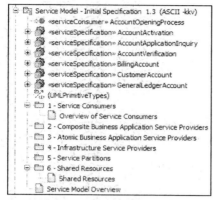

Figure 11-12   Initial service model

As previously described, we made the decision to use service providers as key artifacts to structure our service model around. When we perform the next steps in the structure service architecture task, we structure our service model around service providers. For example, you do not see service specifications, enumerations, info types, messages, or parameter types packages under the initial structure, because these packages will be sub-packages of their service provider packages.

We have created separate packages for the different types of services and service consumers:

▶   Service Consumers
▶   Composite Business Application Service Providers
▶   Atomic Business Application Service Providers
▶   Infrastructure Service Providers
▶   Service Partitions
▶   Shared Resources

We made the decision to keep the analysis-level service model, and create a new model for the (design-level) service model. However, we copied the identified service consumers and specifications from the analysis-level service model into the service model. They are currently at the root of the service model and will be moved to appropriate packages as we perform the next steps in this task.

Note also that we have created diagrams that will be used to provide different views of the service model.

Step 2: Identify service partitions

Now that we have an accepted set of service specifications, the next step involves identifying the service partition (or service partitions) required in our service model. Let us now look at how we use the tool to achieve this task step.

Find the functional areas

We start by examining the functional areas that are in scope. These are modeled in our business architecture model, so let us open this in Rational Software Architect. From the Project Explorer, select the `Business Architecture Model` model, right-click, and select *Open Model*.

Navigate to the `JK Enterprises BusinessArchitectureMap` diagram under `Business Architectures\JK Enterprises\`, and double-click to open the diagram (shown in Figure 11-13).

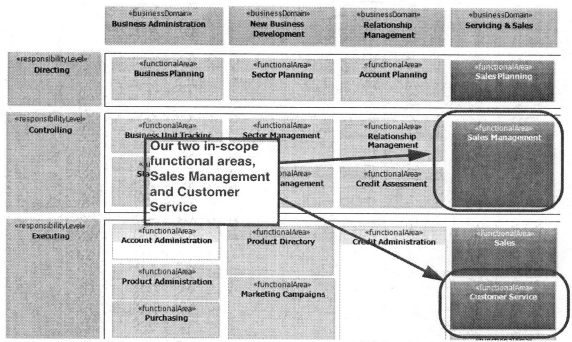

Figure 11-13   A partial view of the business architecture map, highlighting the in-scope functional areas

Our two in-scope functional areas can be seen: `Sales` and `Customer Service`.

Create a service partition for the SO system

A service partition is used in the service model to model the structure of a system made up of service-oriented parts. From "Pattern 5: Manage complexity using SO systems" on page 86, we note that we term an IT system made up of service-oriented parts as an SO system.

From "Pattern 4: Base architecture on business relevant elements" on page 84 we further note that we can look to the business architecture model to see what IT systems have been identified as business relevant. This model defines the various functional areas in the business along with the people, processes and IT systems that support its business function. Note that for the sake of simplicity in our example we assume that there is a single in-scope SO system for each of the functional areas named the same as the functional area.

For each SO system that is in scope, and for which we do not already have one, we create a service partition to represent the structure of each of these SO systems. To do this, let us turn the attention back to the service model that we created during "Step 1: Validate and classify services" on page 308.

In the `Service Model`, navigate to the empty `Service Partitions` package.

Right-click, select *Add UML → Package*. Name the new package `SalesManagement`. This package holds the specification elements of our `SalesManagement` SO system.

Selecting this new package, right-click, *Add UML → Class*. Name the new class `SalesManagement`. Selecting this new class first, select the *Properties* tab, and then the *Stereotypes* section. Click *Apply Stereotypes* and select *servicePartition* from the list (see Figure 11-14).

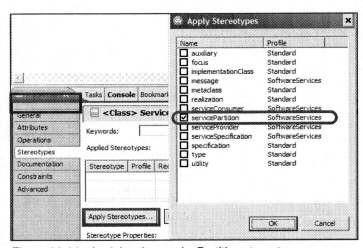

Figure 11-14   Applying the servicePartition stereotype

We have now created a service partition for our `SalesManagement` SO system.

We now trace this back to the functional area that it is based on by creating a *<<derive>>* relationship back to the `SalesManagement` functional area.

Select the `SalesManagement` package and *Add Diagram → Freeform Diagram*. Keep the default name as this is a temporary diagram.

Drag our `SalesManagement` service partition from the Project Explorer into the diagram. Drag the `SalesManagement` functional area from the Project Explorer into the same diagram (it lives in `BusinessArchitectureModel\Business Functional Areas\`).

Hover the mouse over the `SalesManagement` service partition in the diagram until the drag-arrows appear. Click the arrow pointing away from the service partition and drag the line to the `SalesManagement` functional area. Select *Create Derive* from the menu (Figure 11-15).

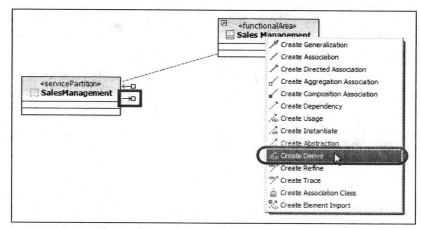

Figure 11-15 Creating the <<derive>> relationship

Now that the <<derive>> relationship has been created, you can delete the temporary freeform diagram.

You can verify that the relationship is there by selecting the SalesManagement service partition in the Project Explorer and *Visualize → Explore in Browse Diagram*. You should see a browse diagram appear as shown in Figure 11-16.

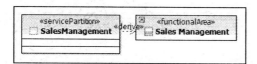

Figure 11-16 Using the browse diagram feature in Rational Software Architect

Create an empty SOA structure diagram

Let us now prepare an empty SOA structure diagram for us to add our service architecture parts to later.

Select the service partition and *Add Diagram → Composite Structure Diagram* (Figure 11-17). Name the diagram SalesManagement SOAStructure.

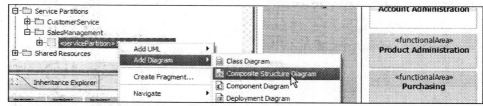

Figure 11-17 Adding an empty SOA structure diagram

Open the diagram. Add four horizontal sections to the diagram to represent the standard sections to our service architecture:

► Service consumers
► Composite business application services
► Atomic business application services
► Infrastructure services

The horizontal layers can be added using the *Geometric Shapes* section in the palette. Select *Rectangle* from the *Rectangle Types* drop-down. The diagram should be made to look like Figure 11-18.

The rationale behind what goes into each of these layers is described by "Pattern 1: Factor composition logic away from process logic" on page 76, "Pattern 2: Factor atomic reusable logic into lower reuse layers" on page 79, and "Pattern 3: Factor application-specific logic out of reuse layers" on page 81.

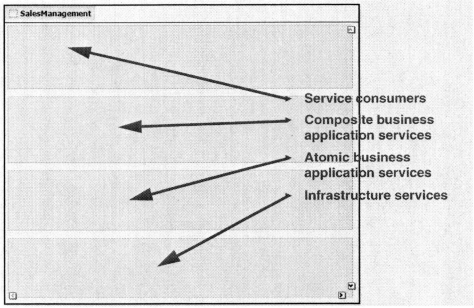

Figure 11-18 Empty SOA structure diagram with four sections

Create a service partition and diagram for the CustomerService SO system

Repeat the same steps to create a service partition and empty SOA structure diagram for the `CustomerService` SO system.

Let us look at what we have now. Figure 11-19 shows us our service model with the two new service partitions added, along with their SOA structure diagrams.

Figure 11-19   Service model with empty service partitions added for each SO system

Step 3: Model atomic service providers

Having identified our SO systems and created service partitions for them, we need service architectural elements to add as parts to these service partitions (see discussion in "Different forms of a service" on page 49). Specifically, we must have service consumers and service providers.

We start by looking at the atomic service providers.

To recap, these come in two different type depending on the services they provide:

► Atomic business application services
► Infrastructure services

In this section we focus on service providers that provide atomic business application services.

First we note the guidance provided by the architectural patterns defined in "Architectural patterns" on page 74.

The following two patterns describe factoring rules to adhere to when defining the atomic service providers:

► "Pattern 2: Factor atomic reusable logic into lower reuse layers" on page 79
► "Pattern 3: Factor application-specific logic out of reuse layers" on page 81

The next two patterns describe how to derive these service providers and to model their data ownership:

► "Pattern 6: Derive atomic services from domain model" on page 89
► "Pattern 8: Model data ownership" on page 94

Let us now look at how we use the tool to achieve this task step.

Study the domain model

First we open the domain model. Select `Domain Model` model and *Open Model*.

Navigate to the `ServicingAndSales Domain` diagram (`Domain Model\Domain Packages\ServicingAndSales\`) and open it. You should have a diagram as shown in Figure 11-20.

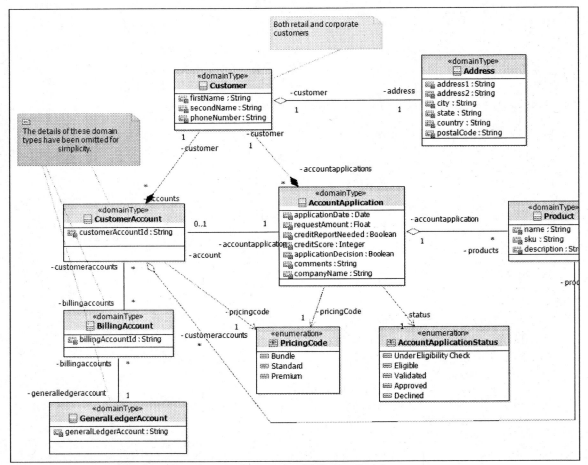

Figure 11-20   *SalesAndServicing domain diagram for JK Enterprises*

Note that this domain model describes the business *things* that exist in the scope of `SalesAndServicing` domain. It is possible that not everything in this domain is in scope for the SOA solution that we are building. But we do not worry about that for the moment. The important thing is that it provides a visual representation of the structure of the information that is important in this domain.

First we make sure that we have reflected aggregation in our domain model because this can provide useful information about the nature of the relationships between the domain type. Examining the domain diagram in Figure 11-20 we make some changes:

▶ The association between AccountApplication and Customer should be a composite aggregation as an instance of a customer is part of the instance of a customer account.

▶ The same holds true for the association between CustomerAccount and Customer. Note that it is a composite aggregation, because it has its own instance of Customer, a separate instance from the snapshot that is a part of the AccountApplication.

▶ The association between Customer and Address should be a shared aggregation as an instance of a customer would have an instance of an address as a part of it. However more than one instance of customer can be related to the same Address.

▶ The association between AccountApplication and Product should be a shared aggregation as an instance of an account application would have one or more instances of product as a part of it. However more than one instance of account application can be related to the same product.

▶ Again, the same holds true for the association between CustomerAccount and Product.

We can see the changes that have been made encircled in Figure 11-21.

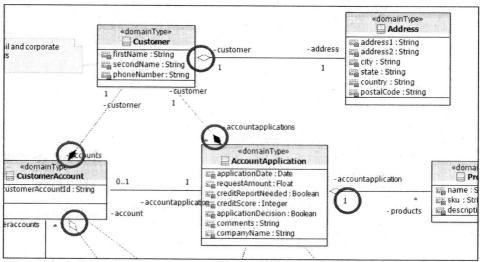

Figure 11-21   Changes made to association aggregation

Derive atomic services from domain model

Note: One may argue that what is described in this section belongs to service identification (we are actually identifying services). However, because the work involved is at the design level (as opposed to the analysis level), we describe it as part of the service specification activity.

Next we identify those domain types that our SOA solution needs to manipulate some persistent state (in other words, data instances).

Let us go through this list one-by-one:

► `CustomerAccount`: We know we care about data instances of `CustomerAccount` as we are already storing instance of this domain type in the COBOL program identified during existing asset analysis.

► `AccountApplication`: At first it may not be clear as to whether we have to store `AccountApplications`. We ask someone representing the `SalesAndServicing` domain for clarification and they tell us that we have to store `AccountApplications` during the application and review process as this can go on for quite some time. Additionally they must have a process for dealing with inquiries on account applications, even after the application has been accepted or rejected.

► `Product`: We know we have to include a reference to products in the `AccountApplications` that we have determined that we have to persist, so for the moment we can assume that we have to persist products as well.

► `BillingAccount`: The same argument holds as did for `CustomerAccount` as we identified that billing accounts are currently stored in a COBOL existing asset.

► `GeneralLedgerAccount`: Again, the same argument holds as did for `CustomerAccount` as general ledger accounts are currently stored in a SAP existing asset.

► `Address`: `Addresses` are a special case as we know that we require at least three types of address data instances:

1. We need access to a set of address data instances that describe the set of possible addresses for validation purposes. When we receive an account application, it contains a description of the customer and related address. This address has to be validated to verify that it is a real and correct address.

2. We have to store the customer address received with an account application.

3. For those account applications that are successful we continue to create a customer account for the customer which includes the customer address.

So for now we accept that we are interested in address state in our solution.

► Customer: Although we are interested in storing information about customers, we note that this is done as part of storing information of both customer accounts and account applications. Therefore we do not store any information about customers separate from these two domain types.

Note that the enumerations defined on the diagram are excluded from our list for consideration as they only exist to provide a set of possible values to type attributes on our domain types, and therefore do not have data instances themselves. This is always true of enumerations.

We now do a simple one-to-one mapping, creating a service specification for each of the in-scope domain types for our SOA solution. This gives us the following list:

► Address <<serviceSpecification>>
► CustomerAccount <<serviceSpecification>>
► BillingAccount <<serviceSpecification>>
► GeneralLedgerAccount <<serviceSpecification>>
► AccountApplication <<serviceSpecification>>
► Product <<serviceSpecification>>

We note that CustomerAccount, BillingAccount, and GeneralLedgerAccount already exist in our service model as they were identified during "Perform existing asset analysis" on page 292, as part of the service identification activity.

> **Note:** As an aside, you may think it fortunate that the names used when identifying these service specifications exactly match our domain model. This is not a coincidence! The domain model should become your primary point-of-reference for names of things that exist in the business. And indeed, when the existing assets were considered and we had to name the services that would represent them, the question asked was "which of our domain types do these existing assets manage data instances of?" If there is no matching domain type, one should be added at this point as in this case you have found a hole in the domain model (in other words, there is some significant business thing not described in the domain model).

As these three service specifications already exist in our model, all we have to do is create service specifications for the remaining three. Note that for the moment we add these to the root of the service model with the other service specifications—they are moved later on.

Let us start with Address. Select *Add UML → Class* and name the class Address.Add the <<serviceSpecification>> stereotype to this new class. Repeat this for AccountApplication and Product.

Identify domain type encapsulation clusters

Now that we have a set of atomic business application services, we have to define the service providers that provide these services. To scope these, we consider the *encapsulation boundaries* that we want (or are forced into choosing).

What do we mean when we talk about encapsulation boundaries here?

► Specifically we are interested in ownership of data instances. For any given data instance we assign ownership of it to a single service provider in our architecture. And therefore we say that for a given service provider, the data instances that it owns are <u>inside</u> its encapsulation boundary while any other data instances are <u>outside</u>. Any access to the data instances inside a service providers encapsulation boundary can only be via the services provided by that service provider.

► Note that if two services are provided by the same service provider, we allow their implementations shared access to the data instances owned by that service provider. In contrast, if the services were on separate service providers, then they would each have to go through the other service to access its state.

There are two factors to consider when determining encapsulation boundaries:

► What encapsulation boundaries are desirable?
► What encapsulation boundaries are forced on us?

We define domain type clusters on our domain diagram to determine our encapsulation boundaries. See Figure 11-22 for the finished artifact for our example where the domain type clusters have been super-imposed.

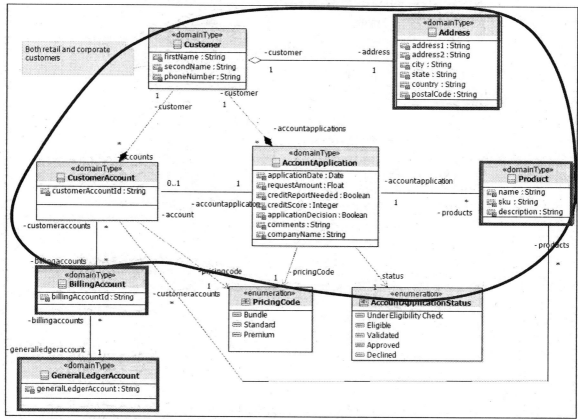

Figure 11-22 Defining encapsulation boundaries using domain type clusters

The reasoning behind creating these domain type clusters is as follows:

► As a starting point, we place each core domain type in its own domain type cluster.

► The data instances of GeneralLedgerAccount, BillingAccount and CustomerAccount are all owned by individual existing assets. In our example we have just a single domain type owned by each. However note that if, for example, we had a domain type called Posting that was also in-scope for our solution, then it would have to be included in the same domain cluster as GeneralLedgerAccount as we have to assume that all state owned by the COBOL asset is shared, and therefore should be in one domain type cluster.

► CustomerAccount and AccountApplication are closely related. In fact an AccountApplication turns into a CustomerAccount (although note that we still have to keep our AccountApplication snapshot in this case). We say that they have a high affinity with each other and should be included in the same domain type cluster.

► Further we note that instances of `Address` form a part of instances of `Customer`, and instances of `Customer` form part of either CustomerAccount or `AccountApplication`. Because of this we expand our domain type cluster to include these as well.

► In the same way, instances of `Product` form a part of instances of `AccountApplication` and instances of `CustomerAccount` so we include them in the same domain type cluster.

► As well as forming part of instances of `Customer`, instances of `Address` have their own life span as we have to keep track of the set of allowed `Addresses` as well as snapshots of `Address` as used to describe the address of a customer. Therefore we create a new domain type cluster around `Address`.

► `Product` also appears in its own domain type cluster.

We now have the following five domain type clusters describing our encapsulation boundaries. We have noted in parenthesis the domain core types:

1. Customer, (CustomerAccount), (AccountApplication), Address, Product
2. (BillingAccount)
3. (GeneralLedgerAccount)
4. (Address)
5. (Product)

Identify a service provider for each domain type encapsulation cluster

For each of the domain type clusters, identify the core domain type in the cluster. We underline these in the list above to get:

1. Customer, (<u>CustomerAccount</u>), (AccountApplication), Address, Product
2. (<u>BillingAccount</u>)
3. (<u>GeneralLedgerAccount</u>)
4. (<u>Address</u>)
5. (<u>Product</u>)

It is now a simple one-to-one mapping from our underlined domain types to the set of service providers. As a naming convention, we append Mgr (for Manager) to the end each of the above to get names for our service providers. As is implied by this name, the service provider manages the domain type that it is named after (along with the related set of domain types in the same domain type cluster). Our resulting list of atomic business application service providers is:

- ▶ `CustomerAccountMgr <<serviceProvider>>`
- ▶ `BillingAccountMgr <<serviceProvider>>`
- ▶ `GeneralLedgerAccountMgr <<serviceProvider>>`
- ▶ `AddressMgr <<serviceProvider>>`
- ▶ `ProductMgr <<serviceProvider>>`

Create service providers along with standard package structure and diagrams

> **Note:** In this example there are no atomic service providers that already exist. If previous SOA projects had delivered solutions that had already produced atomic service providers in the same domain, then some of the service providers that we require would already exist and we would most likely be adding to them.
>
> The topic of reuse as it is relevant to this case is described in "Reusing architecture and design experience" on page 73.

We start with the `CustomerAccountMgr`:

- ▶ In the `Service Model\3 - Atomic Business Application Service Providers\` package, create a new package (right-click, *Add UML → Package*) and name it `CustomerAccountMgr`. This is the package that holds all the UML model elements and diagrams for the `CustomerAccountMgr`.

- ▶ Rename the `Main` diagram (created by default) to `CustomerAccountMgr ServiceProviderSpec`. This diagram is our service provider specification diagram (see Figure 9-8 on page 256).

- ▶ In this new package select *Add UML → Component* and name it `CustomerAccountMgr`. Apply the `<<serviceProvider>>` stereotype to it. This model element represents our `CustomerAccountMgr` service provider.

- ▶ Create a `<<derive>>` relationship to the domain type that the service provider is derived from (and named from). An example of how to do this was provided in "Classify services by functional area" on page 310.

- ▶ Drag the `CustomerAccountMgr` element onto the `CustomerAccountMgr ServiceProviderSpec` diagram.

- ▶ Create the remaining standard packages and empty freeform diagrams as shown in Figure 11-23.

Figure 11-23   Standard package structure and diagrams applied to the provider

We do the same for each of the remaining identified service providers: BillingAccountMgr, GeneralLedgerAccountMgr, AddressMgr, and ProductMgr. The result is in the Service Model - Structure Service Architecture (1).

In Software Architect, and under the Modeling perspective, open the Service Model - Structure Service Architecture (1), and explore its packages, model elements, and diagrams in the Project Explorer (Figure 11-24).

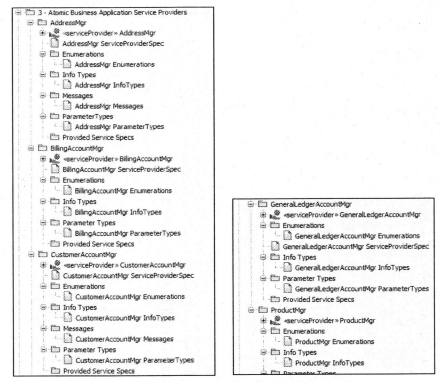

Figure 11-24   Service Model - Structure Service Architecture (1)

Match up service specifications with the service providers

Our list that we created in the previous step allows us to do this easily:

1. Customer, (CustomerAccount), (AccountApplication), Address, Product
2. (BillingAccount)
3. (GeneralLedgerAccount)
4. (Address)
5. (Product)

The service specification that matches each core domain type (in parenthesis) is assigned to the service provider that was identified from the domain type cluster that it lives in.

This results in the mapping between service providers and service specifications:

Service provider	Service specifications
CustomerAccountMgr	CustomerAccount, AccountApplication
BillingAccountMgr	BillingAccount
GeneralLedgerAccountMgr	GeneralLedgerAccount
AddressMgr	Address
ProductMgr	Product

In line with this mapping, we now have to move the service specifications so that they are under the package of the service provider that it has been mapped to. Let us do this for the CustomerAccount service specification:

▶ Open the Service Model - Structure Service Architecture (1) model.

▶ Create a new package called CustomerAccount under the Service Model\3 - Atomic Business Application Service Providers\CustomerAccountMgr \Provided Service Specs\ package.

▶ Rename the default Main diagram to CustomerAccount ServiceSpecification. This diagram is our service specification diagram for the CustomerAccount service specification (see "Diagram: Service specification diagram" on page 253).

▶ Move the CustomerAccount service specification to this new package, and then drag the CustomerAccount service specification from the Project Explorer onto the service specification diagram.

We do the same for the remaining service specifications: `AccountApplication`, `BillingAccount`, `GeneralLedgerAccount`, `Address`, `Product`. The result is in the Service Model - Structure Service Architecture (2) model.

Open the Service Model - Structure Service Architecture (2), and explore its packages, model elements, and diagrams in the Project Explorer (Figure 11-25).

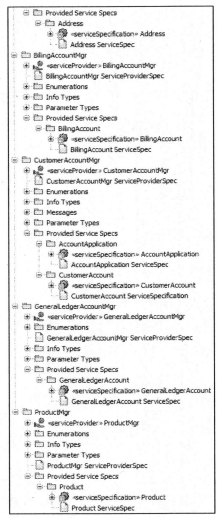

Figure 11-25   Service Model - Structure Service Architecture (2)

Model services for the service providers

The magical link between a service provider and the service specifications that it exposes is provided by services (see "Model element: Service" on page 242). Here we explain how to create these for atomic services, using the `AccountApplication` service specification on the `CustomerAccountMgr` service provider as our example:

► Open the Service Model - Structure Service Architecture (2) model.

► Select the `CustomerAccountMgr` service provider and *Add UML → Port*. Select *Select Existing Element* and then type `AccountApplication` in the search box shown (Figure 11-26). Make sure you select the `AccountApplication` service specification that is owned by the `CustomerAccountMgr`.

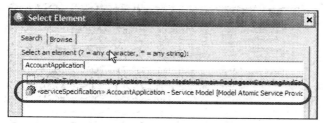

Figure 11-26   Selecting the AccountApplication service specification to type the service

► Rename the port that gets created to be `AccountApplicationService`. Apply the `<<service>>` stereotype.

Do the same for the remaining service specification/service provider combinations:

Service provider	Service specification	Service
CustomerAccountMgr	CustomerAccount	CustomerAccountService
BillingAccountMgr	BillingAccount	BillingAccountService
GeneralLedgerAccountMgr	GeneralLedgerAccount	GeneralLedgerAccountService
AddressMgr	Address	AddressService
ProductMgr	Product	ProductService

Model info types for the service providers

As per "Pattern 8: Model data ownership" on page 94 we model the data owned by each of our atomic business application service providers using info types.

Info types are described in "Model element: Information type" on page 246.

Let us use the `CustomerMgr` service provider as an example.

We refer back to the domain type clusters drawn in Figure 11-10 on page 311. The domain type cluster from which we derived the encapsulation boundary for the `CustomerMgr` service provider contains the following domain types:

- ► `Customer`
- ► `AccountApplication`
- ► `CustomerAccount`
- ► `Product`
- ► `Address`

Before we create info types for these, we note that we require local copies of the `PricingCode` and `AccountApplicationStatus` enumerations. Using the Project Explorer, copy these from the `Domain Model\Domain Packages \ServicingAndSales` package to the `Service Model\3 - Atomic Business Application Service Providers\CustomerAccountMgr\Enumerations\` package.

Now, for each of the domain types listed above, we want to create an equivalent info type in the `Service Model\3 - Atomic Business Application Service Providers\CustomerAccountMgr\Info Types\` package. The easiest way to do this is to copy across the domain types and modify those so we do this. Make sure you do this as a single copy action with all of the types selected otherwise the info types have relationships back to the domain types in the domain model.

Once you have copied across the domain types, you have to make three modifications:

- ► First you have to change their stereotype from <<domainType>> to <<infoType>>.

- ► Then you must replace any references to the enumerations in the domain model with references to the corresponding copies in the `CustomerAccountMgr` enumerations package.

- ► Next, in the Project Explorer, find the `Product` info type that you have created and delete its sku and description attributes. This is done because the full view of a product is not stored in the `CustomerAccountMgr`. We only store the names of products that appear on account applications and customer accounts. Note that the `ProductMgr` owns the full view of products.

Once you have done this, open the `CustomerAccountMgr` information diagram and drag the info types onto it. With a bit of rearranging you should arrive at Figure 11-27.

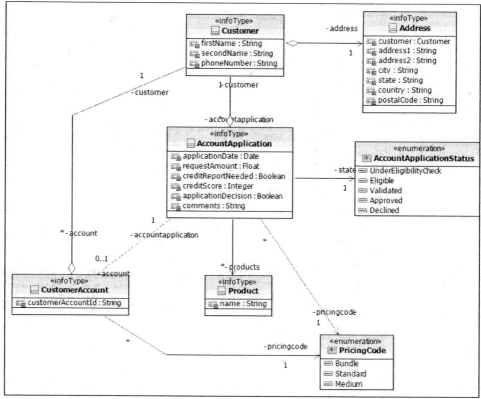

Figure 11-27   CustomerAccountMgr information diagram

Let us look at what we have now. In the Project Explorer, we should now have a set of model artifacts as shown in Figure 11-28 (with detail showed for only the CustomerAccountMgr service provider).

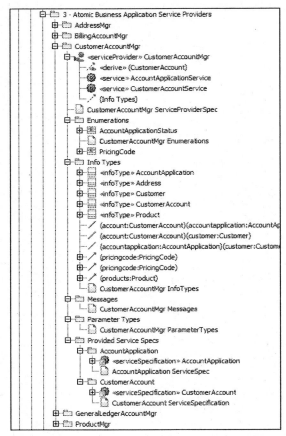

Figure 11-28   Service model with atomic business application service providers added

We do the same for the other atomic business application service providers. The result is provided in the Service Model - Structure Service Architecture (3) model.

Step 4: Model composite service providers

Next we model our composite business application service providers.

To recap, these are service providers that provide services which make use of other services in providing their specified behavior.

First we note the guidance provided by the architectural patterns defined in "Architectural patterns" on page 74.

The following two patterns describe factoring rules to adhere to when defining the composite service providers:

- ▶ "Pattern 1: Factor composition logic away from process logic" on page 76
- ▶ "Pattern 3: Factor application-specific logic out of reuse layers" on page 81

Let us now look at how we use the tool to achieve this task step.

Identify the processes and functional areas

As noted in "Business process model" on page 189, the following two business processes are in scope for our solution:

- ▶ Account Opening
- ▶ Account Application Inquiry

Armed with the business architecture model (and specifically the business architecture map—Figure 11-9 on page 310), we inquire of the business process analyst as to who the owners are of these processes, and we are told that:

- ▶ The Account Opening process is owned by the SalesManagement functional area.
- ▶ The Account Application Inquiry process is owned by the CustomerService functional area.

Find the sub-processes and locate the services for them

Next we consult the business process models in WebSphere Business Modeler to see what the sub-processes are for each of these processes.

Taking the account opening process as an example, we find the process diagram shown in Figure 11-29.

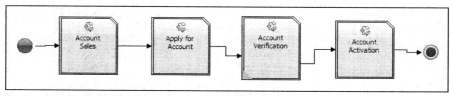

Figure 11-29   Account Opening business process

From here we can see that the sub-processes are Account Sales, Apply for Account, Account Verification and Account Activation. Of these four, we know that only Account Activation and Account Verification are in scope for our project.

Taking a look in the root of our service model, this is verified by the fact that those are the only two of the sub-processes for which we already have identified service specifications (Figure 11-30). To recap, we have a composite business application service for business sub-processes (refer to "Pattern 4: Base architecture on business relevant elements" on page 84, factoring rule 3).

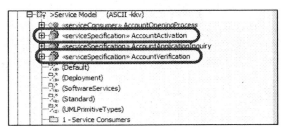

Figure 11-30   Existing service specifications in the root of our service model

Note that we are working on the Service Model - Structure Service Architecture (3) model at this stage.

Note that the remaining service specification in Figure 11-30 (`AccountApplicationInquiry`) corresponds to a sub-process in the `AccountApplicationInquiry` process, and was identified during the service identification activity.

Identify a composite service provider for each SO system

As we have determined that the processes that are in scope are owned by the `SalesManagement` and `CustomerService` functional areas, we look to see what SO systems in those areas we have to support behavior for. This detail will normally be defined in a use case model where you will have captured system use cases for each of the SO systems for which some behavior is required.

Now create a composite service provider for each of these SO systems (note that for the sake of simplicity in our example there is a single service-oriented IT system for each of our functional areas that is named the same as the functional area):

► `SalesManagementComposite` <<serviceProvider>>

► `CustomerServiceComposite` <<serviceProvider>>

Create service providers along with standard package structure and diagrams

> **Note:** In this example there are no composite service providers that already exist. If previous SOA projects had delivered solutions that had already touched one of the functional areas and SO systems that we touch on here, then the service providers would already exist and we would most likely be adding to them.
>
> The topic of reuse as it is relevant to this case is described in "Services and reuse" on page 62.

We follow the same procedure as in Step 3: Model atomic service providers ("Create service providers along with standard package structure and diagrams" on page 327). Apply these instructions to the list of service providers above. We note four modifications to the instructions:

► The service providers we create in this step should go under `Service Model\2 - Composite Business Application Service Providers\` instead of `Service Model\3 - Atomic Business Application Service Providers\`.

► When creating the sub-packages, do not create an `Info Types` package because we do not model info types for composite business application service providers as they do not own any state.

► When creating the sub-packages, create a `Composite Service Specs` package.

► Instead of creating a `<<derive>>` relationship to a domain type, the `<<derive>>` relationship should link the service provider to the functional area that it was derived from (note that these exist in `Business Architecture Model\Business Functional Areas\`).

By way of example, we show the result for the `SalesManagementComposite` in Figure 11-31.

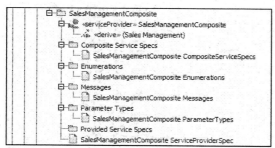

Figure 11-31   Package structure and diagrams for SalesManagementComposite

Match up service specifications with the service providers

We now have to decide what services to expose from each of our composite service providers. As our composite services providers have been based on SO systems and the services that we are considering have been based on sub-processes, we do this by matching the sub-processes to SO systems.

This is done by taking the process diagrams for our two in-scope processes (account opening and account application inquiry) and reviewing them with their relevant process owners (as noted previously). What we have to determine is which SO systems mainly support each of the sub-processes. The owning SO system for each sub-process should be annotated onto each sub-process.

In our example the mapping turns out to be as follows:

Service provider	Service specifications
SalesManagementComposite	AccountActivation, AccountVerification
CustomerServiceComposite	AccountApplicationInquiry

The resulting service model at this stage is provided in Service Model - Structure Service Architecture (4).

Model services for the service providers

This sub-step is a bit different to what we did for our atomic business application services. This is because an atomic service is only related to a provided service specification whereas for a composite service it additionally needs to be related to the service specifications that it requires.

First we have to determine which service specifications are required for each of our composite services.

To start it is important for us to point out that you will only know for sure which service specifications are require once you have completed your service interaction modeling (as described in "Step 2: Design service interactions" on page 359). However we take a stab at it now as it makes it easier to draw the service interactions, and use them to refine our decisions.

To perform the mapping, we have to look at two things:

1. The list of composite services needed along with the service operations from their provided service specifications.

We identify a new composite service for each of the service specifications listed in the previous sub-step, and note the service operations for each composite service.

Composite service	Composite service operations
AccountActivation	activateAccount()
AccountVerification	determineApplicantEligibility() verifyCustomerAddress()
AccountApplicationInquiry	searchAccountApplications()

2. The list of atomic service specifications to choose from (these all come from "Step 3: Model atomic service providers" on page 319):

   — Address
   — BillingAccount
   — CustomerAccount
   — AccountApplication
   — GeneralLedgerAccount
   — Product

We now have to achieve a mapping between our composite service operations to the atomic services they require. Note this is quite a *rough* mapping as the composite service operations actually have to be mapped to atomic service operations. This will be done when we model our service interactions.

A simple mapping is achieved by considering the composite service operations one at a time, looking at what business logic or data instances are needed to support its behavior, and then taking a stab at which atomic service that business logic or data instance is owned by. Not much more science to it than that at this stage.

Further hints that would help us do this can be found by looking at the system use case that matches the service operation (as we do in more detail later when modeling our service interactions) and also by consulting the information diagrams for each of our atomic business application service providers (these were created in "Step 3: Model atomic service providers" on page 319, see the "Model info types for the service providers" sub-step).

The mapping of the composite services is complete (Table 11-1).

Table 11-1   Mapping of composite services

Composite service	Composite service operations	Atomic service specifications
AccountActivation	activateAccount()	BillingAccount, CustomerAccount, GeneralLedgerAccount
AccountVerification	determineApplicantEligibility()	AccountApplication
AccountVerification	verifyCustomerAddress()	Address
AccountApplication Inquiry	searchAccountApplications()	AccountApplication

We capture each row in this table in our model in the form of a composite service specification (see "Model element: Composite service specification" on page 243).

Let us use the AccountActivation composite service as an example:

► Navigate to the Service Model\2 - Composite Business Application Service Providers\SalesManagementComposite\Composite Service Specs\ package.

► Select *Add UML* → *Class*. Name the class AccountActivationCompServSpec and set the keyword of the class to <<compositeServiceSpec>> (Figure 11-32).

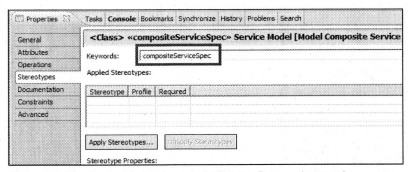

Figure 11-32   Setting the <<compositeServiceSpec>> keyword

► Place this class on the SalesManagementComposite CompositeServiceSpecs diagram.

► From the Project Explorer, drag the AccountActivation service specification onto the same diagram. Then drag the three atomic service specifications onto the diagram as per the mapping table (Table 11-1).

- ▶ Draw an <Interface Realization> between AccountActivationCompServSpec and AccountActivation.
- ▶ Draw a <Usage> relationship between AccountActivationCompServSpec and each of the required service specifications. This should result in Figure 11-33.

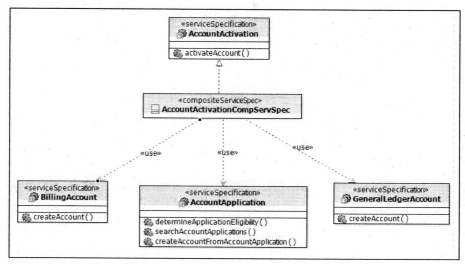

Figure 11-33 AccountActivationCompServSpec and its service specifications

Now that we have our composite service specifications, we go on to create the composite services using them:

- ▶ Select the SalesManagementComposite service provider and *Add UML → Port*. Choose *Select Existing Element* and type AccountActivationCompServSpec in the search box shown. Make sure you select the service specification that is owned by the SalesManagementComposite.

- ▶ Note that when we did this for the atomic services, we selected a service specification (based on an interface) to type the port. Now we use a composite service specification (based on a class) instead.

- ▶ Rename the port that gets created to be AccountActivationService. Apply the <<service>> stereotype.

Do the same for the remaining service specification/service provider combinations as shown in Table 11-2.

Table 11-2   Service specification to service provider mapping

Service provider	Service specification	Service
SalesManagement Composite	AccountVerification	AccountVerificationService
CustomerService Composite	AccountApplication Inquiry	AccountApplicationInquiryService

Let us look at what we have now.

Looking in the Project Explorer, we should now have a set of model artifacts as shown in Figure 11-34 (with detail showed for only the SalesManagementComposite service provider).

Figure 11-34   Service model with composite business application service providers

Similarly, we design the other composite service specifications. At the end, we have:

► AccountActivationCompServSpec (Figure 11-33)
► AccountVerificationCompServSpec (Figure 11-35)
► AccountApplicationInquiryCompServSpec (Figure 11-36)

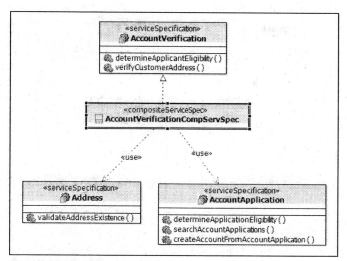

Figure 11-35   AccountVerificationCompServSpec

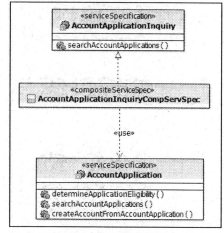

Figure 11-36   AccountApplicationInquiryCompServSpec

The resulting service model at this stage is provided with `Service Model - Structure Service Architecture (5)`.

Step 5: Model service consumers

Having modeled the service providers that appear in our service architecture, we move our attention to the consumers of the services that we have defined.

First we note the guidance provided by the architectural patterns defined in "Architectural patterns" on page 74. Two relevant patterns are:

- ► "Pattern 4: Base architecture on business relevant elements" on page 84, factoring rule 2
- ► "Pattern 12: Drive applications using business processes" on page 101

Let us now look at how we use the tool to achieve this task step.

Locate the processes identified previously

This is easy to do. They were described in "Step 4: Model composite service providers" on page 334. The two processes that we are interested in are:

- ► Account opening
- ► Account application inquiry

Identify a service consumer for each process

As suggested in "Pattern 4: Base architecture on business relevant elements" on page 84 and "Pattern 12: Drive applications using business processes" on page 101, we identify a single service consumer for each of our business processes. This gives us the following two service consumers:

- ► AccountOpeningProcess <<serviceConsumer>>
- ► AccountApplicationInquiryProcess <<serviceConsumer>>

> **Note:** In this example there are no service consumers that already exist. If previous SOA projects had delivered solutions that had already touched the same business processes, then the service consumers would already exist and we would most likely be adding to them.
>
> The topic of reuse as it is relevant to this case is described in "Reusing architecture and design experience" on page 73.

Let us use the AccountOpeningProcess as an example.

In the Service Model\1 - Service Consumers\ package, create a new package (select *Add UML → Package*) and name it AccountOpeningProcess. This is the package that holds all the UML model elements and diagrams for the AccountOpeningProcess.

Rename the `Main` diagram (created by default) to `AccountOpeningProcess ServiceConsumerSpec`. This diagram is our service consumer specification diagram (see "Diagram: Service consumer specification diagram" on page 254). Open the diagram and drag the `AccountOpeningProcess` from the Project Explorer into it.

In this new package select *Add UML → Component* and name it `AccountOpeningProcess`. Apply the `<<serviceConsumer>>` stereotype to it. This model element represents our `AccountOpeningProcess` service consumer.

Do the same for the `AccountApplicationInquiryProcess`.

Model the required service specifications for the service consumer

Determining the required service specifications for each of our service consumers is now very easy. All the work was done in "Step 4: Model composite service providers" on page 334. From this we know:

1. What the in-scope sub-processes are for each of our processes.
2. What composite services provide automation support for these sub-processes (these are the services that have the same names as our sub-processes and which are exposed by our composite business application service providers).

All we have to do is to create the appropriate links in the tool. These are summarized below.

Service consumer	Required service specifications
`AccountOpeningProcess`	`AccountActivation,` `AccountVerification`
`AccountApplicationInquiryProcess`	`AccountApplicationInquiry`

Let s use the `AccountOpeningProcess` as an example:

► Open the `AccountOpeningProcess ServiceConsumerSpec` diagram. It should already have the `AccountOpeningProcess` service consumer on it. From the Project Explorer, drag the `AccountActivation` and `AccountVerification` service specifications (these can be found in the corresponding sub packages within the `Service Model\2 - Composite Business Application Service Providers\SalesManagementComposite\Provided Service Specs\` package) into the same diagram.

▶ Then draw <Usage> between the AccountOpeningProcess and the two required service specifications. The result is shown in Figure 11-37.

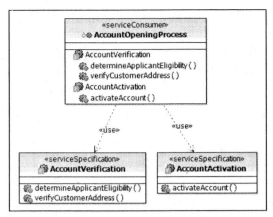

Figure 11-37   AccountOpeningProcess service consumer and its service specifications

Let us look at what we have now. In the Project Explorer we should now have a set of model artifacts as shown in Figure 11-38.

Figure 11-38   Service model with service consumers added

The resulting service model at this stage is provided with Service Model - Structure Service Architecture (6).

Step 6: Assign parts to service partition

Having modeled the various bits and pieces that form a part of our service architecture, we now model how all these things fit together!

To reiterate what the purpose of the current task is, we took in an unstructured service model as input and we want to produce a service model that is structured and ready for further refinement. Note that the structure we produce in this task is a straw man or candidate architecture, which is verified and refined during the task "Task 2: Refine service architecture" on page 356. So in this task we are capturing an initial idea as to what the service architecture looks like.

Let us quickly recapitulate what we have so far (Figure 11-39):

► A set of service consumers, one for each of our business processes

► A set of composite business application service providers, one for each of our SO systems, and each exposing the service specifications identified for the sub-processes that they support

► A set of atomic business application service providers that have been derived from the domain model, specifically supporting those domain types for which our solution is interested in data instances

► Two SO system (identified from the business architecture model) and a service partition for each one of these

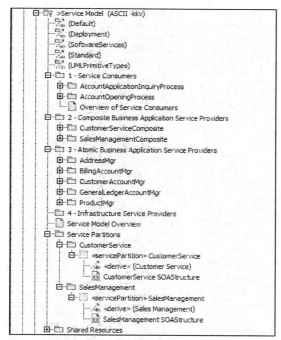

Figure 11-39   Service model so far...

Note that we are now working with Service Model - Structure Service Architecture (6).

Before we go any further, we note the following relevant architectural pattern:

► "Pattern 5: Manage complexity using SO systems" on page 86

Let us now look at how we use the tool to achieve this task step.

Allocate composite business application services to the service partitions

Let us start with the SalesManagement SO system. We model its structure by adding detail to the SalesManagement service partition.

To do this, we open the SalesManagement SOAStructure diagram. Note that it is empty at the moment as shown in Figure 11-18 on page 318.

We start adding parts to this diagram (and therefore the service partition representing the SO system) by dragging on service consumers and service providers from the Project Explorer:

► We start with the easiest first, the composite service provider. To verify which composite service provider we require for the service partition, we make use of the Browse Diagram functionality in Rational Software Architect.

► In the Project Explorer, select the SalesManagement service partition and *Visualize → Explore in Browse Diagram*.

► Set the degrees of separation to 2 using the diagram controls at the top (see Figure 11-40). Then click *Apply.*

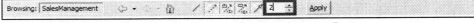

Figure 11-40 Setting the degrees of separation on a browse diagram

► The resulting diagram is shown in Figure 11-41.

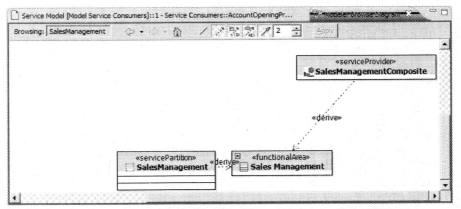

Figure 11-41 Browse diagram for the SalesManagement service partition

From this diagram we can deduce that the service provider that provides composite services to support the sub-processes owned by the `SalesManagement` functional area is the `SalesManagementComposite` service provider.

Therefore, using the Project Explorer, we select the `SalesManagementComposite` service provider and drag it onto our SOA structure diagram resulting in Figure 11-42.

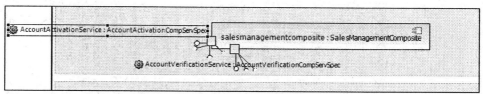

Figure 11-42   Drag-and-drop of the SalesManagementComposite service provider

The first thing we do is clean this up a bit. We resize the text box that the service name appears in, and rearrange the services themselves to give a result that looks more like Figure 11-43.

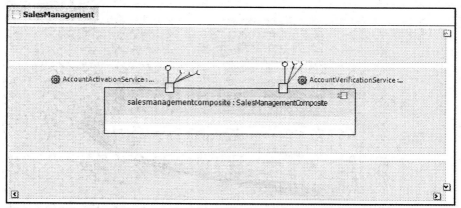

Figure 11-43   Cleaned-up result of the SalesManagement service partition

Allocate service consumers to the service partitions

To determine which service consumer to place on our diagram, we have to know which processes own the sub-processes that correspond to the composite services that we have placed on the diagram. In our example the composite services are the `AccountActivationService` and the `AccountVerificationService`, meaning that the corresponding sub-processes are `AccountActivation` and `AccountVerification`. These are both part of the account opening process, which means that the service consumer we should be using is the `AccountOpeningProcess` service consumer.

Using the Project Explorer we drag and drop this service consumer onto the diagram. The result is shown in Figure 11-44.

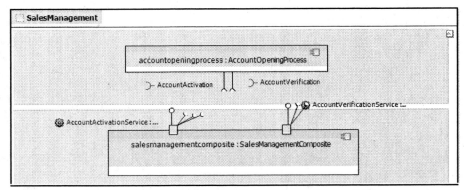

Figure 11-44 AccountOpeningProcess added to our service partition

Allocate atomic business application services to the service partitions

To determine which atomic services to place on the diagram, we refer to the composite service specification design performed in a previous step. For example, we know that the AccountVerificationCompServSpec uses the Address and AccountApplication service specifications. Therefore, we have to add to the diagram the atomic service providers for these specifications. In our case, they are AddressMgr and CustomerAccountMgr. Similarly, we know that we need BillingAccountMgr and GeneralLedgerAccountMgr for AccountActivationCompServSpec.

Using the Project Explorer, we drag AddressMgr, CustomerAccountMgr, BillingAccountMgr, and GeneralLedgerAccountMgr onto the atomic service layer of the diagram (Figure 11-45).

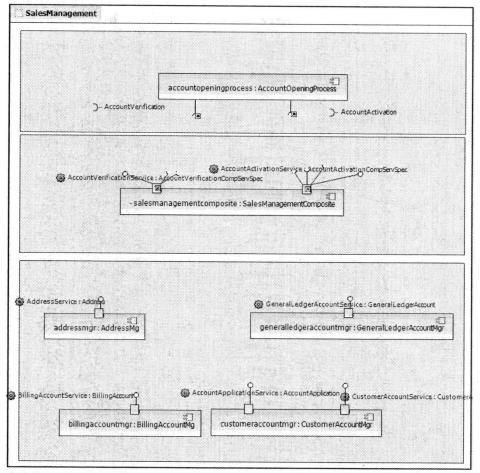

Figure 11-45   Service consumers, composite, and atomic services for SalesManagement

Create candidate service channels

Before we create the service channel, we look at the graphical notation used to represent services. Figure 11-46 shows the `AccountVerificationService` of `SalesManagementComposite`.

Figure 11-46   AccountVerification service

The graphical representation used is called *lollipop*, where a provided interface is represented as a circle, and a required interface as a semi-circle. In Figure 11-46 we can see that `AccountVerificationService`, typed as `AccountVerificationCompServSpec`, provides one interface, `AccountVerification`, and requires two interfaces, `Address`, and `AccountApplication`.

The `AccountOpeningProcess` service consumer has `AccountVerification` as one of its required interfaces. We now connect `AccountOpeningProcess`'s `AccountVerification` required interface to `AccountVerificationService`'s provided `AccountVerification` interface.

Select the `AccountVerification` required interface in `AccountOpeningProcess` (Figure 11-47).

Figure 11-47   AccountOpeningProcess's required AccountVerification interface

Drag it into the `AccountVerification` interface of `AccountVerificationService`. Release your mouse button when the lines are highlighted in green (Figure 11-48).

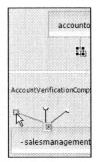

Figure 11-48   Creating a connector

A connector, `AccountVerification1`, is created. Stereotype the connector as `<<serviceChannel>>` (Figure 11-49).

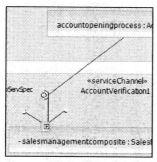

Figure 11-49   AccountVerification1 service channel

Create the other service channels as shown in Figure 11-50. Alternatively, look at the solution in Service Model - Structure Service Architecture (7), where we have created the CustomerService service partition as well (Figure 11-51).

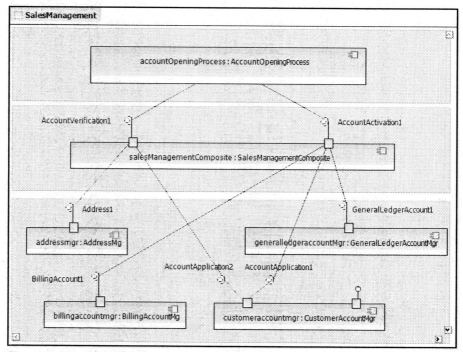

Figure 11-50   Sales Management service partition

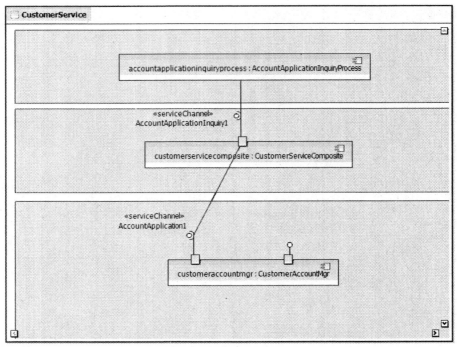

Figure 11-51   The CustomerService service partition

Note that you can see the new service channels in the Project Explorer (Figure 11-52).

Figure 11-52   Service channels under the SalesManagement service partition

Also note that we removed the bottom layer because we do not have infrastructure service providers in our example.

Step 7: Consider service policies

Service policies are explained in "Service policies" on page 220. In this section, we discuss how service policy needs are addressed when designing the service model.

The IBM Systems Journal article on service-oriented architecture (listed under resources) defines *policy* as follows:

> *A policy is a high-level statement of how things are managed or organized, including management goals, objectives, beliefs, and responsibilities. Policies are normally defined at an overall strategy level and can be related to a specific area, for example, security and management policies.*

Services have policies associated to them, as well as service-level agreements and quality-of-service (definitions from the same article):

► **Service-level agreement (SLA)**: A service-level agreement is an agreement between an IT service provider and the business that includes:

- Performance and capacity (such as user response times, business volumes, throughput rates, system sizing, and utilization levels)

- Availability (mean time between failure for all or parts of the system, disaster recovery mechanisms, mean time to recovery, and so on)

- Security (for example, response to systematic attempts to break into a system)

► **Quality of service (QoS):** Quality of service addresses all features and characteristics of a product or service that bear on its ability to satisfy stated or implied objectives (from International Organization for Standardization [ISO] 8402)

You can consider these as non-functional requirements that have to be addressed by your service-oriented architecture.

Note that JK Enterprises has enterprise-level IT policies (defined in the SOA SDP Redbook Enterprise Content RequisitePro project), as well as business process-specific policies, derived from the business policy defined by the Account Opening business process (how different parts of the business process interact).

One of the service policies that comes the JK Enterprises requirement effort is described as follows:

> *All messages must be encrypted.*

For example, we add a service policy statement (as defined in the UML 2 profile for software services) to the `SalesManagementComposite` service provider:

► Open the Service Model - Structure Service Architecture (7).

► Double-click the `SalesManagementComposite` package under the `2 - Composite Business Application Services` package. This should open the `SalesManagementComposite ServiceProviderSpec` diagram, which shows `SalesManagementComposite`.

► On the diagram, select *SalesManagementComposite* and *Add UML* → *Constraint*.

► Name the constraint `Messages must be encrypted`.

► Stereotype the constraint as `<<policyStatement>>`.

The resulting diagram is shown in Figure 11-53.

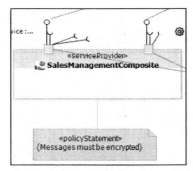

Figure 11-53   Policy statement of SalesManagementComposite

Note that we have not address the policy in our architecture. We simply captured the fact that messages to and from SalesManagement must be encrypted.

Task 2: Refine service architecture

This task takes the output of the structure service architecture task and fully specify the service architecture in terms of structure and behavior.

The constituent steps of this task are listed in Figure 11-54 and are described further in this section.

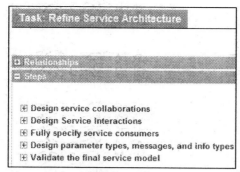

Figure 11-54   Refine service architecture steps

Step 1: Design service collaborations

In this section, we design the service collaborations (as described in "Model element: Service collaboration" on page 250) and interactions between service consumers and services.

The inputs for service collaboration and interaction design are the system use case model (as described in "System use cases" on page 224), and the service partitions created during "Task 1: Structure service architecture" on page 307.

Note that using system use cases is not mandatory, but it has value, as described in this section.

For JK Enterprises, we have two sets of system use cases, one for each of the IT systems in-scope (and specifically here for the service-oriented IT systems or SO systems):

► Sales Management system use cases (Figure 11-55).

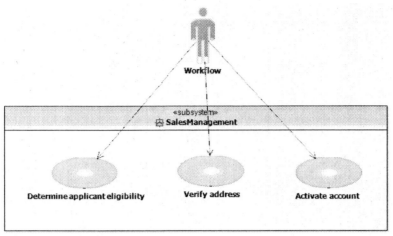

Figure 11-55   Sales Management system use cases

► Customer Service system use case (Figure 11-56).

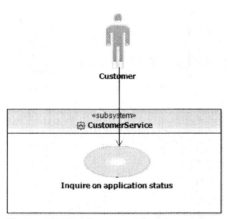

Figure 11-56   Customer Service system use case

One of the first questions to answer about service interaction is: How many service interactions do we have to create? The technique we use is to create one service collaboration (as defined in the UML 2.0 profile for software services) per system use case. We thus have to create four service collaborations for JK Enterprises.

Then, we detail each service collaboration with service interactions, one for each use case flow. Detailing service interactions allows us to specify the behavior of composite services, which act as service providers (usually to a business process) and also as service consumers (of atomic services). During this exercise, we are likely to identify new required operations on atomic services.

We now focus on Sales Management's Determine applicant eligibility system use case.

We create a service collaboration and interaction for Determine Applicant Eligibility:

▶ From the Project Explorer, select the *Service Partitions → Sales Management* package and *Add Diagram → Sequence Diagram*.

Software Architect creates collaboration, interaction, and sequence diagram.

▶ Rename the collaboration to Determine Applicant Eligibility, the interaction to Determine applicant eligibility (basic flow), and the sequence diagram to Determine applicant eligibility (basic flow) service interaction.

Note that for this exercise, we only design the basic flow service interaction.

▶ Select the *Determine Applicant Eligibility* collaboration, and stereotype it as serviceCollaboration (*Properties → Stereotypes → Add Stereotypes... serviceCollaboration*).

Step 2: Design service interactions

As a starting point, we have the initial service partition for Sales Management, as described in the previous section (Figure 11-57).

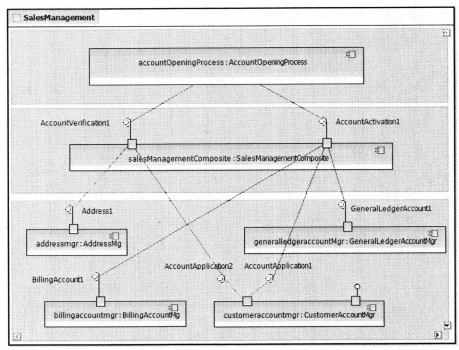

Figure 11-57   Initial Sales Management service partition

We drag all of the composite and atomic services and consumers (including business processes) required to determine an applicant's eligibility into the interaction diagram. Note that to be complete, we also include in the service interaction the workflow that triggers the business process:

▶   From the use case model, we know that workflow is required. Drag the workflow actor from the use case model into the diagram.

Software Architects creates an interaction lifeline for workflow (Figure 11-58).

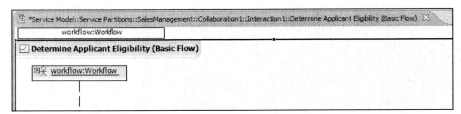

Figure 11-58   Workflow lifeline

▶ Drag the `Account Opening` service consumer into the diagram (from the *1-Service Consumers → AccountOpeningProcess* package).

▶ To improve the layout, we decrease the width of the lifeline. Select the *AccountOpeningProcess* lifeline and select *Filters → Stereotype and Visibility Style → Stereotype: Decoration* (Figure 11-59).

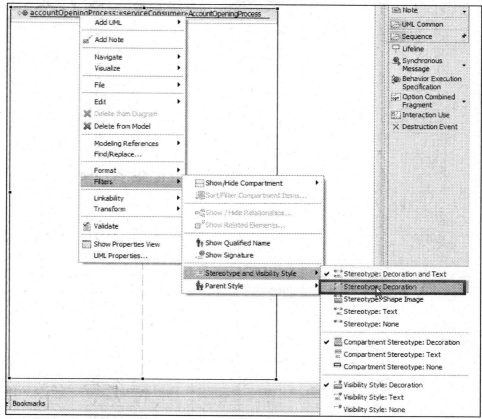

Figure 11-59   Changing the appearance of a lifeline

From our service identification exercise and the structure of the service architecture, we know that `AccountOpeningProcess` is a consumer of the `AccountVerification` composite service. Also, we know that `AccountVerification` is in turn a consumer of the `AccountApplication` service.

▶ Drag the `AccountVerification` serviceSpecification into the diagram (from the *2- Composite Business Application Services → SalesManagementComposite → Provided Services Specs → AccountVerification* package).

- ▶ Perform the step described in Figure 11-59.
- ▶ Optionally, rename the lifeline to `proc` (to improve visibility and decrease the overall width of the diagram.
- ▶ Repeat the previous three steps for `AccountApplication` (located under the *3 - Atomic Business Application Service Providers → CustomerAccountMgr → Provided Service Specs → AccountApplication* package).

The resulting diagram is shown in Figure 11-60.

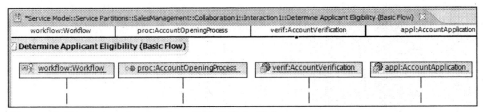

Figure 11-60   *Determine Applicant Eligibility's lifelines*

Note that we have not used the palette to create new lifelines, but instead we dragged existing model elements onto the diagram. This is very important because during our next step, we may create new operations on service specifications, as required by the interaction.

We know that `workflow` interacts with `AccountOpeningProcess`, and the initial service architecture already specified that `AccountOpeningProcess` invokes the `determineApplicantEligibility` operation of the `AccountVerification` service. We now capture that in the interaction diagram:

- ▶ Select the workflow lifeline, and mouse over the dotted line. You should see the *Click and drag to create a message* arrow (Figure 11-61).

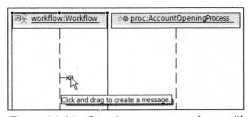

Figure 11-61   *Creating a message from a lifeline (1)*

- ▶ Click and hold the small square, then mouse over the `AccountOpeningProcess` lifeline (dotted line) and release the mouse button.
- ▶ Select *Create Message* from the contextual menu (Figure 11-62).

Figure 11-62   Creating a message from a lifeline (2)

► When presented with the list of operations, select
  determineApplicantEligibility. The resulting diagram is shown in Figure 11-63.

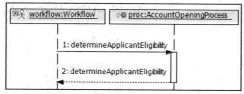

Figure 11-63   determineApplicantElligibility message between workflow and process

► Repeat previous steps to create the `determinApplicantEligibility`
  message between `AccountOpeningProcess` and `AccountVerification`
  (Figure 11-64).

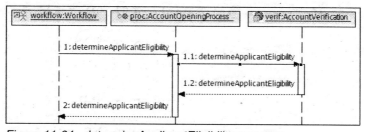

Figure 11-64   determineApplicantEligibility message

For the previous message, the operation was already available to us because of
how the `AccountVerification` composite service's
`determinApplicantEligibility` operation was identified from the business task.
It is usually the case with composite services identified from business processes
that you have the operations already available at this stage.

For the atomic services, however, operations would typically not be defined yet if the services are new (not being reused from another project). We now create an operation on the `AccountApplication` atomic service from the interaction diagram:

► Create a new message between *AccountVerification* and `AccountApplication`.

► Select *Create new operation*. In the pop-up dialog type `determineApplicantEligibility` and click *OK*.

Software Architect creates a new `determineApplicantEligibility` operation in the Project Explorer. We specify in details what the operation parameters and return type are in the next section.

► Save the work. The resulting diagram is shown in Figure 11-65.

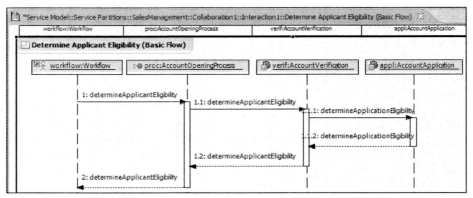

Figure 11-65   Determine applicant eligibility (basic flow) service interaction

Note that for `Determine Applicant Eligibility`, there is only one message between the composite service and one atomic service. Typically, a composite service would interact with more than one atomic services, as shown in the `Activate Account` service interaction (Figure 11-66).

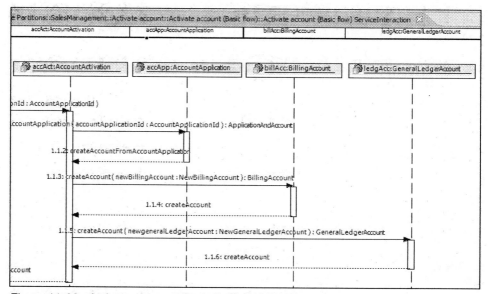

Figure 11-66   Activate account (basic flow) service interaction

For the `Activate Account` service interaction, the `AccountActivation` composite service invokes three atomic services' operations (in order):

▶ `createAccountFromAccountApplication` (from `AccountApplication`)
▶ `createAccount` (from `BillingAccount`)
▶ `createAccount` (from `GeneralLedgerAccount`)

Using the same technique, we also design service interactions for the remaining system use cases. The result is that we have created four service interaction diagrams, and identified required operations for atomic services. and show the service interactions for the Verify address (Figure 11-67) and Inquire on application status (Figure 11-68) respectively.

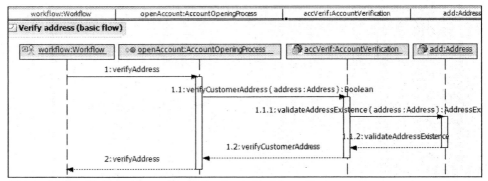

Figure 11-67   Verify address (basic flow) service interaction

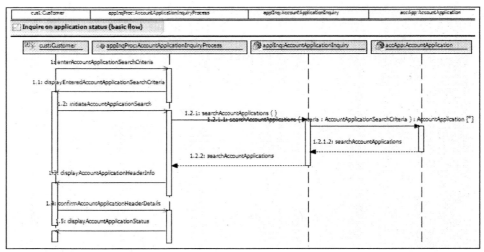

Figure 11-68   Inquire on application status (basic flow) service interaction

Note that we used service specifications for lifelines. Theoretically, we should use service instead of service specification, as described in "Service model work product" on page 234. We used service specifications, because it makes it easier to create new operations on composite services.

Step 3: Fully specify service consumers

Designing service collaborations and interactions also allows us to verify service consumers, and fully specify how they interact with services. For example, we identified a service consumers named `AccountOpeningBusinessProcess` (now renamed to `AccountOpeningProcess`) during service identification.

From the Activate account, Determine applicant eligibility, and Verify address service interactions, we now know exactly what operations it calls (`activateAccount`, `determineApplicantEligibility`, and `verifyCustomerAddress`), and what service specifications it requires (`AccountVerification`, and `AccountActivation`). This is shown in Figure 11-69:

1. Called operations
2. Required service specifications

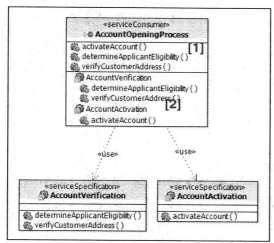

Figure 11-69   AccountOpeningProcess service consumer

Note that in this case, all of the three operations defined in the service specifications are called by the service consumer. This is not always the case.

For example, the required service specifications could define more operations than would be triggered by the consumer. Because `AccountVerification` and `AccountActivation` were identified from a top-down business process, the triggered and defined operations are very much aligned. Also, in the case of non automated human tasks, triggered operations exist for which there are no corresponding operation on a service specification, as in the `AccountApplicationInquiryProcess` service consumer (Figure 11-70).

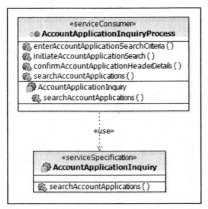

Figure 11-70   AccountApplicationInquiry service consumer

We have completed the design of service collaborations and interactions. From this task, we have fully specified the service consumers, and we have identified all of the required service operations. The next step is to specify what the service operation parameters, messages, and info types are.

Step 4: Design parameter types, messages, and info types

The inputs to this task are the domain model, service interactions (as described in the previous section), and initial service specifications.

Design parameter types

As described in "Model element: Parameter type" on page 245, parameter types are used to model information structures that are passed in and out of service specifications' operations.

In this section, we look in details at the `CustomerAccountMgr` service provider.

From the JK Enterprises service interaction design, we know that the `AccountApplication` service specification has a `determineApplicationEligibility` operation that takes an application as input parameter. We also know that `determineApplicationEligibility` must return a message containing information about whether or not the customer is eligible to open the account. At this stage, we start to fully specify what this input application and output eligibility message are.

JK Enterprises also defines a domain model, from which we derive the parameter types. It is important to design parameter types, and not just use the domain types because the information that is passed in and out of service operations is different from the information defined in a domain model.

The JK Enterprises domain model is shown in Figure 11-71.

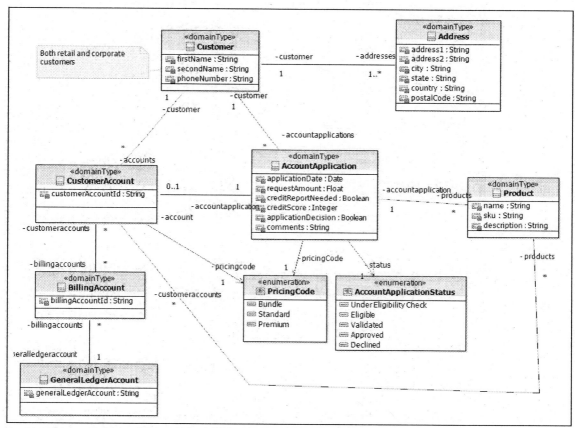

Figure 11-71   JK Enterprises's Servicing and Sales domain model

We can reuse the AccountApplication domain type to design our parameter types. We design the AccountApplication parameter type, as shown in Figure 11-72.

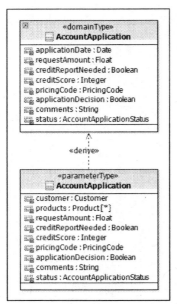

Figure 11-72   AccountApplication parameter type

Note that although the `AccountApplication` parameter type is derived from and has the same name as the `AccountApplication` domain type, it is does not have the same attributes. For example, we define a products attribute, which specifies which products the customer is applying for.

Note also that parameterType and domainType are not stereotypes (defined in a profile), but keywords.

The other parameter types for `CustomerAccountMgr` can be found under the *3- Atomic Business Application Service Providers → CustomerAccountMgr → Parameter Types* package. Note that patterns and transformations would help derive parameter types from domain types.

Specify operation parameter types

After designing the `AccountApplication` parameter type, we specify that the *AccountApplication* service specification's `determineApplicationEligibility` operation takes an `AccountApplication` as input parameter type.

► Open the `AccountApplication` ServiceSpec diagram from under the *3 - Atomic Business Application Service Providers → CustomerAccountMgr → Provided Service Specs → AccountApplication*.

► Drag the `AccountApplication` parameter type from the Project Explorer into the diagram.

- ► On the diagram and select the AccountApplication's `determineApplicationEligibility` operation.
- ► From the Properties view, select the Parameters tab, and click *Insert new parameter* (Figure 11-73).

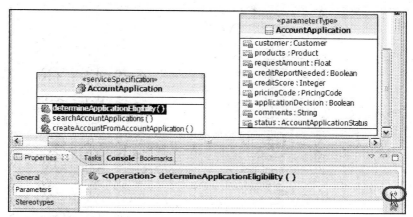

Figure 11-73   Insert new parameter

- ► Type `application` in the Name cell.
- ► Click `...` in the `Type` cell.
- ► In the Select Element for Type window, type `AccountApplication`, and select the *AccountApplication* parameter type. Click *OK*.
- ► To see the signature of the operation, select the `AccountApplication` service specification, right-click, and select *Filters → Show signature*.

Design messages

Designing messages is optional.

Message is a stereotype defined in the UML 2.0 profile for software services. As described in "Model element: Message" on page 244, a message is a container which identifies a subset of an information model which is passed into or out of a service invocation. A message is always passed by value and should have no defined behavior.

During service identification, the return type that was specified for the `determineApplicationEligibility` operation was boolean (true or false). By looking at the Determine applicant eligibility service interactions (Figure 11-74) we realize that the `AccountVerification` composite service must have the `AccountApplication` returned from the `AccountApplication` atomic service, and not just a true or false.

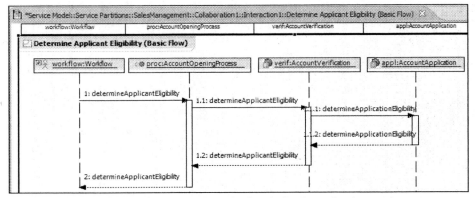

Figure 11-74   Determine applicant eligibility (basic flow) service interactions

Sometimes, an application may be approved, but the application was almost not approved. In that case, it would be very useful if the determineApplicationEligibility operation returned a warning message that would describe that even though it is approved, the application is risky.

Create messages

We design a message for the determineApplicationEligibility operation's return type:

► Open the CustomerAccountMgr messages diagram under the *3 - Atomic Business Application Service Providers → CustomerAccountMgr → Messages* package.

► From the diagram, create a new class stereotyped as Message and name it EligibilityMessage.

► Drag the AccountApplication parameter type into the diagram.

► Create another Message class named CreditWarning.

► Add an attribute named creditScoreComment of type String to the CreditWarning message.

The resulting diagram is shown in Figure 11-75.

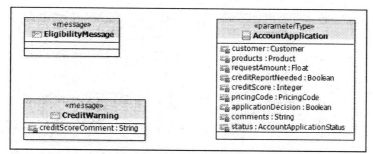

Figure 11-75   Intermediary EligibilityMessage diagram

We now design EligibilityMessage so that acts as a container of AccountApplication and CreditWarning.

▶ Mouse over EligibilityMessage. When the outbound arrow appears, click the mouse button on the small square, drag over to AccountApplication, and release the mouse button (Figure 11-76).

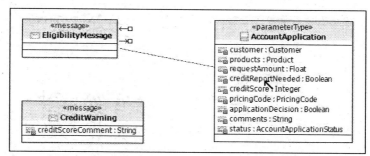

Figure 11-76   Creating an association: EligibilityMessage to AccountApplication

▶ Select *Create Composition Association* from the pop-up menu.

Creating a composition association from EligibilityMessage to AccountApplication means that an instance of AccountApplication does not live without an EligibilityMessage, and is always contained by an EligibilityMessage. In our case, we want the message to only contain one AccountApplication. We specify that in the model:

▶ From the diagram, select the new association. You should see its details in the Properties view (Figure 11-77).

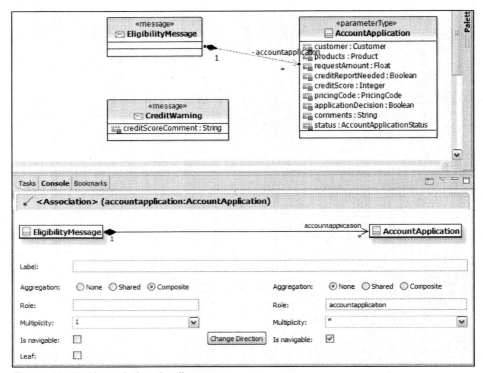

Figure 11-77   Association details

► On the *AccountApplication* side (right-hand side), change the value of Multiplicity from * to 1.

► Using the same technique, create a composition association between `EligibilityMessage` and `CreditWarning`. Make sure that an `EligibilityMessage` can contain zero or more warnings.

The resulting diagram is shown in Figure 11-78.

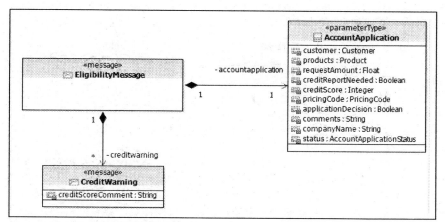

Figure 11-78   Design of EligibilityMessage

Note that designing a message in this case is useful partly because operations only have one return type (message), and we want to return information about `AccountApplication` and `CreditWarning`.

We also design an `ApplicationAndAccountMessage` for the `createAccountFromAccountApplication` operation of `AccountApplication` (Figure 11-79).

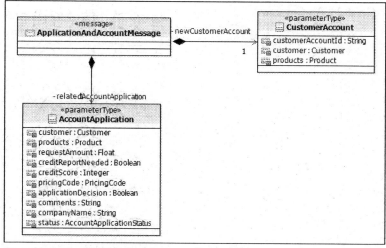

Figure 11-79   ApplicationAndAccountMessage

We design the `AddressExistenceMessage` for the return type of the `validateAddressExistence` operation of the Address service specification (Figure 11-80).

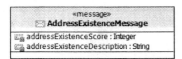

Figure 11-80   AddressExistenceMessage

Now that we have designed the messages, we are ready to use them in the definition of service specification operations.

Use messages in operation definitions

We specify that the `AccountApplication determineApplicationEligibility` operation returns `EligibilityMessage`:

► Open the `AccountApplication` ServiceSpec diagram from under the *3 - Atomic Business Application Service Providers → CustomerAccountMgr → Provided Service Specs → AccountApplication.*

► Drag `EligibilityMessage`, `AccountApplication`, and `CreditWarning` into the diagram.

► Select the `AccountApplication determineApplicationEligibility` operation. From the General tab of the Properties view, click *Set Return Type...* and select the `EligibilityMessage`. The result is shown in Figure 11-81.

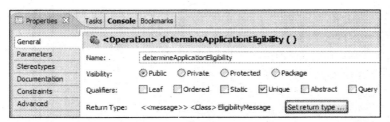

Figure 11-81   General properties of the determineApplicationEligibility operation

We also fully specify the other two operations of the `AccountApplication` service specification. The resulting `AccountApplication` ServiceSpec diagram is shown in Figure 11-82.

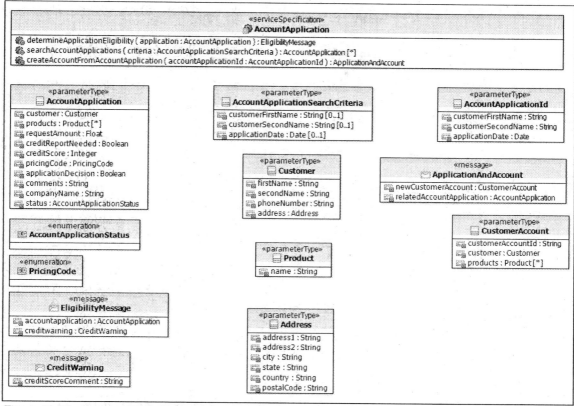

Figure 11-82   *AccountApplication service specification*

Note that in service specification diagrams, we do not represent messages with associations (as in the messages diagrams), but with attributes instead. This does not make a difference to the Message model elements; it is a different way to present the service specification. We use attributes because developers (implementers) are going to use this diagram and they typically prefer textual to graphical notations. If you prefer to see the associations, select a message attribute, right-click, and then select *Filters → Show as Association*.

We also fully specify the other service specifications. The resulting service specifications are:

▶ AccountApplication (Figure 11-82)
▶ AccountApplicationInquiry (Figure 11-83) -
▶ AccountActivation (Figure 11-84)
▶ AccountVerification (Figure 11-85)
▶ Address (Figure 11-86)

- ► `BillingAccount` (Figure 11-87)
- ► `CustomerAccount` (Figure 11-88)
- ► `GeneralLedgerAccount` (Figure 11-89)

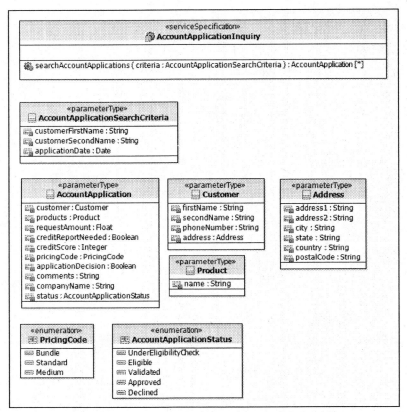

Figure 11-83   AccountApplicationInquiry service specification

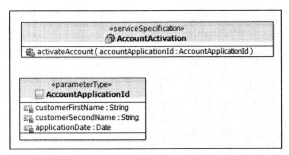

Figure 11-84   AccountActivation service specification

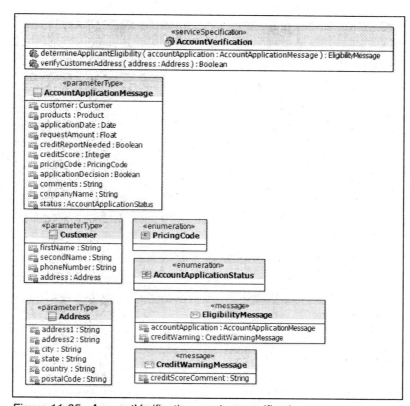

Figure 11-85 AccountVerification service specification

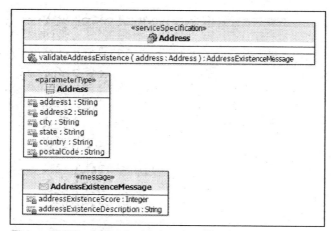

Figure 11-86 Address service specification

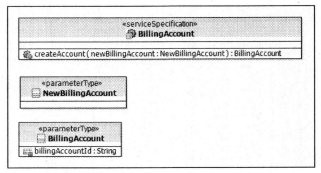

Figure 11-87   BillingAccount service specification

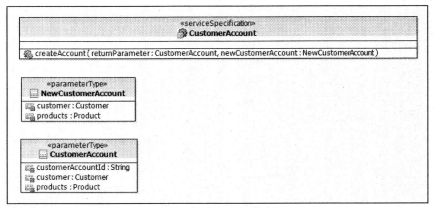

Figure 11-88   CustomerAccount service specification

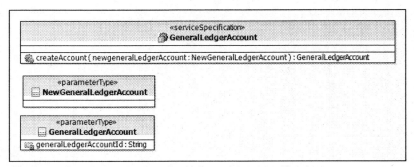

Figure 11-89   GeneralLedgerAccount service specification

At this stage, when we have defined all of the service specifications, operations, parameter types, and messages, we have completed the design of service specifications.

Design info types

Designing info types is optional.

As described in "Model element: Information type" on page 246, info types are used to specify a black-box view of information structures that are persisted.

Note that we decided to have info types owned by service providers, so that they provide a consolidated black-box view of the data managed by a service provider across all of its provided service specifications. It also means that service providers are responsible for the state of their info types.

The inputs used to specify info types are mainly the domain model and the service specifications.

Note that because composite services do not typically persist data, we design info types for atomic services only.

Note also that info types are not explicitly associated with parameter types and messages. Parameter types and messages are about the information being exchanged between service consumers and providers, whereas info types are about the information that is persisted by service providers. Service implementers (developers), however, make the connection between parameter types and info types when they write the code. Code could for example create a new instance of an info type, populate the info type instance with information from a parameter type instance, and then persist the info type instance.

In this section, we use a `Product` info type example to illustrate info types. Figure 11-90 shows the `Product` info type for the `ProductMgr` service provider.

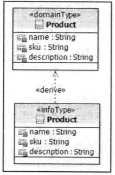

Figure 11-90   ProductMgr: Product info type

Figure 11-91 shows the info types for the `CustomerAccountMgr` service provider, including a `Product` info type as well.

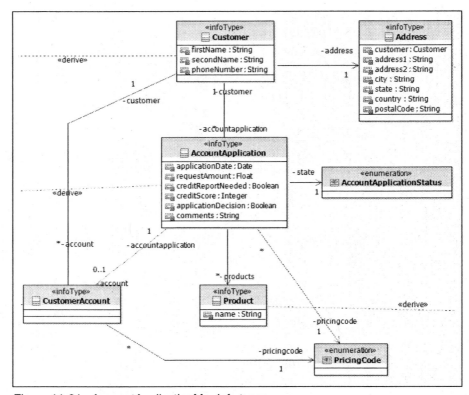

Figure 11-91   AccountApplicationMgr info types

As you can see in Figure 11-90, a product is defined by the domain model as having three parameters:

name   Name of the product

sku   Stock-keeping-unit for the product

description   Description in English for the product

The `Product` info type defined under `ProductMgr` derives from the `Product` domain type. In our case, it actually has the exact same three attributes. It makes sense for the `ProductMgr` service provider, which is responsible for persisting products.

The `Product` info type (Figure 11-91) under the `AccountApplicationMgr` service provider, however, only has one parameter (product name). This means that `AccountApplicationMgr` does not persist full product information. This makes sense because `AccountApplicationMgr` is about account applications and not products. `AccountApplicationMgr` only needs to persist the information necessary to get the full product information from `ProductMgr`.

We also specify info types for other service providers. To summarize, we have info types for:

► `ProductMgr` (Figure 11-90 on page 381)
► `AccountApplicationMgr` (Figure 11-91 on page 382)
► `AddressMgr` (Figure 11-92)
► `BillingAccountMgr` (Figure 11-93)

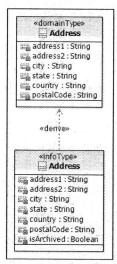

Figure 11-92   AddressMgr info types

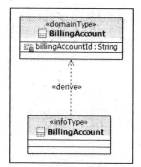

Figure 11-93   BillingAccountMgr info types

As described in "Service model work product" on page 234, we could also define the persistence behavior provided by a service operation where this behavior is described in terms of pre-conditions and post-conditions which refer to the info types. In other words, the info types are used when an operation has persistence behavior. We are not describing this in details.

Step 6: Validate the final service model

We started the service specification activity by validating the analysis level of the service model, which is a set of identified candidate services specifications and their operations. We then created the *real* service model and fully specified all of its elements and diagrams. We also created the initial version of the design model (the service components). We now complete service specification by validating the service model that we have fully specified.

We have to make sure that all services are:

▶ **Self-contained**: Although we have not worked on the deployment model yet, by looking at our service model and more specifically our services providers and their services, we have to make sure that the services can be deployed independently, and that a service provider can be replaced by another service provider in our architecture.

▶ **Implementable:** Are all services operations in the architecture implementable? For example, is there enough information in the parameter types or request messages for developers to implement the operation as a Java method?

Note that validation does not stop here and services have to be validated throughout their life cycle. For example, we want to make sure that services, once deployed, meet the non-functional requirements specified by the business at all times.

Task 3: Model service assemblies

This task populates the deployment model with assemblies and assembly parts (as introduced in "Different forms of a service" on page 49). These are used to model the deployable pieces of software (assemblies) and the parts that they are made up of (assembly parts).

The detail of this task is outside of the scope of this book.

Task 4: Model service deployment

This task models the deployment infrastructure (in terms of physical and logical nodes), and then models the deployment of assemblies onto these infrastructures.

The detail of this task is outside of the scope of this book.

Output of service specification for JK Enterprises

The output of service specification is a fully specified and validated service model work product, with all of its elements and diagrams. The result of the different service specification activities have been described under each section of this chapter (as a list and set of diagrams). Refer to "Service model work product" on page 234 for a complete description of what should be in the service model.

In Chapter 15, "Creating reusable assets" on page 533 we describe packaging and publishing the service model as a reusable asset.

Next steps

At the end of service specification, most of the architecturally significant elements have been specified, and designers and implementers use the output of service specification to perform their job. The activities that follow service specifications are:

► **Service realization:** Designers use the fully specified service model to create and fully specify the design model. They design how the service providers are realized.

► **Service implementation:** Service implementers use the service model to implement the service binding (typically Web services with WSDL, XML Schema, and then code implementation such as Java 2 Enterprise Edition or .NET). They also use the design model to implement the code.

References

Read the IBM Systems Journal, volume 44, number 1, *Toward an on-demand service-oriented architecture*:

```
http://www.research.ibm.com/journal/sj/441/crawford.html
```

12

Service realization

This chapter provides a detailed explanation and description about *how* to fully specify the design model starting from the service model. This is the service realization activity.

This chapter is structured around:

► Tools used

► Input to service realization

► Design model creation and structure

► Design service components

► Refine design model

Additionally, this chapter describes the service realization activity for one of the services in our JK Enterprises case study.

Introduction

In Chapter 9, "Service and design model work products" on page 231 we showed the results of the service realization phase, the design model. Thus, we already know what to expect in term of work product from this activity.

In this chapter we walk through this activity, starting from input work products and initial tasks, going to core tasks, such as service components design and realization decisions, and apply patterns. The result is a fully specified design model that is the input for implementation.

As a reminder, we want to point out that we are following an iterative development process. Thus, you should not expect that activities described here happen in a serialized way with respect to other activities (disciplines) for all services belonging to our SOA solution. However you can expect that, for a single service, it has already been identified and specified.

Tools and capabilities used for service realization

In this phase we use several Rational Software Architect capabilities:

1. Modeling
2. Patterns
3. Transformations
4. Reusable Asset Specification (RAS)
5. Architectural analysis

Some of these capabilities belong to Rational Software Modeler (such as 1 and 2), others belong to Rational Application Developer (such as 5). Refer to "Overview of IBM architect tools" on page 159 for a more detailed product description.

Inputs to service realization

We are supposed to play the *designer* role in this phase. As a designer we receive a service model. This model is detailed enough and complete, specifically for the parts we are interested, which are the services we have to realize. The service model, by exploiting the Software Services profile, fully defines all service characteristics:

- ► Service specifications defined
- ► Service providers defined
- ► Services defined
- ► Messages defined

Note that by having the service specifications defined, all service interfaces are defined: Operation signatures, input parameters, and return types.

Thus, we can say that we have the service defined from a *black-box* view. Indeed we know everything about *what* to send and to expect from that service, but we still do not know anything about *how* it is realized (*white-box* view). Therefore this is exactly what we are beginning to face now.

Important: By saying that the service model is ready, we do not exclude that feedback arises from this phase. Indeed, it is quite normal in an iterative software development project to have feedback on previous levels when we move on the realization level.

Creating the design model

Although we stressed that we are in an iterative development process, we are assuming this is the *first iteration*, and consequently we have to create a design model from scratch.

With Rational Software Architect (or Modeler in this case) we can create a new model in several ways and one is:

► In the Project Explorer, select the models project and *New → UML Model* (Figure 12-1).

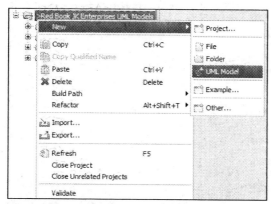

Figure 12-1   Creating a new UML model

► In the next dialog, select *Blank model* as a template, type Design Model for file name, and click *Finish*.

The design model is added under the `Red Book JK Enterprises UML Models` project.

In Rational Software Architect Version 7, depending on your Eclipse setting, you may see two elements named "Design Model" in the Project Explorer.

► **Design Model.emx**—Represents the physical resource (file) that keeps your model.

► **Design Model**—Represents the real UML model. This is a logical element, recognized by the tool as a proper UML element.

> **Tip:** You can show only logical models by setting the Project Explorer filter: click the ▽ icon at the top of the Project Explorer, select *Filters* and then select *UML Model files* in the pop-up dialog.

Create the model structure

As you likely noticed, we did not use a model template when creating the new model. This is because, for the scope of this book, we want to start from scratch to better understand all the necessary steps. However, in other cases you may want to exploit an existing template, such as Enterprise IT Design Model. This template applies the typical model structure that classical RUP defines for a design model.

As described in Chapter 9, "Service and design model work products" on page 231, we have to create a UML package for each service component identified. Following our traceability strategy, we have one service component for each service provider specified in the service model.

For the scope of this chapter, we are focusing on service realization for a service that we completely develop in a top-down fashion: `AccountApplication`.

Following this approach, we create a package named `AccountApplicationSC`. This package contains all UML elements, such as classes, diagrams, interactions, collaborations, and components, which are necessary to realize the service component.

We put all the component packages under a root package, named `Service Components`.

To create these two nested packages:

► Select the Design Model and *Add UML → Package*.

► Type `Service Components` an the package name.

► Select the new package and *Add UML → Package*.

► Type `AccountApplicationSC` as the package name.

If you want to create all packages for the remaining components, repeat these steps and create sub-package of `Service Components` for each service component, until you obtain the structure shown in Figure 12-2.

Figure 12-2   Package structure for JK Enterprises design model

Prepare the model for transformations

We configure the model to be ready for the next steps, such as transformation to a Java project. To do this we have to perform a few simple steps:

► Apply a Java transformation profile.
► Import the Java type library for primitive types (from deployed libraries).
► Import the `RoseJavaDataTypes` (from deployed libraries).

Apply a Java transformation profile

To apply a Java transformation profile, perform these steps:

► Select the Design Model.

► In the Properties view select the *Profiles* tab.

► Click *Add Profile*.

► Select *Deployed Profile* (pre-selected) and select *EJBTransformProfile* from the drop-down menu.

► Click *OK*.

Although in our service development we are exploiting Java transformation and not EJB transformation, we have chosen this profile because it can be used for both transformations.

Conceptually, this profile defines all stereotypes necessary to represents in a design model the classes that can act as EJBs (session, entity, or message-driven beans). Furthermore, the profile adds all stereotype properties necessary to create deployment descriptors. Although part of this content improves the semantic of the model, detailed information are strictly necessary for the transformation itself.

Import Java primitive type library

To import the Java primitive type library perform these steps:

► Select the Design Model and *Import Model Library*.
► Select *Deployed Libraries* (preselected) and select *Java Primitive Types*
► Click *OK*.

This operation allows the model to know other UML types, which correspond to Java primitive types (for example, `int` or `boolean`).

Repeat this step for the `RoseJavaDataTypes`.

Create service components

Now we create all component realization elements for a single component, `AccountApplicationSC`. We are decreasing the level of abstraction with respect to the service model. A key factor is to start from what represents our input, the service model. We create one service component (in the design model) for each service specification (in the service model).

Manual creation

In particular we start from two key elements of the service model: *service specification* and *service provider*.

Our component is to be *traced* to the service provider and has to *realize* the service specification.

We create the component using these steps:

► Create a class diagram under the `AccountApplicationSC` package by selecting the package and *Add Diagram → Class Diagram*.

► For the class diagram name, type `Traceabilities`.

► Expand the Service Model in the Project Explorer and navigate to *3 - Atomic Business Application Service Providers → CustomerAccountMgr → Provided Service Specs → Account Application → <<serviceSpecification>> AccountApplication* (Figure 12-3).

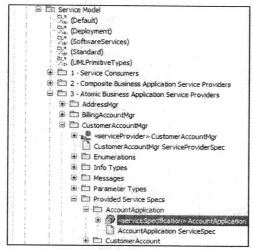

Figure 12-3   Navigate to service specification

► Drag and drop `AccountApplication` service specification to the newly created diagram in the Design Model. The <<`serviceSpecification`>> is added to the class diagram. There is a little arrow in the top left ▣ , indicating this element comes from an external model.

► In the same way, drag and drop the `CustomerAccountMgr` service provider to the diagram.

► In the Palette, under *Component*, select *Component*.

► Click anywhere on the class diagram to create a component.

► Name the new component `AccountApplicationSC` (Figure 12-4).

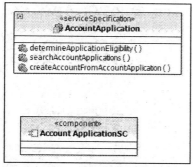

Figure 12-4   Add a component to the class diagram

- Select the component. In the Properties view select the *Stereotypes* tab and type `serviceComponent` for Keywords.

- Next we create the traceability link: Under the *Class* tab of the Palette select *Dependency* → *Abstraction*. Create a connection from the `AccountApplicationSC` component to the `CustomerAccountManager` service provider. Select *Create Derive* when prompted.

- Next we represent the realization: In the Palette, *Class* tab, select *Realization*. Create a connection from the `AccountApplicationSC` component to the `AccountApplication` service specification.

- The resulting diagram is shown in Figure 12-5.

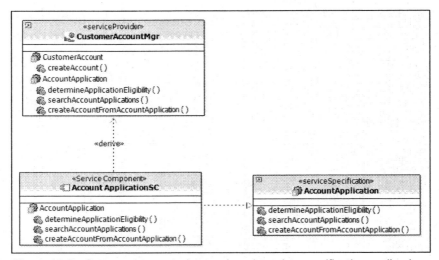

Figure 12-5   *Component created, traced, and service specification realized*

Conceptually, we have just created what is becoming part of our *white-box* view of the service provider. This component directly comes (derive) from it and also realizes the service specification.

Notes:

- When you draw the realization relationship, the component immediately adds the service specification in its provided interfaces (this is an UML component compartment).

- Although `CustomerAccountMgr` provides two service specifications (`CustomerAccount` and `AccountApplication`) we are only realizing one of the two specifications. The `<<derive>>` association does not imply that we are realizing all of the provided service specifications.

Transformation

In this book we introduced model-driven development (MDD) concepts, such as patterns and transformations, in "Model-driven development" on page 145.

Another way to achieve what we just explained in the previous section is to use an automated transformation.

Rational Software Architect provides transformations out-of-the-box, but furthermore, it provides pattern and transformation authoring tools. Several software development organizations exploit these model driven mechanisms to automate the job of creating a model (or code) from another model. This way we can obtain several benefits, such as:

► Improve productivity by automating all target model creation tasks.

► Enforce standards compliancy by decreasing human errors or misunderstandings.

► Enforce architecture is respected by service realizations.

► Ensure all traceability links are in place.

Generally speaking, all these points enforce SOA governance.

Going back to our example, we could use automated transformations for all service components generation, including realization relationship, and also more detailed realization elements that are explained later in the chapter.

Furthermore, by creating a customized transformation, we can address our organization (or project) architecture, creating a standard solution for each service.

Traceability

By creating a <<derive>> relationship between our component and the service provider, we are ensuring that what we implement is directly related to what the higher level of abstraction (on its own directly related to business) is expecting from this service component. At the same time we continue this traceability chain through lower levels to ensure they also respect the specification.

Refine service components

Next we specify the AccountApplicationSC service component in more details.

Create realization classes

As designers we are identifying two classes and one interface to realize this component:

- A facade class named `AccountApplicationServiceFacade` designed to directly realize the service specification.

- An implementation class named `AccountApplicationServiceImpl` designed to realize the detailed structure and tasks of the service component.

- An interface named `AccountApplicationService` that represent a realization view of the service specification.

> **Note:** On the design abstraction level we are slightly changing class names by appending the word `Service` to the original service name. This is because, at the design level, we also have other classes that reside at a lower architectural layer. These classes are *entity* types and they typically represents persistent information of a service, or a service partition. Typically these (kind of) classes assume the same name of business items they come from. In this case we have an `AccountApplication` entity class as well. Therefore, we (as designers) decide to have this naming convention: Services classes are named using the `Service` suffix, whereas entity classes are named with their proper name.

Now we continue with the services class creation. We work with the same `Traceabilities` diagram that was open before:

- In the Palette, under the *Class* tab, select *Class → Stereotyped Class*.
- Click anywhere on the diagram and select *Create <<service>> Class*.
- Type `AccountApplicationServiceFacade` as the class name.
- In the Palette, under the *Class* tab, select *Class → Class*.
- Type `AccountApplicationServiceImpl` as the name.
- Create an interface by selecting *Interface* under the Class tab.
- Name this interface `AccountApplicationService`.
- The resulting diagram is shown in Figure 12-6.

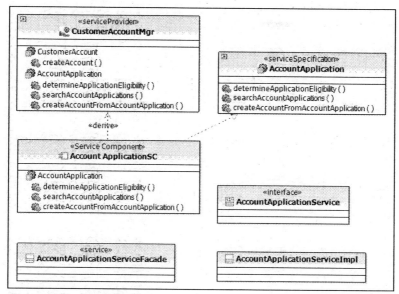

Figure 12-6   Class diagram

Now, we want to assign appropriate dependency relationships between the component and these new classes:

▶ Select *Dependency → Abstraction* under the Class tab (you may already see *Abstraction* directly).

▶ Create a connection from the `AccountApplicationService` interface to the `AccountApplicationSC` component. When prompted select *<<refine>>*.

▶ Repeat this step for the two remaining classes.

▶ The resulting diagram is shown in Figure 12-7.

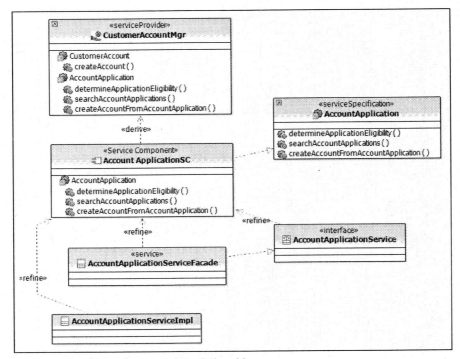

Figure 12-7   Class diagram with relationships

Note that by introducing new classes in this diagram, we have put these classes into the model as well, in the same `AccountApplicationSC` package.

> **Tip:** In Rational Software Architect (and Modeler) there are several ways or gestures to create model elements (classes, operations, properties). Besides the steps we described in this section, you can:
>
> ► **Right-click any UML element** in the Project Explorer and select *Add UML*. Only valid UML classifiers for that kind of elements appear on the context menu.
>
> ► **Action bar**: The modeling surface of Software Architect has a context graphical menu that is displayed automatically by hovering the mouse on the diagram or on an element of the diagram. This pop-up menu, the action bar, shows only UML elements valid for the context, such as diagram type, selected object, or possible relations for elements.

Refining the interface

The `AccountApplicationService` interface represents the *design level* service specification. Thus we want to add to this interface the operations coming from service specification:

► Select the interface and *Add UML* → *Operation*. Type `determineApplicationEligibility` as the operation name.

► Complete operation signature by selecting the operation in the diagram and *Navigate* > *Show in* → *Project Explorer*.

> **Tip:** This gesture can be very useful: it takes you to the model explorer for any UML element present in a diagram.

► Select the operation in Project Explorer and *Add UML* → *Parameter*. In the Properties view, leave the default options. Click *Select Type*. Select the parameter type from the service model (Figure 12-8).

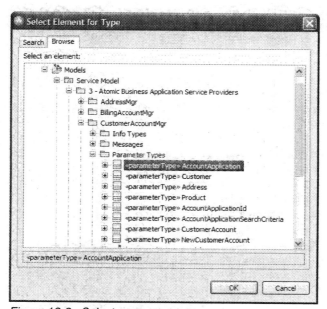

Figure 12-8   Select a parameter type

► Select the operation and in the Properties view click *Set return type*.

► Select `EligibilityMessage` from *Service Model* → *CustomerAccountMgr* → *Messages*.

▶ Repeat these steps by adding operations corresponding to the `AccountApplication` <<`serviceSpecification`>> in the service model to the `AccountApplicationService` interface.

The interface with all operations is shown in Figure 12-9.

Figure 12-9   Interface refined

Tip: To show the complete signature, select the interface and *Filters* → *Show Signature*.

All these tasks can be automated by using a transformation from the service model to the design model.

Apply design patterns

We introduced patterns and their importance in software development.

A *pattern* is a common solution for a recurring problem. Today, many software development organizations have their own standard and architecture customization. By using patterns they enforce those standards, and ensure greater productivity and quality. Thus patterns can help to achieve better SOA governance.

For the case study we, as designers, have to follow our SOA architecture. By reading its definition, we know we have to design a component that has to realize directly the interface corresponding to the service specification.

Following this constraint we want to apply a facade design pattern to our new classes. But first we want the facade class to have the same operations as the interface. To achieve these two goals, we apply two different design patterns that are available in Rational Software Architect:

▶ A sample design pattern called *Interface*
▶ A design pattern called *Facade*

To obtain the interface pattern:

▶ Select menu *Help* → *Sample Gallery*.

▶ Expand *Patterns*, click *patterns to apply*.

▶ Click *Import the sample*.

▶ Click *Finish*.

> **Important:** Please be aware this could be not working, depending on your Rational Software Architect installation. If you cannot see the sample patterns in the Pattern Explorer, you can work around this problem by exporting the imported project ("Patterns to apply sample") as a RAS asset with deployable plug-in and then importing the same RAS asset.
>
> You can find detailed instruction about how to do these operations in "Using the Reusable Asset Specification (RAS) to distribute and manage assets" on page 573.

Interface design pattern definition

▶ **Problem solved:** If an interface is already present and a class has to realize it, the class must provide implementation for each operation defined in the interface. Doing it manually can be less productive and error prone.

▶ **Solution**: Interface pattern creates realization relationship and copies all interface operation signatures to the class.

▶ **Parameter interface**: the defined interface.

▶ **Parameter implementation**: the class implementing the interface.

Applying a design pattern in Software Architect is straightforward:

▶ Open the Pattern Explorer by selecting *Window → Show View → (Other) → Modeling → Pattern Explorer*.

▶ In the Project Explorer create a class diagram named `Pattern Instances` under the `AccountApplicationSC` component.

▶ In the Pattern Explorer, expand *Sample Patterns*, select *Interface* and drop it into the new diagram.

▶ In the Project Explorer drag and drop the `AccountApplicationServiceFacade` into the diagram, to the right of the small `Implementation` box (it is ok when the corresponding line becomes gray).

▶ In the Project Explorer drag and drop the `AccountApplicationService` into the diagram to the right of the small `Interface` box.

After both the facade class and the interface are in the diagram there is a realization relationship between the two and moreover, the facade class has now all the interface operations (Figure 12-10).

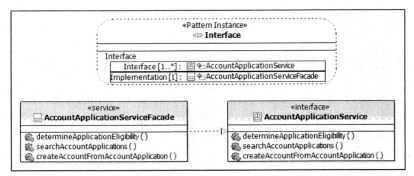

Figure 12-10   Interface pattern applied

Tip: With Rational Software Architect V7 you can also avoid to create all necessary elements *before* to apply the pattern. Indeed, you can let the pattern engine to do it for you, while applying the pattern. By hovering the mouse on a particular parameter on the pattern instance, you will find a button that creates an element corresponding to that parameter type.

Facade design pattern definition

▶ **Problem solved:** Dealing with complex subsystem can create too many dependencies on specific subsystem details, such as different methods with different parameters types and so on. This does not allow to have a clear and well defined interface for the subsystem.

▶ **Solution**: Facade provides a unified interface that hide a set of interfaces in a subsystem. A higher level interface, easier to use is defined for clients.

▶ **Parameter facade**: this class knows all subsystem details and it delegates all client requests to appropriate subsystem objects.

▶ **Parameter subsystem**: this is the actual subsystem implementation classes. There is no dependency to the facade.

Note: If you are interested in knowing more about pattern theory and applications, refer to Chapter 16, "Pattern-based engineering with Rational Software Architect   ." on page 545.

Next we apply the facade design pattern. We want the facade class to realize the service specification. We already realized the service interface. We want to allow the external world to access our service with the expected interface and hide all internal implementation details and interfaces.

Let us apply the facade design pattern:

▶ Bind `AccountApplicationServiceFacade` to the `Facade` pattern formal parameter.

▶ Bind `AccountApplicationServiceImpl` to the Subsystem pattern formal parameter.

Figure 12-11 shows the resulting diagram.

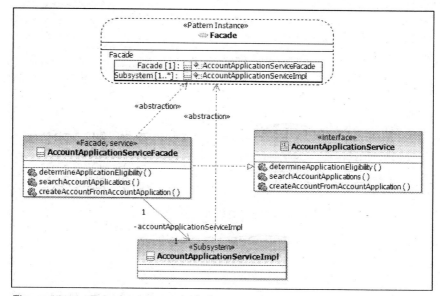

Figure 12-11   Facade pattern applied

Using the Reusable Asset Specification (RAS)

Rational Software Architect has powerful features to manage assets through RAS.

The content of a Reusable Asset Specification (RAS) asset can be a pattern or group of patterns, but also:

▶ Transformations
▶ Models
▶ Code libraries
▶ Code samples
▶ Project configurations
▶ Network descriptors
▶ Frameworks

An important part of RAS format is its powerful documentation. You have the appropriate space and tools to exhaustively document and explain your assets.

Typically organizations use RAS repositories in these basic ways:

► To share, within the organization, internal reusable assets such as project patterns, transformations, frameworks, and so forth.

► To share internal assets with other organizations, for example, in a customer/contractor relationship.

► To reuse public assets, such as those IBM Rational provides through the developerWorks RAS repository.

Software Architect provides you with a perspective to manage RAS repositories. Select *Window → Open Perspective → RAS (Reusable Asset)* to open the perspective.

In the Asset Explorer you find all available repositories. Initially you have one repository named `Patterns Repository`. You can click it and browse it. For example you can expand to *Design Patterns → Structural → Facade*. Select *Facade* and *View → Documentation*. This way you can learn about any available design pattern you are interested in.

Furthermore, you can import other repositories, for example from developerWorks:

```
http://www.ibm.com/developerworks/
```

To import developerWorks patterns:

► In the Asset Explorer select *New → Repository*.
► Select *DeveloperWorksRepository* and click *Next*.
► Click *Finish*.

Browse the new repository in the Asset Explorer and import patterns of interest by selecting a pattern and *Import*.

Design class structure

Our design model begins to have its own meaningful structure and content. Next we improve this model by designing the entity classes, which usually represents business items used by a service.

Following our architecture we want our service provider to completely encapsulate structure and behavior of services. Therefore, we provide with this component (or those components that are part of the same service provider) a set of *entities* that are owned by the service provider:

- Under the AccountApplicationSC package, create a package and name it Entities.

- Create a class diagram in this package and name it CustomerAccountMgrEntities.

- In the diagram create a stereotyped <<entity>> class and name it AccountApplication.

- Navigate to Service Model and drag the *<<infotype>> AccountApplication* from the package *3 - Atomic Business Application Service Providers → CustomerAccountMgr → Infotypes* into the diagram.

- Create a <<derive>> traceability from the new AccountApplication <<entity>> class to corresponding <<infotype>>.

Begin to add attributes:

- Select the entity class and *Add UML → Attribute*. Name the attribute applicationDate and select the RoseJavaDatatypes::java::util::Date type.

- Create another <<entity>> class and name it Customer.

- Trace it to corresponding <<Infotype>> in the service model through a <<derive>> dependency relation.

- Create an association using the Palette, *Class* tab, *Association*. Create a connection from Customer to AccountApplication.

- Select the association and in the Properties view on the AccountApplication side, select * from the Multiplicity combo box.

  In the last step you created an UML association from AccountApplication to Customer. This association is navigable in both direction and has a * multiplicity on the AccountApplication side, meaning that for each Customer instance, there can be many AccountApplication instances.

Figure 12-12 shows the entity diagram.

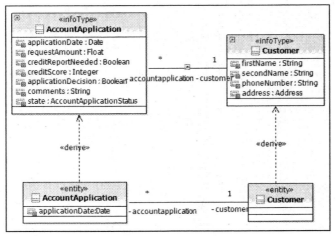

Figure 12-12   Entity diagram with entities created

You should now continue this task until you have recreated the info types structure that is in the service model.

Again, please note that all these tasks can be automated through a transformation.

Note: We have derived entity classes from info types belonging to service model. However, in the JK Enterprises case study, info types are considered optional, and, therefore, we could derive entities directly from our domain model.

Design class behavior (interaction diagrams)

Until now we have mainly designed the *structural* part of the model, meaning that we have represented static aspects of the solution: properties such as attributes or associations, dependencies and so on. Indeed we have mainly used a type of UML diagram, the class diagram, which is a structural diagram.

Remember that we are in the middle of the top-down development of a service called AccountApplication and we have to develop a particular service operation, named determineApplicationEligibility.

Now, as designers, after we having designed the service component and its class structure, we want to represent the realization of this operation. Thus we can now open this operation and try to figure out how it works. To do this, we use a sequence diagram that, which belongs to the interaction diagrams family.

In particular, we want to represent the *basic flow* of this operation. Basic flow means the default behavior of the operation in the case everything works as expected and we follow a default path in the operation execution.

To create a sequence diagram:

▶ In the project explorer, select the `AccountApplicationSC` component.

▶ Add a sequence diagram by selecting *ADD UML > Sequence Diagram*.

▶ Name this diagram `determineApplicationEligibility - Basic Flow`.

▶ Find the Generic Consumer actor in the model.

▶ Drag and drop this actor to the sequence diagram.

▶ Drag `AccountApplicationServiceFacade` from the Project Explorer and drop it to the diagram.

▶ Drag and drop also `AccountApplicationServiceImpl` into the diagram.

▶ Locate the `EligibilityMessage` in the service model from *service model → CustomerAccountMgr → Messages*, and drag and drop it to the diagram.

Now you should see the skeleton diagram shown in Figure 12-13.

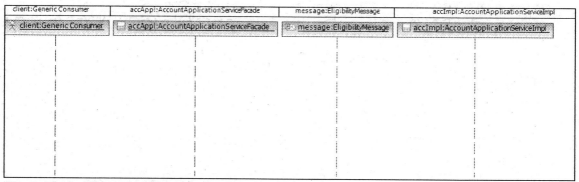

Figure 12-13   First step of sequence diagram creation

Please note a sequence diagram, because it represents a behavior, does not contain classes, but objects (class instances) and thus the UML representation is different.

Now we learn how to create messages in a sequence diagram:

► Select the life line (dash vertical line) for the Generic Consumer actor.

► Drag from this line and drop to the life line of AccountApplicationServiceFacade. Select *create message*.

► From the operation combo box in the diagram, select the *determineApplicationEligibility* operation.

► Now repeat this step from AccountApplicationServiceFacade object to AccountApplicationServiceImpl object.

► This time you don't have a yet ready operation. Select *Create new operation* just type the operation name on the message box editing.

► Complete the signature by putting AccountApplication (from service model) parameter type as either input and return type of this operation. You can find this class as we showed in Figure 12-8 on page 399.

► Now draw a <<create>> message from AccountApplicationServiceFacade object to EligibilityMessage. You should see the life line of EligibilityMessage starts now from the creation message (Figure 12-14).

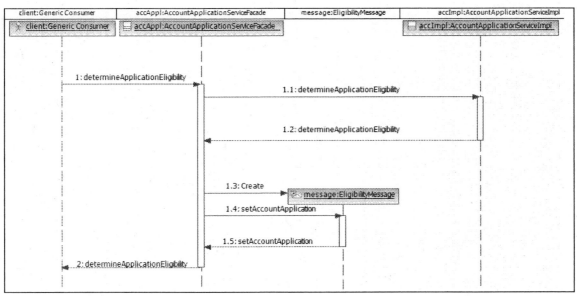

Figure 12-14   Sequence diagram completed

As designers, we just created the facade pattern and sequence diagram. By doing this we have put in place an initial solution. As we can note from the sequence diagram the facade object provides the service interface, where as the internal *impl* object does not provide it. Indeed, the facade object creates the message to be returned to a generic consumer. This is an initial representation of a facade behavior. However, once developers take ownership of the implementation, the internal behavior is likely more complicated. The only thing that does not have to change is, as usual, the facade interface, because it represents the service interface and directly comes from service model done during the service specification phase.

Comparison with traditional RUP object-oriented approach

If you already know RUP and the typical object-oriented analysis and design approach, you may have noticed that we are following a slight different workflow.

In classical RUP approach, the greatest part of the process is driven by *use cases*. Indeed if the focus of your software development is an *application*, this approach is very consistent and has years of successful experiences in many development organizations.

Thus, using a classical RUP approach we have different models on different abstraction levels like:

- ▶ Business model
- ▶ Use Case model
- ▶ **Analysis model**
- ▶ Design model
- ▶ Implementation model

During the execution of Analysis and Design discipline, you are expected to *identify* initial *analysis* classes (very abstract classes, as they appear from a requirement point of view, free of any technological detail). These classes are a *first draft* of your use case realization. Design activities will develop these classes by putting all the necessary details, patterns, and solution requested.

However, in an SOA world, the main focus of your development could not be an application but, generally speaking, a realization of a business process or part of it, through *services*. Therefore, there will be a greater emphasis on services, along the complete development life cycle. Indeed we already explained—by introducing services directly linked to business processes—we are raising the level of abstraction to achieve alignments between business needs and IT solutions.

Therefore, the development workflow in an SOA RUP development, such as our case study, there is more emphasis on different models, such as:

- ► Business (process) model
- ► Use Case model (optional)
- ► **Service model**
- ► Design model
- ► Implementation model

As you can see, levels of abstraction are slightly different and this difference reflects exactly the greater and fundamental emphasis on services we have now. Although for the JK Enterprises case study, service model seems to replace analysis model, we want to point out the two are different:

- ► The service model is less abstract than analysis model, since it defines precisely all service specifications, including complete and detailed service operation signatures (operation return and parameter types are completely defined). Typical RUP analysis model is more generic on this: signatures are not completed and well defined. Types are not necessary defined.

- ► The service model does not "open the box" for a single, atomic service. Instead analysis model, from a use case point of view, creates an initial, sketched and abstract use case realization.

However these two different models have one similarity: they both represent a bridge from business requirements to the solution. Going back to our design model we may say design versus analysis is a similar to design versus service (model). Indeed, before we were realizing *analysis classes* and now we are realizing *services*.

Finally, service model responsibilities also imply that the design model *inherits* more elements: All elements related to service specification, such as operation signatures, parameter types, and messages. In this sense we may say the design model has less responsibility, but it always represents service detailed realization in term of subsystem design, class design, patterns used, internal structures, and so forth.

From a realization point of view (design and implementation), we want to point out that we are not loosing characteristics and strength points of *component based* and *object-oriented* development. Moreover, when appropriately used, these paradigms help and enforce our SOA solution. Thus, at the design level we can exploit object-oriented characteristics, such as polymorphism, encapsulation, abstraction, and modularity.

However we have to be careful: We are building *services*. These are business-aligned, repeatable, and loosely coupled. Thus we have to pay attention to architectural dependencies, associations used, and so forth, to achieve service decoupling. In other words we may say we can fully exploit object oriented paradigm inside a service component or a group of components that belongs to the same service provider.

Output of service realization for the JK Enterprises example

After completing the service realization phase we have produced a **refined design model**. We say a *refined* design model because, being in an iterative development process, we realize one or a set of services that were already fully specified by the service model. Therefore we can expect this model will be further refined by:

► Other service realizations

► Feedback and updates coming from implementation

For a complete description of the design model, refer to "Design model work product" on page 263.

Therefore our primary output for this phase is the design model and it contains important realization elements such as:

► Service components

► Classes refining components, their structure and operations.

► Service operations realizations, in terms of detailed structure and behavior.

► Patterns applied for each realized service.

> **Important:** For the scope of this document, is important to understand that our design model is very simple: it contains only one service operation realization where as other models like service model are spanning the entire JK Enterprises solution. Although design model is simple, it shows as a single service operation is realized through detailed design. A complete design model will include much more classes, details and patterns applied.

Validate model

Going back to our case study, we may say we have a design model, consistent and detailed enough to be transformed to initial code for developers.

Thus, the design model is the primary work product that constitutes the output from service realization phase and the input for implementation activities, as we described in our development case. The next implementation activities (for example, transforming the model to code) are formally owned by developers. However, we are on the boundaries between these two disciplines and many interactions among designers and developers are expected. For example designers could informally test transformations to verify they are working on the design model, and make sure all of the details are there.

An important step, not always emphasized enough, is model *validation*. Rational Software Architect allows us to validate models that have different profiles, constraints and so on. By validating models we ensure:

► **Completeness**: The model has fully specified UML content.

► **Correctness:** The model is *well formed*.

► **Integrity**: There are no broken or missing references, referenced models are reachable, and so forth.

► **Profile conformance**: A model is valid against a particular profile. Profiles introduce stereotypes and constraints and thus a model has to respect them.

► **Transformations-ready**: The model is valid for a particular transformation.

> **Tip:** In Rational Software Architect you can explicitly request a model validation by selecting a model (or a model element) and *Validate*.

We suggest to periodically validate models because it enforces integrity and consistency among several models owned by different roles. Therefore this is another task that helps achieve SOA governance.

Transform model and refine design with developers

As we previously stated, we are in an iterative software development process, and several interactions between developers and designers are expected.

As developers run transformations to code, they begin implementation and typically, new details arise. It is quite impossible that a designer puts all of the details before at least one implementation iteration is run on a service component. As new elements appear we, as designers, have to decide how to incorporate them (or not). For example, we have to verify that the architecture is always respected, and that no invalid dependencies have been created.

In the JK Enterprises case study, we are using the following transformations (among models and code) (Figure 12-15):

► Service model to WSDL
► Design model to Java (and reverse)

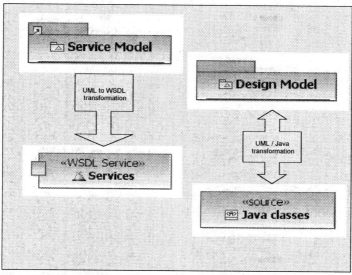

Figure 12-15 JK Enterprises code transformations

Note that the implementation gets the *specification* part of services directly from the service model, where as implementation parts are coming from the design model. Thus, all those parts belonging to specifications, such as operation names, parameters types, and messages, come from the service model. In other words all service interfaces are coming from the service model.

Therefore developers can exploit both transformations and have all generated elements merged and working together as we show in Chapter 13, "Service implementation" on page 419.

Reverse transformation from Java code

We said that in an iterative development process we have to incorporate what developers have produced during the implementation phase.

Rational Software Architect Version 6 provides UML to code transformations but does not provides an (out-of-the-box) *reverse* transformation.

Over the past two years we have observed an interesting debate in software development organizations about how to update models and keep them consistent with code, or generally speaking, underlying abstraction levels. Someone was saying that a reverse transformation was needed, whereas someone else disagreed by saying this is not needed in a model-driven development approach.

From our experience we say that having accurate models is an important aspect that can strongly help in respecting software architecture and improving our solution quality. Non accurate models have very limited value.

Rational Software Architect Version 7 provides a reverse Java transformation.

First of all, we want to point out that having a (Java) reverse transformation does not necessary mean that you have to update all of the design model with everything that comes from the code, for several reasons:

▶ Design model and code are two different abstraction levels and, by definition, not all the code details are needed in the design model.

▶ Developers can add something that is wrong or not compliant with the architecture or with organization standards.

▶ Assuming that the design model is *closer* to requirements, developers may alter requirement interpretation.

For these reasons it is necessary to have capabilities in the tool that allow one to verify what the model content will be *before* updating the model itself. Indeed we may call reverse transformation a *reconciliation* between code and model.

Going back to our case study, assuming there has been an implementation iteration of the AccountApplication service, we now want to update our model with significant elements coming from the first implementation.

> **Note:** In Software Architect Version 7 you can setup your UML to Java transformation and its reverse by selecting *Modeling → Transform → New Configuration → UML to Java V5.0*.
>
> Refer to Chapter 13, "Service implementation" on page 419 where you can find detailed instruction about how to set up this transformation.

At this time your transformation is already configured (developers have already used it). However, when setting up the transformation, pay attention on the mapping packages between UML and Java and to transformation configuration information.

So what we have to do to run the reverse transformation is simple:

▶ From the implementation EJB project, you can find the transformation descriptor, named UML to Java V5.0 for JK Enterprises.tc.

▶ Select this descriptor and *Transform → Java to UML*.

▶ The merge model window opens (Figure 12-16).

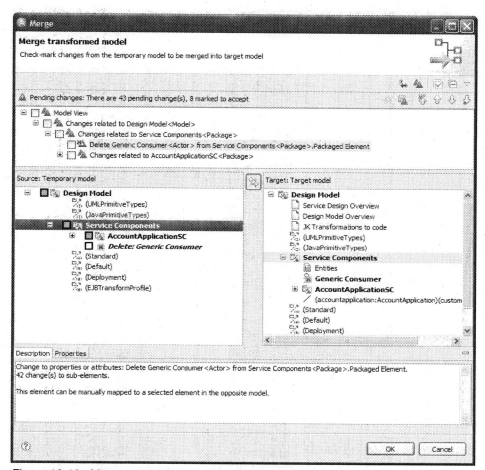

Figure 12-16   Merge model during reverse transformation

► Note that something has changed. However, as we already anticipated, many aspects and elements are different from model to code. For example, some model element like stereotypes do not exists in the code. All we have to do is ignore these changes.

The merge window is structured in this way:

– The upper part shows which changes would happen to the model, if selected.

– The middle-left part show the temporary model, as a UML representation of parsed Java elements, and what would the corresponding action be in the target model.

- The middle-right part shows the target model and meaningful icons representing the potential new model content.

- The bottom part explains the changes of the selected element.

- The space between these two parts shows matching lines between these two model versions.

► Analyze the major changes coming from the code.

► Select pending changes you want to accept and click *OK*.

Your model is now up to date!

> **Important:** In our case study we generate WSDL from the service model and implementation classes from the design model. EJBs are generated from within Application Developer starting from WSDL. In this way we also obtain all wrapping code necessary to call EJBs business methods from the Web service. When the reverse transformation runs, it will find all EJB classes. In this kind of workflow we can simply avoid to gather them back in the design model. Additionally, it is a good practice to avoid to launch the reverse transformation with all of the EJB deployed (generated) code into the project (this is not necessary and not significant at the design level), so reading which model elements have to be gathered back to design will be easier.
>
> Finally, if you decide to not always generate a WSDL, you can exploit the UML to EJB transformation, obtaining also EJBs directly from the design model.

Architectural analysis

We are talking about interactions with developers. Besides the capability that allows us to update our model, we want to show here another powerful Rational Software Architect capability.

Periodically, after developers do their work, we can exploit automated tasks that allow us to verify code content, structure, dependencies and patterns.

This can be done from two different points of view corresponding to two Software Architect capabilities:

► **Code review**: This can be considered a code quality automatic control. It is related also to quality aspects and the test discipline. Basically it allow us to define a set of customized rules to verify which classes and methods can be used, which dependencies are forbidden or from a language point of view, to define things like naming convention rules or syntax rules.

- **Architectural analysis**: This capability allows us to discover existing patterns or *anti-patterns* on our code. We may say anti-patterns are something the architect wants to verify. Sometimes it is normal to have it or even expected (for example we have a component that is designed to act as an hub). Instead sometimes they are a risk or a mistake. This often depends on the architecture.

In this section we are assuming developers have done their work and we, as designers, want to verify this work by exploiting this architectural analysis capability.

For the first time, we have to configure the Software Architect Analysis functionality for our EJB project.

To configure an analysis set:

- Select any project in your workspace and *Analysis*.
- A window opens. Create a new configuration by selecting *Analysis → New*.
- Type JK EJB Architectural analysis in the name field.
- Click *Analyze selected project*.
- Select *RedBook JK Enterprises EJB Project*.
- Select the *Rules* tab.
- Select only *Architectural Discovery for Java*.
- Click *Apply*, click *Close*.

To perform architectural discovery on the EJB project now and in the future:

- Select the project. and *Analysis*.
- Click *JK EJB Architectural analysis*.

Rational Software Architect scans your code looking for patterns (and anti-patterns). At the end it display the results in the Analysis results view. You can browse this view looking for applied design patterns, object-oriented patterns (for example, hierarchies), and structural pattern (such as global or local butterfly).

If you expand *component global butterfly* and double-click AccountApplication, you should see the diagram shown in Figure 12-17.

This diagram represents all dependencies to a single component, the AccountApplication class in this case. These dependencies may be expected or not. However, the architect should know and with this kind of tool, he can verify that the code is respecting the architecture.

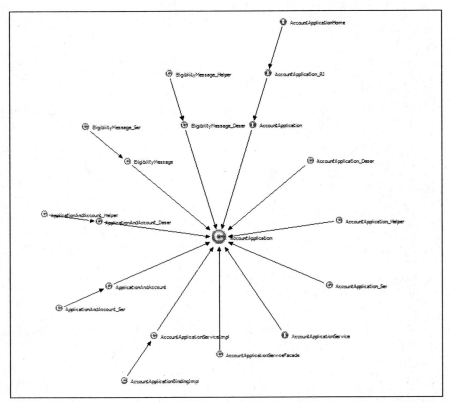

Figure 12-17   Component Global Butterfly for JK Enterprises architectural analysis

13

Service implementation

This chapter discusses the different implementation options for our SOA based solution. We demonstrate how to use the tools.

This chapter describes these topics:

► Inputs to service implementation
► Implementation options
► Tooling options
► Set up our development environment
► Top down development of a service
► Using a third-party service
► Using an enterprise service indirectly
► Updating your design
► Output of service implementation

Introduction

In this chapter we describe the options available to implement an atomic service. Using the JK Enterprises sample, we demonstrate how to build a service top-down, how to subscribe to an external service, and how to integrate an existing function based on CICS.

Figure 13-1shows the activities involved in Implementation. This chapter focuses specifically on the Implement Atomic Services activity.

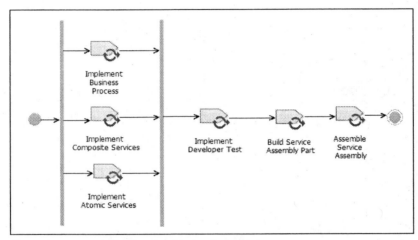

Figure 13-1   Activities involved in implementation

The output of implementation results in an implementation model, developer test and build. In this chapter we briefly touch on developer test and build. We provide links to more information about developer test and build.

The Implementation model consists of three parts (Figure 13-2):

► Business Process Implementation

► Composite Service Component Implementation

► Atomic Service Component Implementation

We focus on the Atomic Service Component Implementation in this chapter.

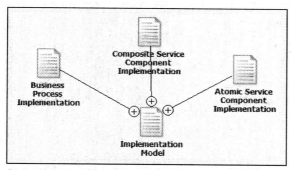

Figure 13-2   Parts of the Implementation model

The roles involved in implementation are shown in Figure 13-3. The chapter focuses on the Developer role. The Integrator role is responsible for the component services and business process implementation, which was briefly discussed in the Introduction chapter and is out of scope for this book.

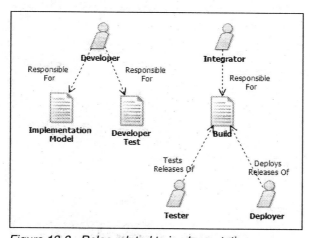

Figure 13-3   Roles related to implementation

Inputs to service implementation

We are supposed to play the *developer* role in this phase. We receive multiple inputs to produce the services:

▶ We receive the requirements and system use case requirements which define the flow and business logic we need to implement.

▶ We receive the service, design, and deployment models. From the models we perform transformations, which produce WSDL and skeleton implementation code.

► We receive the business process model.

Figure 13-4 show the work products related to the implementation.

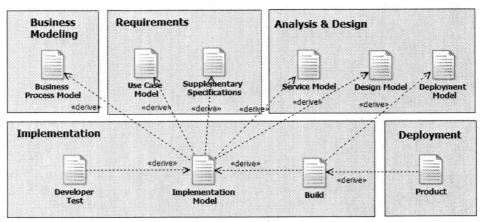

Figure 13-4   Implementation related work products

We should now have all the information required to implement the service.

Implementation options

In this section we describe the implementation options available to realize our services. The flexible nature of a SOA allows for many service implementation options. The basic service implementation options are:

► **Build**—Implementing a service from scratch.

► **Buy**—Purchasing a service implementation from a third-party vendor.

► **Integrate**—Wrapping an existing system's function

► **Subscribe**—Purchasing the capability to use a service or integrating an existing service.

► **Transform**—Refactoring existing code to better expose functionality as a service.

> **Note:** For more information about different options for service creation, the SOA Foundation Service Creation Scenarios provides in-depth, look at:
> - Realization options
> - How to leverage the e-business patterns in the realization of those options
> - Best practices in service creation
>
> Refer to the IBM Redbooks publication *SOA Foundation Service Creation Scenario,* SG24-7240.

Which implementation of a service is the best? The correct answer is, the one that best aligns with the business goals. For example, it might not make sense to spend thousands of dollars building new service implementation when you can integrate existing system functions. How you implement your service depends on your business goals. Odds are your SOA solution consists of a combination of these implementation options.

When you move to an SOA based solution you can do it in stages using existing systems and functionality, as well as new services or services you obtain from third-party vendors.

In this chapter we build a service top-down, we subscribe to an external service, and we integrate an existing function based on CICS.

Now let us look at our different tooling options.

Tooling options

In this section we describe the relationship between Rational Software Architect and Rational Application Developer. We discuss what roles and capabilities are available in Rational Application Developer and then provide role examples.

Overview

All the IBM tooling we discuss here is based on the Eclipse platform. This provides a consistent and common user interface and a common integration platform for the tools to work together.

In previous chapters we have been using Rational Software Architect. However, when we get to implementing we have other tooling options available.

Rational Software Delivery Platform (SDP) has a role-based approach to its tooling offerings. Through the use of roles, we can provide capabilities that are specific to a user's role, and we can hide capabilities that are not. This reduces the cluttering and complexity of the user's workspace. A user can have multiple roles enabled at a time, which exposes all the capabilities assigned to each role.

▶ **Rational Software Architect** has everything an architect, designer, or developer needs to complete a SOA solution. We use Rational Software Architect to visually design a software application using UML models. Based on our design, we can transform our design into code and continue to develop our solution. We can also update our design from the final code implementation.

▶ **Rational Application Developer** is a tool for developers. It provides a single comprehensive development environment designed to meet a variety of development needs, from Web interface to server-side application, from individual development to advanced team environments, from Java development to application integration.

When should you use Rational Software Architect and when should you use Rational Application Developer? The answer to this question is, it depends on the roles and capabilities required for the given person to perform their tasks.

Let us look at an example. In an organization you have an architect who is leveraging model driven development to design an SOA solution. You have a lead developer that takes the models created by the architects and performs model to code transformations. The roles and capabilities required to perform these tasks requires Rational Software Architect. Once the lead developer has the skeleton code (from the transformation), this can now be passed off to an internal development team or outsourced to a development team. The roles and capabilities required by the development team to finish the solution only requires the capabilities of Rational Application Developer.

Rational Application Developer is a subset of Rational Software Architect and all the roles and capabilities available in Rational Application Developer are available in Rational Software Architect.

Rational Application Developer roles and capabilities

In the previous section we talked about roles and capabilities. How do roles and capabilities work? Capabilities are logical sets of tools that are available in the workbench. These capabilities can have hierarchical relationships, meaning some could include other capabilities. Roles are a set of capabilities. You can enable multiple capabilities at one time by selecting one or more roles. Rational Application Developer has multiple roles and capabilities.

Below is a partial list of the roles available in Rational Application Developer and the capabilities they enable. For a complete list of roles and capabilities see the Rational Application Developer's Info Center:

```
http://publib.boulder.ibm.com/infocenter/rtnlhelp/v6r0m0/index.jsp?topic=/c
om.ibm.rational.rad.books/icwelcome_product_rad.htm
```

► **Advanced J2EE**: Enables support for developing typical Web applications

► **Enterprise Java Developer**: Enables support for developing enterprise applications, Enterprise JavaBeans™ and Application clients

► **Java Developer**: Enables support for developing typical Java applications

► **Team**: Enables the use of the supported source-code management systems, such as CVS and ClearCase

► **Web Developer (advanced)**: Enables support for developing typical Web applications and adds support for Struts development, Web services development, and database access

► **Web Developer (typical)**: Enables support for developing basic, J2EE-compliant Web applications

► **Web Service Developer**: Enables support for developing and consuming Web Services

► **XML Developer**: Enables support for building and incorporating XML applications, including DTDs, XSLTs, and XML schemas

There are a multiple ways in which we can enable roles and capabilities:

► If we use a resource that requires a role or a capability we are prompted to add the associated capabilities to our workspace.

► We can add capabilities by selecting *Window → Preference → General → Capabilities.*

► We can add sets of capabilities by enabling additional user roles from the *Enable roles* menu in the Welcome view.

As an example of how to enable capabilities in the Eclipse-based tools, we demonstrate how to enable the Web services capabilities in "Enable the Web services development capability" on page 428.

Note: For a full list of Rational Application Developer features refer to:

```
http://www-306.ibm.com/software/awdtools/developer/application/features/i
ndex.html
```

Setup the development environment

This section describes the tasks that need to be completed prior to developing the services for the JK Enterprises application. The tasks defined here apply to every development section in this chapter. Additional setup task maybe required in some sections and are called out where appropriate. This enables you to focus on a section without additional setup tasks which are not required.

Complete the following tasks to prepare for the sample application development:

► Install the model transformation feature
► Download the sample code
► Create a test server within Rational Software Architect
► Enable the Web services development capability

Install the model transformation feature

The model transformation feature is an option feature of Rational Software Architect. To complete sections in this chapter we have to have this feature installed. Refer to the Rational Software Architect's InfoCenter for steps to install this feature.

Download the sample code

This chapter references files and database scripts supplied with the additional material. For instructions about how to download the sample code, see Appendix A, "Additional material" on page 575.

Create a test server in Rational Software Architect

If you already have a test server defined, you can continue to the next section. After a typical full installation you already have a test server defined.

If you do not have a test server configured, create a test server configuration by following these steps:

► Open the J2EE perspective.

► In the Servers view right-click a blank area and select *New → Server*.

► When the Define a New Server dialog appears, select *WebSphere V6.1 Server* and click *Next* (Figure 13-5).

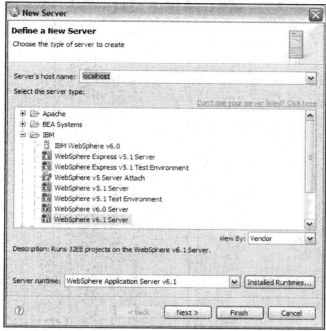

Figure 13-5   Create new server

► Accept the default values in the WebSphere Server Setting dialog and click
   Finish (Figure 13-6).

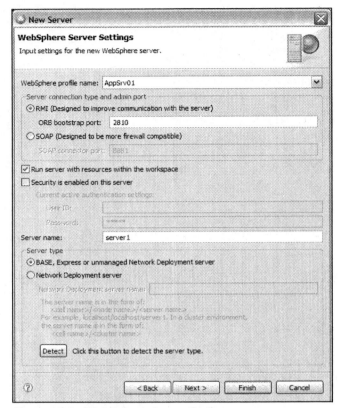

Figure 13-6   WebSphere Server Settings

Enable the Web services development capability

If the Web Service Development capability is already enabled you can skip this section.

To enable the Web Service Development capability, perform these steps:

► In the Workbench, select *Window → Preferences*.

► Expand *General* and select *Capabilities*.

► Click *Advanced*.

► In the Advanced dialog select *Web Service Developer*. Click *OK* (Figure 13-7).

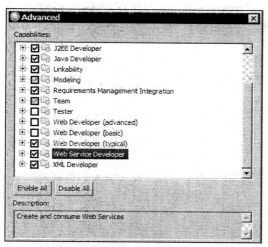

Figure 13-7   Enable Web service development

► The Preferences Dialog is shown in Figure 13-8. Click *OK*.

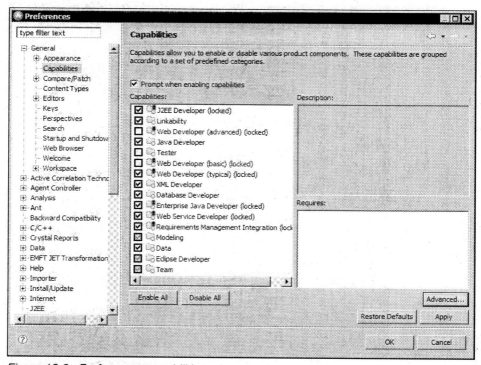

Figure 13-8   Preferences capabilities

Top-down development of a service

In this section we describe the process for top-down development of the Account Application service from the JK Enterprises example (Figure 13-9).

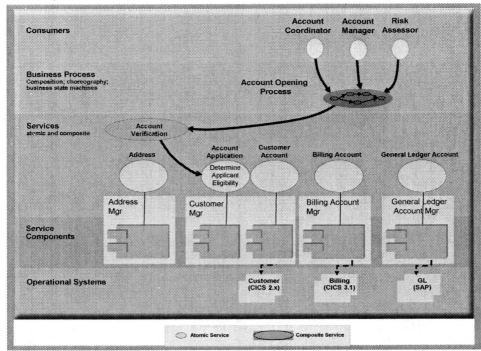

Figure 13-9   Determine Application Eligibility operation of the Account Application Service

Transformations help move from one level of abstraction to another. We use two transformations to speed up the implementation of the `AccountApplication` Web service.

1. The first transformation takes us from the UML service model to the WSDL that defines the service.

2. The second transformation takes the UML design model and generates skeleton code that is used to implement the service.

3. From the WSDL that was produced in the model to code transformation, we use the Web Service wizard to generate the EJB Web service skeleton code.

Figure 13-10 shows the transformations in the order that we perform the transformations.

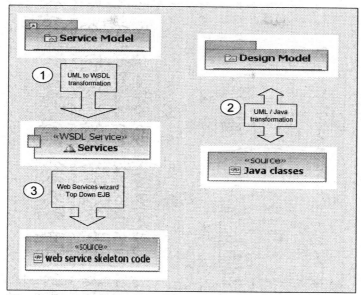

Figure 13-10   Steps to generate skeleton code from models

We use the skeleton code that was generated by the Web Service wizard and the transformations to glue our service together.

► We implement the business logic inside of a plain old Java object (POJO). We get the business logic from the system use case requirements.

► Using the facade pattern, we wrapper the POJO in an EJB session bean to isolate any interface discrepancies.

► From there we wrap the EJB with a Web service.

Application that have to use the service can reach the service either by going through the Web service interface or by talking directly to the EJB.

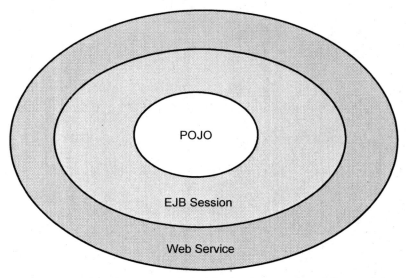

Figure 13-11   Visual representation of the implementation of the service.

In this section we perform the following:

- ► Create a configuration for a UML to WSDL transformation
- ► Create a configuration for a UML to Java V5.0 transformation
- ► Run the UML to WSDL transformation
- ► Run the UML to Java V5.0 transformation
- ► Visualize and modify the WSDL
- ► Create a skeleton EJB Web service from a WSDL
- ► Implement the EJB Web service
- ► Unit test the EJB Web service

Prepare for top-down development

Before we can being implementing the top-down Web service sample, we have to import the Account Application project interchange file into the workspace and import two code templates.

Import the project interchange file for the Account Application

To import the project interchange file perform the following steps:

- ► Select *File → Import*.
- ► In the Import dialog, expand *Other* and select *Project Interchange*.

- Click *Browse* to locate and open the file:

  `c:\SG247356\sampcode\SoftwareArchitect\topdown\AccountApplicationSC.zip`

- Select `AccountApplicationSC` and `AccountApplicationSCEJB`, and click *Finish.*

> **Note:** The EJB project shows an error because there is no EJB defined at this point. We do create an EJB in the sections that follow.

Import the project interchange file for the UML Models

Repeat the same steps to import the interchange file for the UML Models from:

`c:\SG247356\sampcode\SoftwareArchitect\UMLModels.zip`

Select the `Red Book JK Enterprises UML Models` project.

Import code templates

Templates are sections of code that occur frequently enough that we want to be able to insert them with few key strokes, known as *content assist* function. In this section we leverage templates to remove the need for copying and pasting code. For more information about creating a template refer to the Rational Application Developer InfoCenter.

Import code templates by performing the following steps:

- Select *Window → Preferences.*

- In the navigator of the Preferences dialog, expand *Java → Editor* and select *Templates.*

- Click *Import* and locate and select the file:

  `c:\SG247356\sampcode\SoftwareArchitect\topdown\`**`daeImpl.xml`**

  Click *Open.*

- Click *Import* and locate and select the file:

  `c:\SG247356\sampcode\SoftwareArchitect\topdown\`**`daeService.xml`**

  Click *Open.*

- Click *OK* (Figure 13-12).

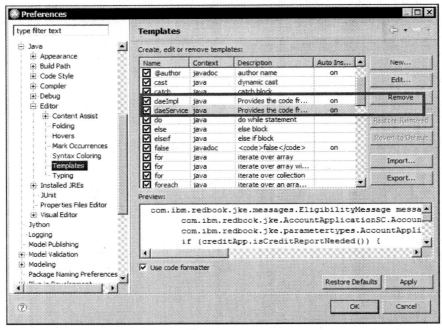

Figure 13-12   Importing code templates

Model transformations

A model transformation is a way to generate output from a source model. The transformation interprets elements in the source model and based on rules, generates output to a target model. The source and target models can be text files, code models, or UML models.

We can have different types of transformations:

▶ **Model to model**—These transformations are used (typically) to create (or update) a model starting from a higher level of abstraction. Typical examples are business to use case model and use case to analysis model.

▶ **Model to code**—These transformations are used to generate code (Java, XML, XSD, WSDL, and so forth) starting from (typically UML) models. This transformation is also called *model to text*.

▶ **Refactoring**—These transformations are used for a particular task on a single model; examples include changing a class name, moving a package, changing stereotypes, and so forth.

Note: For more information about transformations, as they relate to architecture see "Transformations" on page 148.

Rational Software Architect has the following transformations available:

- ► C++ to UML
- ► Java to UML
- ► UML to C++
- ► UML to CORBA
- ► UML to EJB
- ► UML to Java V1.4
- ► UML to Java V5.0
- ► UML to WSDL
- ► UML to XSD

Transformations help take you from one level of abstraction to another. Rational Software Architect provides the capability to perform forward transformations and reverse transformations. A forward transformation takes us from a higher level of abstraction to a lower level. A reverse transformation helps us move from a lower level of abstraction to a higher.

In this section we focus on the model to code forward transformations. We demonstrate how we cannot only save developers time but ensure developers implement the design. We provide an example of a reverse transformation in "Reverse transformation from Java code" on page 413.

How do transformations add value at implementation time? Imagine this: Your architects have just done a brilliant job designing your SOA solution. They have produced well defined service and design models. The service model contains over fifty service specifications and the design model has over a hundred classes. Now it is time for developers to implement. They could read the design model and code, by hand, each of the classes defined by the models or they can use a model-to-code transformation to speed up the process. Using a transformation saves developer's time by generating the skeleton code from the design model and generating WSDL from our service model. These transformations run in seconds rather than hours.

We use two model to code transformations to generate a WSDL and supporting code for the JK Enterprises example.

Before we use a transformation, we have to configure the transformation to specify what to transform and where to transform to. There may also be other special settings that the transformation requires such as namespace to Java package mappings.

Now we configure the transformation for the JK Enterprises example.

UML to WSDL transformation configuration

This section describes how to configure a new UML to WSDL transformation for the JK Enterprises sample application. We then use the WSDL generated by the transformation in the Web Service wizard to generate an EJB Web service.

Before we can configure the transformation the following setup must be completed:

► With Rational Software Architect open, switch to the Modeling perspective by selecting *Window → Open Perspective → Modeling*.

We have to open the service model so that its contents is available to the New transformation configuration dialog.

► From the Project Explorer expand *Red Book JK Enterprises UML Models → Models → Service Model*.

► Select the *Service Model* and *Open Model*.

To configure a new UML to WSDL transformation perform these steps:

► Open the New Transformation Configuration dialog by selection *Modeling → Transformation → New Configuration*.

► In the Name field type: UML to WSDL for JK Enterprises.

► Select *UML to WSDL* from the list of transformations under IBM Rational Transformations.

► For the Configuration file destination click *Browse* and select */AccountApplicationSCEJB*, then click *Next* (Figure 13-13).

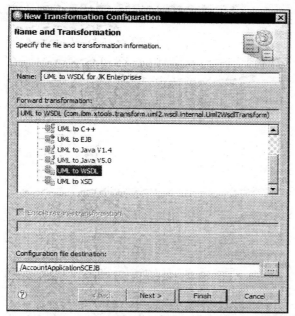

Figure 13-13   New Transformation Configuration: Name and transformation

► Set the transformation source by expanding *Red Book JK Enterprise UML Models → Models → Service Model → 3 - Atomic Business Application Service Providers → CustomerAccountMgr* and selecting *<<serviceProvider>> CustomerAccountMgr*.

► Set the transformation target by selecting *AccountApplicationSCEJB* from the right pane. Click *Next* (Figure 13-14).

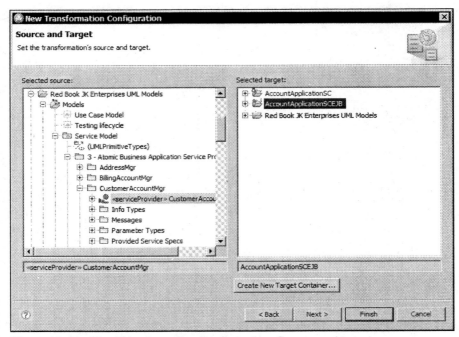

Figure 13-14   New Transformation Configuration: Source and target

▶ In the WSDL options dialog leave the default binding set to
  SOAP-DOCUMENT-LITERAL and click *Next*.

▶ Leave all the default settings in the Properties dialog and click *Next*.

▶ Click *Finish*.

When the transformation finishes the UML to WSDL for JK Enterprises.tc file
opens. Close the file and verify the new transformation configuration by
expanding *AccountApplicationSCEJB* in the Project Explorer to locate the UML to
WSDL for JKEnterprises.tc file (Figure 13-15).

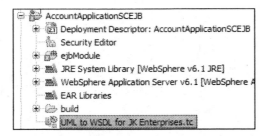

Figure 13-15   New transformation configuration: Verification

Run the UML to WSDL transformation

This section describes how to run the UML to WSDL transformation. We use the resulting WSDL with the Web Service wizard in "Create a skeleton EJB Web service from a WSDL" on page 451.

To run the UML to WSDL transformation perform these steps:

► From Project Explorer, expand `AccountApplicationSCEJB` and find the `UML to WSDL for JK Enterprises.tc` file.

► Select the `UML to WSDL for JK Enterprises.tc` file and *Transform → UML to WSDL*.

A new folder named `_3AtomicBusinessApplicationServiceProviders` is created under `AccountApplicationSCEJB` and it contains the WSDL and related files (Figure 13-16).

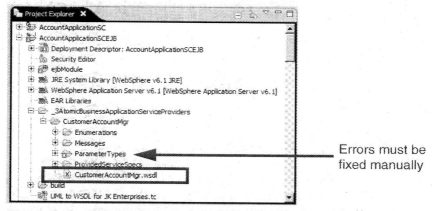

Errors must be fixed manually

Figure 13-16   UML to WSDL transformation resulting file structure

The transformation results in three errors in `ParameterTypes.xsd` in the `ParameterTypes` folder. Open the `ParameterTypes.xsd` file and correct the errors as follows:

```
From:
    <xsd:element name="requestAmount" type="xsd:Float"/>
    <xsd:element minOccurs="0" name="applicationDate" type="xsd:Date"/>
    <xsd:element name="applicationDate" type="xsd:Date"/>
To:
    <xsd:element name="requestAmount" type="xsd:float"/>
    <xsd:element minOccurs="0" name="applicationDate" type="xsd:date"/>
    <xsd:element name="applicationDate" type="xsd:date"/>
```

> **Note:** You can now jump to "Create a skeleton EJB Web service from a WSDL" on page 451 to generate the Web service or continue to the next section.

UML to Java V5 transformation configuration

This section describes how to configure a new UML to Java V5.0 transformation. We use this transformation on the design model to generate our skeleton Java classes. We then use these skeleton Java classes to implement the determineApplicationEligibility service component in "Implement the business logic" on page 456.

To configure a new UML to Java V5.0 transformation perform these steps:

► Switch to the Modeling perspective.

► From the Project Explorer expand *Red Book JK Enterprises UML Models →
  Models → Design Model.*

► Select the *Design Model* and *Open Model.*

► Open the New Transformation Configuration dialog by selection *Modeling →
  Transformation → New Configuration.*

► In the Name field type UML to Java V5.0 for JK Enterprises.

► Select *UML to Java V5.0* from the list of transformations.

► Select *Enable reverse transformation.*

► For the Configuration file destination click *Browse* and select
  /AccountApplicationSCEJB, then click *Next.* The Name and Transformation
  dialog is shown in Figure 13-17.

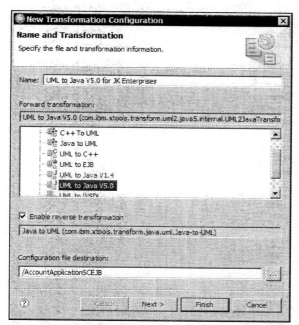

Figure 13-17   New Transformation configuration: Name and transformation

▶ Set the transformation source by expanding *Red Book JK Enterprise UML Models → Models* and selecting *Design Model*.

▶ Set the transformation target by selecting *ApplicationAccountSCEJB* from the right pane and click *Next* (Figure 13-18).

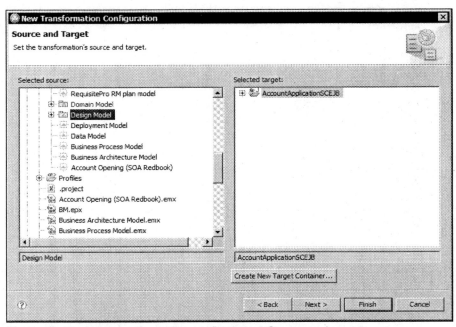

Figure 13-18   New transformation configuration: Source and target

► Leave all of the defaults in the UML to Java Options dialog and click *Next*.

► Leave all of the defaults in the Collections dialog and click *Next*.

► On the Mapping view, select *Enable mapping*.

The UML to Java V5.0 transformation, by default, uses the package structure of the model for the Java package names. The package structure of the model might not make the best Java package name. Because of this, we define custom mapping of the model elements to Java packages.

► Click *New* to create a new mapping model file.

► Using the Windows Explorer in the dialog, browse to find *AccountApplicationSCEJB/mappings* and type the file name `JKModelMapping.emx`.

The Mapping dialog of the New Transformation Configuration is shown in Figure 13-19.

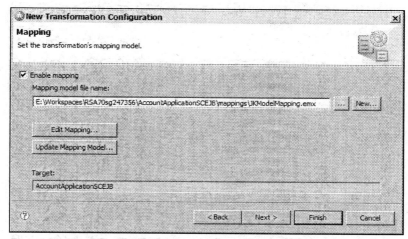

Figure 13-19   New transformation configuration: Create mapping file

Next we add the packages.

► Click *Edit Mapping*.

► Expand *Red Book JK Enterprises UML Models → Models → Design Model*. Select *Service Components,* type `com.ibm.redbook.jke` in the Mapped Name field and click *Apply*.

► Expand *Red Book JK Enterprises UML Models → Models → Service Model → 3 - Atomic Business Application Service Providers → CustomerAccountMgr*:

  – Select *Parameter Types*, type `com.ibm.redbook.jke.parametertypes` in the Mapped Name field and click *Apply*.

  – Select *Messages*, type `com.ibm.redbook.jke.messages` in the Mapped Name field and click *Apply*.

► The Edit Mapped Name dialog is shown in Figure 13-20. Click *OK*.

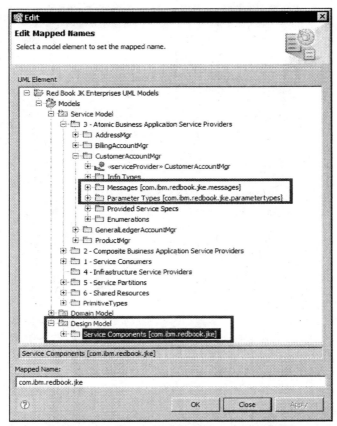

Figure 13-20   New transformation configuration: Add package mapping

► Click *Next*.

► Leave the defaults for Java to UML Options (if *Enable reverse transformation* is selected).

► To have traceability of the skeleton classes created by the transformation back to the design model, select *Create source to target relationships* in the Transformation options section as shown in Figure 13-21.

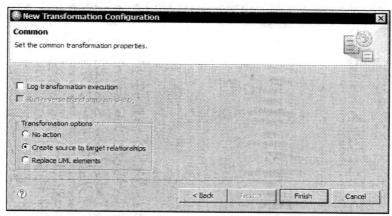

Figure 13-21 New transformation configuration: traceability

▶ Click *Finish*.

▶ Close the generated file. You can find the generated `UML to Java V5.0 for JKEnterprises.tc` file in the `AccountApplicationSCEJB` project.

▶ The mapping, `JKModelMapping`, can be found in a new `Models` folder in the project (although the `JKModelMapping.emx` file is in the `mappings` folder).

Note: We could have also used the UML to EJB transformation on our design model and generated EJBs instead of plain Java objects. We have assigned the EJB stereotypes to our model elements which the UML to EJB transformation uses to generate the EJBs. The UML to Java V5.0 transformation just ignores these stereotypes and generates plain Java objects.

Run the UML to Java V5.0 transformation

This section describes how to run the UML to Java V5.0 transformation. We use the generated skeleton code to implement the Web service in "Implement the business logic" on page 456.

To run the UML to Java V5.0 transformation select the `UML to Java V5.0 for JK Enterprises.tc` file and *Transform → UML to Java V5.0*.

Figure 13-22 shows the directory structure of the `AccountApplicationSCEJB` module after the transformation. You notice there are errors markers on the module and on some of the packages. There are a few reasons for these errors:

▶ We do not have an EJB defined in the deployment descriptor.

► Classes in the packages have references to classes which have not been created yet.

► Import of `java.util.Date` is required in some of the Java classes.

The errors are resolved by completing "Visualization and traceability of generated Java classes" (below) and "Create a skeleton EJB Web service from a WSDL" on page 451.

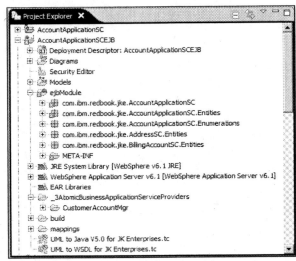

Figure 13-22 UML to Java V5.0 transformation resulting file structure and files.

Visualization and traceability of generated Java classes

Rational Software Architect provides the capability to visualize the generated Java classes and provides traceability back to the models.

We can visualize a class and then show traceability to the design model by performing the following steps:

► Select `com.ibm.redbook.jke.AccountApplicationSC.AccountApplication-Service` and *Visualize → Add to New Diagram File → Class Diagram*. When prompted click OK to enable selected activities. This creates a new class diagram for `AccountApplicationService` (Figure 13-23).

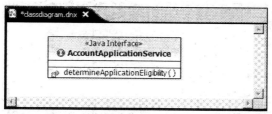

Figure 13-23   Visual representation of AccountApplicationService

Now we can show traceability.

► Select AccountApplicationService in the class diagram and *Filters* → *Show Related Elements.*

► Click *Details.*

► Select and then clear *All Relationships*, to remove all selections.

► Expand Java and select *Trace (Abstraction)*. The configuration is shown in Figure 13-24.

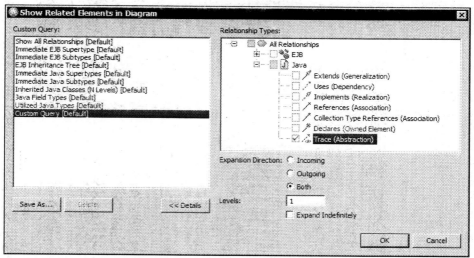

Figure 13-24   Show related elements in diagram configuration

► Click *OK*. The resulting diagram shows that the AccountApplicationService is derived from the AccountApplicationService Java interface defined in the design model (Figure 13-25).

► Save the class diagram.

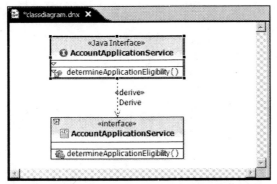

Figure 13-25   Trace of the AccountApplicationService back to the design model

Note: Rational Software Architect has the capability to visualize the Java classes in UML and then work with the UML to continue with development.

Resolve compilation errors

Now is a good time to resolve some of the compilation errors:

► From Project Explorer, open the `AccountApplication` class in the Java editor:

   `com.ibm.redbook.jke.AccountApplicationSC.Entities.AccountApplication`

   Insert `import java.util.Date` (Figure 13-26), then save the changes.

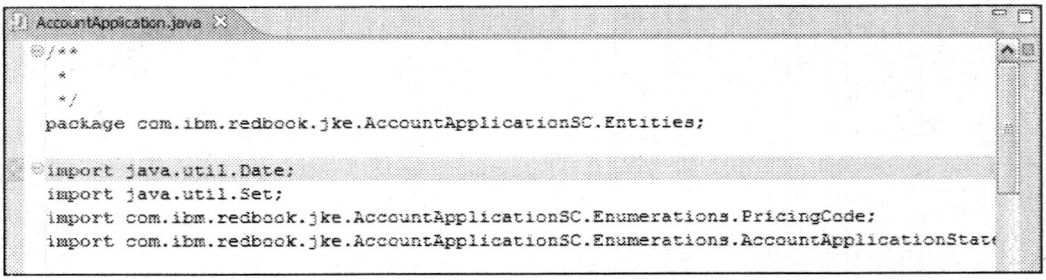

```
AccountApplication.java
/**
*
*/
package com.ibm.redbook.jke.AccountApplicationSC.Entities;

import java.util.Date;
import java.util.Set;
import com.ibm.redbook.jke.AccountApplicationSC.Enumerations.PricingCode;
import com.ibm.redbook.jke.AccountApplicationSC.Enumerations.AccountApplicationState
```

Figure 13-26   Import java.util.Date

Tip: To resolve compile errors you can select an error mark and *Quick Fix*, then select one of the suggested actions, such as `import java.util.Date`.

Visualize and modify the WSDL

In this section we utilize the visualization and editing capabilities in Rational Software Architect. We view and edit the WSDL we generated in "Run the UML to WSDL transformation" on page 439.

► In Project Explorer, select CustomerAccountMgr.wsdl and *Visualize → Add to New Diagram file → Class Diagram* (Figure 13-27).

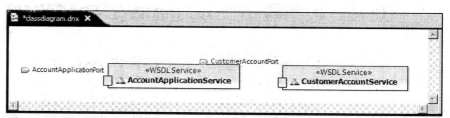

Figure 13-27   Visual representation of the services found in CustomerAccountMgr.wsdl

► In the class diagram, double-click the AccountApplicationService to open it in the WSDL editor. Select *Detailed* from the View pull-down (Figure 13-28).

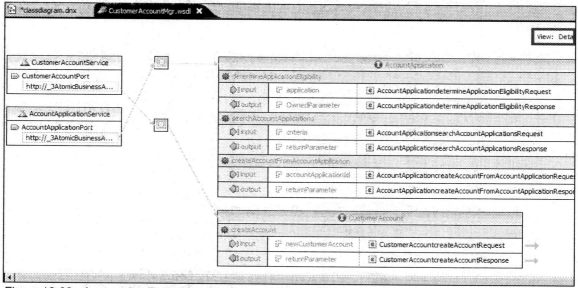

Figure 13-28   AccountApplicationService in the WSDL editor

► At this point, if we wanted to add a new port, we would select one of the services and *Add Port* (Figure 13-29).

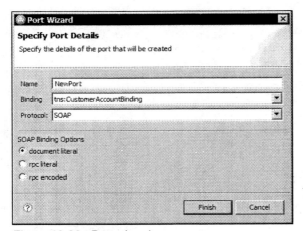

Name
Binding
Protocol

Protocol options

Figure 13-29   Port wizard

► Click *Cancel* to dismiss the dialog.

We can also use this view to add and configure the messages associated with the service:

► In the WSDL editor double-click the `AccountApplication` port type (with the Interface icon). This opens the port type in a view where we can add operations.

► Select the `AccountApplication` port type and *Add Operation*. A new operation appears as shown in Figure 13-30.

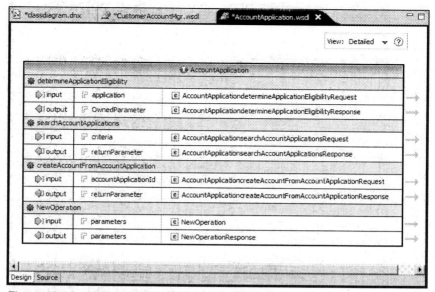

Figure 13-30   Adding an operation to the service

► Close this editor without saving a new operation.

In this section we described how to visualize a WSDL and modify the WSDL using the visualization and editing capabilities in Rational Software Architect. In the next section we use the Web Service wizard to generate code from the WSDL.

Create a skeleton EJB Web service from a WSDL

In this section we describe how to use the Web Service wizard to create an EJB Web service top down from the WSDL we created in "Run the UML to WSDL transformation" on page 439.

► Switch perspective by selecting *Window → Open Perspective → J2EE.*

► In the Project Explorer expand *AcountApplicationSCEJB →
_3AtomicBusinessApplicationServiceProviders → CustomerAccountMgr* to
find the CustomerAccountMgr.wsdl file.

► Select the CustomerAccountMgr.wsdl file and *New → Other.*

► Expand the *Web Service* directory and select *Web Service.* Click *Next*
(Figure 13-31).

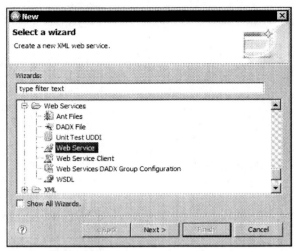

Figure 13-31   Web Service wizard: Launch

Now we begin configuring the Web Service wizard to generate our EJB Web service.

► For the Web service type field, select *Top down EJB Web Service*.

► The Service definition field should be automatically filled with the selected WSDL file `/AccountApplicationSCEJB/.../CustomerAccountMgr.wsdl`.

► Select *Monitor the Web service*. This enables us to use the TCP/IP Monitor to view the request and the response SOAP messages.

► Leave all the other configuration at their defaults. The Web Service wizard is shown in Figure 13-32. Click *Next*.

Note: We do not select to generate the Web service client. The client is usually generated by the consumer of the Web service.

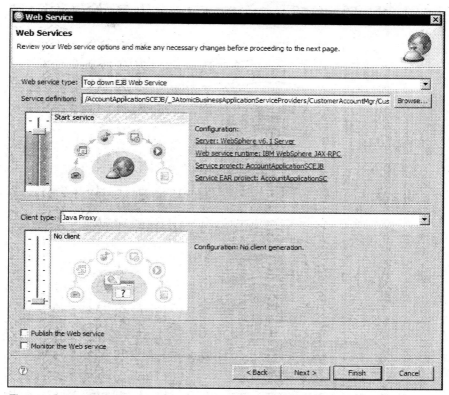

Figure 13-32 Web Service wizard: Top-down EJB Web service configuration

► In the Web Service Skeleton EJB Configuration panel, select *Define custom mapping for namespace to package*.

The Web Service wizard uses the namespaces defined in the WSDL to create package names for the Java classes it generates. These namespaces, as in our example, can be complex and not well suited for Java package names. The Web Service wizard enables you to provide a namespace to Java package mapping to generate meaningful Java package names.

► Leave all the other configuration at their defaults. The Web Service wizard is shown in Figure 13-33. Click *Next*.

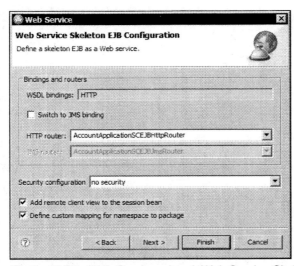

Figure 13-33   Web Service wizard: Web Service Skeleton EJB Configuration

► On the Web Service Skeleton namespace to package mapping panel, click *Import*.

► We have provided a namespace to package properties file for you. In the Browse Files dialog, expand *AccountApplicationSCEJB → mappings* to find `jkemappings.properties` file.

► Select `jkemappings.properties` and click *OK*.

► The namespace to package mappings have been imported. The Web Service wizard is shown in Figure 13-34. Click *Next*.

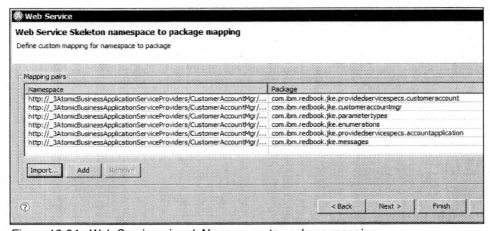

Figure 13-34   Web Service wizard: Namespace to package mapping

- ► Be patient, parsing the WSDL file and generating code takes a while.
- ► In the Start Server panel, we start the test server to deploy and test the Web service we are creating. Click *Start server*.
- ► Once the server has started and the application is deployed, click *Next*.
- ► On the Web Service Publication panel, you have the option to publish this Web service to a UDDI Registry. For this sample, we do not publish the Web service to a UDDI Registry. Click *Finish*.

  The Web Service wizard created a Web module named `AccountApplicationSCEJBHttpRouter`. This module performs the routing of the Web service calls to the EJB Web service.

- ► Expand *AccountApplicationSCEJB* → *ejbModule* to view the packages and Java classes that were created by the wizard. The Project Explorer is shown in Figure 13-35.

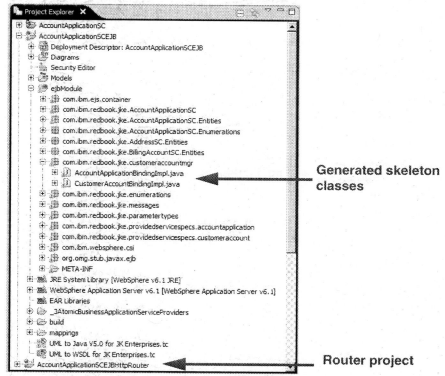

Figure 13-35   Project Explorer after EJB Web Service generation

We have completed the EJB Web service skeleton creation. We implement the EJB Web service using the Web service skeleton and the skeleton code that we generated in "Run the UML to Java V5.0 transformation" on page 445.

Implement the business logic

From our service and design models we use transformations from Rational Software Architect to move from a higher level of abstraction to a lower level of abstraction:

► We use the UML to WSDL transformation on the service model to generate the WSDL.

► We then use the WSDL2Java transformation, with the help of the Web Service wizard, to generate the skeleton interfaces for our Web service.

► For the design model, we use a UML to Java V5.0 to generate skeleton code that is used for the implementation of the determineApplicationEligibility operation for the AccountApplication service.

► Now we implement the business logic that will glue these pieces together.

We have been leveraging the capabilities in Rational Software Architect to model and transform our models. Depending on the transformation, these can either be executed by an architect or a developer role. We now transition to a pure developer role and utilize Rational Software Architect to implement the business logic and glue the pieces together.

We have created code templates with the business logic and miscellaneous code fragments to limit the amount of copying and pasting we have to do for this implementation.

Implement the Web service by performing the following steps:

► Open the J2EE perspective (*Window → Open Perspective → J2EE*).

When we performed the UML to Java V5.0 transformation, Rational Software Architect put tasks into a task list as reminders to us that we may have to modify the code. We use the Tasks view to find the methods we must implement. The Tasks view appears at the bottom of the product window (Figure 13-36).

► If the Tasks view is not visible, open it by selecting *Window → Show View → Tasks.*

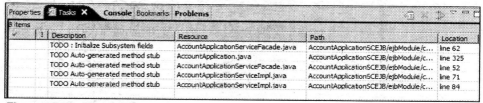

✓	!	Description	Resource	Path	Location
		TODO : Initialize Subsystem fields	AccountApplicationServiceFacade.java	AccountApplicationSCEJB/ejbModule/c...	line 62
		TODO Auto-generated method stub	AccountApplication.java	AccountApplicationSCEJB/ejbModule/c...	line 325
		TODO Auto-generated method stub	AccountApplicationServiceFacade.java	AccountApplicationSCEJB/ejbModule/c...	line 52
		TODO Auto-generated method stub	AccountApplicationServiceImpl.java	AccountApplicationSCEJB/ejbModule/c...	line 71
		TODO Auto-generated method stub	AccountApplicationServiceImpl.java	AccountApplicationSCEJB/ejbModule/c...	line 84

Figure 13-36   Tasks lists

From the Tasks view we implement the TODO items for the
AccountApplicationServiceImpl class.

> **Note:** We introduce a signature change on the
> determinApplicationEligibility method made by the developer. We do this
> to simulate the iterative nature of development and the need for reverse
> transformation to keep your design model current. More information about
> reverse transformation and an example transformation can be found in "Refine
> service components" on page 395.

To complete the AccountApplicationServiceImpl class perform these steps:

▶ Double-click the task for the AccountApplicationServiceImpl.java resource
to open the class at the location of the determineApplicationEligibility
TODO method.

▶ Change the method signature to:

```
public AccountApplication determineApplicationEligibility
                        (AccountApplication application, float limit)
```

▶ Delete the existing two lines of code.

```
//TODO Auto-generated method stub
return null;
```

▶ Use the code template daeImpl to add code to the method. (Type dae and
press Ctrl+SpaceBar to select the daeImpl template as in Figure 13-37.)

The sample code prints log messages to the Console and decides if a credit
report is required based on company name and requested amount.

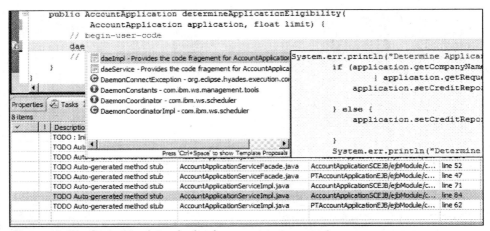

Figure 13-37   Code template: daeImpl

▶ Optionally remove the TODO line in the getApplication method.

▶ Press Ctrl+S to save the changes.

We now link the implementation to the Web service skeleton by performing these steps:

▶ Open the AccountApplicationBindingImpl class at the determineApplicationEligibility method. You can do this by expanding *AccountApplicationSCEJB → ejbModule → com.ibm.redbook.jke.customeraccountmgr → AccountApplicationBindingImpl* and double-clicking the determineApplicationEligibility method.

▶ Delete the line of code: return null;

▶ Use the code template daeService to add code to the method. Type dae and press Ctrl+SpaceBar to select the daeService template.

The sample code returns an eligibility message with application status and comment (eligible or credit report required).

▶ Press Ctrl+S to save the changes.

You have completed the implementation of the Web service. If you have any compilation errors, you must resolve them before you can continue to testing.

Test the service

Unit testing is traditional performed by the developer. Rational Software Architect has many features to assist the developer in unit testing. In this section we describe the following features to assist in unit testing Web services:

- ▶ Web Services Explorer
- ▶ TCP/IP Monitor
- ▶ Component Test
- ▶ JUnit

> **Note:** A unit test plan should be created for unit test. This test plan should then be reviewed and static testing of the unit test plan should be done to reveal any missing scenarios. For more information about testing, see the Rational Unified Process Test discipline.

Web Services Explorer

We unit test the `determineApplicationEligibility` service by using the Web Services Explorer.

The Web Services Explorer allows you to explore, import and test WSDL document. You can use this tool to aid in unit testing your own Web service operations or those of a third-party Web service.

The Web Service Explorer also allows you to publish the business entities and Web services to a registry. The Web Services Explorer comes populated with several registries, you can also add additional registries to your list of favorites.

> **Note:** Refer to the Rational Application Developer InfoCenter for information about exploring and importing WSDL and for publishing your business entities and Web services to a registry.

Start the test server

Start the server if not already started, in the Servers view start the WebSphere Application Server V6.1 test server by clicking the *Start* icon ◉ .

Locate and open the WSDL file

To test the Web service from the WSDL file perform these steps:

- ▶ Start Web Services Explorer by selecting *Run → Launch the Web Services Explorer.*
- ▶ Click the WSDL page 📄 icon located in the upper right corner of the Web Service Explorer.
- ▶ In the Navigator pane, select *WSDL Main*. This opens the Open WSDL view in the Actions pane.
- ▶ Enter the URL of a WSDL document:
  - Click *Browse.*
  - For the Category select *Workspace WSDL documents.*

- For Workspace Projects select *AccountApplicationSCEJB*.
- For WSDL URL use the pull-down to locate the correct WSDL file:

  ```
  platform:/resource/AccountApplicationSCEJB/ejbModule/META-INF/wsdl/Custo
  merAccountMgr.wsdl
  ```

- Click *Go* (Figure 13-38).

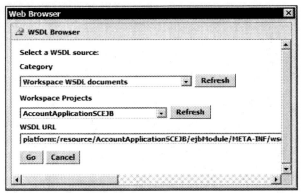

Figure 13-38   Select WSDL file

► Click *Go* in the Actions pane to work with the selected WSDL file.

Note: The Web Service Explorer enables you to browse the WSDL operations and set additional endpoints for the service. This is covered in detail in "Browse operations and set WSDL endpoints" on page 467.

Invoke the determineApplicationEligibility WSDL operation

In this section we describe how to test the determineApplicationEligibility operation using the Web Service Explorer.

► From the Navigator pane, expand *AccountApplicationService* → *AccountApplicationBinding* and select *determineApplicationEligibility* (Figure 13-39).

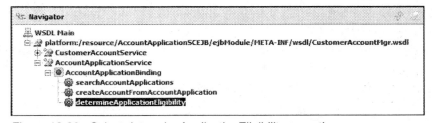

Figure 13-39   Select determineApplicationEligibility operation

► In the Actions pane, enter the account application test data into the fields, for example:

    — Customer: Laura, Olson, 123-456-7890
    — Address: 4400 N First Street, San Jose, CA, USA, 95134
    — Request amount: 4444.44
    — Credit report needed: true
    — Credit score: 777
    — Pricing code: Medium
    — Application decision: true
    — Company name: IBM
    — Status: UnderEligibilityCheck

► Click *Go*.

► The Web service runs and the status window displays the formatted results (Figure 13-40).

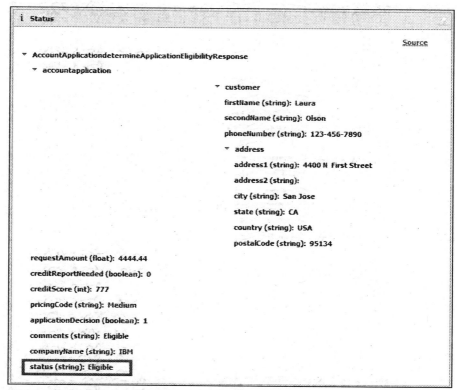

Figure 13-40   Result of the Web service call

Also note the test output of the Web service in the Console view.

TCP/IP Monitor

TCP/IP Monitor is a simple server that monitors all request and response between the Web browser and the server. It is another way, besides the Web Services Explorer, to monitor the SOAP request and response messages.

To use TCP/IP Monitor to test our Web service, we have to send the message to the TCP/IP Monitor port:

► In the Servers view select the server and *Monitoring → Properties.* You should see that the Monitor is started, the server port, and the monitor port.

► In the Web Services Explorer, select *AccountApplicationBinding* in the Navigator. In the Actions pane click Add for Endpoints and add an endpoint using the same syntax but changing the port to the monitor port. Then select the new port and click *Go.*

► Select the *determineApplicationEligibility* method in the Navigator and run the Web service with some data.

► The TCP/IP Monitor view opens and you can see the input and output messages. Select *XML* for both input and output messages to see the formatted XML messages (Figure 13-41).

► We can also open the TCP/IP Monitor view by selecting *Window → Show View → Debug → TCP/IP Monitor.*

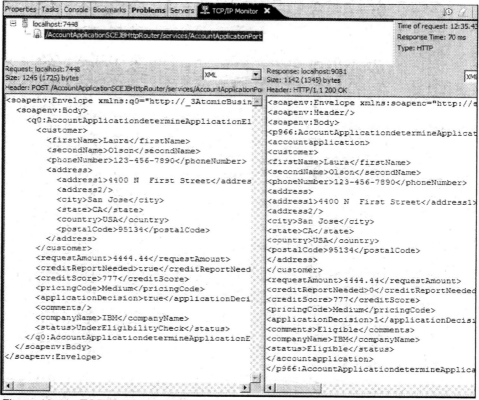

Figure 13-41 TCP/IP Monitor view

Alternatively, we could generate a client for the Web service using the Web Service wizard and selecting the Monitor service option.

Component test

In software development it is well known that component testing allows us to find and fix defects early. In a SOA solution it becomes crucial to find and fix defects early. The impact of a defect can have a cascading effect because the service could be used by multiple critical systems.

Rational Application Developer comes with automated component testing features that allow us to create, edit, deploy, and run automated tests of Java components, EJB components, and Web services.

For an in-depth information about the component test features in Rational Application Developer refer to IBM developerWorks:

- Tutorial: DEV341: *Essentials of IBM Rational Application Developer*:

  http://www-128.ibm.com/developerworks/rational/library/05/dev341/dev341.html

- Article: *Component testing with IBM Rational Application Developer for WebSphere Software*:

  http://www-128.ibm.com/developerworks/rational/library/05/kelly-stoker/

JUnit

Rational Application Developer has support for JUnit testing. JUnit is a simple testing framework that creates repeatable tests. The JUnit tests are created and run by the developer to validate their code and also used to perform regression testing. For more information about how to use JUnit, refer to the Rational Application Developer InfoCenter.

Summary of top-down development of a service

In this section we described the top-down development of a service:

- We introduced model transformations.
- We configured a UML to WSDL and a UML to Java V5 transformation
- We performed transformations on our service and design models.
- We leveraged the Web Service wizard to generate and EJB Web service from a WSDL
- We implemented the service from the skeleton code that was produced by the transformations
- We unit tested our service using the Web Services Explorer.

Third-party service

In the JK Enterprises sample application we are using a third-party service for the address verification service. We received the WSDL from the third-party and we have to test the *validate* operation on AddressVerification service.

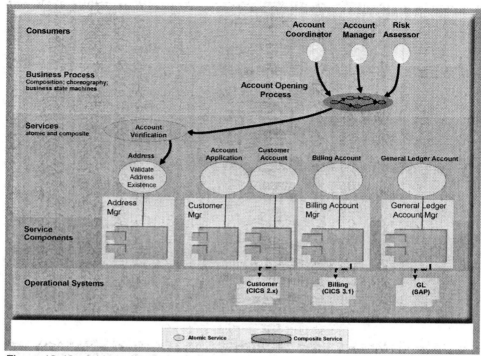

Figure 13-42   Address Verification service

> **Note:** For this book we have provided a stubbed out sample address verification Web service. The are multiple address verification services available today. For a real address verification server, refer to the internet.

Prepare for sample third-party sample

We have provided an address service to simulate using a third-party service.

Import the project interchange file

To import the project interchange file perform the following steps:

► Select *File → Import*.

► In the Import dialog, expand *Other* and select *Project Interchange*.

► Click *Browse* to locate and open file:

```
c:\SG247356\sampcode\SoftwareArchitect\thirdparty\AddrVerification.zip
```

► Select *AddrVerification* and *AddressVerificationServiceEAR* and click *Finish*.

Add the project to the test server

We use the WebSphere Application Server to host the third-party service.

Add the project to the test server by performing these steps:

► Open the *Servers* view.

► Right-click the WebSphere Application test server and select *Add and Remove Projects*.

► Select *AddrVerificationServiceEAR* and click *Add*. Click *Finish*.

Start the test server

Start the WebSphere Application Server in the Servers view by selecting the server and *Start*.

Validating the WSDL file

When you create a WSDL file through the Web Service wizard the WSDL that is generated should be valid. However, if you have imported a WSDL file, or if you are creating a WSDL file, you should validate the WSDL to ensure it is valid.

In the JK Enterprises sample solution we are using a third-party service for the Address Verification service. We received the WSDL from the third party and we have to validate the WSDL to make sure it is valid and complies with the Web Services Interoperability (WS-I) Basic Profile.

WS-I Basic Profile is an outline of requirements to which a WSDL and a Web service protocol traffic must comply to claim WS-I conformance. Rational Application Developer allows us to configure the level of compliance that we require our WSDLs to meet. For more information about how to configure WS-I compliance, refer to the Rational Application Developer's InfoCenter.

> **Note:** WS-I is an organization designed to promote Web service interoperability across, platforms, operating systems and programing languages. For more information about WS-I, refer to:
>
>   http://www.ws-i.org

The WSDL file is stored under:

    AddrVerficitionService/WebContent/WEB-INF/wsdl/AddressVerification.wsdl

Validate the WSDL file by selecting the file and *Validate WSDL*.

Testing the third-party Web service

In this section we demonstrate how to use the Web Services Explorer to test the third-party service.

Locate and open the WSDL file

Locate and open the third-party WSDL by performing the following:

- ► Select the `AddressVerification.wsdl` file and *Web Services → Test with Web Services Explorer*.

- ► The Web Services Explorer opens (Figure 13-43).

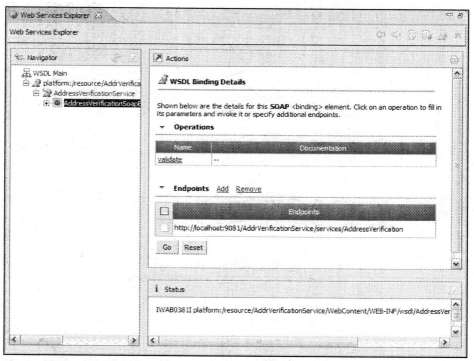

Figure 13-43   Web Services Explorer for third-party Web service

Browse operations and set WSDL endpoints

You can browse the available endpoints and add additional endpoint to test through the WSDL Binding Details view. Here are the steps to view the available endpoints and to add an endpoint.

- ► Select *AddressVerificationSoapBinding* in the Navigator pane (Figure 13-44).

Figure 13-44   Web services Explorer: Selecting the service binding

▶ You are now able to view the available operations and the endpoints. You can
   add an endpoint by clicking *Add*. A copy of the endpoint is made, which you
   can modify to:

```
http://localhost:9080/AddrVerificationService/services/AddressVerification
```

▶ Click *Go* and the new endpoint is added to the list (Figure 13-45).

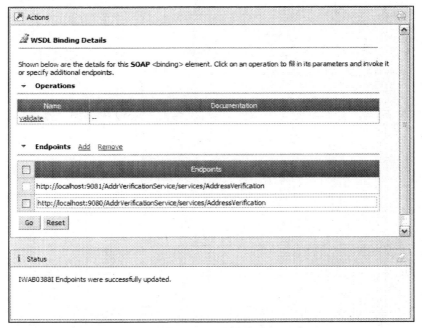

Figure 13-45   Web services Explorer: Adding an endpoint

Invoking a WSDL operation

In this section we test the *validate* operation on the `AddressVerification`
service. To perform these steps, the WebSphere test server must be started.

► From the Navigator pane expand *AddressVeficationSoapBinding* and select *validate* (Figure 13-46).

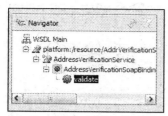

Figure 13-46   Web service Explorer: Select the validate operation

► In the Actions pane select the endpoint:

`http://localhost:9081/AddrVerificationService/services/AddressVerification`

► Enter any values into the address fields (Figure 13-47).

Figure 13-47   Web services Explorer: Validate operation parameter entry

▶ Click *Go.*

▶ The Status pane displays the Web service operations response (Figure 13-48).

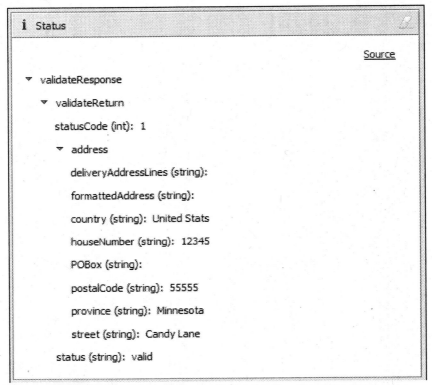

i Status

Source

▾ validateResponse

  ▾ validateReturn

    statusCode (int): 1

    ▾ address

      deliveryAddressLines (string):

      formattedAddress (string):

      country (string): United Stats

      houseNumber (string): 12345

      POBox (string):

      postalCode (string): 55555

      province (string): Minnesota

      street (string): Candy Lane

    status (string): valid

Figure 13-48   Web services Explorer: Test validation operation status

▶ Click *Source* in the Status pane and the SOAP Request and Response Envelopes are displayed (Figure 13-49).

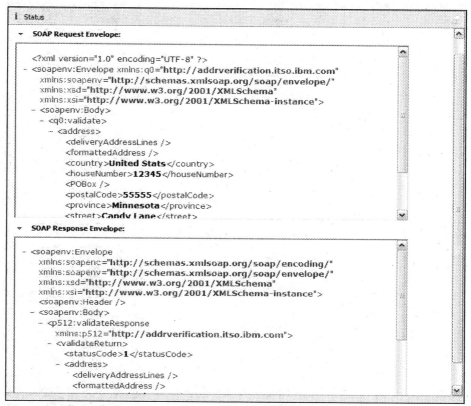

Figure 13-49   Web services Explorer: Validation operation SOAP envelopes

Summary of third-party service

In this section we simulated the validation and testing of a third-party service. We looked a the WSDL validation and the Web Services Explorer.

Rational Application Developer's WSDL validation capabilities enables us to validated a WSDL we import or that we have created. We can configure the WS-I level of compliance we want the validator to verify.

The Web Services Explorer tool is a good tool to use when we are supplied with a WSDL and we need to import and test the Web service. It is also helpful in testing Web services we have created with the Web Service wizard.

Indirectly exposing an enterprise service

In this section we show how to indirectly expose an enterprise service. We illustrate how to create a J2C bean and a Java data binding that is used to call the CICS Transaction Gateway, which in turn accesses the CICS Transaction Server. We expose the J2C bean as a Web service endpoint, which receives SOAP requests.

> **Note:** We are demonstrating the techniques to expose enterprise server in this section. This section does not provide a sample CICS Transaction Gateway or a CICS Transaction Server. We use a fictitious CICS system and sample configuration values which would need to be replaced by real CICS system and configuration values to run the resulting Web service. This section is here to demonstrate the steps and techniques.

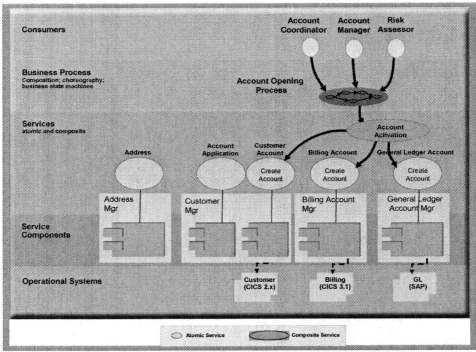

Figure 13-50   Create Account operation on the Customer Account service

We expose an older CICS application (running on CICS 2.3) through a tightly-coupled J2C adaptor. In this case, the CICS program we are calling represents the customer master record.

As we open the account in the Open Account business process at JK Enterprises we must create a customer record. We build the service in this section that will later be called by the business process.

> **Note:** It is important to note that the techniques we use here can also be used to expose IMS programs.

Preparing for sample

We have to create a new Dynamic Web Project called CICSCustomerWeb, which we use to build a Web service connecting to our fictitious CICS system. We highlight in the chapter in which steps the configuration values would need to be replaced by real configuration values.

To create an Enterprise Application Project perform the following:

► Select *File → New → Project → Web → Dynamic Web Project*.

► Type CICSCustomerWeb as Project Name.

► Create a new EAR Application by clicking *New*, and name it CICSCustomer, Click *Finish*.

► Click *Finish*.

We must have the Java Connector Tools installed and the capabilities enabled.

Implementation

In this section, we perform these steps:

► Create a Java data binding
► Create a J2C bean
► Create a Web service to use the J2C bean

Create Java data binding

We use a wizard to create a mapping from a COBOL structure to a Java object, and vice-versa. This is necessary because the COBOL executing on CICS is expecting a COBOL record structure, in EBCDIC, whereas our Web application manipulates Java objects in ASCII.

► In Project Explorer, select CICSCustomerWeb and *New → Other*. In the Select a Wizard dialog, under *J2C* select *CICS/IMS Java Data Binding* (Figure 13-51).

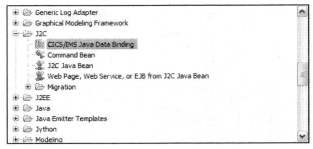

Figure 13-51   CICS/IMS Java data binding

► In the Data Import window perform these steps:

 – Chose mapping field: Select *COBOL to Java*.

 – COBOL file:

```
c:\SG247356\sampcode\SoftwareArchitect\cics\CUSTPROG.cbl
```

► The Import dialog is where you select the code page conversion:

 – For Platform select *z/OS®*.

 – For Data Structures, click *Query*. When the list has been populated, select *DFHCOMMAREA*. Click *Next* (Figure 13-52).

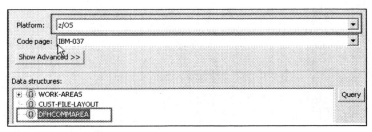

Figure 13-52   Select data structure

DFHCOMMAREA is the default name giving to the CICS COMMAREA (communication area).

► On the next page, leave Generation Style as *Default*. The Project name should be CICSCustomerWeb. Enter a package name, for this example use: com.jke.cics. Change the class name to CreateAccount (Figure 13-53).

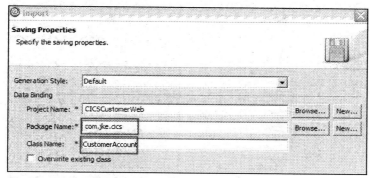

Figure 13-53   Saving properties

These changes simply make the package names conforming to JK Enterprises and what the application is actually doing. None of these names reflect what is exposed in the WSDL file.

▶ Click *Finish*. This creates an `CreateAccount.java` file in the Web project. You use this class later to pass and receive data from CICS.

Create J2C JavaBean and a Web service to use the J2C bean

Now we use the wizard to create a J2C JavaBean and a Web service to use the J2C JavaBean, which means you do not have to write any code to use the CICS Transaction Gateway to call the program on CICS. This wizard uses the Java data binding we created in the previous section.

▶ Under Dynamic Web Projects, select the `CICSCustomerWeb` project and *New → Other*. In the wizard select *J2C Java Bean*. Click *Next* (Figure 13-54).

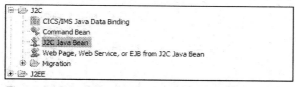

Figure 13-54   Select J2C Java Bean wizard

▶ The Resource Adapter Selection page is where you select the resource adapter. Select *1.5 > ECIResourceAdapter (IBM:6.0.2)*. Click *Next* (Figure 13-55).

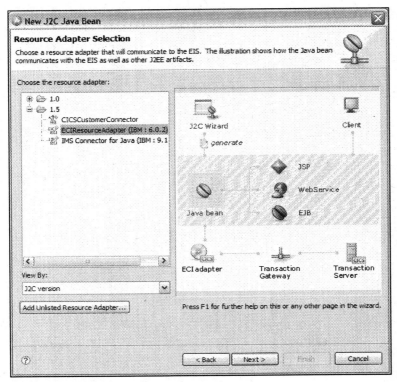

Figure 13-55   Resource adapter selection

Note: Resource adapters are a set of related classes that let an application access a resource such as data, or an application on a remote server, often called an enterprise information system (EIS).

In the Connection Properties page we use a managed connection:

► Next to the JNDI lookup name field click *New*.

A wizard opens and takes you through creating a connection factory in the WebSphere Application Server Test Environment.

► In the Server Selection page select *WebSphere Application Server V6.1* and click *Next*.

► In the New J2C Connection Factory page, you enter the values for the connection factory that will be created in WebSphere. Expand the window and click *Show Advanced* to configure advance properties (Figure 13-56).

- In JNDI Name field type `CICS/CustProg`.
- Leave the Connection class name as the default value.
- In Connection URL field type `tcp://demomvs.itso.ibm.com`.

  This is the URL for CICS Transaction Gateway with which the Resource Adapter communicates.

- In the Server name field type `CICSACB3`.
- For the Port number type `12006`.
- For User name type `TEAM99`.
- For the Password type `t6y7u8i9`.
- Under Advance Properties, for TPN Name type `DSMI`.

The above values depend on the installation. The server name should match the server that is created using the configuration tool, and a Connection URL of `local:` means it uses the Gateway in local mode on the local machine. For more information about these parameters, consult the CICS Transaction Gateway documentation.

- Click *Finish* (Figure 13-56).

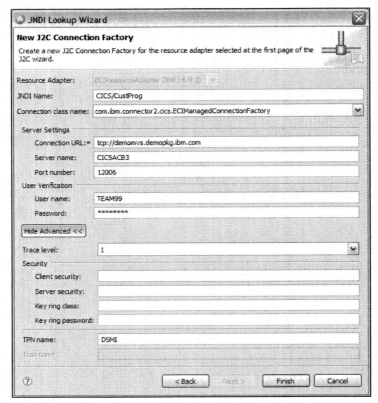

Figure 13-56   New J2C Connection Factory

► This step takes some time, because it starts the test server, and then creates a connection factory. When this has finished it should have filled in the JNDI lookup name in the Connection Properties window. Click *Next*.

► The J2C Java Bean Output Properties window enables us to select names for the generated classes. The Project name should be `CICSCustomerWeb`. Click *Browse* next to the Package Name to select `com.jke.cics`.

► For the Interface Name type `CustProgJ2Bean` and the Implementation Name is filled as `CustProgJ2CBeanImpl`. Click *Next* (Figure 13-57).

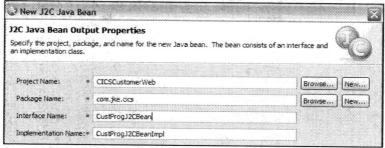

Figure 13-57   J2C Java Bean output properties

► In the Java Methods page you can add a method for each program you want to access in CICS:

   – Click *Add.* In the Java method name field type `custProg`. Click *Next* (Figure 13-58).

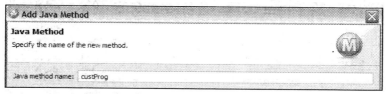

Figure 13-58   Add Java method

   – On the next page, you select the inputs and outputs for the method. These should be the data type(s) you created earlier. Next to Input type click *Browse*.

   – In the pop-up dialog select the `CreateAccount` class you created earlier (Figure 13-59).

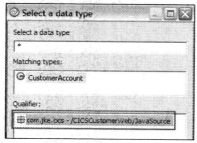

Figure 13-59   Select data type

- Click *Ok*. To use the same structure for input and output, select *Use the input type for output*. Click *Next*.

- Select both parameters and click *Finish*.

► Click *Next*.

► For J2EE Resource Type, select *Web Service*. Click *Next* (Figure 13-60).

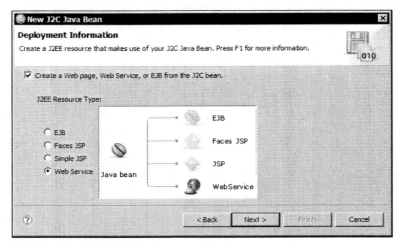

Figure 13-60   Deployment information

► In the Web service Creation dialog (Figure 13-61):

- Service Web Project: `CICSCustomerWeb`

- Click *Show Advanced* and set the Resource Reference to `CustProgRef` and the JNDI lookup name to `CICS/CustProg`.

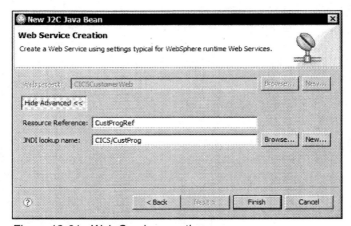

Figure 13-61   Web Service creation

- Click *Finish* to generate the Web service. (If you get an error indicating the Connection Factory already exists, ignore the error and click *Close*.)
- This should open the `CustProgJ2CBeanImpl.java` implementation class that has been created.

We can now test the Web service by using the Web Services Explorer. The Web Services Explorer is detailed in "Test the service" on page 458 and "Testing the third-party Web service" on page 467.

Note: You would require an actual CICS system to run the test.

Summary of indirectly exposing an enterprise service

In this section we demonstrated how to indirectly expose an enterprise service by creating a Java data binding, a J2C JavaBean, and then wrapping the bean with a Web service.

The techniques we demonstrated here can be applied to expose function in other systems (such as IMS) as a service.

Note: For more information about the options available to expose existing enterprise service, refer to the IBM Redbooks publication *Patterns: SOA Foundation Service Creation Scenarios*, SG24-7240:

- Realization options
- How to leverage the e-business patterns in the realization of those options
- Best practices in service creation

Updating the design

In this chapter we have covered the service implementation options of top-down development, third-party outsourcing, and indirectly exposing an enterprise service. In each of these situations Java code has been changed and created that is not reflected in the design model. To keep an accurate view of our solution we have to be able to perform a reverse transformations.

Rational Software Architect provides the capability to perform reverse transformations. It can perform reverse transformation to update an existing model in the case of top-down development. It can also perform reverse transformations to create new model elements in the case of bottom-up development.

Reverse transformations are covered in detail in "Reverse transformation from Java code" on page 413.

Output of service implementation

In this chapter we described the options available to implement a service. We demonstrated how to build a service top-down, how to subscribe to an external service, and how to integrate an existing function based on CICS.

We demonstrated the value of transformations as a way of moving from a higher level of abstraction to a lower level. We configured a UML to WSDL and a UML to Java V5 transformation. We ran the transformations to generate a WSDL and the skeleton Java code, which was used by the developers to implement the Web service.

We used the Web Service wizard to generate a top-down EJB Web service from the WSDL that was generated from the UML to WSDL transformation.

We implemented the business logic of the service using the skeleton Java code from the transformation and the Web service skeleton Java code.

We were introduced to the unit testing features in Rational Application Developer for Web services.

At the end of service implementation we have as outputs the implementation model and the developer tests for the service. The next step would be composite service implementation. In composite service implementing we use WebSphere Integration Developer to compose our services. Building composite services is mentioned briefly in the Introduction chapter of this book.

Another important output of implementation is the build. Rational Build Forge™ is a tool that provides a way for development teams to standardize and automate repetitive tasks, manage compliance mandates and share information. Rational Build Forge streamlines the software delivery throughout the development life cycle.

For more information about build, see the following:

► Rational Build Forge product Web site:

   `http://www-306.ibm.com/software/awdtools/buildforge/index.html`

► White paper: *Agile configuration management for Large Organizations*:

   `ftp://ftp.software.ibm.com/software/rational/web/whitepapers/wp-agile-cm4lrg-orgnzs.pdf`

14

Service testing

This chapter provides a look into testing SOA applications. It is organized into these sections:

► Introduction

► Testing SOA systems from a technology and architecture perspective

► SOA test strategy

► IBM products for SOA testing

► Test work products

► Test roles

► Test process

► Managing testing artifacts

► Creating reusable test scripts with Rational Manual Tester

► Designing and executing functional tests with Rational Functional Test

► Where to find more information

Introduction

In this chapter we cover the testing challenges and strategy in SOA. We do not cover the testing discipline in detail, but we outline the different aspects that an SOA brings to the table. We introduce the JK Enterprises testing process and then provide hands on examples using Rational's testing tools.

Inputs to testing

Test receives input from multiple sources. Figure 14-1, shows the inputs received from Requirements and Analysis & Design. We use these inputs to generate the Test Case work product. We describe the key work products of the RUP Test discipline in "Test work products" on page 507.

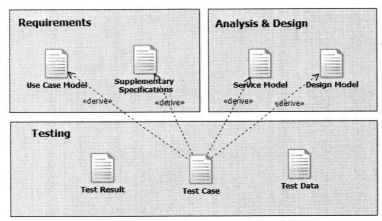

Figure 14-1   Testing related work products

The roles responsible for the above work products are shown in Figure 14-2. We describe these roles and additional roles in the Test discipline in "Test roles" on page 509.

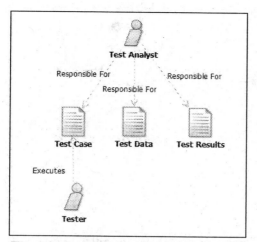

Figure 14-2   Roles responsible for Test work products

SOA testing from a technology and application perspective

Testing an SOA application is not just a simple variation of traditional testing. Testing is no longer just about testing our components, we also need to make sure they work with all the other layers and components in the business services space. Figure 14-3, the SOA solution stack, shows the different architectural layers in an SOA.

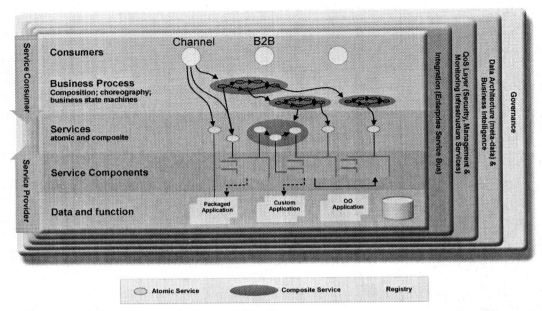

Figure 14-3   SOA solution stack: A layered architecture

Note: For more information about the SOA foundation, refer to "SOA foundation reference architecture" on page 6.

Below are some characteristics of an SOA that present unique challenges in testing its solution adequately from a technology and architectural perspective. Each item by itself may not be entirely unique to SOA, but taken together they create a unique package of qualities to address.

Loose coupling between services and requesters

What does it mean to have loose coupling between services providers and requesters? Loose coupling implies that the underlying implementation is hidden from the application that invokes the service. In a loosely coupled system you are not required to have the same technological implementation at each end of the connection. This implies that there is a minimum dependency between service providers and requesters.

How does this affect our testing? With a loosely coupled system we cannot make assumptions about the system when it comes to testing, because a service could be reused in an environment or reused with technologies not originally intended.

Take for example a small job search application which was built for one human resources administrator when JK Enterprises was a small company of only 40 employees. Today this job search functionality is re-used in a new technology and exposed as a service to company's intranet where all employees have access to perform job searches. The company has now grown to over 11,000 employees. The service that was designed with a single user base and technology in mind is now being used by a much larger user base and new technology. With loosely coupled systems we don't control both ends of the system as we once did.

Consequence: Test designs have to follow the same coding disciplines (that is, be loosely coupled). In order for the test cases to be re-used in different technologies, they need to comply to the same interfaces and coding standards. Just as the code needs to be used by all technologies, the test, designed to run that code, needs to be reused by all technologies.

Heterogeneous technologies intertwined in the same solution

SOA systems are often composed of both new and existing services and their business goals. The system could be a collection of heterogeneous existing or earlier systems or applications with heterogeneous networks and environments, distributed across global and geographical cultural boundaries and across various communication protocols.

Most companies do not have the time or resources to rewrite from scratch, re-engineer or refactor everything at the same time. Take for example JK Enterprises, which has CICS and SAP applications. These applications hold many companies policies, rules, and procedures. It may not be strategical or economical to replace entire applications to fit the new technologies *right now*. SOA allows you to have new and existing or earlier applications in the same model. The existing or earlier applications are looked at as black-box services. This allows the company to replace or revamp the existing or earlier applications when it has the resources by using a phased approach. This leads to heterogeneous environments.

Consequence: Test cases have to be environment neutral. One of the concepts behind SOA is the ability to react and to adapt to changes in the future, because of this, you cannot make the assumption that just because the business is run like this today, it will always be this way.

Lack of total control over all elements of a solution

An SOA gives applications the flexibility to outsource services to third parties. This causes an interesting challenge when determining the source of a problem, it could be within the third party service. Another challenge is when a problem is found, who is responsible to fix it? An SOA also gives the flexibility to distribute the services. Distributing the services can bring up issues such as geographical and cultural differences which result in increased communication and administrative challenges. It also causes issues when determining who owns the testing. With SOA the systems need to comply with standards and agreed-upon interfaces. You now need to be aware of changes in the interfaces and standards. Overall, the lack of total control over all elements of a solution increases the need for collaboration.

Consequence: We have to monitor changes at all levels of interfaces whether service or policy oriented. We also must have service contracts.

New standards and technologies

There are many standards and technologies to understand and to deal with; WSDL, SOAP, UDDI, HTTP, JMS, and WS-Security, just to name a few. With these comes many versions and implementations, which raises issues with interoperability.

Consequence: Every time a new version is released, you have exponentially increased the testing. You now have to test on the currently released standards and you need to test on the new version of the standards/API/interfaces. Customers may or may not be upgraded to the newest version, so you have to work with both versions.

Asynchronous nature

SOA systems often have multiple activities occurring at the same time which can result in no single point of failure. SOA system also have a combination of synchronous connectivity and distributed routing which is difficult to map and model. This brings up a complex array of integration issues. With this combination of factors comes an increased difficulty to duplicate a problem. We see an increase in time and effort trying to reproduce the problem. The problem cannot be fixed until it can be reproduced consistently.

Consequence: You need test cases that exercise and emulates asynchronous behavior. Test should be created with serviceability and better diagnostics tools up-front to help debug these asynchronous and difficult issues.

Application failures

The previous characteristics of loose coupling, lack of control of all elements, heterogeneous technologies and asynchronous nature can each lead us to application failure. What happens when the service works on most, but not all technologies, environments and platforms. What happens when services are from third parties. What happens when there is no single point of failure? All of these are good questions but, to fix a bug which causes the failure we need to be able to consistently duplicate the bug. As mentioned above, the ability to do this in an SOA takes increased time and effort.

In pre SOA systems, six to seven percent of product failures are marked as unreproducible. Therefore we are releasing seven percent of our defects to our customers. Because application failure points in SOA are difficult to find this *unreproducible number* increases.

In reality, there are no intermittent bugs. The problem is consistent, you just have not found the right condition to reproduce it.

Consequence: We need test cases that emulate, diagnose, and self-correct failures.

Providing serviceability tools that continually monitor performance, auto-calibrate at the application's degradation thresholds, and automatically send the proper data at the time of degradation, prior to the application actually crashing, reduces both in-house troubleshooting time and customer downtime. Both iterative testing and iterative serviceability activities reduce the business impact of undiscovered bugs.

Better diagnostic and serviceability routines increase the customer value of your product. By proactively monitoring the environment when your product starts to degrade, you can reduce analysis time and even avoid a shutdown by initiating various auto-correcting calibration and work around routines. These types of autonomic service routines increase your product's reliability, endurance, and runtime duration, even if the conditions for reproduction of a bug are unknown.

In a sense, autonomic recovery routines provide a level of continuous technical support. Environment logs and transaction trace information are automatically collected and sent back to development for further defect causal analysis, while at the same time providing important data about how your product is actually being used. If we acknowledge that bugs are inevitable, we also need to realize the importance of appropriate serviceability routines. These self-diagnostic and self-monitoring functions are effective in increasing customer value and satisfaction because they reduce the risk that the customer is negatively affected by bugs. Yet even though these routines increase customer value, few development cycles are devoted to putting these processes in place.

SOA: Testing strategy

An SOA poses some challenges when devising a testing strategy. Below are questions that need to be answered when developing a test strategy.

► At what level to test?

Do you start at the data and function layer, service component layer or do you only test at the services layer? How do you test end to end?

► Who is in charge of the tests?

Do business analysts own the tests because they defined the requirements that should be tested? Do developers own the test because they implement the services? Or how about the tester shouldn't they be the ones that own the test since they run the test?

► How to define the right test cases?

SOA is dynamic and flexible in nature which leaves endless possibilities for test cases.

► What is the integration strategy?

How are you going to handle B2B services? How are you going to handle testing distributed services across global and geographical boundaries?

► Effective test automation?

Which test can be automated? Which test should be automated?

► What are the test completion criteria?

Is it when you can prove reliability? How about availability? Is it when performance meets a certain criteria? What is the measurement on security?

By now you are probably thinking, how do I answer these questions and where do I even begin to define a testing strategy? You need to start off by making finding defects early a primary goal. Finding and fixing defect closest to when they are created reduces cost, time and effort. Now you are thinking this is nothing new, this is the same for every application you test. However, finding defects early is even more important for SOA applications. SOA solutions involve many levels, composites and roles. As we mentioned in "SOA testing from a technology and application perspective" on page 485, it becomes more difficult to locate and reproduce a bug when there are multiple levels, composites and roles. You can see the service layers involved in an SOA in Figure 14-3. So find the defects early.

We can answer the above testing strategy questions by keeping in mind the testing challenges SOA introduces and the fact we need to find defects early. Let us begin answering the SOA strategy questions.

At what level do you test?

You have to test at each level: Service components, atomic and composite services, business composition, and end-to-end. Testing at each level enables you to locate and fix defects at the point where they were introduced which ties in with finding and fixing defect early. Testing should be an iterative process that continues throughout the whole life cycle of the application. Code reviews and inspections should be done for each code drop along with unit and regression testing.

Who is in charge of testing?

Because you need to test at each level in the architecture, there is no one role that is in charge of all testing. Instead, there are multiple roles, each in charge of, or at least sign-offs on tests within their level. The roles need to coordinate and communicate with testers at the levels around them. As with the nature of SOA, this also helps enable alignment of the business with IT because the business analyst needs to be in sync with the technical tester and so forth.

Defining a test team is critical in testing an SOA. There are testing techniques that are unique to SOA testing that require a specific set of skills in the test team. We need to address preparing the test team on both managerial and technical levels. We also need to make sure that the test targets described in the test strategy are used to determine the test team objectives and make-up.

We expand on the testing in each level of the architecture and the roles involved in testing in that level in the following subsections. We must keep in mind the best practices of testing early, performing code review and inspection, and unit testing and regression testing for each code drop.

For this section we have defined the following roles for testing:

- **Technical and non-technical tester**—Expert in testing techniques and test automation
- **Integration and service component developer**—Ensures adequate level of quality of the base services
- **Business analyst**—Understands the business process

Business composition

The role involved at this level of testing is the technical tester.

In this section we focus on the business composition layer as depicted in Figure 14-4

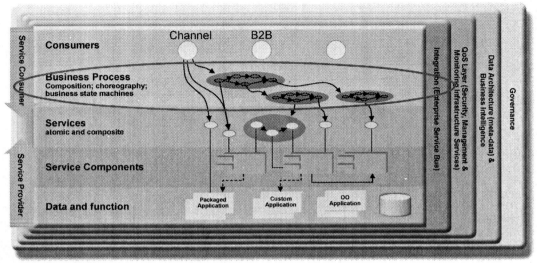

Figure 14-4   Testing business composition services

Below is a list of best practices for testing at the business composition level. Once again there is nothing really novel about this list. They all stem from the best practices around integration system or product testing. We have testing across silos or stand-alone applications, interoperability concerns and service response times when there are failures in the service.

► Test the business logic as soon as possible:

   – Do not wait to have all the UIs already built
   – Make the project more predictable to deliver
   – Test across many different applications
   – Leverage business process models to define test cases

► Focus on potential integration problems:

   – Requirement misunderstanding
   – Error handling
   – Interoperability: Web service conformance testing

► Specific case of business-2-business transactions:

   – No UI is built for those services consumed by another company
   – Validation of both consumed and provided business processes
   – Performance test: Validated against service level agreements

► Need to simulate unavailable services.

What complicates this picture is the loose coupling environment. As we mentioned previously in "Introduction" on page 484, developers cannot make assumptions about the system on the other end because they do not control both ends as they once did.

In an SOA it becomes more important to simulate and test error conditions, error handling and recovery times because we need to better understand and test the unexpected. We have to insert fault insertions to rate reliance and resiliency. We have to be able to determine how likely we can recover and come back online.

Atomic and composite services

The roles involved at this level of testing are the technical tester and the integration and service component developers.

In this section we focus on the atomic and composite services layer as shown in Figure 14-5.

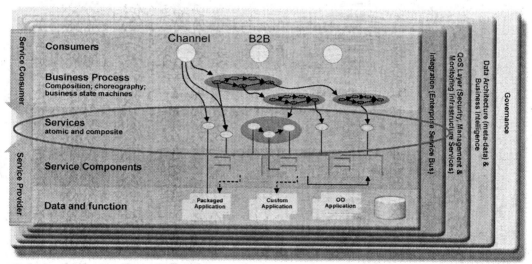

Figure 14-5   Testing atomic and composite services

An SOA application is only as good as its weakest service. SOA is flexible and dynamic in nature, it enables and promotes services to be reused. As you can imagine, because of this service reuse, one small defect in a shared routine disseminates quickly through the entire system. This may cause failures in multiple places and critical product cycles.

As mentioned in "Loose coupling between services and requesters" on page 486, although the original intent of your service was not in the critical path, it can certainly be reused in a totally different environment than it was originally intended. So now your service is in the critical path and its causing all kinds of problems.

Recognizing this important difference in SOA environments, properly aligns the imperative for diligent unit testing, code inspections, and reviews.

How do we go about testing at the atomic and composite service level? You must test each individual service thoroughly. For each service you have to exercise all possible use cases with valid data. For stateless services, your unit tests need to be very data-driven as opposed to state driven. You do not need to vary the order you call these services because they are stateless. For each service you have to perform negative testing to verify the reliability of the service. You also have to performance test each service.

Because some individual services do not have a user interface, you have to create test drivers that call the services and verify the responses. IBM Rational Software Delivery Platform has tool to assist you with your testing. You can find a list of tools in "IBM products for SOA testing" on page 500.

As we have stated many times in this chapter, developers cannot make assumptions about the system on the other end because they do not control it. What does this mean in terms of testing atomic and composite services? It means you have to create stubs associated with the expected standard interfaces of the services you are dependent on. By creating stubs or temporary substitute routines to work around a dependent code area, if the external component is delivered late or is unavailable, you have an acceptable backup to support testing. By reducing your dependency, you make it easier to maneuver past third-party problems.

You can already see that in a multiple-contributing environment like SOA, with many layers, components and activities, diagnosing or pinpointing a problem is challenging. We have to acknowledge that up front and design serviceability directly into our testing framework.

SOA supports the migration to autonomic and on-demand infrastructure by support metering and billing, self-healing, and dynamic routing among other things. Implemented correctly it reacts to events to self-configure, heal, and optimize.

Service component

The roles involved at this level of testing are the integration and service component developers.

In this section we focus on the service component layer as shown in Figure 14-6.

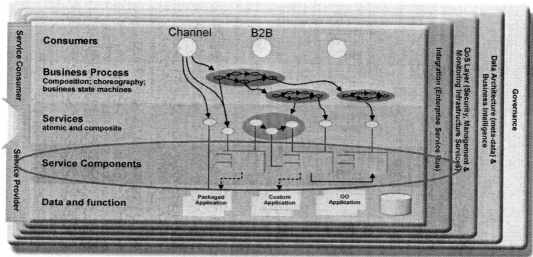

Figure 14-6   Testing service components

Realistically, there will be many useful levels of service granularity in most service-oriented architectures. An example of different levels could be as follows:

► Technical functions (logging)
► Business functions (getBalance)
► Business transactions (openAccount)
► Business processes (applyForMortgage)

It is important to test at each level of granularity to make sure that it is reusable. The most effective way to catch deficiencies and incapabilities among these various levels is through formal code reviews, static analysis and unit testing

Third party services should be tested only to the extent that their installation, configuration and implementation of requirements is verified. It is not necessary to retest the entire service.

The infrastructure (for example, WebSphere) only has to be explicitly tested to verify that it was correctly installed and configured. Its not necessary to fully retest the infrastructure.

Here is a list of developer testing activities and a list of the typical service components to test:

- ► Developer testing activity:
  - – Code review and inspections
  - – Unit testing
  - – Runtime analysis

- ► Typical service components:
  - – EJB
  - – Java classes
  - – Utility Web services

End-to-end

The roles involved at this level of testing are the business analyst, the technical tester and the non-technical tester.

In this section we focus on the consumer as shown in Figure 14-7.

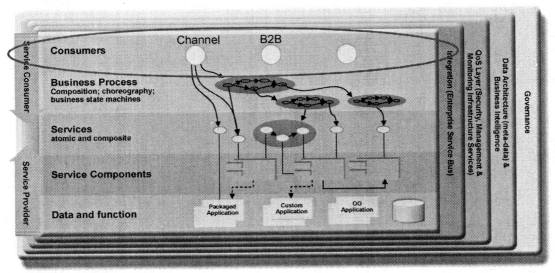

Figure 14-7   Testing end-to-end

The end-to-end testing takes on a new meaning for SOA testing. In traditional (non-services based) application programming, the end points are well defined and it is clear what is expected. This is not necessarily the case for SOA applications. Services are reusable both within an application and across applications.

Consider the case where you have existing services that are used by other applications. Those applications are stable and continue to run in a production environment. The application you are currently testing is invoking these services in a new SOA for the first time. This makes it very important to understand and set your test objectives very carefully to ensure that all possible end-to-end scenarios are covered.

Tests of the end-to-end system should be performed through the user interface, Also, test the complete IT system in an environment that mimics real-world use. For example, all supported browser types and all supported display resolutions should be tested for the user interface. The end-to-end tests are required to validate the system functions, to ensure acceptable usability levels, measure the overall system performance and to verify the system security.

The majority of these testing needs are no different than in traditional testing. But once again the SOA implementation gives rise to learning different approaches to cover similar concepts.

The number of messages needed for an SOA is humongous. The messages are critical to delivering end-to-end service. They must be delivered quickly, accurately and their arrival has to be guaranteed. Ensuring that the message correlations are properly handled by the service receiving them is essential. If this doesn't happen, then the end-to-end service quickly becomes a lack of service. To assure serviceability of these messages, we need to measure service levels, response times and failure frequency.

The only way to know that an application is delivering the service that the business users require is to define the service level expectations. Then we have to measure the applications activity to see whether it is achieving it.

Because application interruptions are sporadic, you can either measure service constantly and then average it out over a period of month or you can simulate a load by emulating multiple users, and then collecting response times and data at an accelerated pace prior to your product's release. This allows you to tune your performance prior to a release, which increases your reliability and reduces your outage risk.

You can also emulate faults or system outages to verify resiliency to see how quickly the product returns to service after a fault is detected.

How to define the right test cases?

To define the right test cases, begin prioritizing test cases in the order in which the function they test bring the most value add to the customer. There are several surveys by Gartner that say only 36% of the features in a product are actually used. The other 64% are rarely or never used. You want to prioritize those activities that customer use higher on your test matrix.

When developing the test cases, get the customers involved early in the process. This not only reinforces that you are investing in the correct test cases but it also reinforces that your requirements are correct.

Where do you get your test cases? You can derive test cases from multiple places. You can derive test cases from design documents, system use cases, WSDLs, services specification artifacts ("Service model work product" on page 234) and business processes. SLA/QoS policy documents are useful in defining workloads to be tested. In addition, supplementary requirements, non-functional requirements and all other types of requirements should also be used to help define the test cases.

For the business processes, the business analysts write or at least review the test cases. Each of the business processes should be tested.

The test completion criteria is that you have tested each user requirement for all the business processes.

What is the integration strategy?

In traditional development applications, integration testing is the test phase in which individual software modules are combined and tested as a group. In traditional testing, it follows unit testing and precedes system testing.

Integration testing takes, as its input, modules that have been unit tested and groups them in larger aggregates. Integration testing then applies tests defined in an integration test plan to the larger aggregates. The output of integration is that we are ready for system testing.

The purpose of integration testing is to verify the functional, performance and reliability requirements placed on major design items. These design items, for example assemblages, are exercised through their interfaces using black box testing. Success and error case are simulated via appropriate parameter and data inputs. Simulated usage of shared data areas and inter-process communication is tested, subsystems are exercised through their input interface. Test cases are constructed to test that all components within assemblages interact correctly, for example, across procedure calls or process activations.

The overall idea is a building block approach, in which verified assemblages are added to a verified base which is then used to support the integration testing of further assemblages.

In the SOA environment, you do not have control over all the building blocks and individual subsystems. You now need a practical method to create stubs and simulate back-end servers, systems, and services to conduct your end-to-end business-to-business integration testing.

All end-to-end testing falls into integration testing.

What are the test completion criteria?

Test completion criteria identify acceptable product quality and identify when the test effort has been successfully implemented. Test completion criteria defines the acceptable level of reliability, availability, performance and security. Test completion criteria include things such as the exit and entry criteria for the test, number of defects we allow at each phase, the test that have to be fixed before we can exit a phase and so forth. If everyone is not on the same page for these test completion criteria, we could implement a component with an unacceptable quality and it might be too late to fix it.

In SOA systems, defining the completion criteria becomes even more important. The service we are implementing can be used in multiple SOA systems that have different product quality standards.

Test completion criteria are best tracked by metrics and checklists.

Effective test automation

Test automation is a must-have in traditional testing, but again, it is especially important in an SOA because we are constantly adopting and absorbing services. To keep pace with rapid deployment of new services and business processes we need some way to quickly verify our acceptance of these new services. In traditional testing we are accustomed to automate our acceptance tests to verify that we are meeting our standards, but in SOA we also have to acknowledge that we have to meet a certain standard or interface. Because of the flexible nature of SOA, these standards and interfaces also change, having upgrades and versions. We can use automation test to detect changes in these standards early. Once detected we can easily accommodate and track the changes required in our code.

Identification of appropriate test paths in the presence of multiple concurrent/synchronization scenarios among the composed services is particularly problematic in an SOA. The individual services may have been developed using heterogeneous technologies (languages and frameworks). Integration testing of such services needs tool support that spans the different technologies used.

> **Note:** Refer to "IBM products for SOA testing" on page 500 for tools that help you with test automation.

IBM products for SOA testing

The IBM Rational SDP supports SOA testing with a portfolio of modular, open standard base products. Use the following tables to help determine the tools that can assist you in unit, functional, and system testing. Descriptions of the products are found after the tables in alphabetical order.

Tools to assist in unit testing are shown in Table 14-1.

Table 14-1   Tools to assist in unit testing

Area	Tools
Defect management / Metrics	Rational ClearQuest
Performance	Rational Performance Tester
Code Inspector / Static Analysis	Rational Application Developer – Code Review
Java Runtime Analysis Metrics	Rational PurifyPlus™ Rational Application Developer
Test Automation	Rational Application Developer with Rational Component Test Automation Rational Functional Tester
Test Management	Rational ClearQuest Rational Manual Tester
Change Management	Rational ClearCase
Requirements Tracking	Rational Requisite® Pro

Tools to assist in functional testing are shown in Table 14-2.

Table 14-2   Tools to assist in functional testing

Area	Tools
Source Control / Change Management	Rational ClearCase
Defect Tracking	Rational ClearQuest
Test Management	Rational ClearQuest Rational Manual Tester
Test Automation	Rational Functional Tester
Code Inspection	Rational Application Developer - Code Review
Metrics	Rational ClearQuest Rational PureCoverage® Rational Application Developer

Tools to assist in system testing are shown in Table 14-3.

Table 14-3   Tools to assist in system testing

Area	Tools
Defect Management	Rational ClearQuest
Performance	Rational Performance Tester
Test Automation	Rational Functional Tester
Test Management	Rational Test Manager Rational Manual Tester
Metrics And Reporting	Rational Project Console (Dashboard)
Requirements Tracking	Rational RequisitePro
Customer Interaction Programs	Design Reviews, Residency, Visitations
Change Management	Rational ClearCase

Rational Application Developer

Rational Application Developer provides a wide variety of testing tool to enable the developer to effectively test their parts. We mention just a few of them here.

Component test

In software development it is well know that component testing allows us to find and fix defects early. In an SOA solution it becomes crucial to find and fix defects early. The impact of a defect can have a cascading affect because the service could be used by multiple critical systems.

Rational Application Developer V6 comes with automated component testing features that allows us to create, edit, deploy, and run automated tests of Java components, EJB components, and Web services. This feature has been removed in Version 7.

JUnit

Rational Application Developer has support for JUnit testing. JUnit is a simple testing framework that creates repeatable tests. The JUnit tests are created and run by the developers to validate their code and to perform regression testing.

WSDL validation

Rational Application Developer provides interoperability testing for Web Services. It can validate WSDL conformance to the WS-I standard and also validate SOAP messages. See "Validating the WSDL file" on page 466 for an example of validating a WSDL.

Web Services Explorer

The Web Services Explorer allows us to explore, import and test WSDL documents. We can use this tool to aid in unit testing our Web service operations or that of a third-party Web service operations. See "Test the service" on page 458 for an example of using the Web Services Explorer to test a Web service operation.

TCP/IP Monitor

TCP/IP Monitor is a simple server that monitors all request and response between the requester Web browser and the provider. It is another way, besides the Web Services Explorer, to monitor the SOAP request and response messages.

> **Note:** For more information about Rational Application Developer testing capabilities, see the product's Information Center.

Rational ClearCase

IBM Rational ClearCase manages and controls all your software development assets. including test plans, test cases and test scripts.

Rational ClearCase is integrated with Rational ClearQuest for a complete change and configuration management solution.

> **Note:** More information about Rational ClearCase can be found in "Rational ClearQuest and Rational ClearCase" on page 35.

Rational ClearQuest

IBM Rational ClearQuest is the hub of the software development life cycle. It manages all the tests, defects and change actives that occur during software development. It also permits users to log defects after the services have been released into production - either directly[1] or via an integration to a help desk system.

Rational ClearQuest enables configurable and enforceable quality projects. Rational ClearQuest is an extensible test management ecosystem that manages your test activities while supporting geographically distributed teams. We provide a demonstration of Rational ClearQuest in "Managing testing artifacts" on page 515.

> **Note:** More on Rational ClearQuest can be found in "Rational ClearQuest and Rational ClearCase" on page 35.

Rational Functional Tester

IBM Rational Functional Tester is an advanced, automated functional and regression testing tool for testers and GUI developers who need superior control for testing Java, Microsoft Visual Studio .NET and Web-based applications.

Rational Functional Tester automate end-to-end tests. It can capture or playback system-user interactions. Because of this automation Rational Functional Tester is able to keep up with the rapid development of new business processes in an SOA environment.

---

[1] IBM Rational product development teams and tech support use ClearQuest for this purpose. Customers may see a reference to RATLC - the name of the ClearQuest database.

Rational Functional Tester minimizes test maintenance with scripts resilient to the frequent changes of an SOA system. We demonstrate this capability with an example from the JK Enterprises solution in "Designing and executing functional tests with Rational Functional Tester" on page 530.

> **Note:** For more information about IBM Rational Functional Tester features and benefits, refer to:
>
>   http://www-306.ibm.com/software/awdtools/tester/manual/features/index.html

Rational Manual Tester

IBM Rational Manual Tester is a manual test authoring and execution tool that promotes test step reuse to reduce the impact of software change on testers and business analysts.

Rational Manual Tester adds organization and control to all activities that comprise a manual testing effort including:

► Test creation and modification
► Test organization and consolidation for distributed team members
► Test execution and result collection
► Test result reporting

Rational Manual Tester V7 is now fully integrated with Rational ClearQuest. This enables us to submit, track, and resolve defects from within Rational Manual Tester. We are also able to associate test results with the defect-tracking system.

Rational Manual Tester V7 adds the capability to publish the test scripts as HTML files to enable easy viewing of the tests by others.

In an SOA system we use Manual Tester to formalize end-end tests that exercise the business process. This ensures test consistency when the SOA system evolves. We also use Rational Manual Tester to assist in unit and system testing.

We implement a sample test script for JK Enterprises' Determine Eligibility Service using Rational Manual Tester in "Designing and executing functional tests with Rational Functional Tester" on page 530.

> **Note:** For more information about IBM Rational Manual Tester's features and benefits, refer to:
>
>   http://www-306.ibm.com/software/awdtools/tester/manual/index.html

Rational Performance Tester

For multi-user Web applicator, reliability efficiency, and performance is a necessity, not a luxury. IBM Rational Performance Tester is the tool we can use to test our multi-user Web applications.

Rational Performance Tester can emulate different volumes of traffic on our system. This enables us to pinpoint bottlenecks of our system before it reaches production. Simulating the traffic to our system also helps to plan for the hardware that is to host our system.

Rational Performance Tester can model and emulate diverse user populations. We need to make sure our test emulated our user base, because the activists and usage patterns of individual users and groups can vary drastically and have a huge impact on our system. It is better to find out sooner rather than later.

Rational Performance Tester has an easy to use interface that does not require any coding knowledge. It has the ability to record our actions and run tests against the actions we took.

Rational Performance Tester provides real-time reporting capabilities for real-time performance problem identification.

> **Note:** For more information about Rational Performance Tester's features and benefits, refer to:
>
> ```
> http://www-306.ibm.com/software/awdtools/tester/performance/features/inde
> x.html
> ```

Rational Tester for SOA

At the time of the publication of this document **IBM Rational Tester for SOA**[2], which is based on Rational Performance Tester and **IBM Rational Performance Tester Extension for SOA**, is in Beta.

Rational Tester for SOA and Rational Performance Tester Extension for SOA enable testing of SOA applications and Web services and allows teams to:

► Validate SOA system functionality and interoperability
► Ensure system performance
► Determine maximum system capacity
► Identify and resolve performance problems of SOA IT solutions

---

[2] Note that the product names are tentative and may change

More information about these products can be found at:

```
https://www14.software.ibm.com/iwm/web/cc/earlyprograms/rational/P1656/
```

```
http://www-306.ibm.com/software/rational/offerings/testing.html
```

IBM Rational testing solution for service-oriented architecture applications automates the creation, execution, and analysis of functional, regression, and performance tests for services of SOA IT solutions.

Features and benefits include:

► A visual test editor delivering both high-level and detailed test views

No programming knowledge is necessary to create, comprehend, modify, and execute a functional or performance test. A test is a sequence of invocations of Web services operations; no code editing is necessary to create a single or multi-user test. However, deeper detail is available—advanced testers have access to all aspects of the Web services messages, including HTTP headers, cookies, and the SOAP envelope.

► Support for testing of services

IBM Rational testing solutions for service-oriented architecture applications creates, executes, and analyzes tests to validate the reliability of atomic or composite non-GUI headless services and business composition of those services. Support for Web services standards, SOAP over HTTP, SOAP over JMS, and WS-Security.

► Automated data correlation and data-driven testing eliminate need for manual coding

Functional tests typically have to vary data during playback to properly simulate true users. IBM Rational testing solutions for service-oriented architecture applications can automatically detect data entered during test recording and prepare the test for data-driven testing. Using a spreadsheet-like data editor, you can then create customized data sets to be inserted into the script during playback. In this way, you can produce highly personalized tests without manual coding.

► Flexible modeling and emulation of diverse service consumers

To ensure that your performance testing accurately mirrors your user base, IBM Rational testing solutions for service-oriented architecture applications provides a flexible test scheduler that specifies the different groups of service consumers, as well as the activities and usage patterns of each of the groups.

► Collection and visualization of server resource data

Testers must be vigilant to detect performance and reliability problems that can be traced to hardware issues rather than to software. IBM Rational testing solutions for service-oriented architecture applications can collect and display multiple server resource statistics, thereby exposing bottlenecks responsible for poor performance.

► Java code insertion for flexible test customization

Advanced testers have the option of inserting custom Java code into their performance tests to perform activities such as advanced data analysis and request parsing.

► Test creation from WS-BPEL business processes

IBM Rational testing solutions for service-oriented architecture applications automatically generates test from business processes defined using the WS-BPEL standard, using from a range of generation possibilities, and enables to quickly get started with testing a complex business process and to make sure all relevant paths are thoroughly tested.

IBM Web Services Navigator

IBM Research has developed a technology called IBM Web Services Navigator (aka Websight), which is also available through the IBM Tivoli® Composite Application Manager for SOA product and alphaworks, to help during the problem diagnosis phase. This technology allows visualization of the traces which capture dynamic interactions among Web services and provides sophisticated pattern analysis capabilities to help in identification of potential bottlenecks.

> **Note:** For more information about IBM Web Services Navigator and IBM Tivoli Composite Application Manager for SOA, refer to:
>
> http://www.alphaworks.ibm.com/tech/wsnavigator
>
> http://www-306.ibm.com/software/tivoli/products/composite-application-mgr-soa/

Test work products

We talk about work products before the test roles and process because these are the things we need to produce.

in this section, we discuss these key work products:

► **Test plan**—This artifact defines the goals and objectives of testing within the scope of the iteration (or project), the items being targeted, the approach to be taken, the resources required and the deliverables to be produced.

- **Test case**—This artifact defines a set of test inputs, execution conditions, and expected results, identified for the purpose of making an evaluation of some particular aspect of a target test item.

- **Test result**—This artifact summarizes the analysis of one or more test logs and change requests, providing a relatively detailed assessment of the quality of the target test items and the status of the test effort.

- **Test data**—This artifact defines a collection of test input values that are consumed during the execution of a test, and expected results referenced for comparative purposes during the execution of a test.

Test plan

The test plan should provide a project context and background. It should describe the goal of the test, for example reduce defects, or validate a service. Then the test plan defines what you are going to test, specific hardware, software or both. The test plan is a high level summary of the planned tests including what we are not going to test. The test plan documents the deliverables, for example what logs, quality reports or other deliverables from the test process. In the test plan we define the specific testing tasks.

In our example, we use the tasks defined in our testing process in "Test process" on page 511. We should defined testing responsibilities, staffing and training in the test plan. We should list the key project milestone that impact our testing. The test plan includes any risks, assumption, dependencies and constraints. And finally the test plan define management processes and procedures including approval and sign-off. The test plan may consist of reference to other test plan and work products. We do not duplicate information here if possible.

Test case

The test case describes the test as well as any condition that is exercised in this test. The condition includes pre-conditions and post-conditions, test inputs, what we should observe during the test, control points, and expected results. The results include correct behavior as well as any error conditions and failures. This test case acts as an outline for any test scripts, either manual or automated.

Test result

The test result records the detailed findings of the test effort. These results are used later to help measure the progress of the testing. We expect test results to show when the test was run, who ran it and in what environment. It should also show the test cases executed and their results, and an indication of pass or fail. We may include response times and trace-data, this all depends on what level of detail we require and the kind of test being executed. For example, test results on test coverage would not require information about response times.

Test data

The test data plays an important role in testing SOA solutions. For stateless services we no longer test the order of execution but the response to a range of inputs. The test data can either be specific values or a range of values. The way we store the test data varies from test to test and project to project. Certain kinds of applications might use simple ascii files of input values while more complex environment might require comprehensive database of data. An example from our JK Enterprises, is our pricing model. We might change the way we price items based on real-time sales results. This is a complex situation to simulate.

Test roles

Throughout this book we have defined the roles involved in each phase of the Rational Unified Process. In this section we describe the role set that RUP has defined for testers. Testing SOA solutions involves not only the test roles but also the other roles that produce the work products we are testing.

For the business process model, we want to plan tests to validate that the business process model is correct. The test analyst role collaborates with the business analyst to create the appropriate test.

Non-functional requirements include the following kind of requirements:

► Usability
► Reliability
► Performance
► Supportability
► Design constraints

These categories maybe familiar to the reader from Chapter 8, "Requirements" on page 207.

For each of these kinds of requirements we need to insure we have the appropriate test. For example if we have a performance requirement of credit checking 500 applications a day, we should have a test that for that specific volume of credit checks. The architect has an understanding how critical these non-functional requirements are and can assist the test analyst in producing the right tests.

The testing of services, is probably the most critical part of our set of tests. Here the architect and the test analyst need to work closely to make sure the services are tested properly. This is because, the services not only impact our SOA-based solution but potentially other business areas across the enterprise and beyond.

We need to test that the service behaves as expected and fulfills the non-functional requirements we specified. We also have to verify that the service complies to our service policies.

If our SOA-based solution has one or more user interfaces, we have to test these as well. These tests involve GUI designers and implementers working with the test analyst.

We do not consider here testing the internals of the service implementation. Testing code is more of a developer's responsibility that is discussed in Chapter 13, "Service implementation" on page 419.

In RUP a role is a set of responsibilities that may be allocated to the same person or team. That person or team may take on multiple roles across the different disciplines. This is a very important part of RUP because it allows the process to scale. One possible approach to staffing our testing roles is to have the individual (or team) who produced the work product we are testing to take on the role of test analyst, designer, or implementer in addition to their primary role. This is a logical extension of the write test first, then code, which is popular in agile methodologies. However, it is essential a professional test person can assist these other roles in writing good tests.

Note that in addition to tests developed by a developer there should always be tests developed by business and system analysts to make sure that all the business requirements are tested.

RUP has defined the following primary role sets for testing:

▶ **Test analyst**—*"..defines the required tests, monitors detailed testing progress and results in each test cycle and evaluates overall quality."* The test analyst role cuts across all lines of test. In our JK Enterprises example, the test analyst would confirm that the `determineApplicationEligibility` service had met the overall quality goals.

▶ **Test designer**—*".. leads defining the test approach and ensuring its successful implementation. This includes identifying the appropriate techniques, tools and guidelines to implement the required tests, and to provide guidance to the test effort on corresponding resources requirements."* For JK Enterprises the test designer has mandated the use of Rational testing tool to provide automated testing and ClearQuest for test management.

▶ **Tester**—*".. conducts tests and logs the outcomes of his/her testing."* For JK Enterprises, the tester would run the performance tests and feedback the results to the test analyst.

- **Test manager**—"_.. leads overall test effort. This includes quality and test advocacy, resource planning and management, and resolution of the issues that impede the test effort._" In our JK Enterprises, make sure the right test environment was available to run the tests.

- **Test architect**—"_.. provides technical leadership for the testing effort._" For JK Enterprises, the test architect would focus on defining the test architecture, identifying a test strategy and providing leadership to the team particularly in the area of test design and specification.

RUP also places emphasis on the importance of the test team and the importance of managing and facilitating the test team. There are testing techniques that are unique to SOA testing that require a specific set of skills in the test team.

Test process

The testing life cycle is integrated into the rest of the SOA development life cycle (Figure 14-8). Testing is not an afterthought but an essential part of developing any SOA-based solution. The test roles are working in parallel with other disciplines, taking feeds off work products to start their activities.

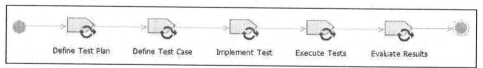

Figure 14-8   Test life cycle

The life cycle starts as soon as there are suitable requirements or business process(es) to be tested. We create a test plan to make sure we define the scope of the iteration or project. We create test cases with inputs and expected results and any exception conditions. We implement the tests. We run the tests and verify the results.

In some cases, the tests themselves are in error, in which case we must fix the tests, the test case or the plan depending on the nature of the error. If there is an error in the element we are testing, that is logged and we wait for a response. The response could range from an updated element to the *works as designed* response with many other possible responses in between. An updated element is retested while a works as designed requires a change to the test or its inputs, data, or results.

This simple process applies to the different kinds of elements we have to test:

- ► Business processes
- ► Non-functional requirements
- ► Services specifications
- ► Compliance to service policies
- ► Service implementations

We do not consider the internals of the code implementing the service. Testing code is more of a developer responsibility that is discussed in Chapter 13, "Service implementation" on page 419.

During the project, we report on progress by looking at the realized requirements that have passed their tests. A realized requirement is the final manifestation of the requirement, and depends on the kind of requirement. For example, a functional requirement is realized by working code. A business process from the business model may be monitored in operation (even if this is running in a test environment). This strong connection between the requirements and test is very important to keep track of real project progress.

In addition to the tests we create in the iteration, we also run regression tests at all levels. Whenever a service is changed (either definition or implementation) it is necessary to identify all the services that could potentially be changed so that regression testing of the impacted services can also be performed.

We have to be pragmatic about how much we can test. It is likely that even with automation of testing, we are unable to run all tests including regression tests. We have to perform a base level of testing (sometimes called a *smoke test*) and then address the areas of highest risk. Having our inputs to test tagged according to priority and risk helps us decide which are the highest risk areas.

Test tooling

So far, we have discussed the process of testing. Now we discuss the use of tooling.

We capture our business process models inside WebSphere Business Modeler. Our requirements such as business goals, service policies, non-functional requirements and others are stored in RequisitePro. We plan our tests in the test management schema for ClearQuest. Tests case are constructed in Manual Tester and either remain in manual tester (for manual tests) or implemented in Functional Tester and Performance Tester.

Setup the test environment

In reality when you test your SOA solution you would set up an environment that closely resembles the production environment. For the purpose of simplicity, we set up the solution in Rational Software Architect's WebSphere Application Server test environment.

Download the sample code

In this chapter we reference files and database scripts supplied with the additional material. For instructions about how to download the sample code, refer to Appendix A, "Additional material" on page 575.

Import the project interchange file

To import the project interchange file perform the following steps:

► Make sure you have opened the J2EE perspective in Rational Software Architect or Rational Application Developer Version 7.

► Select *File* → *Import*.

► In the Import dialog, expand *Other* and select *Project Interchange*.

► Click *Browse* to locate and open the file:

`c:\SG247356\sampcode\SoftwareArchitect\test\PTAccountApplication.zip`

► Select all the projects:
  - PTAccountApplication
  - PTAccountApplicationClient
  - PTAccountApplicationClientWed
  - PTAccountApplicationEJB
  - PTAccountApplicationEJBHttpRouter

► Click *Finish*.

Stat the server and add the projects

In the Servers view select the server and click the Start icon ⏵ (Figure 14-9). Wait until the server is ready.

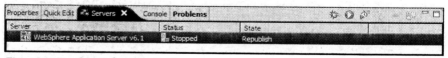

Figure 14-9 Starting the server

To add the project to the test server perform the following:

► In the Servers view select the test server and *Add and Remove Projects*.
► Select the `PTAcountApplication` and click *Add.*
► Select the `PTAcountApplicationClient` and click *Add.*
► Click *Finish.*

Verify the Open Account Application

To start the test server and verify the Open Account Application perform these steps:

► Make sure you have opened the J2EE perspective in Rational Software Architect or Rational Application Developer V7.

► Expand the `PTAccountApplicationClientWeb` application to `WebContent` and `accountApplication`.

► Select the `accountApplication.jsp` and *Run As → Run on Server*. When prompted, select *Set server as project default* and click *Finish.*

► A browser window opens and displays the HTML page (Figure 14-10).

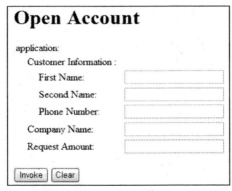

Figure 14-10   Application verification

► Type values into the fields and click *Invoke*. This returns a result of `Eligible` or `Requires Credit Check`.

► The following field values will result in `Eligible`:
  – Company Name: `IBM` and Request Amount: Can be any amount
  – Company Name: Not `IBM` and Request Amount: Less than 5000

► The following field values result in `Requires Credit Check`:
  – Company Name: Not `IBM` and Request Amount: Greater than 5000

Managing testing artifacts

All testing-related artifacts are organized using ClearQuest. Before we start creating testing assets, we set up ClearQuest to manage these items.

As part of JK Enterprises project, we have use the standard ClearQuest Enterprise schema. This schema ships with ClearQuest and include the record types, reports, and other items required for test management. If we had been using another ClearQuest schema, we would have to use the ClearQuest Designer tool to include the Test package. The ClearQuest *schema* is really just a set of tables and fields and other configuration items that configure ClearQuest to provide certain database records with specific fields and other information. The *package* is a new set of tables and fields and other configuration items that can be added to an existing ClearQuest schema.

Assuming we now have the right schema configured in ClearQuest, we can start creating an asset registry for our test assets. There are a few steps in this process:

► Create an asset registry.

► Create a file location.

► Connect to the actual Manual Test, Functional Test, and Performance Test projects with the scripts and executables.

► If required, we create a configuration with details of the types of machines we are using for testing,

Figure 14-11 shows the ClearQuest workspace.

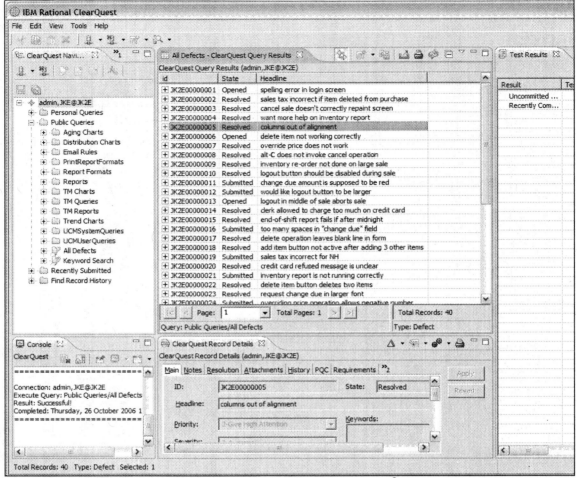

Figure 14-11   IBM Rational ClearQuest, Eclipse-based standalone client[3]

An asset registry is the storage area for the test assets. To create the registry, we select *File → New → TMAssetRegistry* and we then create a new registry (Figure 14-12).

---

[3] A reader familiar with ClearQuest might notice we have loaded the standard ClearQuest sample defects into our JK Enterprises example.

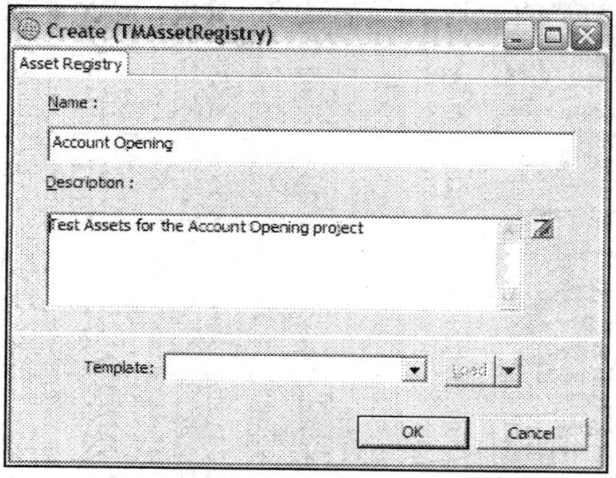

Figure 14-12   Create test asset registry in ClearQuest

At this point, we switch to the Test Manager - Planning Explorer tab because it hides other elements in the Explorer that we may have in our ClearQuest database. The Test Manager view also list a series of folders where we capture our test plans, suites, iterations, and file locations for the various test assets (Figure 14-13).

Figure 14-13   Switch to the Test Manager: Test Planning Explorer

At this point we create Rational Functional Tester, Manual Tester, and Performance Tester projects in a shared directory on our server. We share the directory one level above our Functional Tester, Manual Tester, and Performance projects. We tell ClearQuest where we plan to store our tests.

This allows everyone using ClearQuest for test management to see the test assets.

We also further segment our tests using another category, Iterations. This allows us to assign tests to specific iterations of the development project. This is useful when we have tests that only apply in a specific iteration. We create an Iteration in the ClearQuest, in the Iterations folder. Select the *Iterations* folder in the Planning tab, right-click the folder and select *New Iteration.*

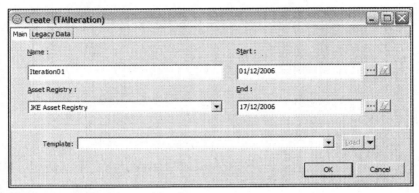

Figure 14-14   Creating an iteration

We have given the iteration a name, a start and end date as well as associating it with a specific asset registry.

We have one more set of actions to complete. A test must be associated with a particular configuration (machine or set of machines). We create a new configuration attribute (Figure 14-15).

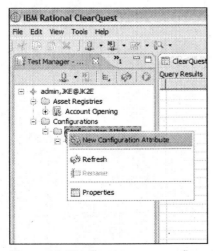

Figure 14-15   Create a new configuration attribute

We can add new possible values to that attribute (Figure 14-16).

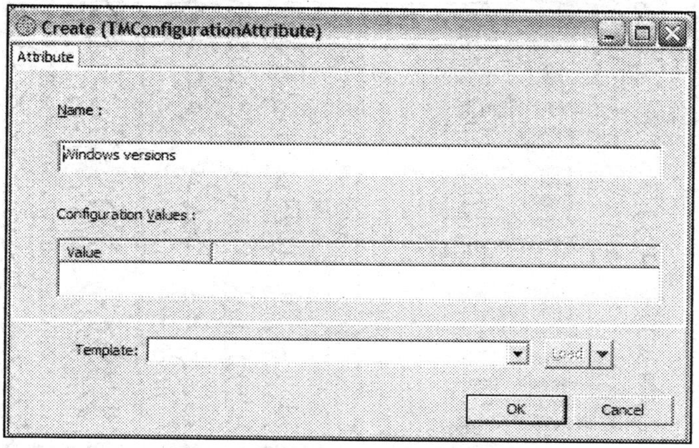

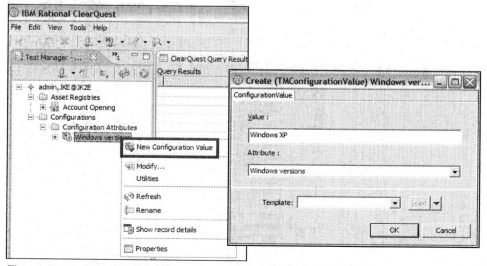

Figure 14-16   New configuration attribute dialog

This attribute is used to denote what kind of test configuration we are working with, for example a Windows XP machine. We create the general category *Windows versions* and then add values for Windows XP and Windows 2000. These are the different machine types we test.

Finally, we add attributes to the configuration value by selecting the configuration attribute and *Add New Configuration Value* (Figure 14-17).

Figure 14-17   Add a new configuration value to the Windows versions

We repeat this to add a new Win2000 value. We can create any number of attributes than helps us understand what kind of machine or other configuration we are testing.

Finally, we can create a configuration instance with various tests associated with it. Add the relevant attributes such as the Windows version (Figure 14-18).

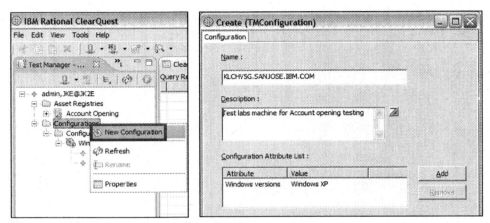

Figure 14-18   Create a new configuration

In summary, we have created an asset registry to store the tests, we have linked to the file server where we are storing our IBM Rational Manual Test, Functional Test, and Performance Test artifacts and we have a configuration to associate our test (Figure 14-19). We can start planning our tests.

Figure 14-19   ClearQuest Test Management setup completed

Creating reusable test scripts with Rational Manual Tester

In this section we create reusable test scripts with Rational Manual Tester to test the `determineApplicationEligiblity` operation on the `AccountApplication` service. Rational Manual Tester was introduced in "Rational Manual Tester" on page 504.

To define the test scripts we utilize the Determine Applicant Eligibility system use case we defined in "Creating a system use case in RequisitePro" on page 225.

We retrieve the system use case from the RequisitePro project. Open the Determine Applicant Eligibility system use case in RequisitePro by:

► Starting RequisitePro.

► Expanding *System Uses Cases* → *Sale Management* and opening *Determine Applicant Eligibility*. This opens the Determine Applicant Eligibility system use case in a word document.

We want to create test scripts that exercise the flow of events for Determine Applicant Eligibility. We need to test the basic flow and any alternative flows.

The basic flow for Determine Applicant Eligibility is as follows:

► The use case starts when the workflow requests the system check of an application.

► The system checks the applicant details for completeness.

► The system checks the applicant details against the business rules for credit limits and confirms or denies eligibility.

► The use case ends when the applicant eligibility is determined.

Determine Applicant Eligibility has two alternate flows which are as follows:

► The applicant is applying for an excessive credit limit

  – The system should reject the application and log this excessive application.

  – The use case ends.

► The applicant has not completed all the details in their application form

  – The application is rejected and the comment field should indicate that the application is incomplete.

  – The use case ends.

We have to create test cases that exercise each route of the use case. From the basic flow and the alternate flow we can see there are three possible routes through the use case.

- ► The application is approved.
- ► The application is rejected because of excessive credit limit.
- ► The application is rejected because of an incomplete application.

We have to create test data which exercise these routes. To do this we look at the business rules for Determine Application Eligibility. The business rules (in this case) was captured in RequisitePro in the Business Rules folder. Determine Application Eligibility has as these business rules:

- ► We accept an account application for less than $5000 from any customer.
- ► Accept all account applications for the company IBM.

Now that we have the routes of the use case and the business rules for the use case, we can see we have four test cases:

- ► Customer account application for loan amount less than 5000
- ► Customer account application for loan amount greater than 5000
- ► Customer is IBM and loan amount greater than 5000
- ► Incomplete account application

These test cases exercise each route of the system use case and the business rules of the use case. We demonstrate how to create a test script for the customer account application for loan amount less than 5000.

We provide the completed solution for all of the above manual test cases in:

```
c:\SG247356\sampcode\test\manualtest.zip
```

Create test scripts in Manual Tester

Now that we have the information needed to create the test scripts for the Determine Application Eligibility system use case. We create the test in Rational Manual Tester.

Rational Manual Tester makes it easy to create manual executable test scripts. Using the Text Editor, we type testing instructions, called *statements*, into a manual test script. There are four statement types we can use in a manual test script:

- ► Steps: Are actions you want the tester to perform when executing the script.
- ► Verification points: Ask question about the application you are testing.

- ▶ Reporting points: Are higher-level verification points whose results often are included in reports.
- ▶ Groups: Signal a block of related statements.

Figure 14-20 shows the Open Account application which leverages the Determine Account Eligibility use case that we are testing (Figure 14-20).

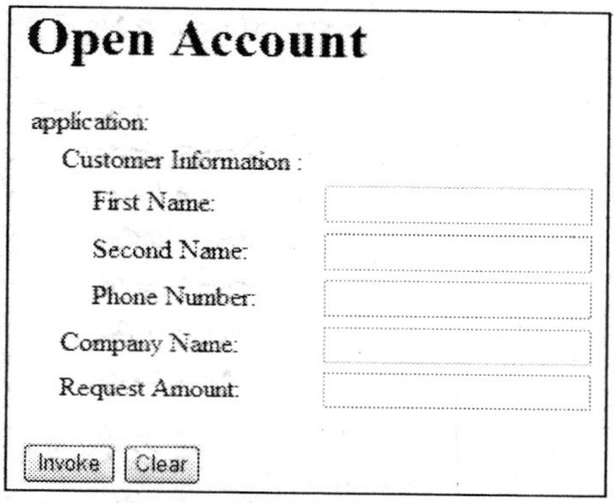

Open Account

application:

    Customer Information :

       First Name: [ ]

       Second Name: [ ]

       Phone Number: [ ]

    Company Name: [ ]

    Request Amount: [ ]

[Invoke] [Clear]

Figure 14-20   Open Account application

Let us begin creating the test script for the customer account application for loan request amount less than 5000 test case.

- ▶ Start Rational Manual Tester. When Rational Manual Tester opens, it creates a new untitled test script that is ready to be edited (Figure 14-21).

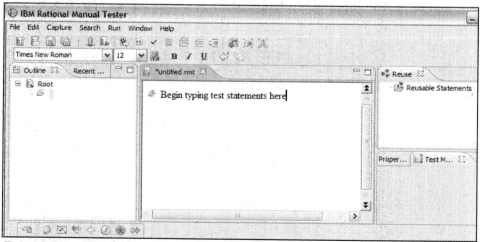

Figure 14-21   Start Rational Manual Tester

Note: If this is the first time Rational Manual Tester is started the Welcome perspective is first thing we see. The Welcome perspective give us an overview of the product and guidance about how to use the product. For now we click the Workbench icon to continue with the JK Enterprises example.

► Delete the text `Begin typing test statements here`.

We now begin to enter the statements that compose our manual test script.

► Type the test statement:

`Launch the application.`

► Press Enter. This creates another statement entry.

The next few test statement we create require the tester to enter specific values into text fields. We can have the tester type the text manually, however, Rational Manual Tester provides the capability for us to capture the data in the test script. When the test statement executes, the data required is copied to the tester clip board. The tester can then paste the data instead of typing the data. This reduces text entry errors.

► Type the test statement:

`Enter the value Laura in the First Name field. Place your curser in the First Name field and press Ctrl^V.`

We now enter the data that is required for the First Name field.

► Have your curser on the statement we created above and select properties view appears at the lower right of the workspace.

► Select *Clipboard*.

► In the Paste Data area type `Laura` (Figure 14-22).

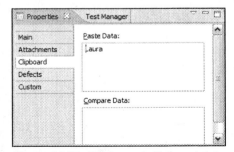

Figure 14-22   Statement clipboard data

We have completed the steps required to associate entry data required by the test statement that can be cut and pasted from the clipboard at test execution time.

We enter the rest of the statements that require paste data by performing the step we completed above for each field:

▶ Second Name:

    – Test statement:

        `Enter the value Olson in the Second Name field. Place your curser in the Second Name field and press Ctrl v.`

    – Test data: `Olson`

▶ Phone Number:

    – Test statement:

        `Enter the value 555-555-5555 in the Phone Number field. Place your curser in the Phone Number field and press Ctrl v.`

    – Test data: 555-555-5555

▶ Company Name:

    – Test statement:

        `Enter the value ITSOWorks in the Company Name field. Place your curser in the Company Name field and press Ctrl v.`

    – Test data: `Olson`

▶ Request Amount:

    – Test statement:

        `Enter the value 3000 in the Request Amount field. Place your curser in the Request Amount field and press Ctrl v.`

    – Test data: `Olson`

The resulting test script is shown in Figure 14-23.

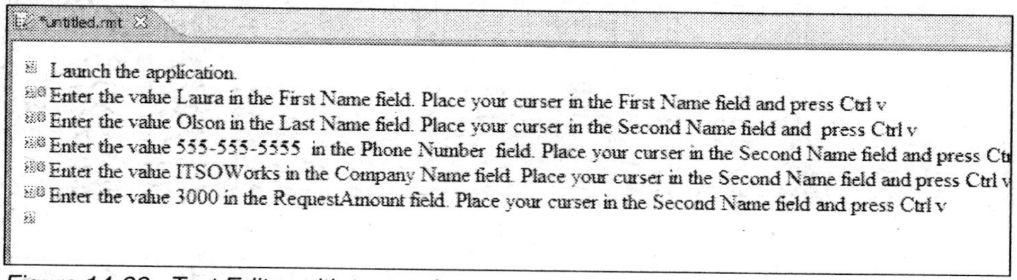

Figure 14-23 Test Editor with test script

We create a verification step to ensure the tester has the correct values in the fields before continuing with the test:

▶ Type the test statement:

   Does your Open Account entry form contain the same field values as in the MTTestVerification.gif file attachment?

▶ Right-click the test statement, select *Statement Type* → *Set as Verification Point*.

▶ We include an image of the Open Account entry form in a file attachment in the statement's properties view by selecting Attachments and then click *Add*. The image is available in:

   c:\SG247356\sampcode\test\MTTestVerification.gif

Now we continue to enter test statements:

▶ Type the test statement:

   Click Invoke

Finally, we create a reporting point statement to capture the final output of the test. It is important to note we can have verification and reporting statements throughout our test script.

▶ Type the test statement:

   Did the application return with the status ELIGIBLE?

▶ Right-click the test statement, select *Statement Type* → *Set as Reporting Point*.

The final test script is shown in Figure 14-24.

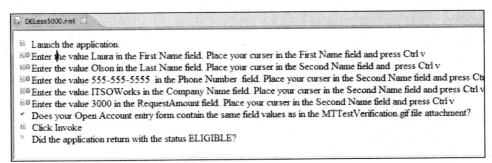

Figure 14-24   Complete test script

One powerful feature of Rational Manual Tester is that you can create reusable statements. This feature saves time when creating multiple test scripts that require similar statements. When the statement requires a change, we change the original test statement and all test scripts with the statement receive the change.

To make a statement reusable, we select the statement and *Add to Reuse*. We have made the following statements reusable to help with the creation of the remaining three test scripts for Determine Application Eligibility (Figure 14-25). To use the reusable test statements we drag and drop the statement into the Test Editor.

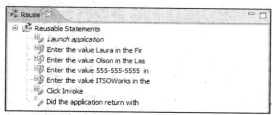

Figure 14-25   Reuse panel

Another powerful feature of Rational Manual Tester is that you can group statements to help create a logical order for the test script.

With the test scripts created, we can let the testers run them.

Run the test script

To run the test script we created in the previous section, select from the menu bar *Run → Run Script*.

This brings up the Run Test Script window as seen in with an gold arrow pointing to the first step (Figure 14-26).

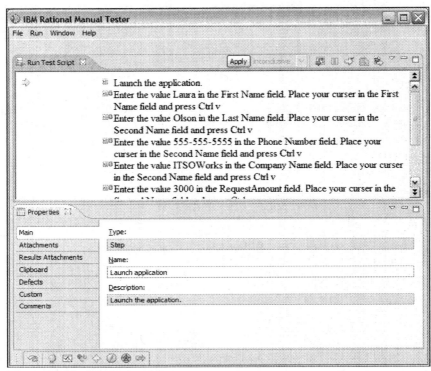

Figure 14-26   Run test script

When we complete a test instruction we click *Apply* and the arrow moves to the next test instruction.

In our test case we have test instructions that require us to enter data into text field. Because of the way we set up our test script, Rational Manual Tester provided this data for us on the clipboard. To enter the data in the text field we paste the data into the field by clicking in the text field and pressing Ctrl-v.

When we encounter a verification point in the test script we must answer by selecting inconclusive, pass, fail or error (Figure 14-27). If the verification produced an error or failed, we can open a defect in Rational ClearQuest by selecting defects in the Properties view and adding a defect. From Rational Manual Tester we can grab screen capture and attach other information which can be used for reporting or aiding in solving the defect.

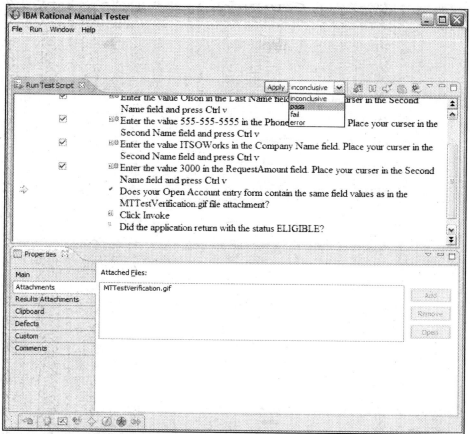

Figure 14-27   Verification test instruction

When we reach a Reporting point instruction, the action is similar to a verification instruction, except that the answer holds greater significance and often is included in reports.

When we have completed the execution of manual test script, Rational Manual Tester prompts us to save the results of the test script. This test script execution can then later be used for reporting and tracking.

Designing and executing functional tests with Rational Functional Tester

IBM Rational Functional Tester is an advanced, automated functional and regression testing tool for testers and GUI developers who need superior control for testing Java, Microsoft Visual Studio .NET, and Web-based applications.

► Provides novice testers with automated capabilities for activities such as data-driven testing.

► Offers advanced testers a choice of scripting language and industrial-strength editor—Java in Eclipse or Microsoft Visual Basic® .NET in Visual Studio .NET—for test authoring and customization.

We did not have the time to use Rational Functional Tester for our sample application.

To learn more about Rational Functional Tester refer to:

`http://www-306.ibm.com/software/awdtools/tester/functional/`

Summary

Software testing an SOA is not that much different than traditional testing. It encompasses the same best practices, such as:

► Testing at each level
► Testing early, often and continuos
► Code inspection, static analysis and behavior modeling
► Error simulation, fault insertion, recovery and response time measuring
► Load and stress testing to verify performance requirements

SOA does not change what we do, but how we do it. It changes how business accomplish their goals, how we do our jobs and how we use our tools. Finally, SOA changes best practices to must practices.

Where to find more information

► *Don't Wait to Test SOA Applications*, by Sergio Lucio, at:

`http://websphere.sys-con.com/read/98059.htm`

- ▶ *Use SLAs in a Web services context, Part 1: Guarantee your Web service with a SLA*, by Judith Myerson, at:

  `http://www-128.ibm.com/developerworks/webservices/library/ws-sla/index.html`

- ▶ *Use SLAs in a Web services context, Part 2: Guarantee second-generation Web services applications with a SLA*, by Judith Myerson, at:

  `http://www-128.ibm.com/developerworks/webservices/library/ws-wssla/index.html`

- ▶ *Performance testing SOAP-based applications*, by Frank Cohen, at:

  `http://www-106.ibm.com/developerworks/webservices/library/ws-testsoap/`

- ▶ *Discover SOAP encoding's impact on Web service performance*, by Frank Cohen at:

  `http://www-128.ibm.com/developerworks/webservices/library/ws-soapenc/`

- ▶ *Web services programming tips and tricks: Stress testing Web services*, by Chris Wilkinson, at:

  `http://www-128.ibm.com/developerworks/webservices/library/ws-tip-strstest.html`

- ▶ *Performance Analysis for Java Web Sites*, S. Joines, R. Willenborg, and K. Hygh, Addison-Wesley, 2002, ISBN 0201844540

15

Creating reusable assets

This chapter describes these topics:

► Assets

► Reusable Asset Specification (RAS)

► Asset life cycle

► Package services as reusable assets

In Chapter 16, "Pattern-based engineering with Rational Software Architect ." on page 545 we also discuss creating reusable assets, such as profiles, transformations, and patterns.

Assets, RAS, and asset life cycle

In this section, we describe assets, the standard specification that supports them, and their life cycle.

Assets

Assets are key to the success of SOA because they enable reuse. In fact, enterprises that adopt an asset-based business model has tremendous growth capabilities. They are no longer limited by the productivity or number of their staff, as in the traditional labor-based business model. The proper use of assets can dramatically change software investments. Anyone who tried to adopt this model, however, can say that it is not straightforward, and requires proper governance and infrastructure support.

Creativity can be counter-productive with SOA. Think for example of people re-inventing the wheel with each new project. Assets are there to allow the proper level or creativity: you reuse proven solutions wherever possible, and then focus all of your time and effort on what needs to be invented.

An asset is a collection of artifacts that provide a solution to a problem in context.

In this context, artifacts can be anything. For example, a requirement, a design model, implementation code, or a test case. Think of an artifact as a file on the file system.

Critical to their success, assets include instructions about how to use, customize, and extend them.

Reusable Asset Specification

Adopted in 2005, the Reusable Asset Specification (RAS) is an Object Management Group (OMG) standard used to describe the structure, contents, and description of reusable software assets.

The goal of RAS is to provide best practices around how to package assets in a consistent and standard way.

As defined in the specification, core characteristics of a RAS asset include:

- **Classification**—The context in which the asset is relevant
- **Solution**—The artifacts contained in the asset
- **Usage**—The rules for installing, using, and customizing the asset
- **Related assets**—How this asset relates to other assets

Artifacts can have a type, determined by their file name suffix (for example, .xml, .txt, .doc, .java), or by their purpose (for example, use case model, analysis model).

Because *software asset* is a very broad term, RAS also provides profiles used to describe specific types of assets. This is the same idea as Unified Modeling Language (UML) profiles. We mentioned that there are UML profiles used to extend the domain-independent UML. In the same fashion, there are domain-specific (for example, Web services) RAS profiles, used to extend the domain-independent RAS.

RAS assets have a .ras file extension, and are packaged like zip files (they have a manifest and can be open by ZIP programs).

Figure 15-1, from the RAS specification, illustrates what the major sections of a core RAS asset are.

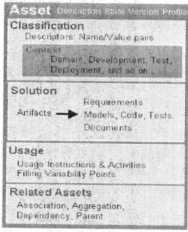

Figure 15-1 Major sections of core RAS asset

Asset life cycle

The JK Enterprises asset life cycle can be described as follows:

► A solution gap is identified.
► An asset specification is created.
► The specification is reviewed by the JK Enterprises' asset board.
► The asset is implemented, and the implementation is reviewed by the board.
► The asset is published to a RAS repository.
► The asset may be deprecated in the future.

Package JK Enterprises services as reusable assets

Several chapters of this book have sections about asset reuse. For example, in "Services and reuse" on page 62 we discuss what can be reused around services, and what has to be in place to support service reuse. In previous sections of this chapter, we describe the concept of an asset, and the RAS specification. "Using the Reusable Asset Specification (RAS)" on page 403 also contains a description of how RAS is supported in Rational Software Architect for browsing, downloading, and using RAS assets.

The JK Enterprises development process includes prescriptive guidance on working with assets. In Chapter 3, "SOA governance" on page 25 we defined a life cycle for JK Enterprises assets, as described in the previous section.

Asset or service?

Assets and services both enable enterprise-level reuse, and share common principles such as the need for description, categorization, life cycle, packaging, extension, or composition. We relate service to asset by thinking of a service as a set of related asset. For example, one of the service assets is the service specification, and another one the service implantation. These services assets are used by different roles and consumed or produced at different stages of service life cycle.

We now described how some of these assets can be created and published to asset repositories.

Package the service model as a reusable asset

In "Service model work product" on page 234 we describe what the service model is composed of.

In this section we do not discuss the concepts behind reuse of the service model or assets, but more how the service model is structured to enable reuse, and how parts of the service model can be packaged as reusable assets.

Structure of the service model

The service model has been structured so that parts of it can be easily packaged as reusable assets. We use Unified Modeling Language (UML) packages to structure the service model. A UML package is used to group related model elements and diagrams, and provide a name space (the name of the package).

Figure 15-2 shows the structure of our service model.

Figure 15-2   Structure of the service model

The first thing that can be packaged as a reusable asset is the complete service model itself. This asset would describe all of the services for the JK Enterprises project (Account Opening).

Individual packages of the service model can also be packaged as reusable assets.

For example, under the 3 - `Atomic Business Application Service Providers` package, we created one sub-package per service provider. The `CustomerAccountMgr` package is expanded in Figure 15-2. By packaging all of what is included in `CustomerAccountMgr` as a reusable asset, we provide all that is necessary to fully specify what that service provider requires and provides. For example, its provided service specifications are included, as well as its parameter types and messages, and also the actual service provider specification. This can be reused by software architects who would want to architect a `CustomerAccountMgr` or similar service.

Note that the structure that we use for the service model can itself be packaged as an asset. This type of asset is called model template, and would be reused by architects who want to specify service models.

Packaging an asset

We now package the `CustomerAccountMgr` service provider package as a RAS asset:

▶ From the Project Explorer, select the *Service Model* and *Export*.

▶ Type ras in the Export window. Select *RAS Asset* and click *Next* (Figure 15-3).

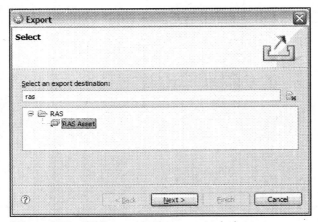

Figure 15-3   RAS asset in the export window

▶ In the RAS Asset (location and manifest) page of the export wizard, select *Repository*, and the JK Enterprises RAS Repository, and click *Next* (Figure 15-5).

JK Enterprises has a RAS asset repository, to which we submit the RAS asset. For the purpose of this exercise, we created a RAS repository. You can also save to the file system instead.

Note: To create a repository, switch to the RAS perspective, and click *Add new Repository connection* (Figure 15-4).

Figure 15-4   Add a new repository connection

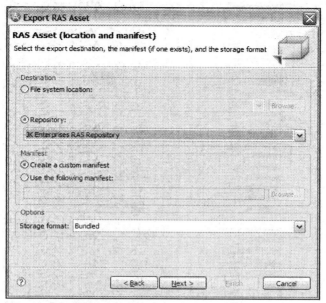

Figure 15-5   RAS asset location and manifest

The next page of the wizard is about specifying the information that is used by the asset repository to produce search results when users looks for assets. Pay attention to providing precise information, otherwise users never find the asset. The information you specify eventually lives in the RAS asset manifest file.

► On the RAS Asset Description page, click ⑦ at the bottom left, and documentation on assets is displayed on the right-hand side (Figure 15-6).

► Specify information about the asset:

    — **Name**: JKEnterpriseServiceModel

    — **Short Description**: JK Enterprises UML Service Model

    — **Description**:

      This asset is the JK Enterprises UML service model. It is composed of
      the following artifacts:
      - Service Consumers Specifications: AccountApplicationInquiryProcess,
        and AccountOpeningProcess.
      - Composite Business Application Service Providers:
        CustomerServiceComposite, and SalesManagementComposite.
      - Atomic Business Application Service Providers: AddressMgr,
        BillingAccountMgr, CustomerAccountMgr, GeneralLedgerAccountMgr,
        ProductMgr.
      - Infrastructure Service Providers

Note that you could also specify the value of default optional descriptors and add new optional descriptors.

► Click *Next*.

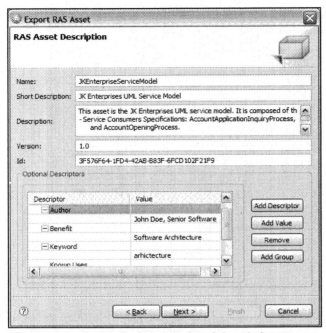

Figure 15-6   Export RAS Asset wizard description page

The last page of the RAS Export wizard is about specifying the artifacts that make up the RAS asset. Artifacts are files on the file system. Software Architect stores UML models in .emx files. The RAS asset we create is made up of one artifact, the service model.

► Select `Service Model.emx` in the RAS Asset Artifact page of the wizard, and click *Finish*.

Note: If you want to package one of the service model packages as a reusable asset, you have to perform a preliminary step to create a new model and then copy the package contents into the new model, or select *Package →* *Create Model*.

Asset repository

The service model asset is now available in the JK Enterprises RAS asset repository. Other JK Enterprises staff can now see the asset description and download it.

Figure 15-7 shows the asset and its description in the Software Architect RAS perspective.

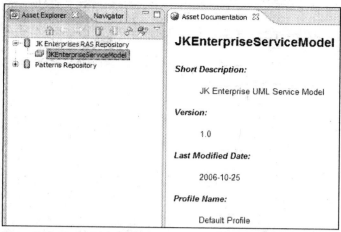

Figure 15-7   Service Model asset description in the RAS perspective

Publish service to Service Registry and Repository

In this section we describe, at a high level, the steps required to publish a service to a service registry and repository, specifically the WebSphere Service Registry and Repository.

At JK Enterprises there are three services registries and repositories: development, production and archive. Also, the service life cycle as defined by JK Enterprises SOA governance includes stages such as awaiting approval, approved, operational, and retired.

Figure 15-8 describes the steps involved in publishing a service.

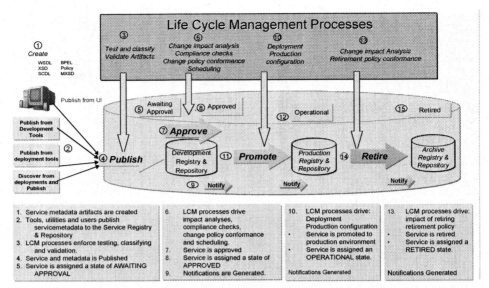

Figure 15-8   Publishing a service to the WebSphere Service Registry and Repository

1. At the beginning of service implementation, the developer generates the WSDL for `AccountApplicationMgr` using Rational Software Architect.

2. Using the Registry and Repository user interface, the software architect browses and makes sure the service does not already exist in the Registry and Repository.

3. The service life cycle management process ensures that the service is tested, validated and classified.

4. The software architect then publishes the service and its description to the development Registry and Repository.

5. At this stage, the service moves to the *Awaiting approval* state of its life cycle.

6. The life cycle management process makes sure that impact analysis, compliance checks and change policy conformance checks have been completed.

7. The JK Enterprises SOA governance board approves the `AccountApplicationMgr` service.

8. The service moves to its life cycles stage of *Approved*.

9. The Service Registry and Repository generates notifications to interested JK Enterprises parties.

Steps 10 to 15 (in Figure 15-8) involve promoting the service to the production registry and repository and finally retiring the service to the archive registry and repository.

Other assets

For JK Enterprises, other services assets that could be created include:

► The JK Enterprises business architecture (Component Business Modeling, CBM) map

► The Account Opening business process model

► The RequisitePro requirements projects

► Parts or all of the domain model

► Parts or all of the design model

References

The Object Management Group (OMG) reusable asset specification can be found at:

```
http://www.omg.org/technology/documents/formal/ras.htm
```

The WebSphere Service Registry and Repository page:

```
http://www-306.ibm.com/software/integration/wsrr/index.html
```

16

Pattern-based engineering with Rational Software Architect

This chapter provides an introduction to pattern-based engineering that uses Rational Software Architect.

This chapter is structured around these topics:

► Pattern-based engineering
► Extensibility
► UML profiles
► Rational Software Architect transformations
► Rational Software Architect patterns

We briefly introduce basic concepts from a theoretical point of view and we provide practical samples and instructions.

For the case study, JK Enterprises requested a custom pattern. We walk through the pattern authoring steps while exploiting the capabilities of Rational Software Architect Version 7.

Pattern-based engineering

Over the years we have come to understand that a pattern is a proven, best practice solution to a known problem within a given context. The industry has embraced the idea of using patterns as they build software solutions.

Up until recently, the patterns that have been used were based on using pattern specifications. A pattern specification is the formal written version of a pattern that has been captured in a book or some other form of documentation. A pattern specification often contains information about the pattern such as:

- ► The **problem** the pattern solves
- ► The **solution** it provides
- ► A **strategy** for applying the pattern in its context
- ► **Consequences**, advantages and disadvantages, or applying the pattern

Over the past decade or so, this was the best approach available in regards to how one could bring patterns to bear on their project. Pattern specifications assisted us in better understanding how to best solve a problem and also assisted us in communicating the solution to others. However, when it came time to apply the pattern, it was a manual effort to use this knowledge. The way one person implemented the pattern would often differ from the way another would implement the same pattern.

To better leverage the power of patterns, we have to take the next step and look at how we can create and use pattern implementations. A pattern implementation is an artifact that automates the application of a pattern. In this way, a pattern becomes a concrete artifact, that is automated, easily applied and results in the same output whether applied by someone down the hall, or someone on the other side of the globe.

Software Architect provides us with a number of tools and features that can be used to build pattern implementations and to further enhance this approach to software development.

Let us look at the different elements that support the building of patterns in Software Architect (Figure 16-1).

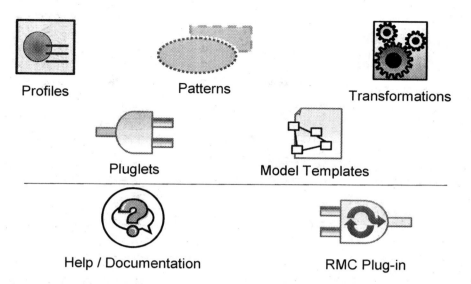

Profiles	Patterns	Transformations
Pluglets	Model Templates	
Help / Documentation		RMC Plug-in

Figure 16-1   Elements within Software Architect supporting Patterns

The elements supporting pattern implementations include:

▶ **Profiles**: The UML, although quite rich in terms of diagrams and notation, is still only a general purpose modeling language. When we look to use it within a specific domain, whether business or technology, we find that there is often a gap between what is provided by UML and what we need to capture aspects and elements within our domain. Rather than trying to create a language that is specific to all domains, the creators of the language took the approach that the it had to be extensible. That is, the UML specification details the ways in which you can extend the language to be specific to a domain. This mechanism is known as *UML profiles*. A UML profile allows you to extend UML through the use of stereotypes, tagged values, and constraints.

▶ **Patterns**: Within Software Architect, there is a specific type of pattern implementation known as a *pattern*. The overloading of the term can be a little confusing at first, but if we state that we are building a pattern implementation using Software Architect's pattern feature, it tends to be much more clear. A Software Architect pattern is used within the scope of a model to interactively modify the model and the elements within. This may mean updating information relating to elements already in the model, adding new elements to the model, or a combination of both.

- **Transformations**: A *transformation* within Software Architect acts much like a Software Architect pattern. It takes elements from a source model and modifies and embellishes them and puts them into a target model. The key differences come down to how the user interacts with the transformation and the scope of its influence. When a user evokes a transformation, its is primarily run as a batch process. The other difference is that it will work its way through all of the elements of a model, or a subset.

- **Pluglets**: Often when creating a pattern or transformation with Software Architect, we find that we have to interact with one of the provided APIs. These APIs allow us to work and interact with Software Architect; this includes query elements in our models, as well as update and create elements within the model. A pluglet is meant to provide a lightweight environment that is quick to use as we interact with these APIs. We are primarily focused on investigation and experimentation when using pluglets. Once we are satisfied that we have created the correct code, we will transition that code to an implementation that is more robust and meant for supporting multiple users, such as an Eclipse plug-in, a transformation or a pattern.

- **Model templates**: When starting to capture a design within Software Architect, it can often be intimidating to start. Faced with a blank model, we are often uncertain about how to structure our model, what information we have to capture and how we should present that information to the people that end up consuming the model. A *model template* is a pre-structured model project that can be selected by the user as they create a new model. A number of model templates ship with Software Architect, assisting us in setting up models targeted to use case analysis, design, and so forth. Software Architect allows us to create our own model templates which can then be shared with others.

- **Help and documentation**: There are two aspects to help and documentation when looking at pattern implementations. The first way to look at the topic is in regard to how you can learn to build your own pattern implementations. There is a great deal of content that ships with Software Architect that helps you in building your own pattern implementations. The other way to look at this topic is when you build your own pattern implementations you want to ensure that you are providing support to the users of your asset. As you build and package the asset that you create you have opportunities and support for providing guidance about how your asset is consumed.

- **Rational Method Composer plug-ins**: When working in a team situation it is imperative that the team is aware of the roles, activities, and work products that are required to successfully complete the project. Method Composer enables you to create and consume content that provides this guidance.

Each of these elements can be used in isolation, however a much higher return on the investment can be achieved when these elements are brought together in combination to assist in building a solution. We can see a basic overview of how features and tools within Software Architect can be brought together in a patterns based solution (Figure 16-2).

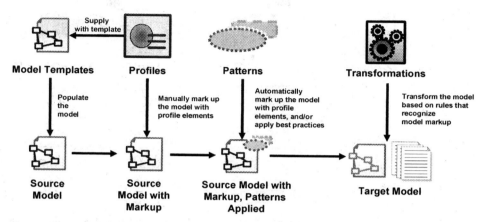

Figure 16-2   *Pattern-based solutions in Software Architect*

One possible workflow that uses all the elements together is as follows:

▶ We start by creating a new model. Rather than starting with a blank slate, we use a model template. As discussed earlier, by selecting to use the template, the new model that is created has a predefined structure that may include a set of packages, default diagrams, a set of reusable model building block, and perhaps some perspective packages. In addition, we often find that model template are already associated with a profile. So in addition to having some structure provide for our model, we find that we have a modeling vocabulary that is particular to the task at hand.

▶ As we work on the design of our solution, we have to add model elements. We may find that we need additional domain related elements. To accomplish this, we attach additional profiles to the model and then manually mark up our model.

▶ At this point we are well on our way to modeling our solution. However, we have seen a very limited way in which we can guide the design of our solution. To further guide how we model, ensuring that we are adhering to best practices, we can look to leverage Software Architect patterns. These patterns are applied within a model, either adding details to existing elements, adding elements, or a combination. In many cases, as we apply a pattern, it uses stereotypes from profiles to add information to the model. So in contrast to the previous step, where we manually added mark up to the model, we use patterns to automate how the markup is added.

► After we have spent time elaborating on the model, we reach a point where we start to focus on the next level of detail. To do so we want to leverage automation again, in this case we use a Software Architect transformation to move from the source model to the target model. The transformation is another pattern implementation. As such it is the automation of a best practice. In this case, the best practice has a wider scope than the Software Architect pattern. It is interesting to note that the transformation also works with the other elements that have been used to this point. A transformation often looks to find the use of stereotypes from particular profiles within the source model. It uses this information to make decisions about what it generates and writes to the target model. In addition, as it writes output to the target model, it may create elements that use stereotypes from a profile, setting things up for the next transformation that is run. The transformation can also leverage Software Architect patterns, expecting input content to adhere to best practice solutions, or even using patterns as it generates content for the target model.

All of these features that surface in support of patterns based development are enabled based on the extensibility that is provided by Software Architect.

Extensibility

As mentioned previously when discussing profiles and UML, a key aspect of the design of UML is that it has a formal extension mechanism. This allows UML to be used in many domains. As we look to build pattern implementations, it is important that there is support to accommodate a wide range or possible pattern implementations. To this end, we find that Software Architect, and its underlying Eclipse platform, are highly extensible. This extensibility is key as we look to support a wide range of domains as we build pattern implementations.

Eclipse extensibility

We already introduced the Eclipse platform in "Overview of IBM architect tools" on page 159. As we stated in that chapter, *Eclipse is designed for extensibility*. Thus, in Eclipse everything is an extension or we may say a plug-in and set of plug-ins. Even the Java development environment or other basic development capabilities are extensions of the Eclipse base platform.

Let us look to the Eclipse architecture to better understand this concept (Figure 16-3).

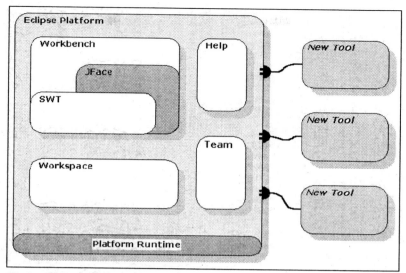

Figure 16-3   Eclipse architecture

Basically, the platform runtime is a plug-in manager. At startup, this component discovers all installed plug-ins, their bundles and creates all necessary runtime configurations (based on XML plug-in descriptors).Through the *extension point* mechanism (refer to "Eclipse" on page 160), the platform runtime creates the plug-in registry that allows the platform to run by finding the extension point *extension*, on demand.

With Eclipse you can develop applications in the desired language (for which there is an Eclipse development environment, such as Java, C++, Cobol and others).

Plug-in Development Environment (PDE)
Eclipse is also used to develop plug-ins that run on Eclipse.

For this task you use the Plug-in Development Environment perspective. This is an extension of Java development perspective. PDE provides an Eclipse *perspective* that allows you to develop plug-ins by managing different information, such as plug-in descriptors with extension, extension points, required plug-in, and plug-in registry.

We can see a snapshot example of the PDE perspective in Figure 16-4.

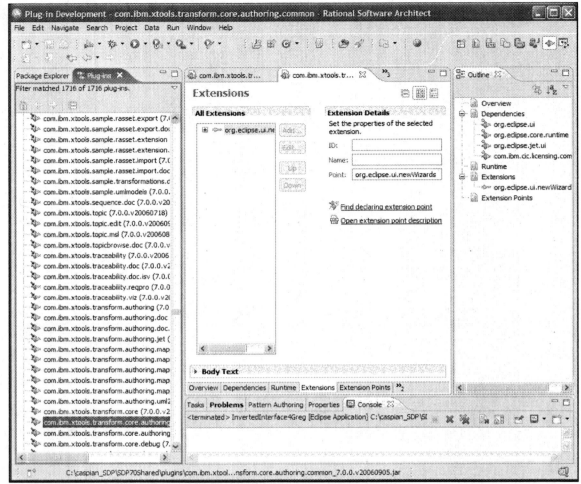

Figure 16-4   Eclipse PDE perspective within Rational Software Architect 7

In Figure 16-4 we can see some important PDE views:

► On the left we have the **Plug-ins** view that basically shows you all installed plug-ins. For each plug-in you can view its descriptor, its dependencies and so on.

► In the middle there is a **plug-in descriptor** open within a manifest editor. A key artifact associated with a plug-in is a manifest file named `plugin.xml`.

The tabs shown at the bottom of the editor represents different plug-in information, such as extensions, extension points, dependencies, and runtime libraries.

In the example we opened the Extensions tab. and we notice that this particular plug-in (`com.ibm.xtools.transform.core.authoring.common`) extends another plug-in through the `org.eclipse.ui.newWizards` extension point.

▶ On the right, we have a typical **Outline** view, which, in this case, shows basic content of descriptor itself.

Testing a plug-in

Furthermore, PDE allows also to run and debug the plug-ins under development.In this phase we test the plug-ins without deployment. Eclipse starts an instance of itself, which is known as the *runtime instance*. The Eclipse instance that was used to launch the runtime instance is known as the host workbench.

The runtime instance has all the plug-ins under development deployed so you can test and debug them. Therefore, for the first time run of the plug-ins, you are expected to configure the runtime instance by specifying:

▶ **Runtime workspace location**: This is a directory path in which you want the runtime workspace resides in.

▶ **List of plug-ins to run**: It is not likely that you need all the plug-ins installed to test your plug-in. Thus you can configure which plug-ins have to run in the runtime instance. However, if you are not sure, keep all plug-ins selected.

▶ **Virtual machine arguments**: Eclipse configuration, enablement of tracing, and so forth.

You can configure the runtime instance using these steps:

▶ From the Java or PDE perspective, select *Run → Run*.
▶ In the left pane, select *Eclipse Application*.
▶ You can now configure the runtime environment.

If you launched the plug-in using Debug, you can use the Debug perspective within the host workbench to manage the interaction with the runtime workbench. As such, you can set break points, inspect variables, and walk through the code as it is running.

Finally, when you think the plug-in is ready to be used in a production environment, you can deploy it so that it is part of the Eclipse installations. This deployment can be done in different ways, one of which is by using the reusable asset specification capability of Rational Software Architect, as we show later in this chapter.

Eclipse modeling

One part of extensibility we are more interested to deeper analyses, is modeling extensibility. Eclipse provides several basic API corresponding to several Eclipse project like:

- **Eclipse Modeling Framework (EMF)**: Provides all the foundation APIs for meta model implementation. It creates a standard for tools to allow them to share a common metadata language. Many eclipse-based tools are depending on this important basic component.

- **Eclipse Modeling Framework Technologies (EMFT)**: Extends EMF by providing capabilities on query, validation, and transactions on models.

- **UML 2**: Is the UML 2 meta model implementation based on EMF.

- **Graphical Modeling Framework** (GMF): Provides the basic API for diagram and visualization capabilities for models.

Rational Software Architect extensibility

As any other tool on Eclipse, Rational Software Architect is realized by a large number of plug-ins. The plug-ins leverage the extension points provided by other plug-ins that are found within the Eclipse platform. In turn, these plug-ins provided by Software Architect also provide extension points that can be extended by other plug-ins.

Figure 16-5 shows the basic architecture of Rational Software Architect.

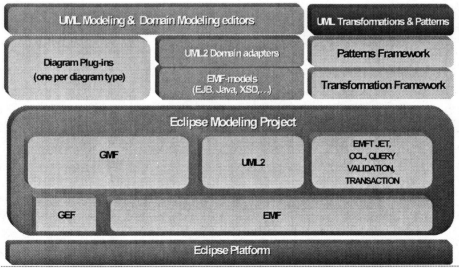

Figure 16-5   Rational Software Architect Version 7

These extension points are our *hooks* to extend IBM tools. For example:

- Modeling tools have profile extension points to allow us to create our own profiles.

- The pattern engine has authoring extensions point that allow us to create new patterns, extend existing ones and so on.

- The transformation engine exposes several extensions point to allow us to define our own transformations and to extend the user interface.

In addition Rational Software Architect offers a way to extend the tool without creating a formal plug-in, by using *pluglets*. A pluglet can be thought of as a lightweight plug-in. The key feature of a pluglet is that it runs within the host workbench; there is no need to launch a runtime workbench to interact with the pluglet. A pluglet can be used to help you in figuring how to interact with the APIs provided by the platform. You can also use a pluglet as a scripting tool that can run in the same eclipse instance against existing models.

Finally, Rational Software Architect provides a full set of public APIs for manipulating models, developing patterns and transformations, and extending existing EMF and UML2 APIs.

Creating profiles

A basic extensibility step that we may need is to create an UML2 profile. For an introduction of profile concepts, refer to "Importance of modeling" on page 138.

Basically, a profile allows us to extend the UML itself, by providing meaningful "types" for our particular domain through definitions of stereotypes, properties and constraints.

To create a profile in Rational Software Architect is straightforward:

- From an existing project (typically this is an extensibility project, such as pattern or transformation authoring), select the project and *New → Other*.

- Expand *Modeling → UML extensibility,* and select *UML Profile* (Figure 16-6).

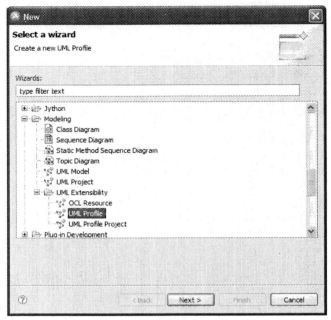

Figure 16-6 Creating a profile

► Click *Next*.

► Leave the default options, type a meaningful name for the profile and for the corresponding file, for example `JK Services Profile` (put spaces in the profile name) and click *Finish*.

Now your profile model exists and you can edit it.

Let us create a simple stereotype. A stereotype is used to extend part of UML meaning. Therefore a stereotype must be related to a *meta class* (this is a part of the UML language), such as Component, Operation, Activity, or Parameter).

► Select the model profile, `JK Services Profile`.

► Select *Add UML → Stereotype*.

► As any UML element, type `compositeServiceSpec` in the name.

► On the properties view, on the Extensions tab, click *Add extension*.

► Select *Class* as a meta class and click *OK*.

Now we have our first stereotype.

Let us assume we want to add a property on this stereotype to represent the version of the service:

- ► Select the stereotype and *ADD UML* → *Attribute*.
- ► Name the attribute `version`.
- ► Select *String* for the type of the attribute.

In this way you can add other stereotypes, properties, or constraint to the profile.

As a typical scenario you likely test your profile (in many case this is associated to a transformation or a pattern) in your development environment, and when you are confident, you deploy it.

We show how to deploy extensibility assets later in this chapter.

Authoring transformations

We already introduced transformations in "Transformations" on page 148, while explaining the model-driven development theory of operations and tools.

Basically, transformations are a powerful tool to transform a model related to a given level of abstraction to a model on a different (typically but not necessary lower) level of abstraction.

Note: By saying *model* we are meaning also the code. Indeed the code is the model on a low level of abstraction!

Like patterns, transformations can be very useful for a software development organization because they:

- ► Improve productivity by automating many deterministic tasks.
- ► Enforce standards because a given model always "becomes" a solution that follows a particular architecture, standard, and so on. Development tasks are less subject to human errors.
- ► Improve software quality and maturity of the development process, by automatically creating traceability links among levels of abstraction.

We may say that all above points help in reaching a more mature SOA governance.

Transformations are made up of rules that, scanning a source model, recognize source elements, meta classes and stereotypes, "know" how to transform it into elements in the target model. Indeed very often transformations are related to particular profiles.

We show examples of transformation usage in this book in Chapter 12, "Service realization" on page 387 and Chapter 13, "Service implementation" on page 419.

In these cases we show transformations from different models to different "code" artifacts.

The transformation engine of Rational Software Architect provides transformations authoring capabilities by defining appropriate extension points.

Moreover, wizards are provided to automatically generate all transformation skeletons, including rules generation.

Where as in Rational Software Architect Version 6, creating a transformation was done almost by hand-coding the overall transformation behavior; Version 7 offers new interesting capabilities:

► Model to model authoring support:
► Model to text authoring support:
► Own transformations

Model to model authoring support

The tool now provides a mapping editor that allows to map models through their meta models. Once this mapping is created, Rational Software Architect is able to generate the transformation.

This allows the user to forget about the detailed implementation and concentrate on the mapping. When this mapping changes, the transformation will be regenerated and ready to use. We can see a sample of this mapping in Figure 16-7. Mapping happens between meta models and UML profiles.

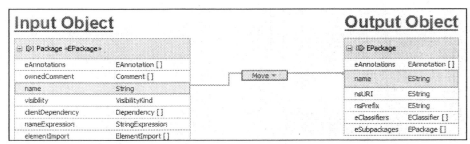

Figure 16-7   A sample of a mapping model

> **Note:** With this capability we are now able to easily create a transformation that, for example, copies elements from one model to another, where these two models represent two different levels of abstraction through two different UML profiles.
>
> For example, for the JK Enterprises case study, we can think a transformation that, starting from the service model, creates the initial design model.

Model to text authoring support

Also in this case, we have new interesting tool capabilities. By exploiting new, open source emerging technologies, such as the Eclipse Modeling Framework Technologies (EMFT) and Java emitter templates (JET2), we can create model-to-text transformation using the authoring tool. In particular is now possible to transform from models not in UML/EMF format.

Own transformations

Finally, Rational Software Architect provides a framework to plug-in your own transformations. In cases where you have more complex transformations to develop, you complete some (Java) methods to implementing your transformation logic (these methods are typically called by the framework itself). To write the logic you have to know basic of some API, such as:

- ► Basics of Eclipse extensibility
- ► UML2
- ► EMF, EMFT
- ► Software Architect extensibility and transformation API

We can exploit a tool wizard to start the transformation implementation. This wizard will prompt us for rules that have to be implemented, and then generates the required plug-in infrastructure.

To browse the API documentation in the product follow these steps:

- ► Select *Help → Help contents*.

- ► Expand *Rational Software Architect functionality*.

- ► From here you can have an overview of all of the extensibility tools provided or you can directly go to transformation informations and API by expanding Rational *Transformation Authoring Developer's Guide*.

If you want to make a first step through transformation authoring, you can also start from the Software Architect samples. You can obtain a sample of transformation by selecting menu *Help → Samples gallery → UML modeler Plug-ins → Model-to-text transformation* (Figure 16-8).

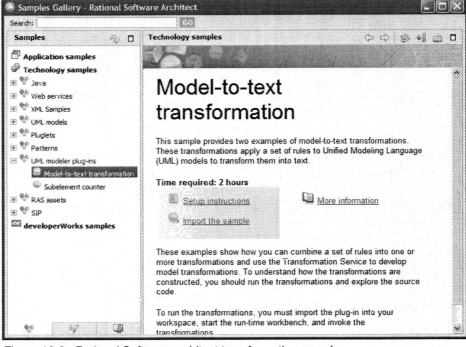

Figure 16-8   Rational Software architect transformation sample

Authoring design patterns (JK Enterprises composite service specification)

Patterns are a similar concept to transformations. The main difference is while a transformation is thought to take a model content from an abstraction level to another (another model), a pattern is executed within the same abstraction level (same model).

Moreover, a transformation has (typically) a large content to transform and can be executed in *batch* mode, where as a pattern is executed through an interaction with the designer.

In the JK enterprises case study we use three different patterns:

► An *Interface* design pattern in the design model, imported from pattern samples (used during service realization).

► A *Facade* design pattern in the design model, taken from official Rational Software Architect patterns (used during service realization).

- A *CompositeServiceSpecification* design pattern in the service model, explicitly built for our case study (used during service specification).

This is a pattern needed to structure a composite service, by updating provided service specification for a given composite service, starting from a composite service specification class. Additionally this pattern creates realization relationship with provided interface and usage dependencies for required interfaces.

This pattern is thought to be used during the service specification phase, in the service model.

Note: For a complete description of this pattern specification refer to "Service model related patterns" on page 259.

So now, we have to author this pattern. Let us go with pattern authoring tools:

- First, create a pattern project by selecting *New → Project → Plug-in development → Plug-in Project*.
- Click *Next*.
- Name the project com.jkenterprises.designpatterns.
- Leave defaults, click *Next*.
- Leave defaults, click *Next*.
- Select *Plug-in with Patterns* (Figure 16-9).

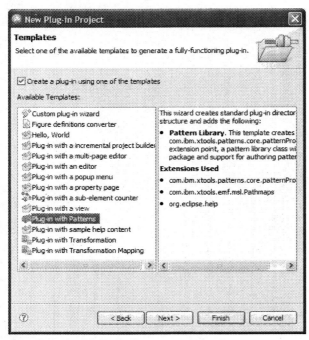

Figure 16-9   Pattern project creation

► Click *Next*.

► Leave the defaults, click *Finish*.

► Open the Pattern Authoring view by selecting *Window → Show View → Other → Modeling → Pattern Authoring*.

Now we have a project that acts as a container for our pattern family and we can see it in the Pattern authoring view.

Now we have to create our pattern:

► In the Pattern Explorer view, select the project and *New → Pattern*.

► Type `CompositeServiceSpecification` in the name field.

► Add a new group and name it `JK SOA Patterns`.

► Optionally, go to Detail tab and type your name as Author and provide a short pattern description:

```
This is a pattern needed to structure a composite service, by creating
"provided" service specification operations for a given composite service.
Additionally it creates realization relationship with provided interface
and USAGE dependencies for required interfaces.
```

- ▸ Click *OK*.
- ▸ Now it is time to add pattern parameters. Select the pattern and *New →
  Parameter*.
- ▸ In the name field, type `CompositeServiceSpecificationClass`.
- ▸ In the Short Description field, type: `This class represents the "type" of a
  composite service. This class realizes the provided service
  specification and uses the required service specifications.`
- ▸ For the type, select *Class* and leave defaults (Figure 16-10).

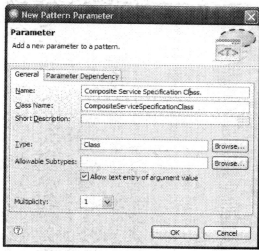

Figure 16-10   Adding a pattern parameter

- ▸ Click *OK*.
- ▸ Add another parameter, name it `ProvidedServiceSpecification`, select
  Interface as type, leave the other defaults.
- ▸ In the Short Description field, type: `The provided service specification.
  Operations of this interface are updated following the Composite
  Service specification class (only public operations are copied).`
- ▸ Select the *Parameter Dependency* tab.
- ▸ Select `CompositeServiceSpecificationClass` as Supplier parameter.

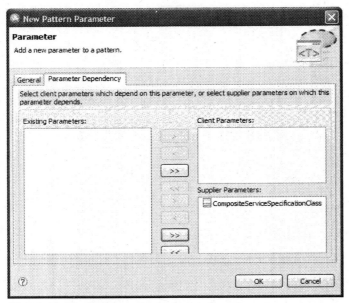

Figure 16-11   Create a dependent parameter

- ► Add another parameter, name it `RequiredServiceSpecification`, select *Interface* as type, select *1..** on multiplicity, leave the other defaults.
- ► In the Short Description field, type: `The list of required service specifications represents all of the service specifications (interfaces) the composite service needs (can use) during its execution.`
- ► Select the *Parameter Dependency* tab.
- ► Select `CompositeServiceSpecificationClass` as Client parameter.
- ► Click *OK* (Figure 16-11).

Now, you should see the pattern in the Pattern Authoring view (Figure 16-12).

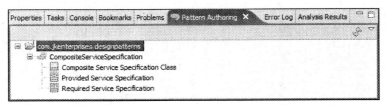

Figure 16-12   The pattern as it appears in pattern authoring view

Important: By creating a dependent parameter, we instruct the framework to generate necessary code to manage events that impact on the parameter itself.

Figure 16-13   CompositeServicespecification pattern in Project Explorer

As we can observe in Figure 16-13, Software Architect has already created all the plug-in structure necessary to implement our pattern.

The first two packages (`com.jkenterprises.designpatterns` and `com.jkenterprises.designpatterns.lib`) contain already implemented structural classes necessary for plug-in activation and pattern library management.

Pattern implementation

The real pattern implementation resides in the class `CompositeServiceSpecification`. Software Architect has already generated this class corresponding to the pattern and three nested classes, that correspond to pattern parameters:

▶ `CompositeServiceSpecificationClass` represents the *class* part of this pattern.

▶ `ProvidedServiceSpecification` represents the *provided interface* part of this pattern. Following our pattern requirements, this interface shall "follow" the above class, by having same operation signatures. In fact, when we visually created this parameter, we checked this parameter as dependent on the first one (that is a *supplier* for this parameter). Thus the framework automatically created hotspot methods called update when the pattern is applied or re-applied by the user.

▶ `RequiredServiceSpecification` represents a list of interfaces that are required by this composite service. Indeed a composite service is likely to use more than one existent service and therefore, to have more than one required interface. The first parameter, `CompositeServicespecificationClass` (that we select as a client), will be dependent on this parameter.

We have to perform two steps in this pattern implementation:

▶ Update the `ProvidedServiceSpecification`, as the *provided* interface of the composite service.

▶ Create USAGE dependencies from the `CompositeServiceSpecificationClass` class to the *required* interfaces.

Update the provided service specification

We want the pattern to copy public operations present in the class to the interface (`ProvidedServiceSpecification`). There are update methods generated for each parameter dependency (inner class of the parameter) in the class:

```
ProvidedServiceSpecification_CompositeServiceSpecificationClassDependency
```

These methods allow us to manage a change in the supplier parameter (`CompositeServiceSpecificationClass` in this case).

Moreover, we want the pattern creates the realization relationship between class and interface.

Therefore—knowing a basic UML 2 API—we implement this method as shown in Example 16-1.

Example 16-1   The hotspot update method implementation

```
public boolean update(PatternParameterValue value,
                      PatternParameterValue dependencyValue) {
  final AbstractPatternInstance instance =
                      (AbstractPatternInstance)value.getOwningInstance();
  final org.eclipse.uml2.uml.Class implValue =
              (org.eclipse.uml2.uml.Class)dependencyValue.getValue();
  final Interface interfaceValue = (Interface) value.getValue();
  instance.ensureInterfaceImplementation(interfaceValue, implValue);
  Utility.ensureClassImplementation(implValue, interfaceValue);
  return true;
}
```

This method receives two parameters that represent the interface parameter itself (corresponding to the class we are implementing) and the parameter this is depending on.

As we can see in the second and third assignment, these two parameters are assigned to the local variable `interfaceValue` and `implValue`.

The method called on the `instance` (the instance of the pattern the framework is currently applying), `ensureInterfaceImplementation` simply checks if a realization relationship exists from the class to the interface.

The last method call refers to our actual implementation of this pattern: The `ensureClassImplementation` method (Example 16-2) has to ensure that operations present on the class (`CompositeServiceSpecificationClass` pattern parameter) are also on the interface (`RequiredServiceSpecification` pattern parameter).

> **Note:** Because the two methods `ensureClassImplementation` and `ensureInterfaceHasOperation` have a generic behavior and can be reused, we put them on a `Utility` class as static methods.

Example 16-2   ensureClassImplementation method from Utility class

```
public static void ensureClassImplementation(Class implValue,
                                             Interface interfaceValue) {
  // retrieve all operations from the class
  EList operations = implValue.getAllOperations();
  //Iterate over class operations
  Iterator iterOps = operations.iterator();
  while (iterOps.hasNext()){
    Operation classOp = (Operation) iterOps.next();
      //if PUBLIC, ensure operation on the Interface
      if (classOp.getVisibility() == VisibilityKind.PUBLIC_LITERAL){
```

```
        Operation intOp = ensureInterfaceHasOperation(
                            interfaceValue, classOp);
        }
    }
}
```

As we note from the code, this method simply loops on the class operations. For each public operation present on the class, it invokes the (Utility) `ensureInterfaceHasOperation` method (Example 16-3) passing the interface and current operation as parameters. Note that only public operations are copied to the interface.

Example 16-3   ensureInterfaceHasOperation method from Utility class

```
public static Operation ensureInterfaceHasOperation(Interface interfaceValue,
                                            Operation classOp) {
    // operation to be returned
    Operation intOp;
    BasicEList listParNames = new BasicEList();
    BasicEList listParTypes = new BasicEList();

    //We gather all parameters types and names in two Elist
    Iterator iterParms = classOp.getOwnedParameters().iterator();
    while (iterParms.hasNext()){
        Parameter classParam = (Parameter) iterParms.next();
        //create ELists for input parameters
        listParNames.add(classParam.getName());
        listParTypes.add(classParam.getType());
    }
    //find or create operation on demand
    intOp = interfaceValue.getOwnedOperation(classOp.getName(),
            listParNames, listParTypes, false, true);

    return intOp;
}
```

As we can see on the provided code, this method:

► Creates two EList to contain parameter types and names.

► Loops over class operation parameters.

► Fills the two lists with all input parameters.

► Using UML2 API on the Interface, invoke `getOwnedOperation` method that, when supplied with all necessary parameters, find or create the requested method.

► Return the (found or created) operation.

Note that although in our example we are not using the returned operation, it is good practice to return it, because this method is expected to find or create such an operation.

Create usage dependencies

Now, we have to work on the third parameter. In particular, we have to create an UML <<use>> dependency from the Class parameter to the required interfaces. We have to remind that at pattern application time, these interfaces will represent the basic services that compose our service.

As we did for the first implementation part, we have to work on the update method of this dependency that is represented by the class:

CompositeServiceSpecificationClass_RequiredServiceSpecificationsDependency

Let us analyze the method implementation (Example 16-4).

Example 16-4   Update method for required interface

```
public boolean update(PatternParameterValue value,
                      PatternParameterValue dependencyValue) {

    //TAKES PATTERN INSTANCE  FROM A PARAMETER
    final AbstractPatternInstance instance = (AbstractPatternInstance) value
        .getOwningInstance();

    Interface requiredIntfc = (Interface) dependencyValue.getValue();
    Class compSrvcClass = (Class)value.getValue();

    //Create USAGE dependency between class and interface
    instance.ensureUsageRelationship(compSrvcClass, requiredIntfc);

    return true;
}
```

First, as we did for the other update method, we retrieve the pattern instance from one parameter.

We initialize the class (CompositeServiceSpecificationClass) and interface (RequiredServiceSpecification) to two meaningful local variables.

Finally, the actual body of the method simply calls the Software Architect API ensureUsageRelationship method on the AbstractPatternInstance (the instance of our pattern). This method create a <<use>> dependency from a class to an interface.

The pattern implementation is now completed and we have to go to test the new pattern.

Pattern test

To test our pattern we have to remind that a pattern is realized as an Eclipse plug-in (that extends Software Architect). As we already explained in Eclipse extensibility, to test a plug-in we have to start an Eclipse runtime instance.

First time, you have to configure your runtime instance:

- From Java or PDE perspective, select *Run → Run*.
- In the left pane, select *Eclipse Application*.
- You can now configure your runtime environment.

Go to the plug-in tab and be sure the pattern under development is selected (Figure 16-14).

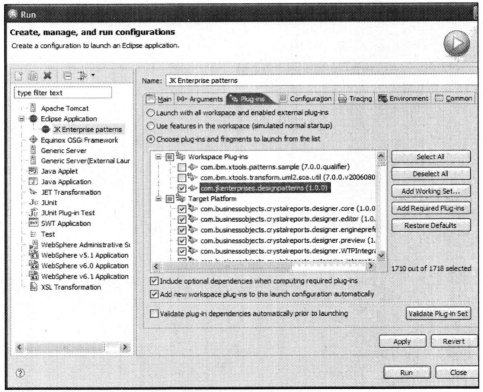

Figure 16-14   Create, manage and run for Eclipse applications

By clicking *Apply* you save the configuration where as by clicking *Run* you save the configuration and start the Eclipse runtime instance.

In the runtime instance you can show the pattern explorer view. You should find our newly defined pattern under the *miscellaneous patterns* group. You can now test this pattern:

- ► Create a model.
- ► Apply the SoftwareServices UML profile to this model.
- ► Create a class (the Composite Service Specification class).
- ► Create some operation on the class.
- ► Create an interface (the provided Service Specification).
- ► StereoType this interface as <<ServiceSpecification>>.
- ► Create a set of interfaces (the required service specifications).
- ► Stereotype these interfaces as <<ServiceSpecification>>.
- ► Apply the pattern.

Note: If you have to know how to apply a pattern, you can find examples of pattern usage in Chapter 12, "Service realization" on page 387.

Tip: With Rational Software Architect V7, you can also avoid to create all necessary elements *before* applying the pattern. Indeed you can let the pattern engine to do it for you, while applying the pattern. By hovering the mouse on a particular parameter on the pattern instance, you will find a button that creates an element corresponding to that parameter type.

As a result of pattern application you should see a realization relationship has been created from the class to the interface and every operation present on the class has been copied to the interface. Additionally all required interfaces are bound to the class through a <<use>> UML dependency.

We can see an example of this pattern application in the context of JK Enterprises service model in Figure 16-15.

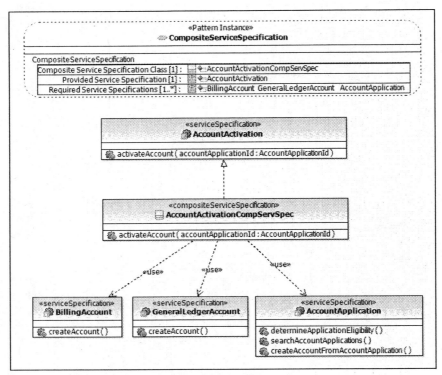

Figure 16-15 The composite service specification pattern applied

The composite service pattern is now working!

Note: This pattern does not enforce the user to apply Software services profile. Indeed, although we are using this profile in this context, the pattern is more generic and can be used whenever a class has to realize one interface and requires a set of other interfaces.

We can think about how to improve it, make all necessary modifications and when we are satisfied with the pattern structure and behavior we can think to deploy it. For example, you can notice if you right-click the pattern in the pattern explorer and select *Show pattern documentation*, no documentation is displayed at this point. Going back to development, in the pattern authoring view, you can right-click the pattern and select *Generate Help Files*. This automatically creates all HTML files containing the pattern documentation. You can use the generated pages as is or improve these pages by writing additional pattern informations.

We are now going to learn how to deploy, manage and distribute our pattern by using Reusable Asset Specification (RAS) tools provided by Rational Software Architect.

Using the Reusable Asset Specification (RAS) to distribute and manage assets

Reusable asset specification is an Object Management Group (OMG) standard that defines format, structure of reusable software assets.

An asset may be any software related element like an UML model, a component, a framework, a service, and so forth.

Being a standard, reusable asset specification ensure that, independently from tools used the asset will be correctly read, managed and interpreted.

One of SOA key principle is about reuse and a correct asset management helps and enforce software reuse.

> **Tip:** You can find a more detailed and complete introduction to reusable asset management in Chapter 15, "Creating reusable assets" on page 533.

Going back to our SOA pattern, now we want to deploy this pattern using reusable asset specification.

As we have explained in the asset related chapter, in Rational Software Architect you can create an asset by using the export functionality:

▶ Select *File → Export*.

▶ Select *RAS → Ras Asset*.

▶ Click *Next*.

▶ Select a destination ras file (we are creating a repository).

▶ Click *Next*.

▶ Give a significant name and description to the asset. You can add information related to asset version, author and so on.

▶ Click *Next*.

▶ Select only the pattern project, `com.jkenterprises.designpatterns`.

▶ Check only *Export as deployable feature, fragment or plug-in*.

▶ Click *Finish*.

This way we have created our RAS asset that, for the moment, contains only one pattern, but in the future you can add other assets to it.

A client that wants to install this pattern has to import this RAS asset using the RAS (Reusable Asset) perspective of Software Architect. The reusable asset that we created is available in the sample code:

```
SG247356\sampcode\SoftwareArchitect\ras\SOARedbookPatterns.ras
```

The instructions on how to install the asset are provided in "Installing the sample pattern RAS asset" on page 588.

References

Eclipse modeling project:

```
http://www.eclipse.org/modeling/
```

Eclipse UML2 project:

```
http://www.eclipse.org/modeling/mdt/?project=uml2-uml
```

IBM Rational pattern solution Web site:

```
http://www-128.ibm.com/developerworks/rational/products/patternsolutions/#model
```

Read *A Rational approach to model-driven development,* by A. W. Brown, S. Iyengar, and S. Johnston, at:

```
http://www.research.ibm.com/journal/sj/453/brown.html
```

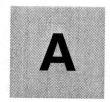

Additional material

This book refers to additional material that can be downloaded from the Internet as described below.

Locating the Web material

The Web material associated with this book is available in softcopy on the Internet from the IBM Redbooks Web server. Point your Web browser to:

```
ftp://www.redbooks.ibm.com/redbooks/SG247356
```

Alternatively, you can go to the IBM Redbooks Web site at:

```
ibm.com/redbooks
```

Select the **Additional materials** and open the directory that corresponds with the Redbooks form number, SG247356.

Using the Web material

The additional Web material that accompanies this book includes the following files:

File name   *Description*
sg247356code.zip   Zipped code samples
correction7356.txt Corrections to the PDF

System requirements for downloading the Web material

The following system configuration is recommended:

Hard disk space: At least 10 GB free space for products
Operating System: Microsoft Windows XP SP2 or greater
Processor: P4-class Pentium®
Memory: 2 Gigabytes RAM

Software requirements

The following tools were used to create the samples. In the case of IBM Rational Software Architect, IBM Rational Functional Test, IBM Rational Performance Test and IBM Rational Manual Test, the pre-release build of Version 7 were used:

► IBM Rational RequisitePro V7.0.0.0-IFIX01 or greater

► IBM WebSphere Business Modeler V6.0.1 or greater

► IBM Rational Software Architect V7.0

How to use the Web material

Unzip the contents of the Web material file **sg247356code.zip** onto your hard drive. This creates a directory **c:\SG247356\sampcode** with these subdirectories:

DevelopmentCase Sample code for RMC plug-in

Modeler   Sample code for WebSphere Business Modeler

RequisitePro   Sample code for Rational RequisitePro

SoftwareArchitect Sample code for Rational Software Architect

Loading the RequisitePro projects

Our sample contain two RequisitePro projects, with cross project traceability and links to the UML models held in Rational Software Modeler or Rational Software Architect.

The projects are saved as zipped RequisitePro baseline files. First unzip the files into a temporary directory:

► `Enterprise.zip`—This project contains information relevant to all SOA-based solutions.

► `Project.zip`—This project contains information specific to the solution discussed in this IBM Redbooks publication.

To load the files, start RequisitePro Baseline Manager by selecting *Start → All Programs → IBM Rational → IBM Rational RequisitePro → RequisitePro Baseline Manager* (assuming we are using Windows XP and have accepted the default tool installation options).

Alternatively, start RequisitePro and select *Tools → RequisitePro Baseline Manager*.

Figure A-1 shows the RequisitePro Baseline Manager.

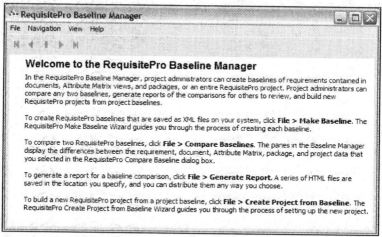

Figure A-1   Use the RequisitePro Baseline Manager to load the RequisitePro files

Use the baseline manager to recreate both projects. Both projects must be recreated to enable the cross-project traceability.

Loading the RequisitePro project templates

The RequisitePro material for this book also contains project templates for the Enterprise project and the Project project. Adding these to our RequisitePro installation provides two additional project templates when creating a new Project:

► The `RequisitePro-outlines.zip` file can be unzipped into the `<installdir>/RequisitePro/outlines` directory.

► The `RequisitePro-templates.zip` file can be unzipped into the `<installdir/RequisitePro/templates` directory.

Loading the WebSphere Business Modeler project

The WebSphere Business Modeler project is stored as a WebSphere Business Modeler project zip file. To import this model, start WebSphere Business Modeler in a new workspace. We do not have to create a new model, this is done as part of the import process.

► Select *File* → *Import*.

► Select *WebSphere Business Modeler Import* and click *Next* (Figure A-2).

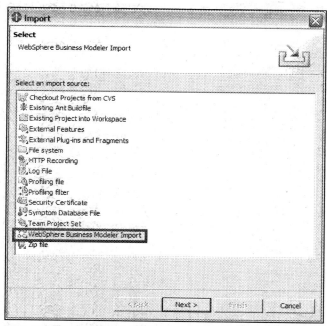

Figure A-2   WebSphere Business Modeler file import

► Select *WebSphere Business Modeler project (.zip)* and click *Next* (Figure A-3).

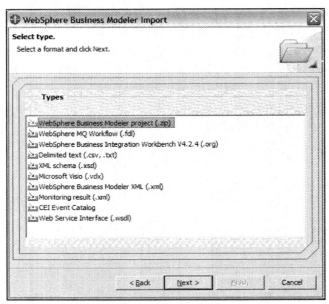

Figure A-3   Select WebSphere Business Modeler project (.zip) import

► Click *New* to create the target project. Enter JK Enterprises Account Opening as project name and click *Finish* (Figure A-4).

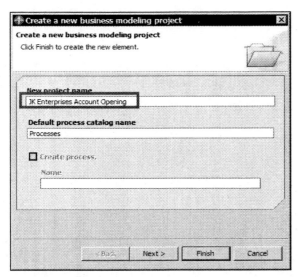

Figure A-4   Create the JK Enterprises project

► Click *Browse* to locate the sample code directory:

`c:\SG247356\sampcode\Modeler`

Then select the ZIP file and click *Finish* (Figure A-5).

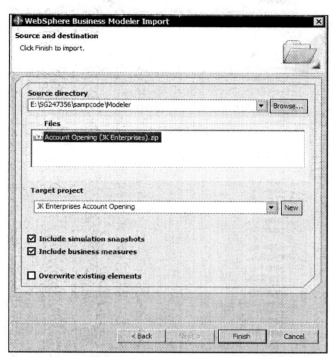

Figure A-5   Enter the import zip files details and create a new model

► When the import is complete, the model is available in the workspace. Figure A-6 shows the project with the business items and processes expanded, and one process opened.

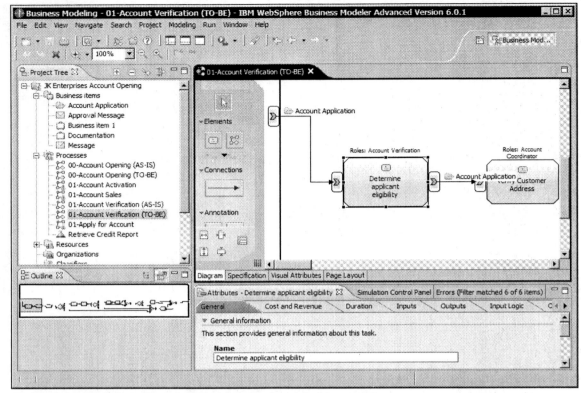

Figure A-6   WebSphere Business Modeler after importing the sample

Loading the models into Rational Software Architect

We provide the UML models in a ZIP file:

```
c:\SG247356\sampcode\SoftwareArchitect\JK Enterprises UML Models.zip
```

To load the models into Software Architect, perform these steps:

► Start Rational Software Architect V7.

► Open the Modeling perspective and close the Resource perspective.

► Select *File → Import*.

► In the Import dialog, select *Other → Project Interchange* and click *Next* (Figure A-7).

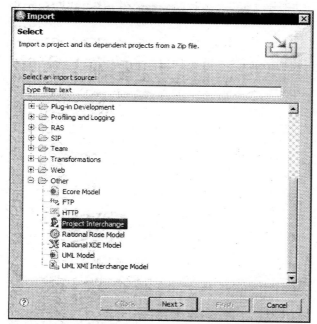

Figure A-7   Select the import type as archive file

► Click *Browse* and locate the file:

```
C:\SG247356\sampcode\SoftwareArchitect\UMLModels.zip
```

Select the project and click *Finish* (Figure A-8).

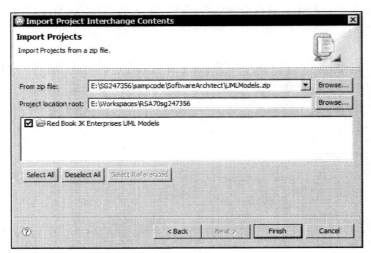

Figure A-8   Importing the UML models

► The models are imported into the project. Expand the project to see the Diagrams, Models, and Profiles (Figure A-9).

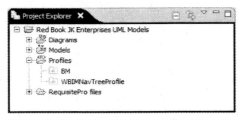

Figure A-9   Project Explorer after import

Loading the implementation into Software Architect

We provide the finished application for testing as a project interchange file in:

```
c:\SG247356\sampcode\SoftwareArchitect\test\PTApplication.zip
```

To load the application into Software Architect perform these steps:

► Open the Web perspective. When prompted click *OK* to enable Web development.

► Select *File → Import*.

► In the Import dialog, select *Other → Project Interchange* and click *Next* (Figure A-7 on page 583).

► Click *Browse* to locate the interchange file. Select all the projects and click *Finish* (Figure A-10).

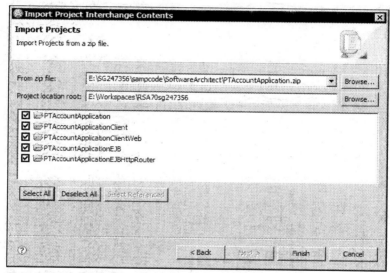

Figure A-10 Importing the application projects

► The projects are imported and built:

– PTAccountApplication is the Web service enterprise application, consisting of PTAccountApplicationEJB and PTAccountApplicationEJBHttpRouter.

– PTAccountApplicationClient is the Web service client enterprise application, consisting of PTAccountApplicationClientWeb.

► Figure A-11 shows the Project Explorer with the application projects and the Web services.

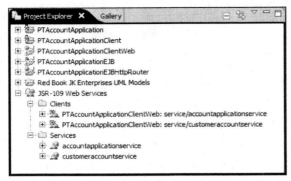

Figure A-11   Project Explorer showing the application projects

Running the application

To run the sample application perform these steps:

► In the Servers view select the server and click the Start icon
(Figure A-12).

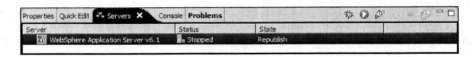

Figure A-12   Starting the server

► Wait until the server is ready.

► Select the server and *Add and Remove Projects*. In the dialog click *Add All*
and click *Finish* (Figure A-13).

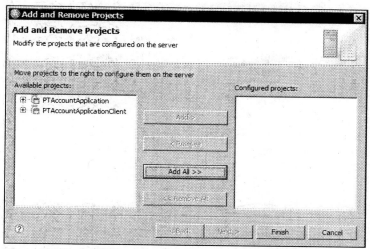

Figure A-13 Add the application projects to the server

► Watch the Console view and wait for the messages that the applications are started:

```
WSVR0221I: Application started: PTAccountApplicationClient
......
WSVR0221I: Application started: PTAccountApplication
```

► To test the application follow the instructions in "Verify the Open Account Application" on page 514.

Loading other projects

We also provide the project interchange files for:

► `topdown\AccountApplicationSCSolution.zip`—See "Top-down development of a service" on page 430 (solution after implementing the service).

► `thirdparty\AddrVerificationService.zip`—See "Third-party service" on page 464.

► `cics\CICSCustomer.zip`—See "Indirectly exposing an enterprise service" on page 472 (solution).

You can import these interchange files in the same way as described for the `PTApplication.zip` file.

Installing the sample pattern RAS asset

In this section we create a local RAS repository that stores a copy of the asset developed in Chapter 16, "Pattern-based engineering with Rational Software Architect   ." on page 545.

We install the asset into Rational Software Architect.

Create a local asset repository

First we create the local asset repository that points to the asset ZIP file of the sample code:

- ► Start Software Architect.
- ► Open the RAS (Reusable Assets) perspective.
- ► In the Asset Explorer click *Add a new Repository connection* 	(Figure A-14).
- ► Select *Local Repository* and click *Next*.
- ► Specify the repository location where the asset ZIP file is:

  `C:\SG247356\sampcode\SoftwareArchitect\ras`

- ► Click *Finish*.

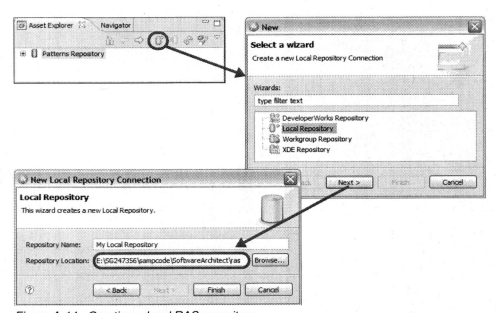

Figure A-14   Creating a local RAS repository

Import the asset

We import the asset into Software Architect:

▶ Select the new repository and *Refresh*, then expand the node. The asset contains both the source project as well as the deployable plug-in.

▶ Select the SOA Redbook patterns and *Import* (Figure A-15).

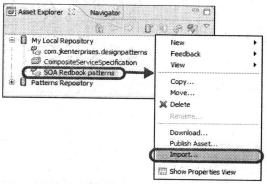

Figure A-15   Creating a local RAS repository

▶ Click *OK* in the information panel (attempt to install the feature com.jkenterprises.designpattern_1.0.0).

▶ You can go through the dialog panels or click *Finish*.

▶ Click *Yes to All* when messages are displayed, and click *OK* to the warning.

▶ Click *Yes* when prompted to restart the workbench.

Confirm that the plug-in is installed

We can confirm that the plug-in is installed properly:

▶ Switch to the Modeling perspective and you can find the source project com.jkenterprises.designpatterns (Figure A-16).

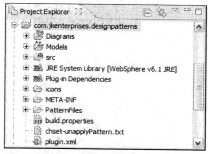

Figure A-16   Project after import

Tip: If you see errors in the project, you have to change the default JDK. Select *Window → Preferences*, expand *Java → Installed JREs*, and select either *WebSphere V6.1 JRE*, or any other JRE that supports Java 5, for example, the JRE that is installed with the product (`C:\IBM\SDP70\jdk`).

► Open the Pattern Explorer view by selecting *Window → Show View → Other → Modeling → Pattern Explorer*.

► Expand *JK SOA Patterns* and select *CompositeServiceSpecification* (Figure A-17).

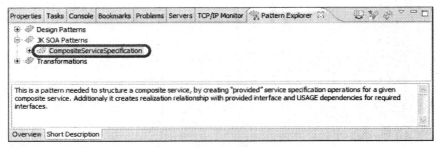

Figure A-17   Pattern Explorer with the sample pattern

► The pattern is now available for you to use from within the JK SOA Patterns library.

Rational Method Composer plug-in

We provide our simple development case codified as a Rational Method Composer plug-in. It is the result of the steps performed in "Codify the development case" on page 116. Note that it does not represent the development case completely, but rather includes the elements necessary to understand how to do this in Method Composer.

To use the plug-in in Method Composer, select *File → Import*. In the Import wizard, select *Method Plug-ins* and click *Next*. In the next page, select the location where you have extracted the DevCase-RMC-plugin-export.zip file. Please note that the plug-in was created using Version 7.0.1 of Method Composer.

We provide the Method Composer plug-in of our development case in:

```
C:\SG247356\sampcode\DevelopmentCase\DevCase-RMC-plugin-export.zip
```

Abbreviations and acronyms

API	application programming interface	**EIS**	enterprise information system
ATM	automatic teller machine	**EJB**	Enterprise JavaBean
BDD	business-driven development	**EMF**	Eclipse Modeling Framework
BPEL	Business Process Execution Language	**EMFT**	Eclipse Modeling Framework Technologies
BPM	business process management	**EPF**	Eclipse Process Framework
BPMN	Business Process Modeling Notation	**ERP**	enterprise resource planning
CBD	component-based development	**ESB**	Enterprise Service Bus
CBDI	component based development and integration	**ETL**	extract, transform, load
CBM	Component Business Modeling	**GB**	gigabyte
CCM	change and configuration management	**GMF**	graphical modeling framework
CDT	C++ development tool	**GUI**	graphical user interface
CEO	chief executive officer	**HR**	human resources
CICS	Customer Information Control System	**HTML**	Hypertext Markup Language
CIO	chief information officer	**HTTP**	Hypertext Transfer Protocol
CORBA	Common Object Request Broker Architecture	**IBM**	International Business Machines
CRM	customer relationship management	**IDE**	integrated development environment
CRUD	create/read/update/delete	**IMS**	Information Management System
CSS	cascading style sheet	**ISO**	International Organization for Standardization
CSV	comma separated values	**IT**	information technology
CVS	Common Version System	**ITSO**	International technical Support organization
DTD	document type definition	**JAR**	Java archive
EAI	enterprise application integration	**JMS**	Java Messaging Service
EAR	enterprise archive	**JNDI**	Java Naming and Directory Interface™
		JSF	JavaServer Faces
		JSP	JavaServer Pages™
		KPI	key performance indicator
		LOB	line of business

593

MDA	model-driven architecture	**WS-I**	Web Services Interoperability Organization
MDD	model-driven development	**WSAA**	WebSphere Studio Asset Analyzer
MOF	meta-object facility	**WSDL**	Web Services Definition Language
OCL	Object Constraint Language	**XML**	eXtensible Markup Language
OMG	Object Management Group	**XSD**	XML Schema Definition
OMT	Object Modeling Technique		
OO	object-oriented		
OOSE	Object-Oriented Software Engineering		
PDE	Plug-in Development Environment		
POJO	plain old Java object		
QoS	quality of service		
RAS	reusable asset specification		
RFP	request for proposal		
RUP	Rational Unified Process		
SCA	service component architecture		
SDP	Software Delivery Platform		
SLA	service-level agreement		
SO	service-oriented		
SOA	service-oriented architecture		
SOMA	Service Oriented Modeling and Architecture		
SPEM	Software Process Engineering		
SQL	Structured Query Language		
TCO	total cost of ownership		
TCP/IP	Transmission Control Protocol/Internet Protocol		
UCM	Unified Change Management		
UDDI	Universal Description Discovery and Integration		
UI	user interface		
UMA	Unified Method Architecture		
UML	Unified Modeling Language		
URL	Uniform Resource Locator		

Related publications

The publications listed in this section are considered particularly suitable for a more detailed discussion of the topics covered in this IBM Redbooks publication.

IBM Redbooks

For information about ordering these publications, see "How to get IBM Redbooks" on page 596. Note that some of the documents referenced here may be available in softcopy only.

- ► *Rational Business Driven Development for Compliance*, SG24-7244
- ► *Business Process Management: Modeling through Monitoring Using WebSphere V6.0.2 Products*, SG24-7148
- ► *Patterns: SOA Foundation - Business Process Management Scenario*, SG24-7234
- ► *Patterns: SOA Foundation Service Creation Scenario*, SG24-7240
- ► *Patterns: SOA Foundation Service Connectivity Scenario*, SG24-7228
- ► *Web Services Handbook for WebSphere Application Server 6.1*, SG24-7257
- ► *Continuous Business Process Management with HOLOSOFX BPM Suite and IBM MQSeries Workflow*, SG24-6590
- ► *Software Configuration Management: A Clear Case for IBM Rational ClearCase and ClearQuest UCM*, SG24-6399
- ► *Rational Application Developer V6 Programming Guide*, SG24-6449

Other publications

These publications are also relevant as further information sources:

- ► *Design Patterns: Elements of Reusable Object-Oriented Software*, Erich Gamma, et al, Addison-Wesley, 1995, ISBN 0201633612
- ► *The Unified Modeling Language User Guide,* Grady Booch, James Rumbaugh, Ivar Jacobson, Addison-Wesley, Second Edition, 2005, ISBN 0321267974
- ► *A Rational approach to model-driven development*, A. W. Brown, S. Iyengar, and S. Johnston, IBM Systems Journal, Volume 45, Number 3, 2006

- *Use Case Modeling*, Kurt Bittner and Ian Spence, Addison-Wesley, 2002, ISBN 0201709139
- *Practical Software Metrics for Project Management and Process Improvement*, Robert Grady, Prentice-Hall, 1992, ISBN 0137203845
- *Performance Analysis for Java Web Sites*, S. Joines, R. Willenborg, and K. Hygh, Addison-Wesley, 2002, ISBN 0201844540

Online resources

These Web sites are also relevant as further information sources:

- IBM software

  ```
  http://www.ibm.com/software/
  http://www.ibm.com/software/rational
  ```

- IBM developerWorks

  ```
  http://www.ibm.com/developerworks/
  http://www.ibm.com/developerworks/rational/
  ```

- Eclipse

  ```
  http://www.eclipse.org/
  ```

- Object Management Group

  ```
  http://www.omg.com/
  ```

- Uniform Modeling Language

  ```
  http://www.uml.org/
  http://www.ibm.com/software/rational/uml/
  ```

How to get IBM Redbooks

You can search for, view, or download Redbooks, Redpapers, Hints and Tips, draft publications and Additional materials, as well as order hardcopy Redbooks or CD-ROMs, at this Web site:

ibm.com/redbooks

Help from IBM

IBM Support and downloads

ibm.com/support

IBM Global Services

ibm.com/services

Index

A

abstraction
    level 146
access
    constraints 4
    services 4, 8
account
    activation 20
    application 20
    sales 20
    verification 21
activities diagram 143
activity 107
application
    failure 488
Application Developer 162, 423
    component testing 463
    EJB generation 416
    features 425
    JUnit 502
    roles and capabilities 424
architect
    tools 159
architectural
    analysis 416
    discovery 417
    elements 98
    patterns 9, 74–75
    significant 57
    styles 73
architecture 43
    business 43
    importance 155
    logical 7
    reuse 73
    specification 49
    styles 43
architecture-driven 113
assemble
    phase 4
assembly
    part 54
asset 4

analysis 224, 292
    life cycle 5, 26, 533
    packaging 538
    registry 515
    repositor 61
    repositories 9
    resuable 68
    stability 68
Asset Analyzer 293
asynchronous 488
atomic
    service providers 319
    services 72, 89
        layer 493
authentication 5
autonomic recovery 489
availability 490

B

baselining 228
behavioral
    policies 220
    specification 238
best practices 492
black-box 144
    view 49, 57
Booch Method 141
Borland 160
bottom-up development 481
BPEL 12, 101
BPMN 78, 198
Building SOA Solutions 117
business
    actor 185
    analyst 4, 491
    application
        services 8
    architecture 43, 174
        model 233, 307
    composition 491
    context 140
    design 3
    domain 208